Mapping Ideology

MAPPING

This series of readers, published in association with *New Left Review*, aims to illuminate key topics in a changing world.

Mapping Ideology

Edited by
SLAVOJ ŽIŽEK

VERSO
London · New York

First published by Verso 1994
© Verso 1994
All rights reserved

Verso
UK: 6 Meard Street, London W1V 3HR
USA: 29 West 35th Street, New York, NY 10001–2291

Verso is the imprint of New Left Books

ISBN 1–85984–955–5
ISBN 1–85984–055–8 (pbk)

British Library Cataloguing in Publication Data
A catalogue record for this book is available from the British Library

Library of Congress Cataloging-in-Publication Data
Mapping ideology / edited by Slavoj Žižek.
p.   cm. — (Mapping)
Includes index.
ISBN 1–85984–955–5 (hard). — ISBN 1–85984–055–8 (pbk.)
1. Political science—History. 2. Right and left (Political science)—History. 3. Ideology—History. I. Žižek, Slavoj. II. Series: Mapping (London, England)
JA83.M265   1994
320—dc20   94-37642
                                                                          CIP

Typeset by Type Study, Scarborough
Printed and bound in Great Britain by Biddles Ltd, Guildford and King's Lynn

Contents

CONTENTS

The Spectre of Ideology

Slavoj Žižek

I   Critique of Ideology, today?

By way of a simple reflection on how the horizon of historical imagination is subjected to change, we find ourselves *in medias res*, compelled to accept the unrelenting pertinence of the notion of ideology. Up to a decade or two ago, the system production-nature (man's productive-exploitative relationship with nature and its resources) was perceived as a constant, whereas everybody was busy imagining different forms of the social organization of production and commerce (Fascism or Communism as alternatives to liberal capitalism); today, as Fredric Jameson perspicaciously remarked, nobody seriously considers possible alternatives to capitalism any longer, whereas popular imagination is persecuted by the visions of the forthcoming 'breakdown of nature', of the stoppage of all life on earth – it seems easier to imagine the 'end of the world' than a far more modest change in the mode of production, as if liberal capitalism is the 'real' that will somehow survive even under conditions of a global ecological catastrophe.... One can thus categorically assert the existence of ideology *qua* generative matrix that regulates the relationship between visible and non-visible, between imaginable and non-imaginable, as well as the changes in this relationship.

This matrix can be easily discerned in the dialectics of 'old' and 'new', when an event that announces a wholly new dimension or epoch is (mis)perceived as the continuation of or return to the past, or – the opposite case – when an event that is entirely inscribed in the logic of the existing order is (mis)perceived as a radical rupture. The supreme example of the latter, of course, is provided by those critics of Marxism who (mis)perceive our late-capitalist society as a new social formation

1

no longer dominated by the dynamics of capitalism as it was described by Marx. In order to avoid this worn-out example, however, let us turn to the domain of sexuality. One of today's commonplaces is that so-called 'virtual' or 'cyber' sex presents a radical break with the past, since in it, actual sexual contact with a 'real other' is losing ground against masturbatory enjoyment, whose sole support is a virtual other – phone-sex, pornography, up to computerized 'virtual sex' . . . . The Lacanian answer to this is that first we have to expose the myth of 'real sex' allegedly possible 'before' the arrival of virtual sex: Lacan's thesis that 'there is no sexual relationship' means precisely that the structure of the 'real' sexual act (of the act with a flesh-and-blood partner) is already inherently phantasmic – the 'real' body of the other serves only as a support for our phantasmic projections. In other words, 'virtual sex' in which a glove simulates the stimuli of what we see on the screen, and so on, is not a monstrous distortion of real sex, it simply renders manifest its underlying phantasmic structure.

An exemplary case of the opposite misperception is provided by the reaction of Western liberal intellectuals to the emergence of new states in the process of the disintegration of real Socialism in Eastern Europe: they (mis)perceived this emergence as a return to the nineteenth-century tradition of the nation-state, whereas what we are actually dealing with is the exact opposite: the 'withering-away' of the traditional nation-state based upon the notion of the abstract citizen identified with the constitutional legal order. In order to characterize this new state of things, Étienne Balibar recently referred to the old Marxian phrase *Es gibt keinen Staat in Europa* – there no longer exists a proper state in Europe. The old spectre of Leviathan parasitizing on the *Lebenswelt* of society, totalizing it from above, is more and more eroded from both sides. On the one hand, there are the new emerging ethnic communities – although some of them are formally constituted as sovereign states, they are no longer states in the proper modern-age European sense, since they did not cut the umbilical cord between state and ethnic community. (Paradigmatic here is the case of Russia, in which local mafias already function as a kind of parallel power structure.) On the other hand, there are the multiple transnational links, from multinational capital to mafia cartels and inter-state political communities (European Union).

There are two reasons for this limitation of state sovereignty, each of which is in itself compelling enough to justify it: the transnational character of ecological crisis and of nuclear threat. This eroding of state authority from both sides is mirrored in the fact that today the basic political antagonism is that between the universalist 'cosmopoliti-cal' liberal democracy (standing for the force corroding the state from

above) and the new 'organic' populism-communitarianism (standing
for the force corroding the state from below). And – as Balibar pointed
out yet again[1] – this antagonism is to be conceived neither as an
external opposition nor as the complementary relationship of the two
poles in which one pole balances the excess of its opposite (in the sense
that, when we have too much universalism, a little bit of ethnic roots
gives people the feeling of belonging, and thus stabilizes the situation),
but in a genuinely Hegelian sense – each pole of the antagonism is
inherent to its opposite, so that we stumble upon it at the very moment
when we endeavour to grasp the opposite pole for itself, to posit it 'as
such'.

Because of this inherent character of the two poles, one should avoid
the liberal-democratic trap of concentrating exclusively on the horrifying facts and even more horrifying potentials of what is going on
today in Russia and some other ex-Communist countries: the new
hegemonic ideology of 'Eurasism' preaching the organic link between
community and the state as an antidote to the corrosive influence of the
'Jewish' principle of market and social atomism, orthodox national
imperialism as an antidote to Western individualism, and so on. In
order to combat these new forms of organicist populism effectively one
must, as it were, turn the critical gaze back upon oneself and submit to
critical scrutiny liberal-democratic universalism itself – what opens up
the space for the organicist populism is the weak point, the 'falsity', of
this very universalism.

These same examples of the actuality of the notion of ideology,
however, also render clear the reasons why today one hastens to
renounce the notion of ideology: does not the critique of ideology
involve a privileged place, somehow exempted from the turmoils of
social life, which enables some subject-agent to perceive the very
hidden mechanism that regulates social visibility and non-visibility? Is
not the claim that we can accede to this place the most obvious case of
ideology? Consequently, with reference to today's state of epistemological reflection, is not the notion of ideology self-defeating? So why
should we cling to a notion with such obviously outdated epistemological implications (the relationship of 'representation' between thought
and reality, etc.)? Is not its utterly ambiguous and elusive character in
itself a sufficient reason to abandon it? 'Ideology' can designate
anything from a contemplative attitude that misrecognizes its dependence on social reality to an action-orientated set of beliefs, from the
indispensable medium in which individuals live out their relations to a
social structure to false ideas which legitimate a dominant political

power. It seems to pop up precisely when we attempt to avoid it, while it fails to appear where one would clearly expect it to dwell.

When some procedure is denounced as 'ideological *par excellence*', one can be sure that its inversion is no less ideological. For example, among the procedures generally acknowledged as 'ideological' is definitely the eternalization of some historically limited condition, the act of discerning some higher Necessity in a contingent occurrence (from the grounding of male domination in the 'nature of things' to interpreting AIDS as a punishment for the sinful life of modern man; or, at a more intimate level, when we encounter our 'true love', it seems as if this is what we have been waiting for all our life, as if, in some mysterious way, all our previous life has led to this encounter . . .): the senseless contingency of the real is thus 'internalized', symbolized, provided with Meaning. Is not ideology, however, also the opposite procedure of failing to notice the necessity, of misperceiving it as an insignificant contingency (from the psychoanalytic cure, in which one of the main forms of the analysand's resistance is his insistence that his symptomatic slip of tongue was a mere lapse without any signification, up to the domain of economics, in which the ideological procedure *par excellence* is to reduce the crisis to an external, ultimately contingent occurrence, thus failing to take note of the inherent logic of the system that begets the crisis)? In this precise sense, ideology is the exact opposite of internalization of the external contingency: it resides in externalization of the result of an inner necessity, and the task of the critique of ideology here is precisely to discern the hidden necessity in what appears as a mere contingency.

The most recent case of a similar inversion was provided by the way Western media reported on the Bosnian war. The first thing that strikes the eye is the contrast to the reporting on the 1991 Gulf War, where we had the standard ideological personification:

> Instead of providing information on social, political or religious trends and antagonisms in Iraq, the media ultimately reduced the conflict to a quarrel with Saddam Hussein, Evil Personified, the outlaw who excluded himself from the civilized international community. Even more than the destruction of Iraq's military forces, the true aim was presented as psychological, as the humiliation of Saddam who was to 'lose face'. In the case of the Bosnian war, however, notwithstanding isolated cases of the demonization of the Serbian president Milosevič, the predominant attitude reflects that of a quasi-anthropological observer. The media outdo one another in giving us lessons on the ethnic and religious background of the conflict; traumas hundreds of years old are being replayed and acted out, so that, in order to understand the roots of the conflict, one has to know not only the history of Yugoslavia, but the entire history of the Balkans from medieval times. . . . In the

Bosnian conflict, it is therefore not possible simply to take sides, one can only
patiently try to grasp the background of this savage spectacle, alien to our
civilized system of values . . . . Yet this opposite procedure involves an
ideological mystification even more cunning than the demonization of
Saddam Hussein.[2]

In what, precisely, consists this ideological mystification? To put it
somewhat crudely, the evocation of the 'complexity of circumstances'
serves to deliver us from the responsibility to act. The comfortable
attitude of a distant observer, the evocation of the allegedly intricate
context of religious and ethnic struggles in Balkan countries, is here to
enable the West to shed its responsibility towards the Balkans – that is,
to avoid the bitter truth that, far from presenting the case of an
eccentric ethnic conflict, the Bosnian war is a direct result of the West's
failure to grasp the political dynamic of the disintegration of Yugo-
slavia, of the West's silent support of 'ethnic cleansing'.

In the domain of theory, we encounter a homologous reversal
apropos of the 'deconstructionist' problematization of the notion of the
subject's guilt and personal responsibility. The notion of a subject
morally and criminally fully 'responsible' for his acts clearly serves the
ideological need to conceal the intricate, always-already operative
texture of historico-discursive presuppositions that not only provide
the context for the subject's act but also define in advance the
co-ordinates of its meaning: the system can function only if the cause of
its malfunction can be located in the responsible subject's 'guilt'. One of
the commonplaces of the leftist criticism of law is that the attribution of
personal responsibility and guilt relieves us of the task of probing into
the concrete circumstances of the act in question. Suffice it to recall the
moral-majority practice of attributing a moral qualification to the
higher crime rate among African Americans ('criminal dispositions',
'moral insensitivity', etc.): this attribution precludes any analysis of the
concrete ideological, political and economic conditions of African
Americans.

Is not this logic of 'putting the blame on the circumstances' however,
taken to its extremes, self-defeating in so far as it necessarily leads to
the unforgettable – and no less ideological – cynicism of Brecht's
famous lines from his *Threepenny Opera*: 'Wir wären gut anstatt so roh,
doch die Verhältnisse, sie sind nicht so!' ('We would be good instead of
being so rude, if only the circumstances were not of this kind')? In other
words, are we, the speaking subjects, not always-already *engaged* in
recounting the circumstances that predetermine the space of our
activity?

A more concrete example of the same undecidable ambiguity is provided by the standard 'progressive' criticism of psychoanalysis. The reproach here is that the psychoanalytic explanation of misery and psychic suffering through unconscious libidinal complexes, or even via a direct reference to the 'death drive', renders the true causes of destructiveness invisible. This critique of psychoanalysis found its ultimate theoretical expression in the rehabilitation of the idea that the ultimate cause of psychic trauma is real childhood sexual abuse: by introducing the notion of the phantasmic origin of trauma, Freud allegedly betrayed the truth of his own discovery.[3] Instead of the concrete analysis of external, actual social conditions – the patriarchal family, its role in the totality of the reproduction of the capitalist system, and so on – we are thus given the story of unresolved libidinal deadlocks; instead of the analysis of social conditions that lead to war, we are given the 'death drive'; instead of the change of social relations, a solution is sought in the inner psychic change, in the 'maturation' that should qualify us to accept social reality as it is. In this perspective, the very striving for social change is denounced as an expression of the unresolved Oedipus complex . . . . Is not this notion of a rebel who, by way of his 'irrational' resistance to social authority, acts out his unresolved psychic tensions ideology at its purest? However, as Jacqueline Rose demonstrated,[4] such an externalization of the cause into 'social conditions' is no less false, in so far as it enables the subject to avoid confronting the real of his or her desire. By means of this externalization of the Cause, the subject is no longer *engaged* in what is happening to him; he entertains towards the trauma a simple external relationship: far from stirring up the unacknowledged kernel of his desire, the traumatic event disturbs his balance from outside.[5]

The paradox in all these cases is that *the stepping out of (what we experience as) ideology is the very form of our enslavement to it*. The opposite example of non-ideology which possesses all the standard features of ideology is provided by the role of *Neues Forum* in ex-East Germany. An inherently *tragic* ethical dimension pertains to its fate: it presents a point at which an ideology 'takes itself literally' and ceases to function as an 'objectively cynical' (Marx) legitimization of existing power relations. *Neues Forum* consisted of groups of passionate intellectuals who 'took socialism seriously' and were prepared to risk everything in order to destroy the compromised system and replace it with the Utopian 'third way' beyond capitalism and 'really existing' socialism. Their sincere belief and insistence that they were not working for the restoration of Western capitalism, of course, proved to be nothing but an insubstantial illusion; we could say, however, that precisely as such (as a thorough

illusion without substance) it was *stricto sensu non-ideological*: it did not
'reflect', in an inverted-ideological form, any actual relations of power.
The theoretical lesson to be drawn from this is that the concept of
ideology must be disengaged from the 'representationalist' problematic: *ideology has nothing to do with 'illusion'*, with a mistaken, distorted
representation of its social content. To put it succinctly: a political
standpoint can be quite accurate ('true') as to its objective content, yet
thoroughly ideological; and, vice versa, the idea that a political
standpoint gives of its social content can prove totally wrong, yet there
is absolutely nothing 'ideological' about it. With regard to the 'factual
truth', the position of *Neues Forum* – taking the disintegration of the
Communist regime as the opening-up of a way to invent some new
form of social space that would reach beyond the confines of capitalism
– was doubtless illusory. Opposing *Neues Forum* were forces who put all
their bets on the quickest possible annexation to West Germany – that is
to say, of their country's inclusion in the world capitalist system; for
them, the people around *Neues Forum* were nothing but a bunch of
heroic daydreamers. This position proved accurate – *yet it was none the
less thoroughly ideological*. Why? The conformist adoption of the West
German model implied an ideological belief in the unproblematic,
non-antagonistic functioning of the late-capitalist 'social state', whereas
the first stance, although illusory as to its factual content (its 'enunciated'), attested, by means of its 'scandalous' and exorbitant position of
enunciation, to an awareness of the antagonism that pertains to late
capitalism. This is one way to conceive of the Lacanian thesis according
to which truth has the structure of a fiction: in those confused months
of the passage of 'really existing socialism' into capitalism, *the fiction of a
'third way' was the only point at which social antagonism was not obliterated.*
Herein lies one of the tasks of the 'postmodern' critique of ideology: to
designate the elements within an existing social order which – in the
guise of 'fiction', that is, of 'Utopian' narratives of possible but failed
alternative histories – point towards the system's antagonistic character, and thus 'estrange' us to the self-evidence of its established
identity.

II   Ideology: the Spectral Analysis of a Concept

In all these *ad hoc* analyses, however, we have already *practicized* the
critique of ideology, while our initial question concerned the *concept* of
ideology presupposed in this practice. Up till now, we have been
guided by a 'spontaneous' pre-comprehension which, although it led
us to contradictory results, is not to be underestimated, but rather

explicated. For example, we somehow implicitly seem to know what is 'no longer' ideology: as long as the Frankfurt School accepted the critique of political economy as its base, it remained within the co-ordinates of the critique of ideology, whereas the notion of 'instrumental reason' no longer appertains to the horizon of the critique of ideology – 'instrumental reason' designates an attitude that is not simply functional with regard to social domination but, rather, serves as the very foundation of the relationship of domination.[6] An ideology is thus not necessarily 'false': as to its positive content, it can be 'true', quite accurate, since what really matters is not the asserted content as such but *the way this content is related to the subjective position implied by its own process of enunciation*. We are within ideological space proper the moment this content – 'true' or 'false' (if true, so much the better for the ideological effect) – is functional with regard to some relation of social domination ('power', 'exploitation') in an inherently non-transparent way: *the very logic of legitimizing the relation of domination must remain concealed if it is to be effective*. In other words, the starting point of the critique of ideology has to be full acknowledgement of the fact that it is easily possible to *lie in the guise of truth*. When, for example, some Western power intervenes in a Third World country on account of violations of human rights, it may well be 'true' that in this country the most elementary human rights were not respected, and that the Western intervention will effectively improve the human rights record, yet such a legitimization none the less remains 'ideological' in so far as it fails to mention the true motives of the intervention (economic interests, etc.). The outstanding mode of this 'lying in the guise of truth' today is cynicism: with a disarming frankness one 'admits everything', yet this full acknowledgement of our power interests does not in any way prevent us from pursuing these interests – the formula of cynicism is no longer the classic Marxian 'they do not know it, but they are doing it'; it is 'they know very well what they are doing, yet they are doing it'.

How, then, are we to explicate this implicit pre-comprehension of ours? How are we to pass from doxa to truth? The first approach that offers itself is, of course, the Hegelian historical-dialectical transposition of the problem into its own solution: instead of directly evaluating the adequacy or 'truth' of different notions of ideology, one should *read this very multitude of the determinations of ideology as the index of different concrete historical situations* – that is, one should consider what Althusser, in his self-critical phase, referred to as the 'topicality of the thought', the way a thought is inscribed into its object; or, as Derrida would have put it, the way the frame itself is part of the framed content.

When, for example, Leninism–Stalinism suddenly adopted the term

'proletarian ideology' in the late 1920s in order to designate not the
'distortion' of proletarian consciousness under the pressure of bourgeois ideology but the very 'subjective' driving force of proletarian
revolutionary activity, this shift in the notion of ideology was strictly
correlative to the reinterpretation of Marxism itself as an impartial
'objective science', as a science that does not in itself involve the
proletarian subjective position: Marxism first, from a neutral distance
of metalanguage, ascertains the objective tendency of history towards
Communism; then it elaborates the 'proletarian ideology' in order to
induce the working class to fulfil its historical mission. A further
example of such a shift is the already mentioned passage of Western
Marxism from Critique of Political Economy to Critique of Instrumental Reason: from Lukács's *History and Class Consciousness* and the early
Frankfurt School, where ideological distortion is derived from the
'commodity form', to the notion of Instrumental Reason which is no
longer grounded in a concrete social reality but is, rather, conceived as
a kind of anthropological, even quasi-transcendental, primordial
constant that enables us to explain the social reality of domination and
exploitation. This passage is embedded in the transition from the
post-World War I universe, in which hope in the revolutionary
outcome of the crisis of capitalism was still alive, into the double trauma
of the late 1930s and 1940s: the 'regression' of capitalist societies into
Fascism and the 'totalitarian' turn of the Communist movement.[7]

However, such an approach, although it is adequate at its own level,
can easily ensnare us in historicist relativism that suspends the inherent
cognitive value of the term 'ideology' and makes it into a mere
expression of social circumstances. For that reason, it seems preferable
to begin with a different, synchronous approach. Apropos of religion
(which, for Marx, was ideology *par excellence*), Hegel distinguished
three moments: *doctrine, belief,* and *ritual*; one is thus tempted to
dispose the multitude of notions associated with the term 'ideology'
around these three axes: ideology as a complex of ideas (theories,
convictions, beliefs, argumentative procedures); ideology in its externality, that is, the materiality of ideology, Ideological State Apparatuses; and finally, the most elusive domain, the 'spontaneous' ideology
at work at the heart of social 'reality' itself (it is highly questionable if the
term 'ideology' is at all appropriate to designate this domain – here it is
exemplary that, apropos of commodity fetishism, Marx never used the
term 'ideology'[8]). Let us recall the case of liberalism: liberalism is a
doctrine (developed from Locke to Hayek) materialized in rituals and
apparatuses (free press, elections, market, etc.) and active in the
'spontaneous' (self-) experience of subjects as 'free individuals'. The
order of contributions in this Reader follows this line that, *grosso modo,*

fits the Hegelian triad of In-itself – For-itself – In-and-For-itself.[9] This logico-narrative reconstruction of the notion of ideology will be centred on the repeated occurrence of the already mentioned reversal of non-ideology into ideology – that is, of the sudden awareness of how the very gesture of stepping out of ideology pulls us back into it.

1. So, to begin with, we have ideology 'in-itself': the immanent notion of ideology as a doctrine, a composite of ideas, beliefs, concepts, and so on, destined to convince us of its 'truth', yet actually serving some unavowed particular power interest. The mode of the critique of ideology that corresponds to this notion is that of *symptomal reading*: the aim of the critique is to discern the unavowed bias of the official text via its ruptures, blanks and slips – to discern in 'equality and freedom' the equality and freedom of the partners in the market exchange which, of course, privileges the owner of the means of production, and so on. Habermas, perhaps the last great representative of this tradition, measures the distortion and/or falsity of an ideological edifice with the standard of non-coercive rational argumentation, a kind of 'regulative ideal' that, according to him, inheres in the symbolic order as such. Ideology is a systematically distorted communication: a text in which, under the influence of unavowed social interests (of domination, etc.), a gap separates its 'official', public meaning from its actual intention – that is to say, in which we are dealing with an unreflected tension between the explicit enunciated content of the text and its pragmatic presuppositions.[10]

Today, however, probably the most prestigious tendency in the critique of ideology, one that grew out of discourse analysis, inverts this relationship: what the tradition of Enlightenment dismisses as a mere disturbance of 'normal' communication turns out to be its positive condition. The concrete intersubjective space of symbolic communication is always structured by various (unconscious) textual devices that cannot be reduced to secondary rhetoric. What we are dealing with here is not a complementary move to the traditional Enlightenment or Habermasian approach but its inherent reversal: what Habermas perceives as the step out of ideology is denounced here as ideology *par excellence*. In the Enlightenment tradition, 'ideology' stands for the blurred ('false') notion of reality caused by various 'pathological' interests (fear of death and of natural forces, power interests, etc.); for discourse analysis, the very notion of an access to reality unbiased by any discursive devices or conjunctions with power is ideological. The 'zero level' of ideology consists in (mis)perceiving a discursive formation as an extra-discursive fact.

Already in the 1950s, in *Mythologies*, Roland Barthes proposed the notion of ideology as the 'naturalization' of the symbolic order – that is, as the perception that reifies the results of discursive procedures into properties of the 'thing itself'. Paul de Man's notion of the 'resistance to (deconstructionist) theory' runs along the same lines: 'deconstruction' met with such resistance because it 'denaturalizes' the enunciated content by bringing to the light of day the discursive procedures that engender evidence of Sense. Arguably the most elaborate version of this approach is Oswald Ducrot's theory of argumentation[11]; although it does not employ the term 'ideology', its ideologico-critical potential is tremendous. Ducrot's basic notion is that one cannot draw a clear line of separation between descriptive and argumentative levels of language: there is no neutral descriptive content; every description (designation) is already a moment of some argumentative scheme; descriptive predicates themselves are ultimately reified-naturalized argumentative gestures. This argumentative thrust relies on *topoi*, on the 'commonplaces' that operate only as naturalized, only in so far as we apply them in an automatic, 'unconscious' way – a successful argumentation presupposes the invisibility of the mechanisms that regulate its efficiency.

One should also mention here Michel Pêcheux, who gave a strict linguistic turn to Althusser's theory of interpellation. His work is centred on the discursive mechanisms that generate the 'evidence' of Sense. That is to say, one of the fundamental stratagems of ideology is the reference to some self-evidence – 'Look, you can see for yourself how things are!'. 'Let the facts speak for themselves' is perhaps the arch-statement of ideology – the point being, precisely, that facts *never* 'speak for themselves' but are always *made to speak* by a network of discursive devices. Suffice it to recall the notorious anti-abortion film *The Silent Scream* – we 'see' a foetus which 'defends itself', which 'cries', and so on, yet what we 'don't see' in this very act of seeing is that we 'see' all this against the background of a discursively pre-constructed space. Discourse analysis is perhaps at its strongest in answering this precise question: when a racist Englishman says 'There are too many Pakistanis on our streets!', *how – from what place – does he 'see' this* – that is, how is his symbolic space structured so that he can perceive the fact of a Pakistani strolling along a London street as a disturbing surplus? That is to say, here one must bear in mind Lacan's motto that *nothing is lacking in the real*: every perception of a lack or a surplus ('not enough of this', 'too much of that') always involves a *symbolic* universe.[12]

Last but not least, mention should be made here of Ernesto Laclau and his path-breaking approach to Fascism and populism,[13] whose main theoretical result is that meaning does not inhere in elements of an ideology as such – these elements, rather, function as 'free-floating signifiers' whose meaning is fixed by the mode of their hegemonic articulation. Ecology, for example, is never 'ecology as such', it is always enchained in a specific series of equivalences: it can be conservative (advocating the return to balanced rural communities and traditional ways of life), etatist (only a strong state regulation can save us from the impending catastrophe), socialist (the ultimate cause of ecological problems resides in the capitalist profit-orientated exploitation of natural resources), liberal-capitalist (one should include the damage to the environment in the price of the product, and thus leave the market to regulate the ecological balance), feminist (the exploitation of nature follows from the male attitude of domination), anarchic self-managerial (humanity can survive only if it reorganizes itself into small self-reliant communities that live in balance with nature), and so on. The point, of course, is that none of these enchainments is in itself 'true', inscribed in the very nature of the ecological problematic: which discourse will succeed in 'appropriating' ecology depends on the fight for discursive hegemony, whose outcome is not guaranteed by any underlying necessity or 'natural alliance'. The other inevitable conse-quence of such a notion of hegemonic articulation is that etatist, conservative, socialist, and so on, inscription of ecology does not designate a secondary connotation that supplements its primary 'literal' meaning: as Derrida would have put it, this supplement retroactively (re)defines the very nature of 'literal' identity – a conservative enchainment, for example, throws a specific light on the ecological problematic itself ('due to his false arrogance, man forsook his roots in the natural order', etc.).

2. What follows is the step from 'in-itself' to 'for-itself', to ideology in its otherness-externalization: the moment epitomized by the Althusserian notion of Ideological State Apparatuses (ISA) that designate the material existence of ideology in ideological practices, rituals and institutions.[14] Religious belief, for example, is not merely or even primarily an inner conviction, but the Church as an institution and its rituals (prayer, baptism, confirmation, confession . . .) which, far from being a mere secondary externalization of the inner belief, stand for *the very mechanisms that generate it*. When Althusser repeats, after Pascal: 'Act as if you believe, pray, kneel down, and you shall believe, faith will arrive by itself', he delineates an intricate reflective mechanism of retroactive 'autopoetic' foundation that far exceeds the reductionist assertion of the dependence of inner belief on external behaviour. That is to say, the implicit logic of his argument is: kneel down and *you shall believe that you knelt down because of your belief* – that is,

your following the ritual is an expression/effect of your inner belief; in short, the 'external' ritual performatively generates its own ideological foundation.[15]

What we encounter here again is the 'regression' into ideology at the very point where we apparently step out of it. In this respect, the relationship between Althusser and Foucault is of special interest. The Foucauldian counterparts to Ideological State Apparatuses are the disciplinary procedures that operate at the level of 'micro-power' and designate the point at which *power inscribes itself into the body directly, bypassing ideology* – for that precise reason, Foucault never uses the term 'ideology' apropos of these mechanisms of micro-power. This abandoning of the problematic of ideology entails a fatal weakness of Foucault's theory. Foucault never tires of repeating how power constitutes itself 'from below', how it does not emanate from some unique summit: this very semblance of a Summit (the Monarch or some other embodiment of Sovereignty) emerges as the secondary effect of the plurality of micro-practices, of the complex network of their interrelations. However, when he is compelled to display the concrete mechanism of this emergence, Foucault resorts to the extremely suspect rhetoric of complexity, evoking the intricate network of lateral links, left and right, up and down . . . a clear case of patching up, since one can never arrive at Power this way – the abyss that separates micro-procedures from the spectre of Power remains unbridgeable. Althusser's advantage over Foucault seems evident: Althusser proceeds in exactly the opposite direction – from the very outset, he conceives these micro-procedures as parts of the ISA; that is to say, as mechanisms which, in order to be operative, to 'seize' the individual, always-already presuppose the massive presence of the state, the transferential relationship of the individual towards state power, or – in Althusser's terms – towards the ideological big Other in whom the interpellation originates.

This Althusserian shift of emphasis from ideology 'in-itself' to its material existence in the ISA proved its fecundity in a new approach to Fascism; Wolfgang Fritz Haug's criticism of Adorno is exemplary here. Adorno refuses to treat Fascism as an ideology in the proper sense of the term, that is, as 'rational legitimization of the existing order'. So-called 'Fascist ideology' no longer possesses the coherence of a rational construct that calls for conceptual analysis and ideologico-critical refutation; that is to say, it no longer functions as a 'lie necessarily experienced as truth' (the sign of recognition of a true ideology). 'Fascist ideology' is not taken seriously even by its promoters; its status is purely instrumental, and ultimately relies on external coercion.[16] In his response to Adorno, however, Haug[17] triumphantly demonstrates how this capitulation to the primacy of the doctrine, far from implying the 'end of ideology', asserts the founding gesture of the ideological as such: the call to unconditional subordination and to 'irrational' sacrifice. What liberal criticism (mis)perceives as Fascism's weakness is the very resort of its strength: within the Fascist horizon, the very demand for rational argumentation that should provide grounds for our acceptance of authority is denounced in advance as an index of the liberal degeneration of the true spirit of ethical sacrifice – as Haug puts it, in browsing through Mussolini's texts, one cannot avoid the uncanny feeling that Mussolini had read Althusser! The direct denunciation of the Fascist notion of the 'community-of-the-people [*Volksgemeinschaft*]' as a deceptive lure that conceals the reality of domination and exploitation fails to take note of the crucial fact that this *Volksgemeinschaft* was materialized in a series of rituals and practices (not only mass gatherings and parades but also large-scale campaigns to help the hungry, organized sports and cultural activities for the workers, etc.) which performatively produced the effect of *Volksgemeinschaft*.[18]

3. In the next step of our reconstruction, this externalization is, as it were, 'reflected into itself': what takes place is the disintegration, self-limitation and self-dispersal of the notion of ideology. Ideology is no longer conceived as a homogeneous mechanism that guarantees social reproduction, as the 'cement' of society; it turns into a Wittgensteinian 'family' of vaguely connected and heterogeneous procedures whose reach is strictly localized. Along these lines, the critiques of the so-called Dominant Ideology Thesis (DIT) endeavour to demonstrate that an ideology either exerts an influence that is crucial, but constrained to some narrow social stratum, or its role in social reproduction is marginal. At the beginnings of capitalism, for example, the role of the Protestant ethic of hard work as an end-in-itself, and so on, was limited to the stratum of emerging capitalists, whereas workers and peasants, as well as the upper classes, continued to obey other, more traditional ethical attitudes, so that one can in no way attribute to the Protestant ethic the role of the 'cement' of the entire social edifice. Today, in late capitalism, when the expansion of the new mass media in principle, at least, enables ideology effectively to penetrate every pore of the social body, the weight of ideology as such is diminished: individuals do not act as they do primarily on account of their beliefs or ideological convictions – that is to say, the system, for the most part, bypasses ideology in its reproduction and relies on economic coercion, legal and state regulations, and so on.[19]

Here, however, things get blurred again, since the moment we take a closer look at these allegedly extra-ideological mechanisms that regulate social reproduction, we find ourselves knee-deep in the already mentioned obscure domain in which reality is indistinguishable from ideology. What we encounter here, therefore, is the third reversal of non-ideology into ideology: all of a sudden we become aware of a For-itself of ideology at work in the very In-itself of extra-ideological actuality. First, the mechanisms of economic coercion and legal regulation always 'materialize' some propositions or beliefs that are inherently ideological (the criminal law, for example, involves a belief in the personal responsibility of the individual or the conviction that crimes are a product of social circumstances). Secondly, the form of consciousness that fits late-capitalist 'post-ideological' society – the cynical, 'sober' attitude that advocates liberal 'openness' in the matter of 'opinions' (everybody is free to believe whatever she or he wants; this concerns only his or her privacy), disregards pathetic ideological phrases and follows only utilitarian and/or hedonistic motivations – *stricto sensu* remains an ideological attitude: it involves a series of ideological presuppositions (on the relationship between 'values' and 'real life', on personal freedom, etc.) that are necessary for the reproduction of existing social relations.

What thereby comes into sight is a third continent of ideological phenomena: neither ideology *qua* explicit doctrine, articulated convictions on the nature of man, society and the universe, nor ideology in its material existence (institutions, rituals and practices that give body to it), but the elusive network of implicit, quasi-'spontaneous' presuppositions and attitudes that form an irreducible moment of the reproduction of 'non-ideological' (economic, legal, political, sexual . . .) practices.[20] The Marxian notion of 'commodity fetishism' is exemplary here: it designates not a (bourgeois) theory of political economy but a series of presuppositions that determine the structure of the very 'real' economic practice of market exchange – in theory, a capitalist clings to utilitarian nominalism, yet in his own practice (of exchange, etc.) he follows 'theological whimsies' and acts as a speculative idealist . . . .[21] For that reason, a direct reference to extra-ideological coercion (of the market, for example) is an ideological gesture *par excellence*: the market and (mass) media are dialectically interconnected;[22] we live in a 'society of the spectacle' (Guy Debord) in which the media structure our perception of reality in advance and render reality indistinguishable from the 'aestheticized' image of it.

III   The Spectre and the Real of Antagonism

Is our final outcome, therefore, the inherent impossibility of isolating a reality whose consistency is not maintained by ideological mechanisms, a reality that does not disintegrate the moment we subtract from it its ideological component? Therein resides one of the main reasons for progressive abandonment of the notion of ideology: this notion somehow grows 'too strong', it begins to embrace everything, inclusive of the very neutral, extra-ideological ground supposed to provide the standard by means of which one can measure ideological distortion. That is to say, is not the ultimate result of discourse analysis that the order of discourse as such is inherently 'ideological'?

Let us suppose that at some political meeting or academic confer-ence, we are expected to pronounce some profound thoughts on the sad plight of the homeless in our big cities, yet we have absolutely no idea of their actual problems – the way to save face is to produce the effect of 'depth' by means of a purely formal inversion: 'Today, one hears and reads a lot about the plight of the homeless in our cities, about their hardship and distress. Perhaps, however, this distress, deplorable as it may be, is ultimately just a sign of some far deeper distress – of the fact that modern man no longer has a proper dwelling, that he is more and more a stranger in his own world. Even if we constructed enough new buildings to house all homeless people, the true distress would perhaps be even greater. The essence of homeless-ness is the homelessness of the essence itself; it resides in the fact that, in our world thrown out of joint by the frenetic search for empty pleasures, there is no home, no proper dwelling, for the truly essential dimension of man.'

This formal matrix can be applied to an infinite multitude of themes – say, distance and proximity: 'Today, modern media can bring events from the farthest part of our earth, even from nearby planets, close to us in a split second. Does not this very all-pervasive proximity, however, remove us from the authentic dimension of human exist-ence? Is not the essence of man more distant from us than ever today?' Or the recurrent motif of danger: 'Today, one hears and reads a lot about how the very survival of the human race is threatened by the prospect of ecological catastrophe (the disappearing ozone layer, the greenhouse effect, etc.). The true danger, however, lies elsewhere: what is ultimately threatened is the very essence of man. As we endeavour to prevent the impending ecological catastrophe with newer and newer technological solutions ('environment-friendly' aero-sols, unleaded petrol, etc.), we are in fact simply adding fuel to the flames, and thus aggravating the threat to the spiritual essence of man, which cannot be reduced to a technological animal.'

The purely formal operation which, in all these cases, brings about the effect of depth is perhaps ideology at its purest, its 'elementary cell', whose link to the Lacanian concept of the Master-Signifier is not difficult to discern: the chain of 'ordinary' signifiers registers some positive knowledge about homelessness, whereas the Master-Signifier stands for 'the truly essential dimension' about which we need not make any positive claim (for that reason, Lacan designates the Master-Signifier the 'signifier without signified'). This formal matrix bears witness in an exemplary way to the self-defeating power of a formal discourse analysis of ideology: its weakness resides in its very strength, since it is ultimately compelled to locate ideology in the gap between the 'ordinary' signifying chain and the excessive Master-Signifier that is part of the symbolic order as such.

Here, however, one should be careful to avoid the last trap that makes us slide into ideology under the guise of stepping out of it. That is to say, when we denounce as ideological the very attempt to draw a clear line of demarcation between ideology and actual reality, this inevitably seems to impose the conclusion that the only non-ideological position is to renounce the very notion of extra-ideological reality and accept that all we are dealing with are symbolic fictions, the plurality of discursive universes, never 'reality' – *such a quick, slick 'postmodern' solution, however, is ideology par excellence*. It all hinges on our persisting in this impossible position: although no clear line of demarcation separates ideology from reality, although ideology is already at work in everything we experience as 'reality', we must none the less maintain the tension that keeps the *critique* of ideology alive. Perhaps, following Kant, we could designate this impasse the 'antinomy of critico-ideological reason': ideology is not all; it is possible to assume a place that enables us to maintain a distance from it, *but this place from which one can denounce ideology must remain empty, it cannot be occupied by any positively determined reality* – the moment we yield to this temptation, we are back in ideology.

How are we to specify this empty place? Perhaps we should take as a starting point the thread that runs through our entire logico-narrative reconstruction of the notion of ideology: it is as if, at every stage, the same opposition, the same *undecidable* alternative Inside/Outside, repeats itself under a different exponent. First, there is the split within ideology 'in-itself': on the one hand, ideology stands for the distortion of rational argumentation and insight due to the weight of the 'pathological' external interests of power, exploitation, and so on; on the other, ideology resides in the very notion of a thought not permeated by some non-transparent power strategy, of an argument that does not rely upon some non-transparent rhetorical devices. . . . Next, this very externality splits into an 'inner externality' (the symbolic order, i.e. the decentred discursive mechanisms that generate Meaning) and an 'external externality' (the ISA and social rituals and practices that materialize ideology) – *the externality misrecognized by ideology is the externality of the 'text' itself as well as the externality of 'extra-textual' social reality.* Finally, this 'extra-textual' social reality itself is split into the institutional Exterior that dominates and regulates the life of individuals 'from above' (ISA), and ideology that is not imposed by the ISA but emerges 'spontaneously', 'from below', out of the extra-institutional activity of individuals (commodity fetishism) – to give it names, Althusser versus Lukács. This opposition between ISA and commodity fetishism – between the *materiality that always-already pertains to ideology as such* (material, effective apparatuses which give body to ideology) and *ideology that always-already pertains to materiality as such* (to the social actuality of production) – is ultimately the opposition between State and Market, between the external superior agency that organizes society 'from above' and society's 'spontaneous' self-organization.

This opposition, whose first philosophical manifestation is provided by the couple of Plato and Aristotle, finds its last expression in the guise of the two modes of cynical ideology: 'consumerist', post-Protestant, late-capitalist cynicism, and the cynicism that pertained to the late 'real Socialism'. Although, in both cases, the system functions only on condition that subjects maintain a cynical distance and do not 'take seriously' the 'official' values, the difference is remarkable; it turns upside down the doxa according to which late capitalism, as a (formally) 'free' society, relies on argumentative persuasion and free consent, 'manipulated' and fabricated as it may be; whereas Socialism resorted to the raw force of 'totalitarian' coercion. It is as if in late capitalism 'words do not count', no longer oblige: they increasingly seem to lose their performative power; whatever one says is drowned in the general indifference; the emperor is naked and the media trumpet forth this fact, yet nobody seems really to mind – that is, people continue to act as if the emperor is not naked. . . .

Perhaps the key feature of the symbolic economy of the late 'real Socialism' was, on the contrary, the almost paranoiac *belief in the power of the Word* – the state and the ruling party reacted with utmost nervousness and panic at the slightest public criticism, as if some vague critical hints in an obscure poem published in a low-circulation literary journal, or an essay in an academic philosophical journal, possessed the potential capacity to trigger the explosion of the entire socialist system. Incidentally, this feature renders 'real Socialism' almost sympathetic to our retrospective nostalgic view, since it bears witness to the legacy of the Enlightenment (the belief in the social efficacy of rational argumentation) that survived in it. This, perhaps, was why it was possible to undermine 'real Socialism' by means of peaceful civil society movements that operated at the level of the Word – belief in the power of the Word was the system's Achilles heel.[23]

The matrix of all these repetitions, perhaps, is the opposition between ideology as the universe of 'spontaneous' experience [*vécu*] whose grip we can break only by means of an effort of scientific reflection, and ideology as a radically non-spontaneous machine that distorts the authenticity of our life-experience from outside. That is to say, what we should always bear in mind is that, for Marx, the primordial mythological consciousness of the pre-class society out of which later ideologies grew (true to the heritage of German classicism, Marx saw the paradigm of this primordial social consciousness in Greek mythology) *is not yet ideology proper*, although (or, rather, precisely because) it is immediately *vécu*, and although it is obviously 'wrong', 'illusory' (it involves the divinization of the forces of nature, etc.); ideology proper emerges only with the division of labour and the class split, only when the 'wrong' ideas lose their 'immediate' character and are 'elaborated' by intellectuals in order to serve (to legitimize) the existing relations of domination – in short, only when the division into Master and Servant is conjugated with the division of labour itself into intellectual and physical labour. For that precise reason, Marx refused to categorize commodity fetishism as ideology: for him, ideology was always of the state and, as Engels put it, state itself is the first ideological force. In clear contrast, Althusser conceives ideology as an immediately experienced relationship to the universe – as such, it is eternal; when, following his self-critical turn, he introduces the concept of ISA, he returns in a way to Marx: ideology does not grow out of 'life itself', it comes into existence only in so far as society is regulated by state. (More precisely, the paradox and theoretical interest of Althusser resides in his conjugation of the two lines: in its very character of immediately experienced relationship to the universe, ideology is always-already regulated by the externality of State and its Ideological Apparatuses.)

This tension between 'spontaneity' and organized imposition introduces a kind of reflective distance into the very heart of the notion of ideology: ideology is always, by definition, 'ideology of ideology'. Suffice it to recall the disintegration of real Socialism: Socialism was perceived as the rule of 'ideological' oppression and indoctrination, whereas the passage into democracy-capitalism was experienced as deliverance from the constraints of ideology – however, was not this very experience of 'deliverance' in the course of which political parties and the market economy were perceived as 'non-ideological', as the 'natural state of things', ideological *par excellence*?[24] Our point is that this feature is *universal*: there is no ideology that does not assert itself by means of delimiting itself from another 'mere ideology'. An individual subjected to ideology can never say for himself 'I am in ideology', he always requires *another* corpus of doxa in order to distinguish his own 'true' position from it.

The first example here is provided by none other than Plato: philosophical *epistēmē* versus the confused doxa of the crowd. What about Marx? Although he may appear to fall into this trap (is not the entire *German Ideology* based on the opposition of ideological chimera and the study of 'actual life'?), things get complicated in his mature critique of political economy. That is to say, why, precisely, does Marx choose the term *fetishism* in order to designate the 'theological whimsy' of the universe of commodities? What one should bear in mind here is that 'fetishism' is a *religious* term for (previous) 'false' idolatry as opposed to (present) true belief: for the Jews, the fetish is the Golden Calf; for a partisan of pure spirituality, fetishism designates 'primitive' superstition, the fear of ghosts and other spectral apparitions, and so on. And the point of Marx is that the commodity universe provides the necessary fetishistic supplement to the 'official' spirituality: it may well be that the 'official' ideology of our society is Christian spirituality, but its actual foundation is none the less the idolatry of the Golden Calf, money.

In short, Marx's point is that there is no spirit without spirits-ghosts, no 'pure' spirituality without the obscene spectre of 'spiritualized matter'.[25] The first to accomplish this step 'from spirit to spirits' in the guise of the critique of pure spiritual idealism, of its lifeless 'negative' nihilism, was F.W.J. Schelling, the crucial, unjustly neglected philosopher of German Idealism. In the dialogue *Clara* (1810), he drove a wedge into the simple complementary mirror-relationship between Inside and Outside, between Spirit and Body, between the ideal and the real element that together form the living totality of the Organism, by calling attention to the double surplus that 'sticks out'. On the one hand, there is the *spiritual element of corporeality*: the presence, in matter itself, of a non-material but physical element, of a subtle corpse, relatively independent of time and space, which provides the material base of our free will (animal magnetism, etc.); on the other hand, there is the *corporeal element of spirituality*: the materializations of the spirit in a kind of pseudo-stuff, in substanceless apparitions (ghosts, living dead). It is clear how these two surpluses render the logic of commodity fetishism and of the ISA: commodity fetishism involves the uncanny 'spiritualization' of the commodity-body, whereas the ISA materialize the spiritual, substanceless big Other of ideology.

In his recent book on Marx, Jacques Derrida brought into play the term 'spectre' in order to indicate this elusive pseudo-materiality that subverts the classic ontological oppositions of reality and illusion, and so on.[26] And perhaps it is here that we should look for the last resort of ideology, for the pre-ideological kernel, the formal matrix, on which are grafted various ideological formations: in the fact that there is no reality without the spectre, that the circle of reality can be closed only by means of an uncanny spectral supplement. Why, then, is there no reality without the spectre? Lacan provides a precise answer to this question: (what we experience as) reality is not the 'thing itself', it is always-already symbolized, constituted, structured by symbolic mechanisms – and the problem resides in the fact that symbolization ultimately always fails, that it never succeeds in fully 'covering' the real, that it always involves some unsettled, unredeemed symbolic debt. *This real (the part of reality that remains non-symbolized) returns in the guise of spectral apparitions.* Consequently, 'spectre' is not to be confused with 'symbolic fiction', with the fact that reality itself has the structure of a fiction in that it is symbolically (or, as some sociologists put it, 'socially') constructed; the notions of spectre and (symbolic) fiction are co-dependent in their very incompatibility (they are 'complementary' in the quantum-mechanical sense). To put it simply, reality is never directly 'itself', it presents itself only via its incomplete-failed symbolization, and spectral apparitions emerge in this very gap that forever separates reality from the real, and on account of which reality has the character of a (symbolic) fiction: the spectre gives body to that which escapes (the symbolically structured) reality.[27]

The pre-ideological 'kernel' of ideology thus consists of the *spectral apparition that fills up the hole of the real.* This is what all the attempts to draw a clear line of separation between 'true' reality and illusion (or to ground illusion in reality) fail to take into account: if (what we experience as) 'reality' is to emerge, something has to be foreclosed from it – that is to say, 'reality', like truth, is, by definition, never 'whole'. *What the spectre conceals is not reality but its 'primordially repressed', the irrepresentable X on whose 'repression' reality itself is founded.* It may seem that we have thereby lost our way in speculative murky waters that have nothing whatsoever to do with concrete social struggles – is not the supreme example of such 'reality', however, provided by the Marxist concept of *class struggle?* The consequent thinking-out of this concept compels us to admit that there is no class struggle 'in reality': 'class struggle' designates the very antagonism that prevents the objective (social) reality from constituting itself as a self-enclosed whole.[28]

True, according to the Marxist tradition, class struggle is the 'totalizing' principle of society; this, however, does not mean that it is a kind of ultimate guarantee authorizing us to grasp society as a rational totality ('the ultimate meaning of every social phenomenon is determined by its position within the class struggle'): the ultimate paradox of the notion of 'class struggle' is that society is 'held together' by the very antagonism, splitting, that forever prevents its closure in a harmonious, transparent, rational Whole – by the very impediment that undermines every rational totalization. Although 'class struggle' is nowhere directly given as a positive entity, it none the less functions, *in its very absence*, as the point of reference enabling us to locate every social phenomenon – not by relating it to class struggle as its ultimate meaning ('transcendental signified') but by conceiving it as (an)other attempt to conceal and 'patch up' the rift of class antagonism, to efface its traces. What we have here is the structural-dialectical paradox of *an effect that exists only in order to efface the causes of its existence*, an effect that in a way resists its own cause.

In other words, class struggle is 'real' in the strict Lacanian sense: a 'hitch', an impediment which gives rise to ever-new symbolizations by means of which one endeavours to integrate and domesticate it (the corporatist translation-displacement of class struggle into the organic articulation of the 'members' of the 'social body', for example), but which simultaneously condemns these endeavours to ultimate failure. Class struggle is none other than the name for the unfathomable limit that cannot be objectivized, located within the social totality, since it is itself that limit which prevents us from conceiving society as a closed totality. Or – to put it in yet another way – 'class struggle' designates the point with regard to which 'there is no metalanguage': in so far as every position within social totality is ultimately overdetermined by class struggle, no neutral place is excluded from the dynamics of class struggle from which it would be possible to locate class struggle within the social totality.

This paradoxical status of class struggle can be articulated by means of the crucial Hegelian distinction between Substance and Subject. At the level of Substance, class struggle is conditional on the 'objective' social process; it functions as the secondary indication of some more fundamental discord in this process, a discord regulated by positive mechanisms independent of class struggle ('class struggle breaks out when the relations of production are no longer in accordance with the development of the productive forces').[29] We pass to the level of Subject when we acknowledge that class struggle does not pop up at the end, as the effect of an objective process, but is always-already at work in the very heart of the objective process itself (capitalists develop means of production in order to lower the relative and absolute value of the labour force; the value of the labour force itself is not objectively given but results from the class struggle, etc.). In short, it is not possible to isolate any 'objective' social process or mechanism whose innermost logic does not involve the 'subjective' dynamics of class struggle; or – to put it differently – *the very 'peace', the absence of struggle, is already a form of struggle*, the (temporal) victory of one of the sides in the struggle. In so far as the very invisibility of class struggle ('class peace') is already an effect of class struggle – that is, of the hegemony exerted by one side in the struggle – one is tempted to compare the status of class struggle to that of the Hitchcockian McGuffin: 'What is class struggle? – The antagonistic process that constitutes classes and determines their relationship. – But in our society there is no struggle between the classes! – You see how it functions!'[30]

This notion of class struggle *qua* antagonism enables us to contrast the real of antagonism with the complementary polarity of opposites: perhaps the reduction of antagonism to polarity is one of the elementary ideological operations. Suffice it to recall the standard New Age procedure of presupposing a kind of natural balance of cosmic opposites (reason–emotions, active–passive, intellect–intuition, consciousness–unconscious, *yin–yang*, etc.), and then of conceiving our age as the age that laid too much stress upon one of the two poles, upon the 'male principle' of activity–reason – the solution, of course, lies in re-establishing the equilibrium of the two principles . . . .

The 'progressive' tradition also bears witness to numerous attempts to conceive (sexual, class) antagonism as the coexistence of two opposed positive entities: from a certain kind of 'dogmatic' Marxism that posits 'their' bourgeois science and 'our' proletarian science side by side, to a certain kind of feminism that posits masculine discourse and feminine discourse or 'writing' side by side. Far from being 'too extreme', these attempts are, on the contrary, not extreme enough: they presuppose as their position of enunciation a third neutral medium within which the two poles coexist; that is to say, they back down on the consequences of the fact that there is no point of convergence, no neutral ground shared by the two antagonistic sexual or class positions.[31] As far as science is concerned: science, of course, is not neutral in the sense of objective knowledge not affected by class struggle and at the disposal of all classes, yet for that very reason it is *one*; there are not two sciences, and class struggle is precisely the struggle for this one science, for who will appropriate it. It is the same with 'discourse': there are not two discourses, 'masculine' and 'feminine'; there is *one* discourse split from within by the sexual antagonism – that is to say, providing the 'terrain' on which the battle for hegemony takes place.

What is at stake here could also be formulated as the problem of the status of 'and' as a category. In Althusser 'and' functions as a precise theoretical category: when an 'and' appears in the title of some of his essays, this little word unmistakably signals the confrontation of some general ideological notion (or, more precisely, of a neutral, ambiguous notion that oscillates between its ideological actuality and its scientific potentiality) with its specification which tells us how we are to concretize this notion so that it begins to function as non-ideological, as a strict theoretical concept. 'And' thus *splits up* the ambiguous starting unity, introduces into it the difference between ideology and science.

Suffice it to mention two examples. 'Ideology *and* Ideological State Apparatuses': ISA designate the concrete network of the material conditions of existence of an ideological edifice – that is, that which ideology itself has to misrecognize in its 'normal' functioning. 'Contradiction *and* Overdetermination': in so far as the concept of overdetermination designates the undecidable complex totality *qua* the mode of existence of contradiction, it enables us to discard the idealist-teleological burden that usually weighs upon the notion of contradiction (the teleological necessity that guarantees in advance the 'sublation' of the contradiction in a higher unity).[32] Perhaps the first exemplary case of such an 'and' is Marx's famous 'freedom, equality, *and Bentham*' from *Capital*: the supplementary 'Bentham' stands for the social circumstances that provide the concrete content of the pathetic phrases on freedom and equality – commodity exchange, market bargaining, utilitarian egotism . . . . And do we not encounter a homologous conjunction in Heidegger's *Being and Time*? 'Being' designates the fundamental theme of philosophy in its abstract universality, whereas 'time' stands for the concrete horizon of the sense of being.

'And' is thus, in a sense, *tautological*: it conjoins the same content in its two modalities – first in its ideological evidence, then in the extra-ideological conditions of its existence. For that reason, no third term is needed here to designate the medium itself in which the two terms, conjoined by means of the 'and', encounter each other: this third term is already the second term itself that stands for the network (the 'medium') of the concrete existence of an ideological universality. In contrast to this dialectico-materialist 'and', the idealist-ideological 'and' functions precisely as this third term, as the common medium of the polarity or plurality of elements. Therein resides the gap that forever separates Freud from Jung in their respective notions of libido: Jung conceives of libido as a kind of neutral energy with its concrete forms (sexual, creative, destructive libido) as its different 'metamorphoses', whereas Freud insists that libido in its concrete existence is irreducibly *sexual* – all other forms of libido are forms of 'ideological' misrecognition of this sexual content. And is not the same operation to be repeated apropos of 'man *and* woman'? Ideology compels us to assume 'humanity' as the neutral medium within which 'man' and 'woman' are posited as the two complementary poles – against this ideological

evidence, one could maintain that 'woman' stands for the aspect of concrete existence and 'man' for the empty-ambiguous universality. The
paradox (of a profoundly Hegelian nature) is that 'woman' – that is, the
moment of specific difference – functions as the encompassing ground
that accounts for the emergence of the universality of man.

This interpretation of social antagonism (class struggle) as Real, not
as (part of) objective social reality, also enables us to counter the worn-
out line of argumentation according to which one has to abandon the
notion of ideology, since the gesture of distinguishing 'mere ideology'
from 'reality' implies the epistemologically untenable 'God's view', that
is, access to objective reality as it 'truly is'. The question of the suitability
of the term 'class struggle' to designate today's dominant form of antagonism is secondary here, it concerns concrete social analysis; what
matters is that the very constitution of social reality involves the 'primordial repression' of an antagonism, so that the ultimate support of
the critique of ideology – the extra-ideological point of reference that
authorizes us to denounce the content of our immediate experience as
'ideological' – is not 'reality' but the 'repressed' real of antagonism.

In order to clarify this uncanny logic of antagonism *qua* real, let us
recall the analogy between Claude Lévi-Strauss's structural approach
and Einstein's theory of relativity. One usually attributes to Einstein the
relativization of space with regard to the observer's point of view – that
is, the cancellation of the notion of absolute space and time. The theory
of relativity, however, involves its own absolute constant: the space–
time interval between two events is an absolute that never varies.
Space–time interval is defined as the hypotenuse of a right-angled triangle whose legs are the time and space distance between two events.
One observer may be in a state of motion such that for him there is a
time and a distance involved between two events; another may be in a
state of motion such that his measuring devices indicate a different distance and a different time between the events, but the space–time interval between the two events does not in fact vary. *This* constant is the
Lacanian Real that 'remains the same in all possible universes (of observation)'. And it is a homologous constant that we encounter in Lévi-
Strauss's exemplary analysis of the spatial arrangement of buildings in
an aboriginal South American village (from his *Structural Anthropology*).

The inhabitants are divided into two subgroups; when we ask an individual to draw the ground-plan of his or her village (the spatial arrangement of cottages) on a piece of paper or on sand, we obtain two
quite different answers, depending on which subgroup he or she belongs to: a member of the first subgroup (let us call it 'conservative-
corporatist') perceives the ground-plan of the village as circular – a ring
of houses more or less symmetrically arranged around the central

temple; whereas a member of the second ('revolutionary-antagonistic') subgroup perceives his or her village as two distinct clusters of houses separated by an invisible frontier . . . . Where is the homology with Einstein here? Lévi-Strauss's central point is that this example should in no way entice us into a cultural relativism according to which the perception of social space depends on the observer's group member-ship: the very splitting into the two 'relative' perceptions implies the hidden reference to a constant – not the objective, 'actual' arrangement of buildings but a traumatic kernel, a fundamental antagonism the inhabitants of the village were not able to symbolize, to account for, to 'internalize', to come to terms with: an imbalance in social relations that prevented the community from stabilizing itself into a harmonious whole. The two perceptions of the ground-plan are simply two mutually exclusive endeavours to cope with this traumatic antagonism, to heal its wound via the imposition of a balanced symbolic structure. (And it is hardly necessary to add that things are exactly the same with respect to sexual difference: 'masculine' and 'feminine' are like the two configurations of houses in the Lévi-Straussian village. . . .)

Common sense tells us that it is easy to rectify the bias of subjective perceptions and ascertain the 'true state of things': we hire a helicopter and photograph the village directly from above . . . . In this way we obtain an undistorted view of reality, yet we completely miss the real of social antagonism, the non-symbolizable traumatic kernel that found expression in the very distortions of reality, in the fantasized displace-ments of the 'actual' arrangement of houses. This is what Lacan has in mind when he claims that *distortion and/or dissimulation is in itself revealing*: what emerges via distortions of the accurate representation of reality is the real – that is, the trauma around which social reality is structured. In other words, if all the inhabitants of the village were to draw the same accurate ground-plan, we would be dealing with a non-antagonistic, harmonious community. If we are to arrive at the fundamental paradox implied by the notion of commodity fetishism, however, we have to go one step further and imagine, say, two different 'actual' villages each of which realizes, in the arrangement of its dwellings, one of the two fantasized ground-plans evoked by Lévi-Strauss: in this case, the structure of social reality itself ma-terializes an attempt to cope with the real of antagonism. 'Reality' itself, in so far as it is regulated by a symbolic fiction, conceals the real of an antagonism – and it is this real, foreclosed from the symbolic fiction, that returns in the guise of spectral apparitions.

Such a reading of spectrality as that which fills out the unrepresen-table abyss of antagonism, of the non-symbolized real, also enables us to assume a precise distance from Derrida, for whom spectrality, the apparition of the Other, provides the ultimate horizon of ethics. According to Derrida, the metaphysical ontologization of spectrality is rooted in the fact that the thought is horrified at itself, at its own founding gesture; that it draws back from the spirit convoked by this gesture. Therein resides *in nuce* his reading of Marx and the history of Marxism: the original impulse of Marx consisted in the Messianic promise of Justice *qua* spectral Otherness, a promise that is only as *avenir*, yet-to-come, never as a simple *futur*, what will be; the 'totalitarian' turn of Marxism that culminated in Stalinism has its roots in the ontologization of the spectre, in the translation of the spectral Promise into a positive ontological Project . . . . Lacan, however, goes a step further here: *spectre as such already bears witness to a retreat, a withdrawal – from what?*

> Most people are terrified when they encounter freedom, like when they encounter magic, anything inexplicable, especially the world of spirits.[33]

This proposition of Schelling can be read in two ways, depending on how we interpret the comparison – in what precise sense is freedom like a spectre? Our – Lacanian – premiss here is that 'freedom' designates the moment when the 'principle of the sufficient reason' is suspended, the moment of the *act* that breaks the 'great chain of being', of the symbolic reality in which we are embedded; consequently, it is not sufficient to say that we fear the spectre – the spectre itself already emerges out of a fear, out of our escape from something even more horrifying: freedom. When we confront the miracle of freedom, there are two ways of reacting to it:

- EITHER we 'ontologize' freedom by way of conceiving it as the terrestrial apparition of a 'higher' stratum of reality, as the miraculous, inexplicable intervention into our universe of another, supra-sensible universe that persists in its Beyond, yet is accessible to us, common mortals, only in the guise of nebulous chimera;
- OR we conceive this universe of Beyond, this redoubling of our terrestrial universe into another *Geisterwelt*, as an endeavour to gentrify the act of freedom, to cope with its traumatic impact – spectre is the positivization of the abyss of freedom, a void that assumes the form of quasi-being.

Therein resides the gap that separates Lacan from Derrida: our primary duty is not towards the spectre, whatever form it assumes.[34] The act of freedom *qua* real not only transgresses the limits of what we experience as 'reality', it cancels our very primordial indebtedness to the spectral Other. Here, therefore, Lacan is on the side of Marx against Derrida: in the act we 'leave the dead to bury their dead', as Marx put it in the 'Eighteenth Brumaire of Louis Bonaparte'.

The problematic of ideology, its very elusive status as attested to by its 'postmodern' vicissitudes, has thus brought us back to Marx, to the centrality of the social antagonism ('class struggle'). As we have seen, however, this 'return to Marx' entails a radical displacement of the Marxian theoretical edifice: a gap emerges in the very heart of historical materialism – that is, the problematic of ideology has led us to the inherently incomplete, 'non-all' character of historical materialism – something must be excluded, foreclosed, if social reality is to constitute itself. To those to whom this result of ours appears far-fetched, speculative, alien to the concrete social concerns of the Marxist theory of ideology, the best answer is provided by a recent work of Étienne Balibar, who arrived at exactly the same conclusion via a concrete analysis of the vicissitudes of the notion of ideology in Marx and the history of Marxism:

> the idea of a theory of ideology was only ever a *way ideally to complete historical materialism*, to 'fill a hole' in its representation of the social totality, and thus a way ideally to constitute historical materialism as a system of explanation complete in its kind, at least 'in principle'.[35]

Balibar also provides the location of this hole to be filled by the theory of ideology: it concerns social antagonism ('class struggle') as the inherent limit that traverses society and prevents it from constituting itself as a positive, complete, self-enclosed entity. It is at this precise place that psychoanalysis has to intervene (Balibar somewhat enigmatically evokes the concept of the unconscious[36]) – not, of course, in the old Freudo–Marxist manner, as the element destined to fill up the hole of historical materialism and thus to render possible its *completion*, but, on the contrary, as the theory that enables us to conceptualize this hole of historical materialism as irreducible, because it is constitutive:

> The 'Marxist theory of ideology' would then be symptomatic of the permanent discomfort Marxism maintains with its own critical recognition of the class struggle.
> . . . *the concept of ideology* denotes no other object than that of the nontotalizable (or nonrepresentable within a unique given order) complexity of the historical process; . . . historical materialism is incomplete and incompletable in principle, not only in the temporal dimension (since it postulates the relative unpredictability of the effects of determinate causes),

but also in its theoretical 'topography', since it requires the articulation of
the class struggle to concepts that have a different materiality (such as the
unconscious).[37]

Can psychoanalysis effectively play this key role of providing the
missing support of the Marxist theory of ideology (or, more precisely,
of accounting for the very lack in the Marxist theory that becomes
visible apropos of the deadlocks in the theory of ideology)? The
standard reproach to psychoanalysis is that in so far as it intervenes in
the domain of the social and/or political, it ultimately always ends up in
some version of the theory of the 'horde' with the feared–beloved
Leader at its head, who dominates the subjects via the 'organic' libidinal
link of transference, of a community constituted by some primordial
crime and thus held together by shared guilt.[38]

The first answer to this reproach seems obvious: was not precisely
this theoretical complex – the relationship between the mass and its
Leader – the blind spot in the history of Marxism, what Marxist
thought was unable to conceptualize, to 'symbolize', its 'foreclosed' that
subsequently returned in the real, in the guise of the so-called Stalinist
'cult of personality'? The theoretical, as well as practical, solution to the
problem of authoritarian populism–organicism that again and again
thwarts progressive political projects is conceivable today only via
psychoanalytic theory. This, however, in no way entails that psychoanalysis is somehow limited in its scope to the negative gesture of
delineating the libidinal economy of 'regressive' proto-totalitarian
communities: in the necessary obverse of this gesture, psychoanalysis
also delineates the symbolic economy of how – from time to time, at
least – we are able to break the vicious circle that breeds 'totalitarian'
closure. When, for example, Claude Lefort articulated the notion of
'democratic invention', he did it through a reference to the Lacanian
categories of the Symbolic and the Real: 'democratic invention' consists
in the assertion of the purely symbolic, empty place of Power that no
'real' subject can ever fill out.[39] One should always bear in mind that the
subject of psychoanalysis is not some primordial subject of drives, but –
as Lacan pointed out again and again – the modern, Cartesian subject
of science. There is a crucial difference between le Bon's and Freud's
'crowd': for Freud, 'crowd' is not a primordial, archaic entity, the
starting point of evolution, but an 'artificial' pathological formation
whose genesis is to be displayed – the 'archaic' character of the 'crowd'
is precisely the illusion to be dispelled via theoretical analysis.

Perhaps a comparison with Freud's theory of dreams could be of
some help here. Freud points out that within a dream we encounter the
hard kernel of the Real precisely in the guise of a 'dream within the

dream' – that is to say, where the distance from reality seems
redoubled. In a somewhat homologous way, we encounter the inherent limit of social reality, what has to be foreclosed if the consistent
field of reality is to emerge, precisely in the guise of the problematic of
ideology, of a 'superstructure', of something that appears to be a mere
epiphenomenon, a mirror-reflection, of 'true' social life. We are
dealing here with the paradoxical topology in which the surface ('mere
ideology') is directly linked to – occupies the place of, stands in for –
what is 'deeper than depth itself', more real than reality itself.

Notes

1. See Étienne Balibar, 'Racism as Universalism', in *Masses, Classes, Ideas*, New York:
Routledge 1994, pp. 198–9.
2. Renata Salecl, *The Spoils of Freedom*, London: Routledge 1994, p. 13.
3. See Jeffrey Masson, *The Assault on Truth: Freud's Suppression of the Seduction Theory*,
New York: Farrar, Straus & Giroux 1984.
4. Jacqueline Rose, 'Where Does the Misery Come From?', in Richard Feldstein and
Judith Roof, eds, *Feminism and Psychoanalysis*, Ithaca, NY and London: Cornell University
Press 1989, pp. 25–39.
5. The very title of Rose's article – 'Where Does the Misery Come From?' – is indicative
here: one of the functions of ideology is precisely to explain the 'origins of Evil', to
'objectivize'-externalize its cause, and thus to discharge us of responsibility for it.
6. For that reason, the 'epochal horizons of pre-understanding' (the big theme of
hermeneutics) cannot be designated as ideology.
7. For a concise account of the theoretical consequences of this double trauma, see
Theodor W. Adorno, 'Messages in a Bottle', in this volume (Chapter 1). As for the way
Adorno's critique of identitarian thought announces post-structuralist 'deconstructionism', see Peter Dews, 'Adorno, Post-Structuralism and the Critique of Identity', in
this volume (Chapter 2).
8. In his *La philosophie de Marx* (Paris: La Découverte 1993), Étienne Balibar drew
attention to the enigma of the complete disappearance of the notion of ideology in
Marx's texts after 1850. In *The German Ideology*, the (omnipresent) notion of ideology is
conceived as the chimera that supplements social production and reproduction – the
conceptual opposition that serves as its background is the one between the 'actual
life-process' and its distorted reflection in the heads of ideologues. Things get
complicated, however, the moment Marx engages in the 'critique of political economy':
what he encounters here in the guise of 'commodity fetishism' is no longer an 'illusion'
that 'reflects' reality but an uncanny chimera at work in the very heart of the actual
process of social production.
   The same enigmatic eclipse may be detected in many a post-Marxist author: Ernesto
Laclau, for example, after the almost inflationary use of the concept of ideology in his
Politics and Ideology (London: Verso 1977), totally renounces it in *Hegemony and Socialist
Strategy* (co-authored with Chantal Mouffe, London: Verso 1985).
9. To avoid a fatal misunderstanding, one must insist that this line of succession is not
to be read as a hierarchical progress, as a 'sublation' or 'suppression' of the preceding
mode. When, for example, we approach ideology in the guise of Ideological State
Apparatuses, this in no way entails the obsolescence or irrelevance of the level of
argumentation. Today, when official ideology is increasingly indifferent towards its own
consistency, an analysis of its inherent and constitutive inconsistencies is crucial if we are
to pierce the actual mode of its functioning.

10. For an exemplary presentation of the Habermasian position, see Seyla Benhabib, 'The Critique of Instrumental Reason', in this volume (Chapter 3).

11. See Oswald Ducrot, *Le dire et le dit*, Paris: Éditions de Minuit 1986.

12. See Michel Pêcheux, 'The Mechanism of Ideological (Mis)recognition', in this volume (Chapter 6). One should bear in mind here that the key source of the critique of ideological evidences in the discourse analysis is Jacques Lacan's 'The Mirror-phase as Formative of the Function of the I' (included in this volume [Chapter 4]), the text that introduced the concept of recognition [*reconnaissance*] as misrecognition [*méconnaissance*].

13. See Laclau, *Politics and Ideology*.

14. See Louis Althusser, 'Ideology and Ideological State Apparatuses', in this volume (Chapter 5).

15. Herein resides the interconnection between the ritual that pertains to 'Ideological State Apparatuses' and the act of interpellation: when I believe that I knelt down because of my belief, I simultaneously 'recognize' myself in the call of the Other-God who dictated that I kneel down . . . . This point was developed by Isolde Charim in her intervention 'Dressur und Verneinung' at the colloquium *Der Althusser-Effekt*, Vienna, 17–20 March 1994.

16. See Theodor W. Adorno, 'Beitrag zur Ideologienlehre', in *Gesammelte Schriften: Ideologie*, Frankfurt: Suhrkamp 1972.

17. See Wolfgang Fritz Haug, 'Annäherung an die faschistische Modalität des Ideologischen', in *Faschismus und Ideologie* 1, Argument-Sonderband 60, Berlin: Argument Verlag 1980.

18. Discourse analysis and the Althusserian reconceptualization of ideology also opened up a new approach in feminist studies. Its two representative cases are Michèle Barrett's post-Marxist discourse analysis (see her 'Ideology, Politics, Hegemony: From Gramsci to Laclau and Mouffe' in this volume [Chapter 11]) and Richard Rorty's pragmatist deconstructionism (see his 'Feminism, Ideology and Deconstruction: A Pragmatist View', in this volume [Chapter 10]).

19. See Nicholas Abercrombie, Stephen Hill and Bryan Turner, 'Determinacy and Indeterminacy in the Theory of Ideology'; and Göran Therborn's critical response, 'The New Questions of Subjectivity', both in this volume (Chapters 7, 8). For a general overview of the historical development of the concept of ideology that led to this self-dispersal, see Terry Eagleton, 'Ideology and its Vicissitudes in Western Marxism', in this volume (Chapter 9).

20. For an approach to this 'implicit' ideology, see Pierre Bourdieu and Terry Eagleton, 'Doxa and Common Life', in this volume (Chapter 12).

21. For the notion of ideology that structures (social) reality, see Slavoj Žižek, 'How Did Marx Invent the Symptom?', in this volume (Chapter 14).

22. See Fredric Jameson, 'Postmodernism and the Market', in this volume (Chapter 13).

23. Cynicism as a postmodern attitude is superbly exemplified by one of the key features of Robert Altman's film *Nashville*: the enigmatic status of its songs. Altman, of course, entertains a critical distance from the universe of country music that epitomizes the *bêtise* of everyday American ideology; one entirely misses the point, however, if one perceives the songs performed in the film as a mocking imitation of 'true' country music – these songs are to be taken quite 'seriously'; one simply has to enjoy them. Perhaps the ultimate enigma of postmodernism resides in this coexistence of the two inconsistent attitudes, misperceived by the usual leftist criticism of young intellectuals who, although theoretically aware of the capitalist machinery of *Kulturindustrie*, unproblematically enjoy the products of rock industry.

24. Note the case of Kieslowski: his films shot in the damp, oppressive atmosphere of late Socialism (*Decalogue*) practise an almost unheard-of critique of ('official' as well as 'dissident') ideology; whereas the moment he left Poland for the 'freedom' of France, we witness the massive intrusion of ideology (see the New Age obscurantism of *La double vie de Véronique*).

25. Within the domain of the law, this opposition between *Geist* and the obscene *Geisterwelt* assumes the form of the opposition between the explicit public written Law and its

superego obverse – that is, the set of unwritten-unacknowledged rules that guarantee the cohesion of a community. (As to this opposition, see Chapter 3 of Slavoj Žižek, *The Metastases of Enjoyment*, London: Verso 1994.) Suffice it to recall the mysteriously obscene institution of fraternities–sororities in the American campuses, these half-clandestine communities with their secret rules of initiation where the pleasures of sex, drinking, and so on, and the spirit of authority go hand in hand; or the image of the English public school in Lindsay Anderson's *If*: . . . the terror imposed by the elder students upon the younger, who are submitted to the humiliating rituals of power and sexual abuse. Professors can thus play the role of good-humoured liberals, amusing students with jokes, entering the classroom on a bicycle, and so on – the true support of power lies elsewhere, in the elder students whose acts bear witness to an indiscernible mixture of Order and its Transgression, of sexual enjoyment and the 'repressive' exercise of power. In other words, what we find here is a transgression that serves as the ultimate support of Order, an indulgence in illicit sexuality that directly grounds 'repression'.

26. See Jacques Derrida, *Spectres de Marx*, Paris: Galilée 1993.

27. This gap that separates the real from reality is what opens up the space for *performative* in its opposition to constative. That is to say, without the surplus of the real over reality that emerges in the guise of a spectre, symbolization would merely designate, point towards, some positive content in reality. In its most radical dimension, performative is the attempt to conjure the real, to gentrify the spectre that is the Other: 'spectre' is originally the Other as such, another subject in the abyss of his or her freedom. Lacan's classic example: by saying 'You are my wife!', I thereby oblige–constrain the Other; I endeavour to entrap her abyss into a symbolic obligation.

28. This notion of antagonism comes, of course, from Laclau and Mouffe, *Hegemony and Socialist Strategy*.

29. What gets lost in the notion of social classes *qua* positive entities that get enmeshed in struggle only from time to time is the genuinely dialectical paradox of the relationship between the universal and the particular: although the whole of history hitherto is the history of class struggle (as Marx claims at the beginning of Chapter 1 of *The Communist Manifesto*), there exists (one is almost tempted to write it: ex-sists) *stricto sensu* only one class, the bourgeoisie, the capitalist class. Prior to capitalism, classes were not yet 'for themselves', not yet 'posited as such'; they did not properly exist but 'insisted' as the underlying structuring principle that found its expression in the guise of states, castes, moments of the organic social edifice, of society's 'corporate body', whereas proletariat *stricto sensu* is no longer a class but a class that coincides with its opposite, a non-class – the historical tendency to negate class division is inscribed into its very class position.

30. For this Hitchcockian analogy I am indebted to Isolde Charim and Robert Pfaller.

31. In the case of sexual difference, the theological name for this third asexual position is 'angel'; for that reason, the question of the *sex of angels* is absolutely crucial for a materialist analysis.

32. This point was developed by Robert Pfaller in his intervention 'Zum Althusserianischen Nominalismus' at the colloquium *Der Althusser-Effekt*.

33. F.W.J. Schelling, 'Clara', in *Sämtliche Werke* IX, Stuttgart: Cotta 1856–61, p. 39.

34. Or, to put this distance of ours towards Derrida in a different way: does not Derrida himself, apropos of the spectre, get caught up in the logic of conjuration? According to Derrida, the ultimate 'source of evil' resides in the ontologization of the spectre, in the reduction of its undecidable status (with reference to the couple reality/illusion) to a 'mere appearance' opposed to some (ideal or real) full existence. Derrida's entire effort is directed into ensuring that the spectre will remain the spectre, into preventing its ontologization – is not Derrida's theory itself, therefore, a conjuration destined to preserve the spectre in the intermediate space of the living dead? Does not this lead him to repeat the classic metaphysical paradox of the conjunction of impossibility and prohibition that he himself articulated apropos of the supplement (the supplement *cannot* endanger the purity of the Origin, which is why we must *fight against it*): the spectre *cannot* be ontologized, which is why this ontologization *must not* happen, one should fight against it . . . .

35. Étienne Balibar, 'Politics and Truth: The Vacillation of Ideology, II', in *Masses, Classes, Ideas*, p. 173.

36. If it is to play this crucial role, the concept of the unconscious is to be conceived in the strictly Freudian sense, as 'trans-individual' – that is, beyond the ideological opposition of 'individual' and 'collective' unconscious: the subject's unconscious is always grounded in a transferential relationship towards the Other; it is always 'external' with regard to the subject's monadic existence.

37. Balibar, 'Politics and Truth', pp. 173–4.

38. One is usually quick to add that this structure of the community of guilt dominated by the feared–beloved paternal figure of the Leader has been faithfully reproduced in all psychoanalytic organizations, from the International Psychoanalytical Association to Lacan's *école freudienne*.

39. See Claude Lefort, *Democracy and Political Theory*, Oxford: Polity Press 1988.

1

Messages in a Bottle

Theodor W. Adorno

I

Key people – The self-important type who thinks himself something only when confirmed by the role he plays in collectives which are none, existing merely for the sake of collectivity; the delegate with the armband; the rapt speechmaker spicing his address with wholesome wit and prefacing his concluding remark with a wistful 'Would that it were'; the charity vulture and the professor hastening from one congress to the next – they all once called forth the laughter befitting the naive, provincial and petty-bourgeois. Now the resemblance to the nineteenth-century satire has been discarded; the principle has spread doggedly from the caricatures to the whole bourgeois class. Not only have its members been subjected to unflagging social control by competition and co-option in their professional life, their private life too has been absorbed by the reified formations to which interpersonal relations have congealed. The reasons, to start with, are crudely material: only by proclaiming assent through laudable service to the community as it is, by admission to a recognized group, be it merely a freemasonry degenerated to a skittles club, do you earn the trust that pays off in a catch of customers and clients and the award of sinecures. The substantial citizen does not qualify merely by bank credit or even by dues to his organizations; he must donate his life-blood and the free time left over from the larceny business, as chairman or treasurer of committees he was half drawn to as he half succumbed. No hope is left to him but the obligatory tribute in the club circular when his heart attack catches him up. Not to be a member of anything is to arouse suspicion: when seeking naturaliz-ation, you are expressly asked to list your memberships. This,

however, rationalized as the individual's willingness to cast off his
egoism and dedicate himself to a whole which is really no more than
the universal objectification of egoism, is reflected in people's behaviour. Powerless in an overwhelming society, the individual experiences himself only as socially mediated. The institutions made by
people are thus additionally fetishized: since subjects have known
themselves only as exponents of institutions, these have acquired the
aspect of something divinely ordained. You feel yourself to the
marrow a doctor's wife, a member of a faculty, a chairman of the
committee of religious experts – I once heard a villain publicly use
that phrase without raising a laugh – as one might in other times have
felt oneself part of a family or tribe. You become once again in
consciousness what you are in your being in any case. Compared to
the illusion of the self-sufficient personality existing independently in
the commodity society, such consciousness is truth. You really are no
more than doctor's wife, faculty member or religious expert. But the
negative truth becomes a lie as positivity. The less functional sense the
social division of labour has, the more stubbornly subjects cling to
what social fatality has inflicted on them. Estrangement becomes
closeness, dehumanization humanity, the extinguishing of the subject
its confirmation. The socialization of human beings today perpetuates
their asociality, while not allowing even the social misfit to pride
himself on being human.

II

Legalities – What the Nazis did to the Jews was unspeakable: language
has no word for it, since even mass murder would have sounded, in
face of its planned, systematic totality, like something from the good
old days of the serial killer. And yet a term needed to be found if the
victims – in any case too many for their names to be recalled – were to
be spared the curse of having no thoughts turned unto them. So in
English the concept of genocide was coined. But by being codified, as
set down in the International Declaration of Human Rights, the
unspeakable was made, for the sake of protest, commensurable. By its
elevation to a concept, its possibility is virtually recognized: an
institution to be forbidden, rejected, discussed. One day negotiations
may take place in the forum of the United Nations on whether some
new atrocity comes under the heading of genocide, whether nations
have a right to intervene that they do not want to exercise in any case,
and whether, in view of the unforeseen difficulty of applying it in
practice, the whole concept of genocide should be removed from the

statutes. Soon afterwards there are inside-page headlines in jour-
nalese: East Turkestan genocide programme nears completion.

III

Freedom as they know it – People have so manipulated the concept of
freedom that it finally boils down to the right of the stronger and richer
to take from the weaker and poorer whatever they still have. Attempts
to change this are seen as shameful intrusions into the realm of the very
individuality that by the logic of that freedom has dissolved into an
administered void. But the objective spirit of language knows better.
German and English reserve the word 'free' for things and services
which cost nothing. Aside from a critique of political economy, this
bears witness to the unfreedom posited in the exchange relationship
itself; there is no freedom as long as everything has its price, and in
reified society things exempted from the price mechanism exist only as
pitiful rudiments. On closer inspection they too are usually found to
have their price, and to be handouts with commodities or at least with
domination: parks make prisons more endurable to those not in them.
For people with a free, spontaneous, serene and nonchalant temper,
however, for those who derive freedom as a privilege from unfreedom,
language holds ready an apposite name: that of impudence.

IV

Les Adieux – 'Goodbye' has for centuries been an empty formula. Now
relationships have gone the same way. Leavetaking is obsolete. Two
who belong together may part because one changes his domicile;
people are anyway no longer at home in a town, but as the ultimate
consequence of freedom of movement, subject their whole lives even
spatially to whatever the most favourable conditions of the labour
market may be. Then it's over, or they meet. To be lastingly apart and
to hold love fast has become unthinkable. 'O parting, fountain of all
words', but it has run dry, and nothing comes out except bye, bye or
ta-ta. Airmail and courier delivery substitute logistical problems for the
anxious wait for the letter, even where the absent partner has not
jettisoned anything not palpably to hand as ballast. Airline directors
can hold jubilee speeches on how much uncertainty and sorrow people
are thereby spared. But the liquidation of parting is a matter of life and
death to the traditional notion of humanity. Who could still love if the
moment is excluded when the other, corporeal being is perceived as an

image compressing the whole continuity of life as into a heavy fruit? What would hope be without distance? Humanity was the awareness of the presence of that not present, which evaporates in a condition which accords all things not present the palpable semblance of presence and immediacy, and hence has only scorn for what finds no enjoyment in such simulation. Yet to insist on parting's inner possibility in face of its pragmatic impossibility would be a lie, for the inward does not unfold within itself but only in relation to the objective, and to make 'inward' a collapsed outwardness does violence to the inward itself, which is left to sustain itself as if on its own flame. The restoration of gestures would follow the example of the professor of German literature who, on Christmas Eve, held his sleeping children for a moment before the shining tree to cause a *déjà vu* and steep them in myth. A humanity come of age will have to transcend its own concept of the emphatically human, positively. Otherwise its absolute negation, the inhuman, will carry off victory.

V

Gentlemen's honour – *Vis-à-vis* women men have assumed the duty of discretion, one of the means whereby the crudity of violence is made to appear softened, control as mutual concession. Since they have outlawed promiscuity to secure woman as a possession, while yet needing promiscuity to prevent their own renunciation from rising to an unendurable pitch, men have made to the women of their class who give themselves without marriage the tacit promise not to speak of it to any other man, or to infringe the patriarchal dictate of womanly reputation. Discretion then became the joyous source of all secrecy, all artful triumphs over the powers that be, indeed, even of trust, through which distinction and integrity are formed. The letter Hölderlin addressed to his mother after the fatal Frankfurt catastrophe, without being moved by the expression of his ultimate despair to hint at the reason for his breach with Herr Gontard or even to mention Diotima's name, while the violence of passion passes over into grief-stricken words about the loss of the pupil who was his beloved's child – that letter elevates the force of dutiful silence to burning emotion, and makes such silence itself an expression of the unendurable conflict of human right with the right of that which is. But just as amid the universal unfreedom each trait of humanity wrung from it grows ambiguous, so it is even with manly discretion, which is reputedly nothing but noble. It turns into an instrument of woman's revenge for her oppression. That men have to keep quiet among themselves, indeed, that the whole erotic sphere takes on a greater air of secrecy the more considerate and well-bred people are, procures for women opportunities from the convenient lie to sly and unhampered deception, and condemns the gentleman to the role of dimwit. Upper-class women have acquired a whole technique of isolation, of keeping men apart, and finally of wilfully dividing all the spheres of feeling, behaviour and valuation, in which the male division of labour is grotesquely reduplicated. This enables them to manipulate the trickiest situations with aplomb – at the cost of the very immediacy that women so pride themselves on. Men have drawn their own conclusions from this, colluding in the sneering *sous-entendu* that women just are like that. The wink implying *così fan tutte* repudiates all discretion, although no name is dropped, and has moreover the justification of knowing that, unfailingly, any woman who avails herself of her lover's gallantry has herself broken the trust he placed in her. The lady who is one, and refuses to make of gentility the mockery of good manners, therefore has no choice but to set aside the discredited principle of discretion and openly, shamelessly take her love upon her. But who has the strength for that?

VI

Post festum – Pain at the decay of erotic relationships is not just, as it takes itself to be, fear of love's withdrawal, nor the kind of narcissistic melancholy that has been penetratingly described by Freud. Also involved is fear of the transience of one's own feeling. So little room is left to spontaneous impulses that anyone still granted them at all feels them as joy and treasure even when they cause pain, and indeed, experiences the last stinging traces of immediacy as a possession to be grimly defended, in order not to become oneself a thing. The fear of loving another is greater, no doubt, than of losing that other's love. The idea offered to us as solace that in a few years we shall not understand our passion and will be able to meet the loved woman in company with nothing more than fleeting, astonished curiosity, is apt to exasperate the recipient beyond all measure. That passion, which breaches the context of rational utility and seems to help the self to escape its monadic prison, should itself be something relative to be fitted back into individual life by ignominious reason, is the ultimate blasphemy. And yet inescapably passion itself, in experiencing the inalienable boundary between two people, is forced to reflect on that very moment and thus, in the act of being overwhelmed by it, to recognize the nullity of its overwhelming. Really one has always sensed futility; happiness

lay in the nonsensical thought of being carried away, and each time that
went wrong was the last time, was death. The transience of that in
which life is concentrated to the utmost breaks through in just that
extreme concentration. On top of all else the unhappy lover has to
admit that exactly where he thought he was forgetting himself he loved
himself only. No directness leads outside the guilty circle of the natural,
but only reflection on how closed it is.

VII

Come closer – The split between outer and inner, in which the individual
subject is made to feel the dominance of exchange value, also affects
the supposed sphere of immediacy, even those relationships which
include no material interests. They each have a double history. That
they, as a third between two people, dispense with inwardness and
objectify themselves in forms, habits, obligations, gives them endurance. Their seriousness and responsibility lie partly in not giving way to
every impulse, but asserting themselves as something solid and
constant against individual psychology. That, however, does not
abolish what goes on in each individual: not only moods, inclinations
and aversions, but above all reactions to the other's behaviour. And the
inner history stakes its claim more forcefully the less the inner and
outer are distinguishable by probing. The fear of the secret decay of
relationships is almost always caused by those involved allegedly or
really finding things 'too hard'. They are too weak in face of reality,
overtaxed by it on all sides, to muster the loving determination to
maintain the relationship purely for its own sake. In the realm of utility
every relationship worthy of human beings takes on an aspect of
luxury. No one can really afford it, and resentment at this breaks
through in critical situations. Because each partner knows that in truth
unceasing actuality is needed, a moment's flagging seems to make
everything crumble. This can still be felt even when the objectified
form of the relationship shuts it out. The inescapable duality of outer
and inner upsets precisely authentic, affectively charged relationships.
If the subject is deeply involved while the relationship's outward aspect
prevents him, with good reason, from indulging his impulse, the
relation is turned to permanent suffering and thus endangered. The
absurd significance of trivia like a missed telephone call, a stinted
handshake, a hackneyed turn of phrase, springs from their manifest-
ing an inner dynamic otherwise held in check, and threatening the
relationship's objective concreteness. Psychologists may well condemn
the fear and shock of such moments as neurotic, pointing out their

disproportion to the relation's objective weight. Anyone who takes fright so easily is indeed 'unrealistic', and in his dependence on the reflexes of his own subjectivity betrays a faulty adjustment. But only when one responds to the inflection of another's voice with despair is the relation as spontaneous as it should be between free people, while yet for that very reason becoming a torment which, moreover, takes on an air of narcissism in its fidelity to the idea of immediacy, its impotent protest against coldheartedness. The neurotic reaction is that which hits on the true state of affairs, while the one adjusted to reality already discounts the relationship as dead. The cleansing of human beings of the murk and impotence of affects is in direct proportion to the advance of dehumanization.

VIII

Depreciation – Kandinsky wrote in 1912: 'An artist, having once "found his form at last", thinks he can now go on producing works in peace. Unfortunately, he usually fails to notice that from this moment (of "peace") he very soon begins to lose the form he has at last found.' It is no different with understanding. It does not live on stock. Each thought is a force-field, and just as the truth-content of a judgement cannot be divorced from its execution, the only true ideas are those which transcend their own thesis. Since they have to dissolve petrified views of objects, the mental precipitate of social ossification, the form of reification which lies in a thought's being held as a firm possession opposes its own meaning. Even opinions of the most extreme radical-ism are falsified as soon as they are insisted upon, as society eagerly confirms by discussing the doctrine and thus absorbing it. This casts its shadow over the concept of theory. There is not one that, by virtue of its constitution as a fixed, coherent structure, does not harbour a moment of reification within it: develop paranoid features. Precisely this makes it effective. The concept of the *idée fixe* touches not only on the aberration but is an ingredient of theory itself, the total pretension of something particular that arises as soon as a discrete moment is held fast in isolation. Ideas related to their antithesis are not exempt. Even theories of the utmost dignity are prone at least to reified interpre-tation. They seem in this to comply secretly with a demand of the commodity society. The *idée fixe*, like persecution mania, usually relates to the attribution of guilt. The mania's system cannot see through the system of mania, the veil of the social totality. It therefore hits out at a single principle: for Rousseau civilization, for Freud the Oedipus complex, for Nietzsche the rancour of the weak. If the theory is not of that kind, its reception can still render it paranoid. To say in a precise sense that someone holds this or that theory is already to imply the stolid, blankly staring proclamation of grievances, immune to self-reflection. Thinkers lacking in the paranoid element – one of them was Georg Simmel, though he made of the lack a panacea – have no impact or are soon forgotten. By no means does this imply their superiority. If truth were defined as the utterly non-paranoid, it would be at the same time not only the utterly impotent and in conflict with itself, to the extent that practice is among its elements – but it would also be wholly unable to evolve a coherent structure of meaning. Flight from the *idée fixe* becomes a flight from thought. Thinking purified of obsession, a thoroughgoing empiricism, grows itself obsessive while sacrificing the idea of truth, which fares badly enough at empiricists' hands. From this aspect, too, dialectics would have to be seen as an attempt to escape the either/or. It is the effort to rescue theory's trenchancy and consequential logic without surrendering it to delusion.

IX

Procrustes – The throttling of thought makes use of an almost inescapable pair of alternatives. What is wholly verified empirically, with all the checks demanded by competitors, can always be foreseen by the most modest use of reason. The questions are so ground down in the mill that, in principle, little more can emerge than that the percentage of tuberculosis cases is higher in a slum district than on Park Avenue. The sneering empiricist sabotage thrives on this, being patted on the back by the budget makers who administer its affairs in any case, and shown the drawn-down corners of the mouth that signify: 'Knew it all along'. But that which would be different, the contribution the scientists claim to thirst for, they deprecate equally, just because it is not known by everyone: 'Where is the evidence?' If this is lacking, a thought can only be vain and idle speculation, whereas research is supposed to caper like reportage. These fatal alternatives induce ill-tempered defeatism. People do science as long as something pays for it. But they have faith in neither its relevance nor the bindingness of its results. They would discard the whole consignment of junk, if changes in the social form of organization made redundant, for example, the ascertaining of statistical averages, in admiration of which formal democracy is mirrored as the mere superstition of the research bureaux. The procedure of the official social sciences is little more now than a parody of the businesses that keep such science afloat while really needing it only as an advertisement. The whole apparatus of book-keeping, administration, annual reports and balance sheets, important sessions and business trips, is set in motion to confer on commercial interests the semblance of a general necessity elicited from the depths. The self-induced motion of such office work is called research only because it has no serious influence on material production, still less goes beyond it as critique. In research the spirit of this world plays by itself, but in the way children play bus conductors, selling tickets that lead nowhere. The assertion of such spirit's employees that one day they will bring off their synthesis of theory and factual material, they just lack the time at present, is a foolish excuse that backfires on them in tacitly acknowledging the priority of practical obligations. The table-embroidered monographs could hardly ever, and then only in a sardonic mode, be elevated to theory by mediating mental operations. The endless collegial hunt, careering between the 'hypotheses' and 'proofs' of social science, is a wild-goose chase, since each of the supposed hypotheses, if inhabited by theoretical meaning at all, breaks through precisely the shaky façade of mere facticity, which in the demand for proofs prolongs itself as research. That music cannot be really experienced over the radio is, to be sure, a modest theoretical idea; but as translated into research, for instance by the proof that the enthusiastic listeners to certain serious music programmes cannot even recall the titles of the pieces they have consumed, yields the mere husk of the theory it claims to verify. Even if a group meeting all the statistical criteria knew all the titles, that would no more be evidence of the experience of music than, conversely, ignorance of the names in itself confirms its absence. The regression of hearing can only be deduced from the social tendency towards the consumption process as such, and identified in specific traits. It cannot be inferred from arbitrarily isolated and then quantified acts of consumption. To make them the measure of knowledge would be oneself to assume the extinction of experience, and to operate in an 'experience-free' way while trying to analyse the change of experience: a primitive vicious circle. As gauche miming of the exact sciences, beside whose results the social sciences seem paltry, research clings fearfully to the reified plaster cast of vital processes as a guarantee of correctness, whereas its only proper task – one thereby improper to the methods of research – would be to demonstrate the reification of the living through those methods' immanent contradiction.

X

Imaginative excesses – Those schooled in dialectical theory are reluctant to indulge in positive images of the proper society, of its members, even of

those who would accomplish it. Past traces deter them; in retrospect, all
social utopias since Plato's merge in a dismal resemblance to what they
were devised against. The leap into the future, clean over the
conditions of the present, lands in the past. In other words: ends and
means cannot be formulated in isolation from each other. Dialectics
will have no truck with the maxim that the former justify the latter, no
matter how close it seems to come to the doctrine of the ruse of reason
or, for that matter, the subordination of individual spontaneity to party
discipline. The belief that the blind play of means could be summarily
displaced by the sovereignty of rational ends was bourgeois
utopianism. It is the antithesis of means and ends itself that should be
criticized. Both are reified in bourgeois thinking, the ends as 'ideas' the
sterility of which lies in their powerlessness to be externalized, such
unrealizability being craftily passed off as implicit in absoluteness;
means as 'data' of mere, meaningless existence, to be sorted out,
according to their effectiveness or lack of it, into anything whatever,
but devoid of reason in themselves. This petrified antithesis holds good
for the world that produced it, but not for the effort to change it.
Solidarity can call on us to subordinate not only individual interests but
even our better insight. Conversely, violence, manipulation and
devious tactics compromise the end they claim to serve, and thereby
dwindle to no more than means. Hence the precariousness of any
statement about those on whom the transformation depends. Because
means and ends are actually divided, the subjects of the breakthrough
cannot be thought of as an unmediated unity of the two. No more,
however, can the division be perpetuated in theory by the expectation
that they might be either simply bearers of the end or else unmitigated
means. The dissident wholly governed by the end is today in any case so
thoroughly despised by friend and foe as an 'idealist' and daydreamer
that one is more inclined to impute redemptive powers to his
eccentricity than to reaffirm his impotence as impotent. Certainly,
however, no more faith can be placed in those equated with the means;
the subjectless beings whom historical wrong has robbed of the
strength to right it, adapted to technology and unemployment,
conforming and squalid, hard to distinguish from the wind-jackets of
Fascism: their actual state disclaims the idea that puts its trust in them.
Both types are theatre masks of class society projected on to the night
sky of the future, and the bourgeois themselves have always delighted
at their errors, no less than their irreconcilability: on one hand the
abstract rigorist, helplessly striving to realize chimeras, and on the
other the subhuman creature who, as dishonour's progeny, shall never
be allowed to avert it.

What the rescuers would be like cannot be prophesied without obscuring their image with falsehood. What can be perceived, however, is what they will not be like: neither personalities nor bundles of reflexes, but least of all a synthesis of the two, hardboiled realists with a sense of higher things. When the constitution of human beings has grown adapted to social antagonisms heightened to the extreme, the humane constitution sufficient to hold antagonism in check will be mediated by the extremes, not an average mingling of the two. The bearers of technical progress, now still mechanized mechanics, will, in evolving their special abilities, reach the point already indicated by technology where specialization grows superfluous. Once their consciousness has been converted into pure means without any qualification, it may cease to be a means and breach, with its attachment to particular objects, the last heteronomous barrier; its last entrapment in the existing state, the last fetishism of the status quo, including that of its own self, which is dissolved in its radical implementation as an instrument. Drawing breath at last, it may grow aware of the incongruence between its rational development and the irrationality of its ends, and act accordingly.

At the same time, however, the producers are more than ever thrown back on theory, to which the idea of a just condition evolves in their own medium, self-consistent thought, by virtue of insistent self-criticism. The class division of society is also maintained by those who oppose class society: following the schematic division of physical and mental labour, they split themselves up into workers and intellectuals. This division cripples the practice which is called for. It cannot be arbitrarily set aside. But while those professionally concerned with things of the mind are themselves turned more and more into technicians, the growing opacity of capitalist mass society makes an association between intellectuals who still are such, with workers who still know themselves to be such, more timely than thirty years ago. At that time such unity was compromised by freewheeling bourgeois of the liberal professions, who were shut out by industry and tried to gain influence by left-wing bustlings. The community of workers of head and hand had a soothing sound, and the proletariat rightly sniffed out, in the spiritual leadership commended to them by figures such as Kurt Hiller, a subterfuge to bring the class struggle under control by just such spiritualization. Today, when the concept of the proletariat, unshaken in its economic essence, is so occluded by technology that in the greatest industrial country there can be no question of proletarian class consciousness, the role of intellectuals would no longer be to alert the torpid to their most obvious interests, but to strip the veil from the eyes of the wise-guys, the illusion that capitalism, which makes them its temporary beneficiaries, is based on anything other than their exploitation and oppression. The

deluded workers are directly dependent on those who can still just see
and tell of their delusion. Their hatred of intellectuals has changed
accordingly. It has aligned itself to the prevailing common sense views.
The masses no longer mistrust intellectuals because they betray the
revolution, but because they might want it, and thereby reveal how
great is their own need of intellectuals. Only if the extremes come
together will humanity survive.

(Translated by Edmund Jephcott)

2

Adorno, Post-Structuralism and the Critique of Identity

Peter Dews

Over the past few years an awareness has begun to develop of the thematic affinities between the work of those recent French thinkers commonly grouped together under the label of 'post-structuralism', and the thought of the first-generation Frankfurt School, particularly that of Adorno. Indeed, what is perhaps most surprising is that it should have taken so long for the interlocking of concerns between these two philosophical currents to be properly appreciated. Among the most prominent of such common preoccupations are: the illusory autonomy of the bourgeois subject, as exposed pre-eminently in the writings of Freud and Nietzsche; the oppressive functioning of scientific and technological reason, not least in its application to the social domain; the radicalizing potential of modernist aesthetic experience; and – in the case of Adorno, at least – the manner in which what are apparently the most marginal and fortuitous features of cultural artefacts reveal their most profound, and often unacknowledged, truths. Furthermore, these affinities have not merely been observed by outsiders, but are beginning to become part of the self-consciousness of participants in the two traditions themselves. Towards the end of his life, Michel Foucault admitted that he could have avoided many mistakes through an earlier reading of Critical Theory, and – in the last of several retrospective reconstructions of his intellectual itinerary – placed his own thought in a tradition concerned with the 'ontology of actuality', running from Kant and Hegel, via Nietzsche and Weber, to the Frankfurt School.[1] Similarly, Jean-François Lyotard has employed Adorno's account of the decline of metaphysics and the turn to 'micrology' in order to illuminate – partly by parallel and partly by contrast – his own interpretation of postmodernity,[2] while even Jacques Derrida, the least eclectic of recent French thinkers, has written appreciatively on Walter Benjamin, whose borderline position between the political and the mystical he clearly finds sympathetic.[3] On the other side, contemporary German inheritors of the Frankfurt School, including Habermas himself, have begun to explore the internal landscape of post-structuralism, and to assess the points of intersection and divergence with their own tradition.[4]

In the English-speaking world, it is the relation between the characteristic procedures of deconstruction developed by Derrida and the 'negative dialectics' of Adorno which has attracted the most attention: a common concern with the lability and historicity of language, a repudiation of foundationalism in philosophy, an awareness of the subterranean links between the metaphysics of identity and structures of domination, and a shared, tortuous love–hate relation to Hegel, seem to mark out these two thinkers as unwitting philosophical comrades-in-arms. However, up till now, the predominant tendency of such comparisons has been to present Adorno as a kind of deconstructionist *avant la lettre*.[5] The assumption has been that a more consistent pursuit of anti-metaphysical themes, and by implication a more politically radical approach, can be found in the French Heideggerian than in the Frankfurt Marxist. It will be the fundamental contention of this essay that, for several interconnected reasons, this is a serious misunderstanding. Firstly, although there are undoubtedly elements in Adorno's thought which anticipate Derridean themes, he has in many ways equally strong affinities with that mode of recent French thought which is usually known as the 'philosophy of desire'. It is only the exaggeration of the constitutive role of the language in post-structuralism, it could be argued, and a corresponding antipathy – even on the intellectual Left – to the materialist emphases of Marxism, which have led to this aspect of Adorno's work being overlooked or underplayed. Secondly, from an Adornian perspective, it is precisely this lack of a materialist counterweight in Derrida's thought, the absence of any account of the interrelation of consciousness and nature, particularly 'inner nature', which can be seen to have brought forth the equally one-sided reaction of the philosophy of desire. From such a standpoint, different post-structuralist thinkers appear as dealing, in an inevitably distorting isolation, with what are in fact aspects of a single complex of problems. Finally, Adorno's concept of reconciliation, while far from immune to criticism, cannot be regarded as a simple 'failure of nerve' on his part, even less as an invitation to 'totalitarianism', to be contrasted with the harsher, less compromising vision of post-structuralism. It is rather the logical consequence of the attempt to think beyond a set of oppositions which – in their Nietzschean provenance – remain vulnerably brittle and abstract. In

short, I hope to show, through an exploration of the central common
theme of the critique of identity, that far from being merely a
harbinger of post-structuralist and postmodernist styles of thought,
Adorno offers us some of the conceptual tools with which to move
beyond what is increasingly coming to appear, not least in France itself,
as a self-destructively indiscriminate, and politically ambiguous, assault
on the structures of rationality and modernity *in toto*.

The Critique of Consciousness

In his 1973 essay on the painter Jacques Monory, Jean-François
Lyotard makes significant use of the following tale from Borges's *Book
of Imaginary Beings*:

> In one of the volumes of the *Lettres édifiantes et curieuses* that appeared in
> Paris during the first half of the eighteenth century, Father Fontecchio of
> the Society of Jesus planned a study of the superstitions and misinformation
> of the common people of Canton; in the preliminary outline he noted that
> the Fish was a shifting and shining creature that nobody had ever caught but
> that many said they had glimpsed in the depths of mirrors. Father
> Fontecchio died in 1736, and the work begun by his pen remained
> unfinished; some 150 years later Herbert Allen Giles took up the interrup-
> ted task. According to Giles, belief in the Fish is part of a larger myth that
> goes back to the legendary times of the Yellow Emperor.
>   In those days the world of mirrors and the world of men were not, as they
> are now, cut off from each other. They were, besides, quite different;
> neither beings nor colours nor shapes were the same. Both kingdoms, the
> specular and the human, lived in harmony; you could come and go through
> mirrors. One night the mirror people invaded the earth. Their power was
> great, but at the end of bloody warfare the magic arts of the Yellow Emperor
> prevailed. He repulsed the invaders, imprisoned them in their mirrors, and
> forced on them the task of repeating, as though in a kind of dream, all the
> actions of men. He stripped them of their power and of their forms and
> reduced them to mere slavish reflections. Nonetheless, a day will come when
> the magic spell will be shaken off.
>   The first to awaken will be the Fish. Deep in the mirror we will perceive a
> very faint line and the colour of this line will be like no other colour. Later
> on, other shapes will begin to stir. Little by little they will differ from us; little
> by little they will not imitate us. They will break through the barriers of glass
> or metal and this time will not be defeated. Side by side with these mirror
> creatures, the creatures of water will join the battle.
>   In Yunnan, they do not speak of the Fish but of the Tiger of the Mirror.
> Others believe that in advance of the invasion we will hear from the depths
> of mirrors the clatter of weapons.[6]

For Lyotard this story condenses a critique of the modern subject which he shares with the majority of post-structuralist thinkers. Subjectivity presupposes reflection, a representation of experience as that of an experiencing self. But through such representation, which depends upon the synthesizing function of concepts, the original fluidity of intuition, the communication between the human and the specular world, is lost. Consciousness becomes a kind of self-contained theatre, divided between stage and auditorium: energy is transformed into the thought of energy, intensity into intentionality. Thus Lyotard writes:

> Borges imagines these beings as forces, and this bar [the bar between representation and the represented] as a barrier; he imagines that the Emperor, the Despot in general, can only maintain his position on condition that he represses the monsters and keeps them on the other side of the transparent wall. The existence of the subject depends on this wall, on the enslavement of the fluid and lethal powers repressed on the other side, on the function of representing them.[7]

This protest at the coercive unification implied by the notion of a self-conscious, self-identical subject is – of course – one of the central themes of post-structuralism. It occurs, in a formulation very close to that of Lyotard, in works such as the *Anti-Oedipus* of Deleuze and Guattari, in which the schizophrenic fragmentation of experience and loss of identity is celebrated as a liberation from the self forged by the Oedipus complex. But it can also be found, in a more oblique form, in the work of Michel Foucault. The models of enclosure and observation which Foucault explored throughout his career are, in a sense, historically specific, institutional embodiments of this conception of a consciousness imposing its order upon the disorderly manifold of impulse. This is clearest in the case of the Panopticon which Foucault describes in *Discipline and Punish*; but, in fact, as far back as *Madness and Civilization*, Foucault had analysed 'the elaboration around and above madness of a kind of absolute subject which is wholly gaze, and which confers upon it the status of a pure object'.[8] Throughout his work the omnipresent look reduces alterity to identity.

Traditionally, within the sphere of philosophy, it is perhaps the stream of dialectical thought derived from Hegel which has most persistently opposed this rigidity of the classifying gaze. Hegel's critique of the 'philosophy of reflection' is based on the view that any assumption abstracted from experience and taken to be fundamental must necessarily enter into contradiction with itself, including the assumption that subjectivity itself is something self-contained, isolated from and standing over against the object of knowledge. In Hegel's conception experience consists in the shifting reciprocal determinations of subject and object, and culminates in an awareness that the very distinction between the two is valid only from a restricted standpoint. As early as his essay on the difference between the systems of Fichte and Schelling, Hegel had established this fundamental principle of his philosophizing. 'The need of philosophy can satisfy itself', he writes, 'by simply penetrating to the principle of nullifying all fixed oppositions and connecting the limited to the Absolute. This satisfaction found in the principle of absolute identity is characteristic of philosophy as such.'[9] However, as this quotation makes clear, the dialectical mobilization of the relation between subject and object in Hegel does not entail the abandonment of the principle of identity. Hence, for post-structuralist thought the reliance on an Absolute which relativizes and reveals the 'reifying' character of conceptual dissection, the operation of the understanding, results in an even more ineluctable form of coercion, since the movement from standpoint to standpoint is orientated towards a predetermined goal. The voyage of consciousness is undertaken only with a view to the treasure of experience which can be accumulated and brought home: the individual moments of the voyage are not enjoyed simply for themselves. This critique of Hegel is also, of course, implicitly or explicitly, a critique of Marxism, which is seen as attempting to coerce the plurality of social and political movements into a single unswerving dialectic of history.

One of the fundamental problems confronting post-structuralist thought, therefore – a problem which accounts for many of its distinctive features – is how to reject simultaneously both the repressive rigidities of self-consciousness and conceptual thought, *and* the available dialectical alternatives. In the quest for a solution to this difficulty, it is Nietzsche who plays the most important role. This is because the central imaginative polarity in Nietzsche's work between the fluidity of the ultimate world of becoming, and the static systems of concepts laid over this fluidity, allows him to reveal the deceptiveness of all partial perspectives on reality, while also blocking the possibility of a historical totality of perspectives that would reveal what cannot be known through any one alone. Nietzsche's characteristic verbal compounds (*hineinlegen, hinzulügen* . . .) render unmistakable his view that all meaning, coherence and teleological movement is projected on to a world which, in itself, is blank, purposeless, indifferent, chaotic. This conception of the relation between thought and reality is common to much of the Nietzsche-influenced philosophy of the 1960s and 1970s in France. Its most striking and systematically elaborated exemplification is perhaps to be found in Lyotard's *Économie Libidinale*, which is centred on the notion of a 'grand ephemeral pellicule' constituted by the deployed surfaces of the body, which are swept by an incessantly mobile libidinal cathexis generating points of pure sensation or 'intensity'. This description of the libidinal band is perhaps best considered as a philosophical experiment, a paradoxical attempt to explore what experience would be like before the emergence of a self-conscious subject of experience. In Lyotard's view, this emergence can take place only through a cooling of intensity, a transformation of energy. Rendering more explicit the assumptions of his commentary on Borges, he writes:

> Theatricality and representation, far from being something one should take as a libidinal given, a fortiori as a metaphysical given, result from a certain kind of work on the labyrinthine and moebian band, an operation which imprints these special folds and creases whose effect is a box closed in on itself, and allowing to appear on the stage only those impulses which, coming from what will from now on be called the exterior, satisfy the conditions of interiority.[10]

Once the representational chamber of consciousness is constituted, then the libidinal band is inevitably occluded: *all* representation is misrepresentation. For Lyotard each segment of the band is 'absolutely singular', so that the attempt to divide it up into conceptual identities 'implies the denial of disparities, of heterogeneities, of transits and stases of energy, it implies the denial of polymorphy'.[11] This ontological affirmation of an irreducible plurality – in more or less sophisticated versions – has been one of the most influential themes of post-structuralism, and has had widespread political repercussions. It is, however, fraught with difficulties, which I would like to explore by looking a little more closely at the Nietzschean thought by which it is inspired.

Knowledge and Becoming in Nietzsche

From the very beginning of his work, Nietzsche is concerned to combat the notion of knowledge as the mere reproduction of an objective reality, believing that forms of knowledge necessarily are – and should be – in the service of and shaped by human interests. The argument is already central to *The Birth of Tragedy*, where Nietzsche draws an unfavourable contrast between Greek tragedy at the height of its powers – a form of artistic creation which, through its blending of Dionysiac insight and Apollonian order, was able to confront the horror and chaos of existence, and yet draw an affirmative conclusion from this confrontation – and the naively optimistic assumption of Socratic dialectic that reality can be exhaustively grasped in concepts. *The Birth of Tragedy* is directed against 'the illusion that thought, guided by the thread of causation, might plumb the furthest abysses of being, and even correct it'.[12] Throughout his work Nietzsche will stress the aversion of the human mind to chaos, its fear of unmediated intuition, and its resultant attempts to simplify the world by reducing diversity to identity. There is, however, an equally strong pragmatic tendency in Nietzsche, which suggests that this process of ordering and simplification takes place not simply because of an 'existential' need for security, but in the interests of sheer survival:

> In order for a particular species to maintain itself and increase its power, its conception of reality must comprehend enough of the calculable and constant for it to base a scheme of behaviour on it. The utility of preservation – not some abstract-theoretical need not to be deceived – stands as the motive behind the development of the organs of knowledge . . . .[13]

It is on such considerations that Nietzsche bases his many paradoxical pronouncements on the nature of knowledge and truth; his statement, for example, that 'Truth is the kind of error without which a certain species of life cannot live.'[14]

A number of commentators have attempted to moderate the perplexing and scandalous effect of these formulations by suggesting that Nietzsche draws a distinction, implicitly at least, between two kinds of truth. His attack is directed against correspondence theories of truth, against the failure to consider the extent to which our language and our concepts shape the world, but does not exclude a deeper insight into the nature of reality which would merit the title 'truth'. Such attempts to render Nietzsche's position coherent are not entirely without textual support, but they also have a tendency to underplay the extent to which Nietzsche's paradoxical formulations betray a genuine dilemma. The Kantian element in Nietzsche's thought pushes him towards a thoroughgoing idealist epistemology, since – like Kant's immediate successors – he rejects the doctrine of the 'thing-in-itself' as incoherent. Thus, in *The Will to Power* he writes:

> The intellect cannot criticize itself, simply because it cannot be compared with other species of intellect and because its capacity to know would be revealed only in the presence of 'true reality' . . . . This presupposes that, distinct from every perspective kind of outlook or sensual-spiritual appropriation, something exists, an 'in-itself'. But the psychological derivation of the belief in things forbids us to speak of 'things-in-themselves'.[15]

Yet, despite these strictures, from *The Birth of Tragedy* onward, where he contrasts the shallow optimism of science to an alternative Dionysiac insight into the nature of things, Nietzsche will repeatedly oppose a vision of ultimate reality to accepted truths. Indeed, in *The Birth of Tragedy* he employs the Kantian concept of the noumenal to illustrate precisely this opposition: 'The contrast of this authentic nature-truth and the lies of culture which present themselves as the sole reality is similar to that between the eternal core of things, the thing-in-itself, and the entire world of appearances.'[16] In general, Nietzsche's critique of metaphysics, and his denial of the ability of philosophy to establish epistemological criteria, drives him towards an idealism which argues that the structures of knowledge are entirely constitutive of the object, while his insistence that all consciousness should comprehend itself as perspectival pushes him back towards a reinstatement of the distinction between appearance and reality.

I would argue that a similar dilemma, encapsulated in Nietzsche's dictum that 'Knowledge and Becoming exclude one another',[17] pervades the work of those post-structuralist thinkers who have been most directly influenced by Nietzschean schemas. We have already examined how Lyotard's motif of the libidinal band, which fuses a Freudian-inspired theory of cathexis with the doctrine of the Eternal Return, makes possible a denunciation of all theoretical discourses as 'apparatuses for the fixation and draining away of intensity'.[18] Lyotard, however, is too conscientious – and too restless – a figure to be satisfied for long with the monistic metaphysics of libido on which *Économie Libidinale* relied. It can be no accident that, shortly after the publication of this work, he began to set off in a new direction, replacing the description of forms of discourse as '*dipositifs pulsionels*' with the less ontologically loaded notion of 'language-games', borrowed from Wittgenstein. In Lyotard's case, the attempt to develop a critique of objectifying theory from the standpoint of an ontology of flux represents an explicit, but only temporary, phase of his thought. With Foucault, however, the tension which this attempt implies is both a more covert, but also a more persistent, feature of his work. It is already apparent in *Madness and Civilization*, where Foucault wishes to develop a critique of the objectifying and alienating nature of modern psychiatric treatment and its theorizations, while also being sensitive to the difficulty of appealing to the 'rudimentary movements of an experience' which would be 'madness itself'.[19] In *The Archaeology of Knowledge* Foucault renounces this approach: 'We are not trying to reconstitute what madness itself might be . . . in the form in which it was later organized (translated, deformed, travestied, perhaps even repressed) by discourses, and the oblique, often twisted play of their operations.'[20] He ostensibly adopts a position in which discourses are entirely constitutive of their objects. And yet the contradiction persists, since it is inherent in his attempt to develop a non-dialectical form of critique. In the first volume of *The History of Sexuality*, for example, the oscillation between the epistemological and the ontological occurs in the form of an opposition between the apparatuses of sexuality and a tentatively – but persistently – evoked pre-discursive 'body and its pleasures'.[21] Foucault is able to avoid this dilemma in his final publications only by returning to a notion of self-constitution and self-reflection which he had denounced up until this point as illicitly Hegelian. One of the fundamental tenets of post-structuralist thought is tacitly abandoned when Foucault reinstates a relation between knowledge and its object internal to consciousness; when he inquires: 'By means of what play of truth does man offer himself to be thought in his own being when he perceives himself as mad, when he considers himself as ill, when he reflects on himself as a living, speaking and labouring being, when he judges and punishes himself as a criminal?'[22] This is an unmistakably 'revisionist' retrospective.

Adorno's Critique of Identity-Thinking

Having explored this fundamental difficulty of the post-structuralist position, I would like now to introduce the comparison with Adorno. One obvious point of entry would be the fact that both the post-structuralists and Adorno owe an enormous debt to Nietzsche, and in particular to his sense of the costs imposed by the forging of a self-identical, morally responsible subject, perhaps most vividly conveyed in the second essay of *On the Genealogy of Morals*. However, as I have already suggested, the full import of these parallels has been misunderstood, because of a failure to appreciate the gap between the general philosophical projects within which they occur. One of the most important distinctions in this respect is that Adorno is not content with a Nietzschean–Freudian, naturalistic critique of consciousness, but takes up the discovery of the early German Romantics that the philosophy of pure consciousness is internally incoherent. In an illuminating article, Jochen Hörisch has shown that the original antecedents for Adorno's acute awareness of the loss of spontaneity imposed by the formation of the modern autonomous individual, his sense that the identity of the self must be coercively maintained against the centrifugal tendencies of impulse, can be traced back beyond Nietzsche to the critical engagement with Fichte's philosophy of Schlegel and Novalis. It is here, in thought partly inspired – like

Adorno's own – by dismay at the failure of an attempted political realization of reason, that Adorno discovers a hidden history of subjectivity, an evocation of the pain of the process of individuation, which is betrayed by logical incoherence. 'Early romanticism', Hörisch argues, 'discovers suffering as the *principium individuationis* and as the "secret of individuality", which transcendental philosophy can only conceal at the cost of becoming entangled in unavowed contradictions. The pain of individuation derives from the inscription of a compulsory identity which passes itself off as an a priori structure of reason . . . .'[23] Both aspects of this critique will be of crucial importance for Adorno: the demonstration of the structure of contradiction which *both* splits and constitutes the subject, and the sensitivity to the repression of inner nature which is demanded by the forging of such a subject. Adorno's critique of the modern subject, therefore, is as implacable as that of the post-structuralists, and is based on not dissimilar grounds: yet – in contrast to Foucault, Deleuze or Lyotard – it does not culminate in a call for the abolition of the subjective principle. Rather, Adorno always insists that our only option is to 'use the force of the subject to break through the deception of constitutive subjectivity'.[24] In order fully to understand the reasons for this difference of conclusion, we must turn to Adorno's account of the relation between concept and object, universality and particularity, and its opposition to that of Nietzsche.

From the very beginning, Nietzsche's work is haunted by a sense of the inherent fictionalizing and fetishizing tendencies of language and conceptual thought. In his early essay 'On Truth and Lies in an Extra-Moral Sense', Nietzsche remarks:

> Every word becomes immediately a concept through the fact that it must serve not simply for the absolutely individualized original experience, to which it owes its birth, that is to say as a reminder, but must straightaway serve for countless more or less similar cases, and that means must be matched to purely dissimilar cases. Every concept arises through the equating of what is not the same. [*Jeder Begriff entsteht durch Gleichsetzung des Nichtgleichen.*][25]

Throughout Nietzsche's work such remarks on the 'coarseness' of language, on the indifference to differences entailed by the use of concepts, are to be found. 'Just as it is certain', Nietzsche continues,

> that one leaf is never quite like another, so it is certain that the concept leaf is constructed by an arbitrary dropping of individual differences, through a forgetting of what differentiates; and this awakens the idea that there is something in nature besides leaves which would be 'leaf', that is to say an

original form, according to which all leaves are woven, drawn, circum-
scribed, coloured, curled, painted, but by clumsy hands, so that no example
emerges correctly and reliably as a true copy of the original form . . . . The
overlooking of the individual gives us the form, whereas nature knows no
forms and no concepts, and also no species, but only an X, which is
inaccessible and indefinable to us.[26]

It is precisely such a view of the deceptive identity forged by concepts,
as we have seen, which motivates Lyotard's evocation of the ineffably
singular points of intensity which constitute the libidinal band, or
Foucault's reluctant but repeated recourse to an uncapturable pre-
discursive spontaneity – whether under the title of 'madness', 'resistance', or 'the body and its pleasures'.

Nietzsche's account of the manner in which real, particular leaves
come to be seen as poor imitations of the concept 'leaf' captures
precisely that process which Adorno refers to as 'identity-thinking'.
'The immanent claim of the concept', Adorno writes, 'is its order-
creating invariance over against the variation of what is grasped under
it. This is denied by the form of the concept, which is "false" in that
respect.'[27] However, Adorno does not believe that this situation can be
remedied simply by counterposing the contingent and particular to the
universality of concepts. Rather, he argues, the assumption that the
'non-identical' left behind by the concept is merely an inaccessible and
undefinable X, the belief that 'nature knows no forms and no concepts',
is itself the result of the primacy of the universal in identity-thinking.
Adorno's philosophical effort is directed towards moving beyond the
split between bare facticity and conceptual determination, through an
experience of the contradiction which that split itself implies. Non-
identity, Adorno suggests, 'is opaque only for identity's claim to be
total'.[28] Thus, in the Introduction to *Against Epistemology* (*Zur Metakritik
der Erkenntnistheorie*), a series of critical essays on Husserlian phenomenology, Adorno employs the following passage from *The Twilight of the
Idols* to demonstrate that Nietzsche 'undervalued what he saw
through':

> Formerly, alteration, change, any becoming at all, were taken as proof of
> mere appearance, as an indication that there must be something which led
> us astray. Today, conversely, precisely insofar as the prejudice of reason
> forces us to posit unity, identity, permanence, substance, cause, thinghood,
> being, we see ourselves caught in error, compelled into error.[29]

Against the bent of this text, which is characteristic of both Nietzsche
and his post-structuralist followers, Adorno insists that

The opposition of the stable to the chaotic, and the domination of nature, would never have succeeded without an element of stability in the dominated, which would otherwise incessantly give the lie to the subject. Completely casting away that element and localizing it solely in the subject is no less *hubris* than absolutizing the schemata of conceptual order . . . . Sheer chaos, to which reflective spirit downgrades the world for the sake of its own total power, is just as much the product of spirit as the cosmos which it sets up as an object of reverence.[30]

Adorno's argument is that pure singularity is itself an abstraction, the waste-product of identity-thinking.

Two major implications of this position are that the attempt by post-structuralist thought to isolate singularity will simply boomerang into another form of abstraction; and that what it mistakes for immediacy will in fact be highly mediated. These pitfalls are clearly exemplified by Lyotard's working through of the 'philosophy of desire' in *Économie Libidinale*. The notion of a libidinal band composed of ephemeral intensities is an attempt to envisage a condition in which, as Nietzsche puts it, 'no moment would be for the sake of another'. But if every moment is prized purely for its uniqueness, without reference to a purpose or a meaning, to a before or an after, without reference to anything which goes beyond itself, then what is enjoyed in each moment becomes paradoxically and monotonously the same: in Lyotard's work of the mid-seventies any action, discourse, or aesthetic structure becomes an equally good – or equally bad – conveyor of intensity. Furthermore, Lyotard's own evocations betray his ostensible intention, since they make clear that such 'intensities' cannot be reduced to pure cathexis, but are symbolically structured, coloured by remarkably determinate situations:

The slow, light, intent gaze of an eye, then suddenly the head turns so that there is nothing left but a profile, Egypt. The silence which settles around her extends to great expanses of the libidinal band which, it seems, belongs to her body. Those zones also are silent, which means that dense, inundating surges move noiselessly and continually to 'her' regions, or come from these regions, down the length of slopes.[31]

It is important to note that Adorno does not avoid these difficulties by espousing a Hegelian position. He agrees with Hegel that, as a unity *imposed* on particulars, the abstract universal enters into contradiction with its own concept – becomes itself something arbitrary and particular. But he argues that even Hegel's solution – an immanent, self-realizing universal – fails to challenge the primacy of the universal as such. Identity-thinking, even in its Hegelian form, defeats its own purpose, since by reducing what is non-identical in the object to itself, it ultimately comes away empty-handed. For Adorno, the experience of this contradiction sparks off a further movement of reflection, to a position in which the non-identical is no longer viewed as the isolated particular which it is forced back into being by identity-thinking. The particular is now seen as standing in a pattern of relations to other particulars, a historically sedimented 'constellation' which defines its identity. 'What is internal to the non-identical', Adorno writes, 'is its relation to what it is not itself, and which its instituted, frozen identity withholds from it . . . . The object opens itself to a monadological insistence, which is a consciousness of the constellation in which it stands . . . .'[32] This consciousness, in its turn, can be expressed only through a 'constellation' – as opposed to a hierarchical ordering – of concepts, which are able to generate out of the differential tension between them an openness to that non-identity of the thing itself, which would be 'the thing's own identity against its identifications'.[33] There is for Adorno, in other words, no necessary antagonism between conceptual thought and reality, no inevitable mutual exclusion of Knowledge and Becoming. The problem is posed not by conceptual thought as such, but by the assumption of the primacy of the concept, the delusion that mind lies beyond the total process in which it finds itself as a moment. The characteristics of reality which post-structuralist thought ontologizes are in fact merely the reflection of a historically obsolete imperiousness of consciousness, a lack of equilibrium between subject and object. 'What we differentiate', Adorno writes, 'will appear divergent, dissonant, negative for just as long as the structure of our consciousness obliges it to strive for unity: as long as its demand for totality will be its measure of whatever is not identical with it.'[34]

Deconstruction and Negative Dialectics

One way of summarizing the argument so far would be to say that, for Adorno, the compulsive features of identity are inseparable from its internal contradictions: identity can become adequate to its concept only by acknowledging its own moment of non-identity. In the more naturalistic of the French thinkers influenced by Nietzsche, however, this logical dimension of the critique of consciousness is entirely absent. The ego is portrayed unproblematically as the internally consistent excluder of the spontaneity and particularity of impulse, with the consequence that opposition can only take the form of a self-defeating jump from the 'unity' of self-consciousness to the dispersal of intensities, or from the Oedipalized subject to a metaphysics of 'desiring

machines'. In the work of Jacques Derrida, by contrast, a complementary one-sidedness occurs: the naturalistic dimension of Nietzsche's
thought is almost entirely excluded in favour of an exploration of the
contradictions implicit in the notion of pure self-identity. Derrida, in
other words, shares a penchant for dialectics with Adorno, is sensitive
to the unexpected ways in which philosophical opposites slide into one
another, but fails to link this concern with an account of the
natural-historical genesis of the self.

The implications of this failure can perhaps best be highlighted by
comparing Adorno's and Derrida's critiques of Husserlian phenomenology. Like Merleau-Ponty, whose account of the relation between
consciousness and nature bears many affinities to his own, Adorno
contests the very possibility of Husserl's transcendental reduction:

> The idealist may well call the conditions of possibility of the life of
> consciousness which have been abstracted out transcendental – they refer
> back to a determinate, to some 'factual' conscious life. They are not valid 'in
> themselves' . . . . The strictest concept of the transcendental cannot release
> itself from its interdependence with the *factum*.[35]

It is important to note, however, that Adorno speaks of 'interdependence': he by no means wishes to effect an empiricist or naturalistic
reduction of consciousness. Rather, his argument is simply that 'the
mind's moment of non-being is so intertwined with existence, that to
pick it out neatly would be the same as to objectify and falsify it'.[36]
Adorno, as a materialist, argues for the anchoring of consciousness in
nature, while resisting any attempt to collapse the dialectic of subject
and object into a metaphysical monism.

In Derrida's thought, however, the possibility of the transcendental
reduction is never questioned as such. Rather, deconstruction incorporates the transcendental perspective, in an operation which Derrida
terms 'erasure', but which – in its simultaneous cancellation and
conservation – is close to a Hegelian *Aufhebung*. Thus in *Of Grammatology* Derrida suggests that there is a 'short-of and a beyond of
transcendental criticism', and that therefore 'the value of the transcendental arché must make its necessity felt before letting itself be
erased'.[37] What this operation implies for Derrida is not the insistence
on an irreducible break between facticity and the transcendental,
which metaphysics has always dreamed of overcoming, but rather a
'reduction of the reduction', a shift to the level of what he explicitly
terms an 'ultra-transcendental text'. For Derrida the incoherence of
the concept of self-presence on which Husserl's theory of transcendental subjectivity is based reveals that the transcendental subject and its

objects, along with the other characteristic oppositions of metaphysical thought, are in some sense – which he finds rather uncomfortable to expound – the 'effects' of a higher principle of non-identity for which his most common name is '*différance*'. The result is a final philosophical position remarkably reminiscent of pre-Hegelian idealism. Since absolute difference, lacking all determinacy, is indistinguishable from absolute identity, Derrida's evocations of a trace which is 'origin of all repetition, origin of ideality . . . not more ideal than real, not more intelligible than sensible, not more a transparent signification than an opaque energy',[38] provide perhaps the closest twentieth-century parallel to the *Identitätsphilosophie* of the younger Schelling.

It appears, therefore, that Derrida's attempt to develop a critique of the self-identical subject which eschews any naturalistic moment results in a position no more plausible that Lyotard's monistic metaphysics of libido. Although Adorno did not live long enough to confront Derrida's position directly, his likely response to current comparisons and inter-assimilations of deconstruction and negative dialectics can be deduced from the critique of Heidegger's thought – undoubtedly the central influence on Derrida – which threads its way through his work. Heidegger is correct to suggest that there is 'more' to entities than simply their status as objects of consciousness, but – in Adorno's view – by treating this 'more' under the heading of 'Being' he transforms it into a self-defeating hypostatization:

> By making what philosophy cannot express an immediate theme, Heidegger dams philosophy up, to the point of a revocation of consciousness. By way of punishment, the spring which, according to his conception, is buried, and which he would like to uncover, dries up far more pitifully than the insight of philosophy, which was destroyed in vain, and which inclined towards the inexpressible through its mediations.[39]

For Adorno, whatever experience the word 'Being' may convey can be expressed only through a constellation of entities, whereas in Heidegger's philosophy the irreducibility of a relation is itself transformed into an ultimate. In the evocation of a Being which transcends the subject–object distinction, 'the moment of mediation becomes isolated and thereby immediate. However, mediation can be hypostatized just as little as the subject and object poles; it is only valid in their constellation. Mediation is mediated by what it mediates'.[40] *Mutatis mutandis*, one could also argue that Derridean *différance* is necessarily differentiated by what it differentiates. While it is true that nature and culture, signified and signifier, object and subject would be nothing without the difference between them, this is not sufficient to ensure the *logical priority* of non-identity over identity which is crucial to Derrida's whole philosophical stance. The distinction between his position, according to which 'subjectivity – like objectivity – is an effect of *différance*, an effect inscribed in a system of *différance*',[41] and that of Adorno, is clearly revealed by the following passage from *Negative Dialectics*:

> The polarity of subject and object can easily be taken, for its part, as an undialectical structure within which all dialectics takes place. But both concepts are categories which originate in reflection, formulas for something which is not to be unified; nothing positive, not primary states of affairs, but negative throughout. Nonetheless, the difference of subject and object is not to be negated in its turn. They are neither an ultimate duality, nor is there an ultimate unity hidden behind them. They constitute each other as much as – through such constitution – they separate out from each other.[42]

The Mirror and the Spell

By this point it will be clear that the frequent attempt of post-structuralist thinkers, and of literary and political commentators influenced by post-structuralism, to oppose the Nietzschean critique of identity to the coercive totalizations of dialectical thought is beset with intractable difficulties. Adorno, no less than recent French thought, criticizes Hegel's dialectic as being in many ways the most insidious, most ineluctable form of identity-thinking. Yet, at the same time, his deeply dialectical sensibility perceives the self-defeating dynamic of a blunt prioritization of particularity, diversity, and non-identity. The dissolution of the reflective unity of the self in Deleuze or Lyotard leads only to the indifference of boundless flux, or to the monotonous repetition of intensity; while in Derrida's work the jettisoning of the materialist ballast of the Nietzschean and Freudian critique of consciousness results in the installation of *différance* as the principle of a new kind of 'first philosophy'. For Adorno, by contrast, non-identity cannot be respected by abandoning completely the principle of identity. 'To define identity as the correspondence of the thing-in-itself to its concept', he writes,

> is *hubris*; but the ideal of identity must not simply be discarded. Living in the rebuke that the thing is not identical with the concept is the concept's longing to become identical with the thing. This is how the sense of non-identity contains identity. The supposition of identity is indeed the ideological element of pure thought, all the way through to formal logic; but

hidden in it is also the truth moment of ideology, the pledge that there should be no contradiction, no antagonism.[43]

Bearing this argument in mind, we are now perhaps in a position to return with more insight to the Borges story with which we began. It will already be apparent that the tale of the subduing of the mirror-animals can be interpreted in terms not only of the libidinal critique of consciousness, but also of the 'Dialectic of Enlightenment' which was first formulated by Horkheimer and Adorno during the early 1940s, and which continues to underpin *Negative Dialectics* and *Aesthetic Theory*. The humanization of the drives, represented by the transformation of the animals into reflections, does indeed result in a kind of mastery by the ego. But this mastery is bought at the price of a terrible isolation: in *Negative Dialectics* Adorno returns repeatedly to the pathos of a self helplessly confined within the circle of its own immanence, unable to make contact with anything external which does not turn out to be simply its own reflection. The need to break out of this isolation generates a tension at the heart of subjectivity itself, which post-structuralism, in general, is reluctant or unable to recognize. This inadequacy suggests that there might be substantive aspects of the story which Lyotard has failed to account for in his interpretation.

Firstly, Lyotard describes the banishment and punishment of the animals as a simple act of force, of repression and containment, whereas Borges describes the Emperor as employing his 'magic arts', as putting the animals under a spell. Significantly, the concept of a spell plays an important role in Adorno's philosophy; since enchantment can constitute a peculiarly intangible and non-apparent form of coercion, to speak of a spell suggests a state of compulsive selfhood in which actions are simultaneously autonomous and heteronomous, accompanied by exaggerated subjective illusions of autonomy, but carried out by subjects nevertheless. The metaphor of the spell, in other words, captures both the repressive and enabling features of processes of socialization, which are portrayed as an aspect of the human conquest of nature in the interests of self-preservation. As Adorno writes in *Negative Dialectics*, 'The spell is the subjective form of the world spirit, the internal reinforcement of its primacy over the external processes of life.'[44] In the later Critical Theory of Habermas, this parallelism of the instrumental domination of outer nature and the repression of inner nature will be contested. Habermas will avoid Adorno's implication that emancipation from nature entails the closing-down of all communicative sensitivity by attributing socializ- ation and instrumental action to categorically distinct dimensions of historical development. Nevertheless, already in its Adornian version, the Critical Theory position has a distinct advantage over that of the post-structuralists; for while figures such as Lyotard force themselves into a corner, where they can only denounce the dominance of the ego as an arbitrary coercion which should be abolished (whether it could is somewhat more problematic), Adorno perceives that compulsive identity, the sacrifice of the moment for the future, was necessary at a certain stage of history, in order for human beings to liberate themselves from blind subjugation to nature. To this extent such identity already contains a moment of freedom. Accordingly, the 'spell of selfhood' cannot be seen simply as an extension of natural coercion; rather, it is an illusion which could, in principle, be reflectively broken through by the subject which it generates – although the full realization of this process would be inseparable from a transformation of social relations. Furthermore, the result of such a breakthrough would not be the self-defeating inrush of the 'fluid and lethal powers' which Lyotard describes, but rather a true identity – one which would be permeable to its own non-identical moment. One of the major differences between post-structuralism and Critical Theory is summarized in Adorno's contention that 'even when we merely limit the subject, we put an end to its power'.[45]

This brings us to a second point. Lyotard describes the mirror-animals as 'monsters', but Borges specifies that the people of Canton believe the creature of the mirror to be a fish, 'a shifting and shining creature that nobody has ever caught'; while in Yunnan it is believed to be a tiger. In Adorno's thought it is under this double aspect that the non-identical appears to identity-thinking: on the one hand as something of tantalizing beauty which perpetually eludes our grasp, on the other as something menacing and uncontrollable, menacing precisely because of our inordinate need to control it. Yet we cannot enter into relation with this creature, either by smashing the mirror (the solution of the 'philosophers of desire'), or by claiming – as does Derrida – that both the human world and the reflected world are merely effects generated by its invisible surface. Rather, the only way to achieve this relation is to revoke the spell cast by the Emperor on the animals – which is also, as we have seen, a spell cast on himself.

It would not do to conclude, however, without stressing an important distinction between the lesson of Borges's tale and the philosophical position of Adorno. The story does contain an evocation of utopia, but Borges sets this in a distant, irrecoverable past. 'In legendary times', he tells us, 'the world of mirrors and the world of men were not . . . cut off from each other. They were, besides, quite different; neither beings nor colours nor shapes were the same. Both kingdoms, the specular and the human, lived in harmony; you could come and go through mirrors.' In Borges's version this initial accord is broken by an unexplained onslaught of nature, temporarily repulsed by human-kind, but destined to triumph in the end: 'a day will come when the magic spell will be shaken off', and this time the animals 'will not be defeated'. Adorno does not deny the possibility of such a calamitous conclusion to history: the 'clatter of weapons' from 'the depths of mirrors', which some believe will precede the final invasion, will undoubtedly sound, to our late-twentieth-century ears, like a four-minute nuclear warning. But Adorno does contest that such a terminus is inevitable. Our historical dilemma consists in the fact that the essential material preconditions for a reconciliation between human beings, and between humanity and nature, could only have been installed by a history of domination and self-coercion which has now built up an almost unstoppable momentum. As Adorno writes in *Negative Dialectics* 'since self-preservation has been precarious and difficult for eons, the power of its instrument, the ego drives, remains all but irresistible even after technology has virtually made self-preservation easy'.[46] To pine for a prelapsarian harmony, in the face of this dilemma, is merely to fall resignedly into conservative illusion. Nevertheless, Borges's evocation of a state of peaceful interchange between the human and the mirror worlds provides a fitting image for that affinity without identity, and difference without domination – rather than coercive unity – which Adorno believes to be implied by the pledge that there should be 'no contradiction, no antagonism'.

Notes

1. See 'Structuralism and Post-structuralism: An Interview with Michel Foucault', *Telos* 55, Spring 1983, p. 200; and 'Un Cours Inédit', *Magazine Littéraire*, 207, May 1984.
2. See Jean-François Lyotard, 'Presentations', in Alan Montefiore, ed., *Philosophy in France Today*, Cambridge 1983, pp. 201–4.
3. See Jacques Derrida, *La Vérité en Peinture*, Paris 1978, pp. 200–09.
4. Axel Honneth, *Kritik der Macht*, Frankfurt 1982; Albrecht Wellmer, *Zur Dialektik von Moderne und Postmoderne*, Frankfurt 1985, Jürgen Habermas, *Der philosophische Diskurs der Moderne*, Frankfurt 1985.
5. See, for example, Rainer Nägele, 'The Scene of the Other: Theodor W. Adorno's Negative Dialectic in the Context of Post-structuralism', *Boundary* 2, Fall–Winter 1982–83; Martin Jay, *Adorno*, London 1984, pp. 21–2; and, above all, Michael Ryan, *Marxism and Deconstruction*, Baltimore, MD 1982, pp. 73–81.
6. Jorge Luis Borges, 'The Fauna of Mirrors', in *The Book of Imaginary Beings*, Harmondsworth 1974, pp. 67–8.
7. Jean-François Lyotard, 'Contribution des Tableaux de Jacques Monory', in Gérald Gassiot-Talabot *et al.*, *Figurations 1960/1973*, Paris 1973, pp. 155–6.
8. Michel Foucault, *Histoire de la Folie à l'Age Classique*, collection TEL edn, Paris 1976, p. 479.
9. G. W. F. Hegel, *The Difference Between Fichte's and Schelling's Systems of Philosophy*, Albany, NY 1977, p. 112.

10. Jean-François Lyotard, *Économie Libidinale*, Paris 1974, p. 11.
11. Ibid., p. 294.
12. Friedrich Nietzsche, *Die Geburt der Tragödie aus dem Geiste der Musik*, in G. Colli and M. Montinari, eds, *Sämtliche Werke, Kritische Studienausgabe*, Berlin/New York 1980, vol. 1, p. 99.
13. Friedrich Nietzsche, Walter Kaufman, eds, *The Will to Power*, New York 1967, pp. 266–7.
14. Ibid., p. 272.
15. Ibid., p. 263.
16. Nietzsche, *Die Geburt der Tragödie*, pp. 58–9.
17. Nietzsche, *The Will to Power*, p. 280.
18. Lyotard, *Économie Libidinale*, p. 295.
19. Michel Foucault, 'Preface', in *Histoire de la Folie à l'Age Classique*, original edn, Paris 1961, p. vii.
20. Michel Foucault, *The Archaeology of Knowledge*, London 1972, p. 47.
21. See, in particular, Michel Foucault, *The History of Sexuality*, Harmondsworth 1981, pp. 150–59.
22. Michel Foucault, *L'Usage des Plaisirs*, Paris 1984, p. 13.
23. Jochen Hörisch, 'Herrscherwort, Gott und Geltende Sätze', in Burkhardt Lindner and W. Martin Lüdke, eds, *Materialien zur ästhetischen Theorie: Th. W. Adornos Konstruktion der Moderne*, Frankfurt 1980, p. 406.
24. Theodor W. Adorno, *Negative Dialectics*, London 1973, p. xx. In quotations from this text the translation has frequently been altered.
25. Nietzsche, 'Ueber Wahrheit und Lüge im äussermoralische Sinne', in *Sämtliche Werke, Kritische Studienausgabe*, vol 1, pp. 879–80.
26. Ibid., p. 880.
27. Adorno, *Negative Dialectics*, p. 153.
28. Ibid., p. 163.
29. Nietzsche, *Götzendammerung*, in *Sämtliche Werke, Kritische Studienausgabe*, vol. 6, p. 77, cited in Theodor W. Adorno, *Against Epistemology*, Oxford 1982, pp. 18–19 (translation altered).
30. Ibid., p. 18.
31. Lyotard, *Économie Libidinale*, p. 40.
32. Adorno, *Negative Dialectics*, p. 163.
33. Ibid., p. 161.
34. Ibid., pp. 5–6.
35. Adorno, *Against Epistemology*, pp. 226–7 (translation altered).
36. Adorno, *Negative Dialectics*, pp. 201–2.
37. Jacques Derrida, *Of Grammatology*, London 1976, p. 61.
38. Ibid., p. 65.
39. Adorno, *Negative Dialectics*, p. 110.
40. Ibid., p. 99.
41. Jacques Derrida, *Positions*, London 1981, p. 28.
42. Adorno, *Negative Dialectics*, p. 176.
43. Ibid., p. 149.
44. Ibid., p. 344.
45. Ibid., p. 183. It is worth noting that the post-structuralist critique of consciousness, while exploiting Nietzsche's opposition of particularity and conceptual identity, is in other respects extremely unfaithful to Nietzsche. Far from advocating a dissolution into impulse, Nietzsche is fully – one might say 'dialectically' – aware that the painfully acquired strength of self-discipline is a precondition for the liberation from discipline.
46. Adorno, *Negative Dialectics*, p. 349.

The Critique of Instrumental Reason

Seyla Benhabib

[. . .]

Members and affiliates of the Institut für Sozialforschung, Max Horkheimer, Theodor Adorno, Herbert Marcuse, Leo Löwenthal, Friedrich Pollock, and Walter Benjamin, developed their theory at a time when the disillusionment with the first experiment of socialism in the Soviet Union, and especially the experiences of European Fascism and the destruction of European Jewry, had blocked off all hopes for a revolutionary transformation of capitalism from within.[1] Critical theory was confronted with the task of thinking the 'radically other'.

In his 1971 Foreword to Martin Jay's *The Dialectical Imagination*, Horkheimer wrote: 'The appeal to an entirely other [*ein ganz Anderes*] than this world had primarily social-philosophical impetus. . . . The hope that earthly terror does not possess the last word is, to be sure, a non-scientific wish'.[2] Here Horkheimer is drawing a distinction between philosophical and scientific truth, and ascribing to philosophy the task of thinking 'the entirely other'. In response to the discussion generated in the *Zeitschrift für Sozialforschung* by the 1937 publication of Horkheimer's 'Traditional and Critical Theory' essay, Marcuse formulates this point even more poignantly:

> When truth is not realizable within the existent social order, for the latter it simply assumes the character of utopia. . . . Such transcendence speaks not against, but for truth. The utopian element was for a long time in philosophy the only progressive factor: like the constitution of the best state, of the most intense pleasure, of perfect happiness, of eternal peace. . . . In critical theory, obstinance will be maintained as a genuine quality of philosophical thought.[3]

Neither formulation captures adequately that unique blend of philosophical reflection and social-scientific research known as 'critical theory' which members of the Frankfurt School developed in the 1930s.[4] Applying 'historical materialism to itself' (Korsch), they were able to analyse the historical conditions of the possibility of Marxian political economy, and were thus confronted with the task of articulating a 'critical theory of the transition' from liberal-market capitalism to a new social formation which they ambiguously named 'state capitalism'. Their efforts altered the very meaning of Marxian social criticism, and of the critique of ideologies.

[. . .]

1. From the Critique of Political Economy to the Critique of Instrumental Reason

The evolution of the research programme of the Institut für Sozialforschung can be divided into three separate phases: the 'interdisciplinary materialism' phase of 1932–37, the 'critical theory' approach of 1937–40, and the 'critique of instrumental reason' characterizing the period from 1940 to 1945.[5] Each of these shifts takes place in the wake of the historical experiences of this turbulent period: the prospects of the working-class movement in the Weimar Republic, the appraisal of the social structure of the Soviet Union, and the analysis of Fascism give rise to fundamental shifts in theory. These developments lead to reformulations in the self-understanding of critical theory: the relation between theory and practice, between the subjects and addressees of the theory, are redefined, while the interdependence of philosophy and the sciences, critical theory and Marxism, are reconceptualized.

The 1937 essay on 'Traditional and Critical Theory' was written in a period when the defeat of the German working-class movement and of its parties by Fascism appeared complete, and when the open Stalinist terror and the ensuing 'purges' in the Soviet power apparatus had destroyed all illusions concerning this first experiment of socialism. These experiences were reflected in a reformulation of the theory–practice relation, as well as in a fundamental redefinition of the addressees of the theory.

Whereas in the period preceding 1937, truth was defined as 'a moment of correct praxis',[6] which none the less had to be distinguished from immediate political success, in 'Traditional and Critical Theory' the relation between theoretical truth and the political praxis of specific

social groups begins to appear increasingly remote. In 1934 Horkheimer could still write:

> The value of a theory is decided by its relationship to the tasks, which are
> taken up [in Angriff genommen] at definite historical moments by the most
> progressive social forces. And this value does not have immediate validity
> for all of mankind, but at first merely for the group interested in this task.
> That in many cases, thought has truly estranged itself from the questions of
> struggling humanity, justifies, among other things, the mistrust against the
> intellectuals. . . . So this charge against the apparently non-committed
> [unbedingte] intelligentsia . . . is insofar correct, as this free-floatingness
> [Beziehungslosigkeit] of thought does not mean freedom of judgement, but a
> lack of control on the part of thinking with respect to its own motives.[7]

In 'Traditional and Critical Theory', by contrast, Horkheimer emphasizes not the commonality of goals, but the possible conflict 'between
the advanced sectors of the class and the individuals who speak out the
truth concerning it, as well as the conflict between the most advanced
sectors with their theoreticians and the rest of the class'.[8] The unity of
social forces which promise liberation is a conflictual one. In place of an
alliance with the progressive forces in society, in relation to whose tasks
the 'value' of the theory would be determined, Horkheimer now
emphasizes the value of the critical attitude of the thinker whose
relation to such social forces is seen as one of potential conflict and
aggressive critique. 'This truth becomes clearly evident in the person of
the theoretician: he exercises an aggressive critique against the
conscious apologists of the status quo but also against distracting,
conformist, or utopian tendencies within his own household.'[9] Between the theory of society with emancipatory intent and the empirical
consciousness of the social class or group who would be the agents of
emancipatory transformation, there is no necessary convergence.

In 'Philosophy and Critical Theory', written in response to the
discussion generated by Horkheimer's essay, Marcuse expresses the
existential situation which isolates and forces the intellectual 'back
upon himself':

> What then, when the developments outlined by the theory do not take place,
> when the forces which should have led to the transformation are pushed
> back and appear to be defeated? The truth of the theory is thereby so little
> contradicted, that instead it appears in a new light and illuminates new sides
> and parts of its object. . . . The changing function of the theory in the new
> situation gives it the character of 'critical theory' in a more poignant sense.[10]

'This changing function of theory' signals the growing gap between the
critical truth of Marxism and the empirical consciousness of the

proletariat, which the theory none the less continues to designate as the objective agent of the future transformation of society.

[. . .]

Horkheimer maintains that the Marxian critical theory of society has continued to be a philosophical discipline even when it engages in the critique of the economy; he names the three aspects which constitute the 'philosophical moment' of the critique of political economy. First, the critique of political economy shows the 'transformation of the concepts which dominate the economy into their opposites'.[11] Second, critique is not identical with its object. The critique of political economy does not reify the economy. It defends 'the materialist concept of the free, self-determining society, while retaining from idealism the conviction that men have other possibilities than to lose themselves to the status quo or to accumulate power and profit'.[12] Third, the critique of political economy regards the tendencies of society as a whole and portrays 'the historical movement of the period which is approaching its end'.[13] Horkheimer names these the 'philosophical moments' in the critique of political economy, for each conceptual procedure aims at more than the empirical comprehension of the given laws and structures of society, and judges and analyses what is in the light of a normative standard, namely, the 'realization of the free development of individuals' through the rational constitution of society. For Horkheimer, it is the critique of the given in the name of a Utopian-normative standard that constitutes the legacy of philosophy.

[. . .]

1. With the claim that the *critique* of political economy shows the 'transformation of the concepts which dominate the economy into their opposites', Horkheimer draws attention to the following aspect of Marx's procedure: beginning with the accepted definitions of the categories used by political economy, Marx shows how these turn into their opposites. Marx does not juxtapose his own standards to those used by political economy, but through an internal exposition and deepening of the available results of political economy, he shows that these concepts are self-contradictory. This means that when their logical implications are thought through to their end, these concepts fail to explain the capitalist mode of production. The categories of political economy are measured against their own content, that is, against the phenomenon which they intend to explain, and are shown to be inadequate in this regard. This aspect of Marx's procedure may be named immanent 'categorial critique'.

2. The purpose of *defetishizing critique* is to show that the social reality of capitalism necessarily presents itself to individuals in a mystified form. Spontaneous, everyday consciousness, no less than the discourse

of classical political economy, proceeds from the assumption that social reality is an objective, law-governed, nature-like sphere. Neither the social relations nor the human activities which give rise to this appearance of a nature-like objectivity are taken into account. 'The materialist concept of a free, self-determining society' emphasized by Horkheimer[14] is possible only on the assumption that individuals are the *constitutive* subjects of their social world. Rather than 'losing themselves in the status quo', they can reappropriate this social reality and shape it in such a way as to make it correspond to human potentials. The 'idealist conviction that men have this possibility'[15] is demonstrated for Horkheimer by Marx's procedure of defetishizing critique. In this sense critique is not identical with its object domain – political economy. By analysing the social constitution of this object domain and its historical transitoriness, it also brings to light the contradictory tendencies within it which point towards its transcendence. The critique of political economy aims at a mode of social existence *freed from the domination of the economy*.

3. The Marxian critique of capitalism exposes the internal contradictions and dysfunctionalities of the system in order to show how and why these give rise to oppositional demands and struggles which cannot be satisfied by the present. Critical theory diagnoses social crises such as to enable and encourage future social transformation. As Horkheimer formulates it: 'Of central importance here is not so much what remains unchanged as the historical movement of the period which is now approaching its end.'[16] He adds: 'The economy is the first cause of wretchedness, and critique, theoretical and practical, must address itself primarily to it.'[17] Yet 'historical change does not leave untouched the relations between the spheres of culture. . . . Isolated economic data will therefore not provide the standard by which the human community [*Gemeinschaft*] is to be judged'.[18]

Although Horkheimer and Marcuse, the co-author of the epilogue to 'Traditional and Critical Theory', perceive 'the economy to be the first cause of wretchedness', they are well aware of the fact that an economic crises theory alone is no longer sufficient to analyse the contradictions of the period between the two world wars; second, as historical change has a cultural dimension, crisis phenomena will not be experienced merely as economic dysfunctionalities, but also as *lived* crises.

[. . .]

Cultural and psychological relations are already singled out as domains in which individuals *live through* the crises generated by the economy. Although caused by the economy, these phenomena are not economic in nature. As their early efforts to integrate Erich Fromm's psychoanalytic studies into the research programme of the Institute show,

Horkheimer and his co-workers are well aware of the need to develop a new social-scientific crisis theory to deal with the historical events confronting them.[19]

This brief analysis of Horkheimer's 1937 essay and the epilogue on 'Philosophy and Critical Theory' co-authored with Marcuse reveals the unresolved tension in these formulations: on the one hand, it is acknowledged not only that there is no convergence between the standpoint of the theorist and that of working-class movements, but, in fact, that there is an ever-widening gap. Although critical theory names certain sectors of the working class its 'addressees', the latter are viewed less and less as an empirical social group; increasingly, all individuals who share a 'critical sense' are designated as the addressees of the theory. On the other hand, Horkheimer holds fast to the critique of political economy as a research paradigm and insists upon the emancipatory interests inherent in this kind of critique.

[. . .]

The precarious balance that Horkheimer brilliantly sustains in his 'Traditional and Critical Theory' essay is upset by historical developments. In view of the realities of World War II, the entire Marxian paradigm of the critique of political economy is thrown into question. The paradigm shift from 'critical theory' to the 'critique of instrumental reason' occurs when this increasing cleavage between theory and practice, between the subjects and potential addressees of the theory, leads to a fundamental questioning of the critique of political economy itself. The transformation in the nature of liberal capitalism between the two world wars and the consequences of this for the Marxian critique of political economy are developed by Friedrich Pollock in an article published in the last issue of the Institute's journal, now appearing as *Studies in Philosophy and Social Science*.

In 'State Capitalism: Its Possibilities and Limitations', Pollock describes the transformations in the structure of political economy that have occurred in Western societies since the end of the First World War as 'transitional processes transforming private capitalism into state capitalism'.[20] Pollock adds:

> the closest approach to the totalitarian form of the latter has been made in National Socialist Germany. Theoretically, the totalitarian form of state capitalism is not the only possible result of the present form of transformation. It is easier, however, to construct a model for it than for the democratic form of state capitalism to which our experience gives us few clues.[21]

The term 'state capitalism' indicates that this formation is 'the successor of *private* capitalism, that the state assumes important functions of the private capitalist, that profit interests still play a significant role, and that it is not socialism'.[22]

State capitalism radically transforms the functions of the market. The market no longer acts as the co-ordinator of production and distribution. This function is now assumed by a system of direct controls. 'Freedom of trade, enterprise and labor are subject to governmental interference to such a degree that they are practically abolished. *With the autonomous market the so-called economic laws disappear.*'[23] If free trade, enterprise, and freedom to sell one's labour-power – in short, the exchange market – are becoming a thing of the past, then the critique of the emergent social and political order can no longer take the form of the critique of political economy. First, *the institutional structure* of this new social order can no longer be defined in relation to the laws of the marketplace, and to the impersonal administration of the rule of law by the state. The increasing etatization of society, and the new prerogatives of the state, create institutional structures whose sociological significance requires new categories of analysis besides those of political economy.[24] Second, if with the 'autonomous market' the so-called economic laws disappear as well, then the dynamics and crisis potentials of the new social order cannot be presented as contradictions immanent in the functioning of the economy alone.[25] Under state capitalism, economic crises are either suspended or transformed. Third, if freedom of exchange in the marketplace once actualized the *normative ideals* of liberal bourgeois society – individualism, freedom, and equality – with the disappearance of the market behind a system of direct controls, the normative ideals of liberalism also disappear. The critique of political economy alone can no longer offer access to the institutional structure, normative ideologies, and crisis potentials of the new social order.

The Marxian critique of political economy was at the same time a critique of the capitalist social formation as a whole. In the period of liberal capitalism, a critique of this social formation could be presented via a critique of political economy for two reasons: first, according to Marx, social relations of production defined the *institutional* backbone of liberal capitalism by legitimizing a certain pattern of the distribution of wealth, power, and authority in the society. Under capitalism, the economy was not only 'disembedded' from the restraints of the social and political domain, but this 'disembedded economy' in turn provided the mechanism for the redistribution of social power and privilege. Second, exchange relations in the capitalist market supplied *normative legitimation* for this society to the extent that ensuing differentials of social power and privilege were viewed as consequences of the activities of freely contracting individuals. The 'autonomous market' embodied the ideals of freedom, consent, and individualism which provided the legitimation of this social order. 'With the disappearance of the autonomous market', as hypothesized by Pollock, the critique of political economy can no longer serve as the basis for a critique of the new social formation.

To put it differently, *a critical social theory of state capitalism cannot be a critique of the political economy of state capitalism, for two reasons*: with the disappearance of the autonomous market under a system of direct state controls, the social distribution of wealth, power, and authority becomes 'politicized'. This distribution is no longer a consequence of the laws of the market but of political directives. To analyse the social structure of state capitalism, one needs not a political economy but a political sociology. With the 'politicization' of the once autonomous market, the normative ideals and ideological foundations of liberal capitalism are also transformed. The forms of legitimation in state capitalism need to be analysed anew: with the decline of the autonomous market, the 'rule of law' also declines; liberalism is transformed into political authoritarianism and eventually into totalitarianism.[26]

The core of what has come to be known as the 'critical social theory of the Frankfurt School' in the English-speaking world since the late 1960s is this analysis of the transformation of liberal nineteenth-century capitalism into mass democracies on the one hand and totalitarian formations of the national socialist sort on the other. Between 1939 and 1947, members of the Frankfurt School devoted themselves to analysing the economic, social, political, psychological, and philosophical consequences of this shift. While Pollock's work centred around political economy, Franz Neumann[27] and Otto Kirchheimer[28] concentrated on political sociology and political theory; Horkheimer, Adorno, and Marcuse focused on developing the sociological, psychological, and philosophical consequences of this transformation.[29]

[. . .]

Although differences exist in this period between Marcuse on the one hand and Horkheimer and Adorno on the other, concerning the appropriate political-economic definition of National Socialism,[30] the following describes the implicit sociological model which all three utilize:

- liberal capitalism and free market competition is correlated with the liberal state, patriarchal bourgeois family, rebellious personality type, or strong superego;
- state capitalism (Adorno and Horkheimer) or monopoly capitalism (Marcuse) is correlated with the Fascist state, authoritarian family, and authoritarian personality type;

● or, the same economic phenomena are correlated with mass democracies, the disappearance of the bourgeois family, the sub-missive personality type, and the 'automatization' of the superego.

Within the framework of this sociological model, which establishes functional relationships between the level of the organization of the productive forces, the institutional structure of society, and personality formations, the concepts of 'rationalization' and 'instrumental reason' are used to describe the *organizational principles* of social formation as well as the *value orientations* of the personality, and the *meaning structures* of the culture.

By 'social rationalization' Adorno, Horkheimer, and Marcuse mean the following phenomena: the apparatus of administrative and politi-cal domination extends into all spheres of social life. This extension of domination is accomplished through the ever more efficient and predictable organizational techniques developed by institutions like the factory, the army, the bureaucracy, the schools, and the culture industry. The efficiency and predictability of these new organizational techniques are made possible by the application of science and technology, not only to the domination of external nature, but to the control of interpersonal relations and the manipulation of internal nature as well. This scientifically and technologically informed control apparatus functions by fragmenting processes of work and production into simple homogeneous units; this fragmentation is accompanied by social atomization within and outside the organizational unit. Within organizations, the co-operation of individuals is subject to the rules and regulations of the apparatus; outside the organizational unit, the destruction of the economic, educational, and psychological function of the family delivers the individual into the hands of the impersonal forces of mass society. The individual must now adapt him/herself to the apparatus in order to be able to survive at all.

Already the fact that the categories of 'rationalization' and 'instru-mental reason' are extended equivocally to refer to societal processes, dynamics of personality formation, and cultural meaning structures indicates that Marcuse, Adorno, and Horkheimer collapse the two processes of rationalization, the societal and the cultural, which Max Weber had sought to differentiate.[31] This conflation on their part leads to a major problem: while accepting Weber's diagnosis of the *dynamics* of societal rationalization in the West, they criticize this process from the standpoint of a non-instrumental paradigm of reason. Yet this non-instrumental reason can no longer be anchored immanently in actuality, and assumes an increasingly Utopian character. With this step, a fundamental change in the very concept of 'critique' takes place.

This theory paradigm, known as 'the critique of instrumental reason', leads to a radical alteration of the procedures of immanent and defetishizing critique, while the third function of a critical theory – namely, crisis diagnosis – disappears.

2. The Critique of Instrumental Reason and Its Aporias

The text in which this new paradigm of critical theory is most explicitly developed, and which contains *in nuce* much of the theoretical position of the Frankfurt School after World War II, is *Dialectic of Enlightenment*. The *Dialectic of Enlightenment* is an elusive text:[32] a substantial part of it was composed from notes taken by Gretel Adorno during discussions between Adorno and Horkheimer. Completed in 1944, it was published three years later in Amsterdam and reissued in Germany in 1969. More than half the text consists of an exposition of the concept of the Enlightenment, with two Excursuses, one authored by Adorno on the *Odyssey* and the other authored by Horkheimer, on the Enlightenment and Morality.[33]

[. . .]

In the *Dialectic of Enlightenment*, Adorno and Horkheimer maintain that the promise of the Enlightenment to free man from his self-incurred tutelage cannot be attained via reason that is a mere instrument of self-preservation: 'The worldwide domination of nature turns against the thinking subject himself; nothing remains of him but this eternally self-identical "I think" that should accompany all my representations.'[34] In order to ground this thesis, they investigate the psychic archaeology of the self. The story of Odysseus discloses for them the dark spot in the constitution of Western subjectivity: the fear of the self from the 'other' – which they identify with nature – is overcome in the course of civilization by the domination of the other. Since, however, the other is not completely alien, but the self as nature is also other to itself, the domination of nature can only signify self-domination. The Homeric self, who distinguishes between the dark forces of nature and civilization, expresses the original fear of humanity in being absorbed by otherness. Myth, relating how the hero constitutes his identity by repressing the manifoldness of nature, also expresses the obverse side of this story. Humanity pays for overcoming the fear of the other by internalizing the victim. Odysseus escapes the call of the Sirens only by subjecting himself willingly to their torturing charm. The act of sacrifice repeatedly enacts the identity of humans with the darker forces of nature, in order to allow them to purge the nature within humanity itself.[35] Yet as the regression from culture to barbarism brought about by National Socialism shows, Odysseus' cunning [*List*], the origin of Western *ratio*, has not been able to overcome humanity's original fear of the other. The Jew is the other, the stranger; the one who is human and subhuman at once. Whereas Odysseus' cunning consists in the attempt to appease otherness via a mimetic act by becoming like it – Odysseus offers the Cyclops human blood to drink, sleeps with Circe, and listens to the Sirens – Fascism, through projection, makes the other like itself:

> If mimesis makes itself like the surrounding world, so false projection makes the surrounding world like itself. If for the former the exterior is the model which the interior has to approximate [*sich anschmiegen*], if for it the stranger becomes familiar, the latter transforms the tense inside ready to snap into exteriority and stamps even the familiar as the enemy.[36]

Western reason, which originates in the mimetic act to master otherness by becoming like it, culminates in an act of projection which, via the technology of death, succeeds in making otherness disappear. '"Ratio" which suppresses mimesis is not simply its opposite; it itself is mimesis – unto death'.[37]

In one of the notes appended to the text, 'The Interest in the Body', Adorno and Horkheimer write:

> beneath the familiar history of Europe runs another, subterranean one. It consists of the fate of those human instincts and passions repressed and displaced by civilization. From the perspective of the fascist present, in which what was hidden emerged to light, manifest history appears along with its darker side, omitted both by the legends of the national state no less than by their progressive criticisms.[38]

This interest in the subterranean history of Western civilization is no doubt the guiding methodological principle for the subterranean history of Western reason which the main body of the text unfolds. The story of Odysseus and that of the Holocaust, the myth which is Enlightenment, and the Enlightenment which become mythology are milestones of Western history: the genesis of civilization and its transformation into barbarism.

Yet Adorno's and Horkheimer's relentless pessimism, their expressed sympathy for the 'dark writers of the bourgeoisie' – Hobbes, Machiavelli, and Mandeville – and for its nihilistic critics – Nietzsche and de Sade – cannot be explained by the darkness of human history at that point in time alone. As they themselves acknowledge in their 1969 Preface: 'We no longer hold unto everything that had been said in this book. This would be incompatible with a theory which ascribes to truth a temporal kernel, instead of juxtaposing it as immutable to the movement of history.'[39] Yet they insist that the transformation of Enlightenment into positivism, 'into the mythology of what the facts are', as well as the thoroughgoing identity of intellect with hostility to spirit, continues to be overwhelmingly the case. They conclude that 'the development towards total integration, acknowledged in this book, has been interrupted but not terminated'.[40] The concept of 'total integration' already echoes Adorno's diagnosis of the 'wholly administered society' and Marcuse's 'one-dimensionality' thesis.[41] The critique of the Enlightenment becomes as totalizing as the false totality it seeks to criticize.

This 'totalizing critique', of the Enlightenment initiates a radical break with the 1937 conception of critical theory. The history of humanity's relation to nature does not unfold an emancipatory dynamic, as Marx would have us believe. The development of the forces of production, humanity's increased mastery over nature, is not accompanied by a diminishing of interpersonal domination; to the contrary, the more rationalized the domination of nature, the more sophisticated and hard to recognize does societal domination become. Labouring activity, the act in which man uses nature for his ends by acting as a force of nature (Marx), is indeed an instance of human cunning. As the interpretation of Odysseus reveals, however, this effort to master nature by becoming like it is paid for by the internalization of sacrifice. Labour is indeed the sublimation of desire; but the act of objectification in which desire is transformed into a product is not an act of self-actualization, but an act of fear which leads to control of the nature within oneself. Objectification is not self-actualization but self-denial disguised as self-affirmation.

These two theses – labour as the domination of nature and as self-denial – taken together mean that the Marxian view of the humanization of the species through social labour must be rejected. Social labour, which for Horkheimer even in 1937 contained an emancipatory moment as well as a kernel of rationality, is no longer the locus of either. Both emancipation and reason have to be sought in another instance. The totalizing diagnosis of *Dialectic of Enlightenment* does not tell us where. This transformation of the activity of labour, from one of self-actualization to one of sublimation and repression, creates a vacuum in the logic of critical theory. It is unclear which activities, if any, contribute to the humanization of the species in the course of its evolution, and furthermore, which activities, if any, critique itself speaks in the name of.

[. . .]

According to Adorno and Horkheimer, the task of culture is to establish identity of the self in view of otherness, and reason is the *instrument* by which this is accomplished.[42] Reason, *ratio*, is the cunning of the name-giving self. Language separates the object from its concept, the self from its other, the ego from the world. Language masters externality – not, like labour, by making it work for humans, but by reducing it to an identical substratum. Whereas in magic, the name and the thing named stand in a relationship of 'kinship, not one of intention',[43] the concept which replaces the magical symbol in the course of Western culture reduces 'the manifold affinity of being' to the relation between the meaning-constituting subject and the meaningless object.[44] The disenchantment of the world, the loss of magic, is not primarily a consequence of the transition from premodernity to modernity. The transition from symbol to concept already means disenchantment. *Ratio* abstracts, seeks to comprehend through concepts and names. Abstraction, which can grasp the concrete only in so far as it can reduce it to identity, also liquidates the otherness of the other. With relentless rhetoric, Adorno and Horkheimer pursue the irrationality of cultural rationalism to its sources, namely, to the identity logic which is the deep structure of Western reason:[45]

> When it is announced that the tree is no longer simply itself but a witness for another, the seat of mana, language expresses the contradiction that something is itself and yet at the same time another beside itself, identical and non-identical. . . . The concept, which one would like to define as the characterizing unity of what is subsumed under it, was much more from the very beginning a product of dialectical thinking, whereby each is always what it is, in that it becomes what it is not.[46]

Here the aporetic structure of a critical theory of society, as conceived by Adorno and Horkheimer, becomes apparent. *If the plight of the Enlightenment and of cultural rationalization only reveals the culmination of the identity logic, constitutive of reason, then the theory of the dialectic of the Enlightenment, which is carried out with the tools of this very same reason, perpetuates the very structure of domination it condemns.* The critique of Enlightenment is cursed by the same burden as Enlightenment itself. This aporia, which is acknowledged by Adorno and Horkheimer themselves,[47] is not resolved, but redeemed through the hope that the critique of Enlightenment can none the less evoke the Utopian principle of non-identity logic, which it must. deny as soon as it would articulate it discursively. The end of Enlightenment, the end of the 'natural sinfulness of humanity', cannot be stated discursively. If Enlightenment is the culmination of identity logic, then the overcoming of Enlightenment can only be a matter of giving back to the non-identical, the suppressed, and the dominated their right *to be*. Since even language itself is burdened by the curse of the concept that re-presses the other in the very act of naming it,[48] we can evoke the other but we cannot name it. Like the God of the Jewish tradition that must not be named but evoked, the Utopian transcendence of the history of reason cannot be named but only reinvoked in the memory of men.

[. . .]

The most far-reaching consequence of the project called the 'dialectic of the Enlightenment' is the transformation of the very concept of critique itself. The 'dialectic of the Enlightenment' is also meant to be a 'critique' of the Enlightenment. When it is maintained, however, that autonomous reason is only instrumental reason in the service of self-preservation, then the Kantian project of critique in the sense of 'the self-reflection of reason upon the conditions of its own possibility' is radically altered. As Baumeister and Kulenkampff rightly observe:

> Classical rationalist philosophy practiced criticism against the dogmatic as-sumptions and untrue contents of reason in the form of reflection upon its own pure concept. However, philosophical thought thereby remained blind to the true essence of reason and to the defect deeply hidden in its funda-mentals. It follows thereby that critical theory, which remains true to this *claim* of reason, can no longer assume the form of transcendental reflection and cannot rely upon the available forms of traditional philosophy. Critique is only possible from a standpoint which allows one to question the constitu-ents of the dominant concept of reason, above all, the fixed universal con-trast between reason and nature. A critical concept of reason cannot be gained out of the self-preservation of reason, but only from the more deeply seated dimension of its genesis out of nature.[49]

The self-reflection of reason upon the conditions of its own possibility now means uncovering the *genealogy* of reason, disclosing the subter-ranean history of the relationship between reason and self-preservation, autonomy and the domination of nature. Since, how-ever, genealogy itself is supposed to be critique and not a mere exercise in historical knowledge, the question returns: what is the standpoint of a critical theory that allows it to engage in a genealogical reflection upon reason by using the very same reason whose pathological history it itself wants to uncover?[50]

The transformation of the critique of political economy into the cri-tique of instrumental reason signals not only a shift in the *object* of cri-tique, but, more significantly, in the *logic* of critique. The three aspects described previously as immanent critique, defetishizing critique, and critique as crisis diagnosis are each thrown into question. Immanent critique becomes negative dialectics, defetishizing critique becomes the critique of culture, and crisis diagnosis is transformed into a retrospective philosophy of history with utopian intent.

Immanent Critique as Negative Dialectics

According to Adorno, the task of immanent critique is to transform 'the concepts, which it brings, as it were, from the outside, into what the object, left to itself, seeks to be, and confront it with what it is. It must dissolve the rigidity of the temporally and spatially fixed object into a field of tension of the possible and the real.'[51] As Hegel had already analysed in the dialectic of essence and appearance, what is, is not mere illusion [*Schein*], but the appearance [*Erscheinung*] of essence.[52] Appearance discloses and conceals its essence at one and the same time. If it did not conceal essence, it would be mere illusion, and if it did not reveal it, it would not be appearance. Conversely, essence is not a mere beyond. It is embodied in the world through appearance. It is 'the as yet non-existent actuality of what is'. Dissolving the rigidity of the fixed object into a field of tension of the possible and the real is to comprehend the unity of essence and appearance as actuality. Essence defines the realm of possibilities of what is. When the reality of appearance is understood in light of essence, that is, in the context of its latent possibilities, reality becomes actuality. It no longer simply is; it becomes the actualization of a possibility, and its actuality consists in the fact that it can always transform an unrealized possibility into actuality.[53]

Undoubtedly, the immanent critique of political economy also aimed at transforming the concepts which political economy brought from the outside 'into what the object, left to itself, seeks to be'. By revealing how the categories of political economy transformed themselves into their opposites, Marx was also dissolving the existent 'into a field of tension of the possible and the real'. In Hegelian terms, immanent critique is always a critique of the object as well as of the concept of the object. To grasp this object as actuality means to show that what the object is, is false. Its truth is that its given facticity is a mere possibility, which is defined by a set of other possibilities, which it is not. Negating the facticity of what is means acknowledging that 'das Bekannte überhaupt ist darum, weil es bekannt ist, nicht erkannt' – 'The well-known is such because it is well-known, not known.[54] This implies that a mode of knowing which hypostatizes what is, is not true knowledge. True speculative knowledge, the standpoint of the concept, is grasping the unity of appearance and essence, and comprehending that the actual, because possible, is also necessary, and because necessary, also a possibility.

Adorno transforms immanent critique into negative dialectics precisely in order to undermine the speculative identity of concept and object, essence and appearance, possibility and necessity, which Hegel postulates.[55] Negative dialectics is the unending transformation of concepts into their opposites, of what is into what could be but is not. Revealing what could be does not mean postulating that it has to be. Quite to the contrary, negative dialectics strives to show that there is no end point of reconciliation and of insight into the necessity of the possible. In fact, Adorno's task is to show the superfluity of what is; to show that the object defies its concept and that the concept is bound to fail in its search for essence. Adorno undermines the very conceptual presuppositions of immanent critique which he practises. Negative dialectics becomes a dialectics of pure negativity, of a perpetual defiance of the actual. The discourse of negativity rejects precisely what Marx could still presuppose: that an insight into the necessity of what is would also lead to an understanding of what could be, and that what could be was worth striving for. Negative dialectics, by contrast, denies that there is an immanent logic to the actual that is emancipatory.[56] Negativity, non-identity, demystifying that passion with which thought strives after identity, guarantee no emancipatory effects. Or, to speak with Adorno, they guarantee that these consequences will be emancipatory, precisely because they refuse to guarantee them at all. Adorno rejects the *logic* of immanence, while preserving immanent critique. In so far as the method of immanent critique presupposed an immanent logical development towards a growing transparency or adequacy between concept and reality, critique became dialectics, a mythology of inevitability guided by a belief in the identity of thought and being. Adorno insists upon the *mediation* between thought and being while denying their *identity*:

> Totality is a category of mediation, not one of immediate domination and subjugation. . . . Societal totality does not lead a life of its own over and above that which it unites and of which it, in turn, is composed. It produces and reproduces itself through its individual moments.[57]

The task of negative dialectics is to reveal the mediated nature of immediacy, without thereby falling into the illusion that all immediacy must be mediated. This could be the case only when the totality would become totalitarian, when all moments of non-identity, otherness, and individuality would be absorbed into the whole.

With the transformation of the liberal market economy into organized capitalism, the economic basis of bourgeois individualism is also destroyed. The individual, who through his own efforts and activities realized his freedom and equality in exchange relations in the marketplace, is now a historical anachronism. The normative critique of bourgeois ideology can no longer be carried out as a critique of political economy. The development of bourgeois society has destroyed its own ideals. The critique of ideologies can no longer juxtapose given norms to actuality; rather, it must demystify an actuality that is in the process of obliterating the norms that once provided its own basis of legitimation. The critique of norms must be carried out as a critique of culture, both to demystify culture and to reveal the latent utopian potential within it.[58]

Defetishizing Critique as Critique of Culture

Although Marx's analysis of the fetishism of commodities continues to provide the model for the critique of culture, this paradigm undergoes serious revisions in the work of Adorno and Horkheimer. The metaphor around which the analysis of the fetishism of commodities is constructed is the reification of the social and the historical as the 'natural'. Since the exchange of commodities conceals the process of the production of commodities, and since the laws of the market conceal the constitution of law-likeness through concrete human activities and relations, defetishizing discourse juxtaposes production to exchange, use value to exchange value, the constitutive activity of humans to the appearances in culture. The disappearance of an autonomous sphere of exchange relations transforms the ontological priority accorded by Marx to production. The sphere of production does not stand to the sphere of circulation as essence to appearance. With the increasing rationalization of the productive sphere and the increasing integration of production and exchange, monopoly capitalism begins to develop into a social reality where all contrasts disappear and alternatives to the present become inconceivable. Horkheimer describes this transformation of social reality as early as 1941 as 'the semantic dissolution of language into a system of signs'.[59] The individual, according to Horkheimer,

> without dreams or history . . . is always watchful and ready, always aiming at some immediate practical goal. . . . He takes the spoken word only as a medium of information, orientation, and command.[60]

With the decline of the ego and its reflective reason, human relationships tend to a point wherein the rule of the economy over all personal relationships, the universal control of commodities over the totality of life, turns into a new and naked form of command and obedience.[61]

This totalization of domination, the totalization of a system of signs in which human language disappears, no longer manifests itself as a sphere of quasi-naturalness that denies its own historicity. Rather, the very contrast between culture and nature, between second nature and first nature, begins to disappear.[62] The totalization of domination means the increasing manipulation of nature itself. The antagonism between nature and culture now turns into the revenge of nature upon culture. Whereas Marx had demystified the naturalization of the historical, critical theorists seek to demystify the historicization of the natural. It is the revolt of suppressed nature against the totality of domination which Fascism manipulates, and it is the revolt of suppressed nature which mass industry recirculates in images of sex, pleasure, and false happiness. The repression of internal and external nature has grown to such an unprecedented proportion that the rebellion against this repression itself becomes the object of new exploitation and manipulation. Under these conditions, the 'fetishism' of commodities does not distort history into nature, but utilizes the revolt of suppressed nature to mystify the social exploitation of the nature within and without us. In Adorno's language, exchange value no longer conceals the production of use values; quite to the contrary, commodities now compete with each other to present themselves in the immediacy of use values and to fulfil the nostalgia for the work of one's hands, for virgin nature, simplicity, and non-artificiality. Whereas in liberal capitalism, use value was a carrier of exchange value, under organized capitalism, exchange value is marketable in so far as it can present itself as the carrier of an unmediated use value, into the enjoyment of whose 'spontaneous' qualities the advertising industry seduces us. The brutalization of nature under Fascism, the seductive exploitation of nature by the mass media and culture industry, and the nostalgia for the natural and the organic, expressed by conservative culture criticism, have this in common: they manipulate the revolt of repressed nature into submission, oblivion, and pseudo-happiness.[63]

Crisis Diagnosis as Retrospective Philosophy of History with Utopian Intent

If organized capitalism has eliminated the autonomous market, if the irrationality of competing individual capitals has been replaced by a system of monopolistic state controls, what then becomes of economic crisis tendencies and potentials in such societies? In his 1941 article, Pollock had already claimed that the capacities of the system to manage and to control crises were unpredictably large.[64] In the postwar period, critical theorists emphasize that organized capitalism has eliminated crisis potentials without eliminating the irrationalities of the system. The systematic irrationalities of capitalism no longer articulate themselves as social crises. For this phenomenon, it is not the economy alone but the transformations in culture as well that are responsible.

In *Eros and Civilization*, Marcuse formulates the impossibility of social crises under conditions of industrial-technological civilization as follows: the very objective conditions that would make the overcoming of industrial-technological civilization possible also prevent the subjective conditions necessary for this transformation from emerging.[65] The paradox of rationalization consists of the fact that the very conditions that could lead to a reversal of loss of freedom cannot be perceived by individuals under conditions of disenchantment. In industrial-technological civilization, the real possibility of ending the loss of freedom is provided by the transformation of science and technology into productive forces and by the subsequent elimination of immediate labour from the work process. Labour is no longer experienced by the individual as the painful exertion of organic energy to accomplish a specific task. The labour process becomes impersonal and is increasingly dependent upon the organization and co-ordination of collective human effort. The diminishing significance of immediate labour in the work process, already analysed by Marx in the *Grundrisse*, does not result in a corresponding decline of sociocultural control over the individual.

Quite to the contrary, the impersonalization and rationalization of authority relations brings with it a corresponding transformation in the dynamics of individual identity formation.[66] With the decline of the role of the father in the family, the struggle against authority loses its focus: the self cannot achieve individuation, for, bereft of personal figures against whom to struggle, he can no longer experience the highly personal and idiosyncratic processes of individuating identity formation. Aggression that cannot be discharged in the Oedipal struggle against a human figure is subsequently internalized and generates guilt.[67]

The most far-reaching consequence of the disappearance of the autonomous personality is the weakening of the 'living bonds between the individual and his culture'.[68] Ethical substance disappears. The disappearance of ethical substance in industrial-technological civilization dries up the cultural sources of group revolt which had hitherto been carried out in the name of the memories of past rebellions. The loss of culture as a repository of collective memory threatens the very dynamic of civilization itself: revolt, repression, and renewed revolt. When culture ceases to be a living reality, the memory of unfulfilled and betrayed promises in the name of which the revolt of the repressed was carried out ceases to be a historical possibility in the present. The transfiguration of modern industrial-technological civilization must begin with an act of *Erinnerung* which sets free the forgotten, repressed, denied meanings, and Utopian hopes and aspirations of past revolts. Instead of a critique of Western ontology and identity logic, Marcuse undertakes to reconstruct the latent Utopian dimension of Western ontology. By revealing the polarities of Logos and Eros, of the endless passage of time and the wish to transcend all time, of the bad infinity of the existent [*die Seienden*] and the fullness of being [*die Vollkommenheit des Seins*] to be the dual structures within which Western ontology unfolds, Marcuse upholds the redemptive function of memory.[69]

But this redemptive memory cannot be reactivated within the continuum of history, precisely because history now unfolds in such a way as to deny its own past, its own history. The one-dimensional society created by the industrial-technological world obliterates the ontological horizon within which it has developed and in which it unfolds. This means that the critical theory of society, which speaks in the name of redemptive theory, is itself outside the historical continuum; in an effort to negate the domination of time, it appeals to the memory of the wish to end all time from a point outside time.[70] Reviving the primordial polarities between Eros and Logos, Narcissus and Orpheus, Marcuse seeks to disclose the revolutionary potential of an emancipated sensuality [*Sinnlichkeit*]. Narcissus emerges as the messenger of a new ontological principle.[71] To be transformed into a new ethics [*Sittlichkeit*], the subversive potential of this new sensuality must be reimmersed in the tissues of history; but according to the one-dimensionality thesis, there can be no collective historical carriers of this process.

If, however, the subversive potential of the redemptive memory evoked by the theory remains outside the historical continuum, then has not critical theory acknowledged a fundamental aporia, namely, the conditions of its own impossibility? Critical social theory analyses a subsisting society from the standpoint of the possible transformation of its basic structure, and interprets emerging needs and conflicts in light of this anticipatory transformation. If it is exactly the continuum of history that critique must reject, then the vision of the emancipated society which it articulates becomes a privileged mystery that cannot be related to the immanent self-understanding of needs and conflicts arising from within the continuum of the historical process. Critical theory must either revise the one-dimensionality thesis or it must question its own very possibility. This was recognized by Claus Offe in

1968: critical theory 'must either limit the argument concerning all-encompassing manipulation and must admit the presence of structural leaks within the system of repressive rationality, or it must renounce the claim to be able to explain the conditions of its own possibility.[72]

This critique applies not only to Marcuse's analysis, but to the theoretical paradigm defined as 'the critique of instrumental reason' in general. If it is assumed that societal rationalization has eliminated crises and conflict tendencies within the social structure, and that cultural rationalization has destroyed the autonomous personality type, then critical theory no longer moves within the horizon of *prospective* future transformation, but must retreat into the *retrospective* stance of past hope and remembrance. Critical theory becomes a retrospective monologue of the critical thinker upon the totality of this historical process, for it views the lived present not through the perspective of possible future transformation, but from the standpoint of the past.

[. . .]

One can interpret this outcome in two ways. First, one could claim that social critique once again becomes mere criticism in the sense ridiculed by Marx in his early works, and that the critical theory of society must justify its explicit normative commitments. Second, one could argue that critical theory does not become mere criticism, for it still appeals to norms and values immanent to the self-understanding of late-capitalist societies, but that the *content* of the norms appealed to has been transformed.

According to the first interpretation, critique becomes mere criticism for the following reasons: if crises and conflict potentials in late-capitalist societies have been eliminated; if this social structure has destroyed the very norms of rationality, freedom, and equality to which the critique of political economy could implicitly appeal; if, furthermore, the very boundaries between history and nature, culture and non-human nature, have become unrecognizable; then where are the normative standards to which critical theory could appeal, and how are they to be justified? The critical theorist must either speak in the name of a future Utopian vision to which he alone has access, or he must play the role of memory and conscience in a culture that has eliminated its own past. Neither this Utopian vision nor retrospective remembrance is based upon norms and values derived from the self-understanding of this culture and social structure. The standpoint of the critic transcends the present and juxtaposes to the existent what *ought* to be or what *could* have been had the past not been betrayed. Critique itself, then, is a mode of explicit criteriological inquiry. Marx's commentary on mere criticism can now be applied to the position of the Frankfurt School itself:

> The reflection of the critical subject, who believes to have preserved for himself a truly free life and the historical future in the form of an appeal, remains self-righteous over and against all instances; Marx, who had already recognized this privilege to be the case of the Bauer brothers, therefore spoke ironically of the 'holy family'.[73]

Against this interpretation, which reduces the position of the Frankfurt School to that of the 'holy family', it can be argued that while the critique of political economy no longer serves as a paradigm for the Frankfurt School, there are still norms and values immanent to the culture of late-capitalist societies that have an emancipatory content. However, these norms and values are no longer provided by rationalist natural law theories, whose embodiment in the institutions of liberal-capitalist society Marx could take for granted. It is no longer the norms of a bourgeois public sphere, of the liberal marketplace and of the liberal state, practising the rule of law, to which critique can appeal. With the transformation of political domination into rational administration, the rational and emancipatory content of the natural law tradition has been emptied out. Emancipatory norms are no longer immanent in public and institutional structures. Instead, they have to be searched for in the unredeemed Utopian promise of culture, art, and philosophy (Adorno), or in the deep structures of human subjectivity that revolt against the sacrifices demanded by an oppressive society (Marcuse).

Adorno, who insists upon the unredeemed Utopian potential of absolute Spirit, could therefore begin *Negative Dialectics* with the following sentence: 'Philosophy, which once seemed to have been overcome, remains alive, for the moment of its actualization has been missed.[74] Since the promise of philosophy to be one with a rational actuality (Hegel) or to be a material weapon of the masses who are about to actualize reason (Marx) has failed, it must engage in ruthless self-criticism. This self-criticism of philosophy must reactivate the illusion to which philosophy owes its continued existence – the illusion, namely, that philosophy could become actuality. This illusion must be demystified, for it betrays the arrogance of conceptual thinking that considers its other, that which is not thought, to be a mere vehicle for the actualization of thought. Actuality is not the vessel into which thought empties itself, although it is this striving towards the unity of thought and actuality that gives philosophy its *raison d'être*. This aporia must not be abandoned, but continually practised and revived through negative dialectics. Adorno himself names his critique one of 'dissonance'. It is the dissonance between thought and actuality, concept and object, identity and non-identity, that must be revealed.[75] The task of the critic is to illuminate those cracks in the totality, those fissures in the social net, those moments of disharmony and discrepancy, through which the untruth of the whole is revealed and glimmers of another life become visible. In an essay on the possibilities of social conflict in late-capitalist societies, Adorno can thus advance the otherwise astonishing claim that the conflict potentials of society are not to be sought in organized, collective protest and struggles, but in everyday gestures like laughter: 'All collective laughter has grown out of such scapegoat mentality, a compromise between the pleasure of releasing one's aggression and the controlling mechanisms of censure, which do not permit this.'[76] When one demands a strict sociological definition of social conflicts, then one blocks access to such experiences which are ungraspable, but 'whose nuances contain likewise traces of violence and ciphers of possible emancipation'.[77]

Through his method of emancipatory dissonance, Adorno becomes an ethnologist of advanced civilization, seeking to reveal those moments of implicit resistance and suffering in which the human potential to defy the administered world becomes manifest. It is unclear that these 'ciphers' of possible emancipation to which Adorno appeals can justify the normative standpoint of critical theory. The charge that the critique of instrumental reason articulates the privileged discourse of a 'holy family' is left unanswered. The transition from the critique of political economy to the critique of instrumental reason alters not only the content criticized but the very logic of social criticism, and of the critique of ideologies.

Notes

1. Max Horkheimer, foreword to Martin Jay, *The Dialectical Imagination: A History of the Frankfurt School and the Institute of Social Research, 1923–1950*, Boston, MA 1973, p. xii.
2. Ibid.
3. Herbert Marcuse, 'Philosophie und kritische Theorie', part two of Horkheimer and Marcuse, 'Philosophie und kritische Theorie', *Zeitschrift für Sozialforschung*, 1937, p. 637; my translation. Marcuse's section of this jointly authored text is not included in the standard English translation of Horkheimer's 'Traditional and Critical Theory' found in *Critical Theory: Selected Essays*, trans. M. J. O'Connell *et al.*, New York 1972.
4. Jay, *The Dialectical Imagination*; David Held, *Introduction to Critical Theory*, Berkeley and Los Angeles 1980; Andrew Arato and Eike Gebhardt, eds, *The Essential Frankfurt School Reader*, New York 1978. Held and Arato and Gebhardt provide helpful bibliographies of works by and on the Frankfurt School. In recent years a number of studies have appeared which, more often than not, are motivated by political impulses to discredit the influence the Frankfurt School has enjoyed in the United States. Among

them Zoltan Tar, *The Frankfurt School: The Critical Theories of Max Horkheimer and Theodor Adorno*, New York 1977; George Freedman, *The Political Philosophy of the Frankfurt School*, Ithaca, NY 1981; and Perry Anderson, *Considerations on Western Marxism*, Atlantic Highlands, NJ 1976, stand out for their misunderstandings. Douglas Kellner and Rick Roderick give a helpful overview of this new literature in their review essay 'Recent Literature on Critical Theory', *New German Critique* 23, Spring–Summer 1981, pp. 141–71. For recent German literature, see the following note.

5. Helmut Dubiel, *Wissenschaftsorganisation und politische Erfahrung: Studien zur frühen kritischen Theorie*, Frankfurt 1978; Alfons Söllner, *Geschichte und Herrschaft: Studien zur materialistischen Sozialwissenschaft*, Frankfurt 1979; Wolfgang Bonß, *Die Einübung des Tatsachenblicks*, Frankfurt 1982.

6. Max Horkheimer, 'Zum Problem der Wahrheit', *Zeitschrift für Sozialforschung*, 1935, p. 345; translated as 'The Problem of Truth' in Arato and Gebhardt, *The Essential Frankfurt School Reader*, p. 429. 'Die Warheit ist ein Moment der richtigen Praxis' is rendered in this translation as 'Truth is an impetus [?] to correct praxis'.

7. Max Horkheimer, 'Zum Rationalismusstreit in der gegenwärtingen Philosophie', *Zeitschrift für Sozialforschung*, 1934, pp. 26–7; my translation.

8. Max Horkheimer, 'Traditional and Critical Theory', in O'Connell, *Critical Theory*, p. 215; originally published in *Zeitschrift für Sozialforschung*, 1937, p. 269.

9. Ibid.

10. Marcuse, 'Philosophie und kritische Theorie', pp. 636–7; my translation.

11. Max Horkheimer, 'Postscript', in O'Connell, *Critical Theory*, p. 247. Originally published as the first part of Horkheimer and Marcuse, 'Philosophie und kritische Theorie', *Zeitschrift für Sozialforschung*, 1937, p. 627.

12. Ibid., p. 248; *Zeitschrift für Sozialforschung*, p. 628.

13. Ibid., p. 247; *Zeitschrift für Sozialforschung*, p. 627.

14. Ibid., p. 248; *Zeitschrift für Sozialforschung*, p. 628.

15. Ibid.

16. Ibid., p. 247; *Zeitschrift für Sozialforschung*, p. 627

17. Ibid., p. 249; *Zeitschrift für Sozialforschung*, p. 628.

18. Ibid., p. 249; *Zeitschrift für Sozialforschung*, p. 629.

19. See Wolfgang Bonß and Norbert Schindler, 'Kritische Theorie als interdisziplinärer Materialismus', in Bonß and A. Honneth, eds, *Sozialforschung als Kritik*, Frankfurt 1982 (an English translation will appear in S. Benhabib and W. Bonß, eds, *Max Horkheimer: A Retrospective*); W. Bonß, 'Kritische Theorie und empirische Sozialforschung: Anmerkungen zu einem Fallbeispeil', Introduction to Erich Fromm, *Arbeiter und Angestellte am Vorabend des dritten Reichs: Eine sozialpsychologische Untersuchung*, ed. W. Bonß, Stuttgart 1980, pp. 7 ff.

20. Friedrich Pollock, 'State Capitalism: Its Possibilities and Limitations', *Studies in Philosophy and Social Science*, 1941, pp. 200.

21. Ibid.

22. Ibid., p. 201.

23. Ibid.

24. G. Marramao, 'Zum Verhältnis von politischer Ökonomie und kritischer Theorie', *Ästhetik und Kommunikation: Beiträge zur politischen Erziehung* 4 (11), April 1973, pp. 79–93; A. Arato, 'Political Sociology and Critique of Politics', in Arato and Gebhardt, *The Essential Frankfurt School Reader*, pp. 3–5.

25. Moishe Postone and Barbara Brick, 'Kritische Theorie und die Grenzen des traditionellen Marxismus', in Bonß and Honneth, *Sozialforschung als Kritik*; a shorter version of this article appeared as 'Critical Pessimism and the Limits of Traditional Marxism', *Theory and Society* 11, 1982, pp. 617–58.

26. In his controversial essay 'Die Juden und Europa', Horkheimer analyses the decline of economic liberalism in Europe, and examines the role of anti-Semitism in allowing segments of the population to express their frustration against the system of free enterprise by identifying the Jews as the representatives of this sphere (*Zeitschrift für Sozialforschung*, 1939–40, pp. 115–37). The essay indicates a certain blindness in Horkheimer's conception of the transition from liberalism to Fascism. He fails to

distinguish between the system of free market and free enterprise, and political principles like representative government, the separation of powers, constitutionality, rule of law, and so on. This denigration of the role of political liberalism is one of the respects in which the Frankfurt School continues the tradition of orthodox Marxism and conflates, or rather reduces, political to economic structures. In this respect, Franz Neumann's work is an exception. Neumann's analysis of the inner contradictions and ambivalences of political liberalism, particularly his exposition of the contradictions between the 'rule of law' and 'sovereignty', remains one of the finest treatments of the history of liberal political thought; see F. Neumann, *Die Herrschaft des Gesetzes*, trans. and ed. A. Söllner, Frankfurt 1980, first submitted as a doctoral dissertation to the London School of Economics and supervised by Harold Laski under the title 'The Governance of the Rule of Law' (1936). See also Neumann's collection of essays, *Wirtschaft, Staat und Demokratie*, Frankfurt 1977.

27. In addition to works mentioned in the preceding note, see Franz Neumann, *Behemoth: Structure and Praxis of National Socialism*, London 1942; and *Democratic and Authoritarian State*, ed. H. Marcuse, Glencoe 1957.

28. After the emigration, Otto Kirchheimer was Professor of Political Science at Columbia University until 1965. His most important publications are *Punishment and Social Structure*, with G. Rushe (New York 1939); *Political Justice: The Use of Legal Procedure for Political Ends* (Princeton, NJ 1961); *Politik und Verfassung* (Frankfurt 1964); *Funktionen des Staates under Verfassung* (Frankfurt 1972).

29. I am referring to the analyses in Theodor Adorno and Max Horkheimer, *Dialektik der Aufklärung* (1947); the 7th edition (Frankfurt 1980) is used here; the English translation by John Cumming, *Dialectic of Enlightenment* (New York 1972) is unreliable, and I will not refer to it in the text; and Max Horkheimer, *The Eclipse of Reason* (1947; New York 1974); trans. into German by A. Schmidt as *Kritik der Instrumentellen Vernunft*, Frankfurt 1974. Also included in this general discussion are Horkheimer's essays 'Die Juden und Europa'; 'Autoritärer Staat' (1940), English translation in Arato and Gebhardt, *The Essential Frankfurt School Reader*, pp. 95–118, and reprinted in Helmut Dubiel and Alfons Söllner, eds, *Wirtschaft, Recht und Staat im Nationalsozialismus*, Frankfurt, 1981; 'The End of Reason', *Studies in Philosophy and Social Science*, 1941, pp. 366–88 (also included in Arato and Gebhardt, *The Essential Frankfurt School Reader*, pp. 26–49). I include Herbert Marcuse's essay 'Some Social Implications of Modern Technology' (*Studies in Philosophy and Social Science*, 1941, pp. 414–39) in this general discussion as well.

30. While Neumann, Gurland and Kirchheimer defended the continuity of the political and economic order of National Socialism with monopoly capitalism, Pollock, along with Adorno and Horkheimer, defended the newness of the social order created by National Socialism. In his essay 'Some Social Implications of Modern Technology', Marcuse on the one hand agrees with Neumann and Gurland's continuity thesis, but on the other introduces a new concept of 'technical' or 'technological' rationality to characterize the new form of domination emerging under National Socialism; see pp. 416 ff.

31. 'Societal rationalization' processes can be analysed at two levels: on the one hand, *institutionally* they initiate a process of differentiation, as a consequence of which the economy and the polity are separated and relegated to independent spheres: market and production on the one hand, the state with its administrative and judiciary bureaucracy on the other (see Max Weber, *Economy and Society*, trans. Günther Roth and Claus Wittich, Berkeley 1978, vol. I, pp. 375 ff.). At the level of *social* action orientations, Weber analyses 'societal rationalization' via the transition in the economy, state administration, and the law from substantive to formal rationality (see *Economy and Society*, vol. I, pp. 85, 107, 178–80, 217–26; vol. II, pp. 666 ff., 875–89). It is this aspect of Weber's analysis which Adorno, Horkheimer and Marcuse integrate with their diagnosis of state capitalism in the 1940s. The interdependence of capitalism and bureaucratically administered political domination, oddly enough, provides them with a model to analyse Fascism and, after 1945, postwar industrial mass democracies.

By 'cultural rationalization' Weber means in the first place the *systematization* of various world-views ('The Social Psychology of World Religions', in *From Max Weber: Essays in Sociology*, ed. and trans. H. H. Gerth and C. W. Mills, New York 1974, p. 293). He describes this process as originating with the demand that 'the world order in its totality is, could and should somehow be a meaningful "cosmos"' (ibid., p. 281). Such efforts at systematization are present in all world religions – resulting at times in monotheism, at times in mystical dualism, and at others in mysticism. Second, common to all such efforts at systematization over the centuries is a *decline in the role of magic [Entzauberung]* (ibid., pp. 290 ff.). Weber appears to have analysed such processes of cultural rationalization in the light of a major distinction, namely, the distinction between those world-views leading to an ethics of world abnegation and those leading to world affirmations. See Weber, 'Religious Rejections of the World and Their Directions', in *From Max Weber*, pp. 233 ff.; originally 'Zwischenbetrachtung' to *Gesammelte Aufsätze zur Religionssoziologie* (1920); W. Schluchter, 'Die Paradoxie der Rationalisierung', in *Rationalismus und Weltbeherrschung*, Frankfurt 1980, pp. 19 ff.

32. See, most recently, Jürgen Habermas, 'The Entwinement of Myth and Enlightenment: Rereading *Dialectic of Enlightenment*', *New German Critique* 126, Spring–Summer 1982, pp. 13 ff.

33. F. Grenz, *Adornos Philosophie in Grundbegriffen. Auflössung einiger Deutungsprobleme*, Frankfurt 1974, p. 275, note 26, as cited by J. Schmucker, *Adorno – Logik des Zerfalls*, Stuttgart 1977, p. 17.

34. Adorno and Horkheimer, *Dialektik der Aufklärung*, p. 27.

35. Ibid., pp. 51, 167.

36. Ibid., p. 167.

37. Ibid., p. 37.

38. Ibid., p. 207.

39. Ibid., p. ix.

40. Ibid.

41. Theodor W. Adorno, *Minima Moralia*, London 1974, p. 50; Herbert Marcuse, *One-Dimensional Man: Studies in the Ideology of Advanced Industrial Society*, Boston, MA 1964.

42. Adorno and Horkheimer, *Dialektik der Aufklärung*, pp. 62–3.

43. Ibid., p. 13.

44. Ibid.

45. The critique of identity logic underlying Western reason had been a concern of Adorno's since his 1931 lecture on the 'Actuality of Philosophy'. Whatever differences may exist between Adorno and Horkheimer in this regard, the search for a non-discursive, non-identitarian logic, be it in an esoteric philosophy of language, in symbol, or in the collective unconscious of the species, characterizes both the *Dialectic of Enlightenment* and *The Eclipse of Reason*.

46. Adorno and Horkheimer, *Dialektik der Aufklärung*, pp. 17–18.

47. Ibid., p. 3.

48. Ibid., pp. 16–17; Horkheimer, *The Eclipse of Reason*, p. 181; *Kritik der instrumentellen Vernunft*, p. 156.

49. Thomas Baumeister and Jens Kulenkampff, 'Geschichtsphilosophie und philosophische Ästhetik: Zu Adornos ästhetischer Theorie', *Neue Hefte für Philosophie* 6, 1974, p. 80; my translation.

50. In this context, Habermas has distinguished between the 'traditional critique of ideology' and 'totalizing critique' as practised by Adorno and Horkheimer: 'The critique of ideology wants to demonstrate that the validity of a theory under investigation has not freed itself from the context of its genesis. It wants to demonstrate that hidden behind the back of this theory is an inadmissible *tension of power and validity* and that it is moreover to this tension that it owes its recognition' ('The Entwinement of Myth and Enlightenment', p. 20). Totalizing critique, by contrast, assumes that reason, 'once instrumentalized, has become the assimilated to power and has thereby given up its critical power' (ibid.). It is forced to renounce 'the totalitarian development of the Enlightenment with its own means – a performative contradiction of which Adorno was well aware' (ibid.).

51. Theodor W. Adorno, 'Sociology and Empirical Research', in *The Positivist Dispute in German Sociology*, trans. Glyn Adey and David Frisby, London 1969, p. 69.

52. G. W. F. Hegel, *Wissenschaft der Logik*, ed. G. Lasson, Hamburg 1976, vol. II, pp. 11–12, 101–2; *Hegel's Science of Logic*, trans. A. V. Miller, New York 1969, pp. 396–7, 479–80.

53. Ibid., pp. 180–84; *Science of Logic*, pp. 550–53.

54. G. W. F. Hegel, *Phänomenologie des Geistes*, ed. J. Hoffmeister, Hamburg 1952; *Hegel's Phenomenology of Spirit*, trans. A. V. Miller, Oxford 1977, p. 18.

55. Theodor W. Adorno, *Negative Dialektik*, Frankfurt 1973, especially pp. 32–42.

56. Ibid., pp. 295–354.

57. Theodor W. Adorno, 'On the Logic of the Social Sciences', in *The Positivist Dispute in German Sociology*, p. 107.

58. Theodor W. Adorno, 'Kultur und Verwaltung', in *Soziologische Schriften*, Frankfurt 1979, vol. I, p. 131.

59. Max Horkheimer, 'The End of Reason', *Studies in Philosophy and Social Science*, p. 377.

60. Ibid.

61. Ibid., p. 379.

62. 'Culture today stamps everything with likeness': Adorno and Horkheimer, *Dialektik der Aufklärung*, p. 108.

63. 'Society perpetrates menacing nature in the form of the ever-lasting organizational compulsion, which reproduces itself in individuals as persistent self-preservation, and thereby strikes back at nature as the social domination over nature' (ibid., p. 162).

64. Pollock, 'State Capitalism', *Studies in Philosophy and Social Science*, pp. 217–21.

65. Herbert Marcuse, *Eros and Civilization: A Philosophical Inquiry into Freud*, New York 1962, p. 84. Since this volume is in fact the third of Marcuse's *Gesammelte Schriften*, I have used it as the main text for the following discussion.

66. Marcuse, *Triebstruktur und Gesellschaft: Ein philosophischer Beitrag zu Sigmund Freud*, trans. M. von Eckhardt-Jaffe, Frankfurt 1979, pp. 80–81.

67. Ibid., pp. 88–9.

68. Ibid., p. 93.

69. Ibid., pp. 198–9.

70. 'Eros which thrusts itself upon consciousness is moved by memory; with memory, it turns against the order of deprivation; it uses memory in its effort to overcome time in a world that is dominated by time'. Ibid., p. 198.

71. Ibid., pp. 146–7.

72. Claus Offe, 'Technik und Eindimensionalität: Eine Version der Technokratie-these', in Habermas, ed., *Antworten auf Herbert Marcuse*, Frankfurt 1978, p. 87.

73. Rüdiger Bubner, 'Was ist kritische Theorie?', in *Hermeneutik und Ideologiekritik*, Frankfurt 1971, p. 179.

74. Adorno, *Negative Dialektik*, p. 15.

75. Adorno, 'Spätkapitalismus oder Industriegesellschaft', in *Soziologische Schriften*, vol. I, p. 369.

76. Adorno, 'Ammerkungen zum sozialen Konflikt heute', in *Soziologische Schriften*, vol. I, p. 193.

77. Ibid.

═══ 4 ═══

The Mirror-phase as Formative of the Function of the I

Jacques Lacan

The conception of the mirror-phase which I introduced at our last congress, thirteen years ago, has since become more or less established in the practice of the French group; I think it nevertheless worthwhile to bring it again to your attention, especially today, for the light that it sheds on the formation of the *I* as we experience it in psychoanalysis.[1] It is an experience which leads us to oppose any philosophy directly issuing from the *Cogito.*

Some of you may perhaps remember our starting point in a feature of human behaviour illuminated by a fact of comparative psychology. The human offspring, at an age when he is for a time, however short, outdone by the chimpanzee in instrumental intelligence, can nevertheless already recognize as such his own image in a mirror. This recognition manifests itself in the illuminatory mimicry of the *Aha-Erlebnis*, which Köhler sees as the expression of situational apperception, an essential moment of the act of intelligence.

This act, far from exhausting itself, as with the chimpanzee, once the image has been mastered and found empty, in the child immediately rebounds in a series of gestures in which he playfully experiences the relations of the assumed movements of the image to the reflected environment, and of this virtual complex to the reality it reduplicates – the child's own body, and the persons or even things in his proximity.

This event can take place, as we have known since Baldwin, from the age of six months, and its repetition has often compelled us to ponder over the startling spectacle of the nurseling in front of the mirror. Unable as yet to walk, or even to stand up, and narrowly confined as he is within some support, human or artificial (what, in France, we call a '*trotte-bébé*'), he nevertheless surmounts, in a flutter of jubilant activity, the obstructions of his support in order to fix his attitude in a more or less leaning-forward position, and bring back an instantaneous aspect of the image to hold it in his gaze.

For us, this activity retains the meaning we have given it up to the age of eighteen months. This meaning discloses a libidinal dynamism, which has hitherto remained problematic, as well as an ontological structure of the human world which accords with our reflections on paranoiac knowledge.

We have only to understand the mirror-phase *as an identification*, in the full sense which analysis gives to the term: namely, the transformation which takes place in the subject when he assumes an image – whose predestination to this phase-effect is sufficiently indicated by the use, in analytical theory, of the old term *imago*.

This jubilant assumption of his mirror-image by the little man, at the *infans* stage, still sunk in his motor incapacity and nurseling dependency, would seem to exhibit in an exemplary situation the symbolic matrix in which the *I* is precipitated in a primordial form, before it is objectified in the dialectic of identification with the other, and before language restores to it, in the universal, its function as subject.

This form would have to be called the *Ideal-I*[2], if we wanted to restore it to a familiar scheme, in the sense that it will also be the root-stock for secondary identifications, among which we place the functions of libidinal normalization. But the important point is that this form situates the instance of the *ego*, before its social determination, in a fictional direction, which will always remain irreducible for the individual alone, or rather, which will rejoin the development of the subject only asymptotically, whatever the success of the dialectical syntheses by which he must resolve as *I* his discordance with his own reality.

The Body as Gestalt

The fact is that the total form of the body by which the subject anticipates in a mirage the maturation of his power is given to him only as *Gestalt*, that is to say in an exteriority in which this form is certainly more constituent than constituted, but in which it appears to him above all in a contrasting size that fixes it and a symmetry that inverts it which are in conflict with the turbulence of the motions which the subject feels animating him. Thus, this *Gestalt* – whose pregnancy should be regarded as linked to the species, though its motor style remains unrecognizable – by these twin aspects of its appearance, symbolizes the mental permanence of the *I*, at the same time as it prefigures its alienating destination; it is pregnant with the correspondences which unite the *I* with the statue in which man projects himself, with the phantoms which dominate him, or finally, with the automaton in which, in an ambiguous relation, the world of his fabrication tends to find completion.

Indeed, where *imagos* are concerned – whose veiled faces it is our privilege to see in outline in our daily experience and the penumbra of symbolic efficacity [3] – the mirror-image would seem to be the threshold of the visible world, if we go by the mirror disposition which the *imago of our own body* presents in hallucinations or dreams, whether it concerns its individual features, or even its infirmities, or its object-projections; or if we notice the role of the mirror apparatus in the appearances of the *double*, in which psychic realities, however heterogeneous, manifest themselves.

That a *Gestalt* should be capable of formative effects in the organism is attested by a piece of biological experimentation which is itself so alien to the idea of psychic causality that it cannot bring itself to formulate its results in these terms. It nevertheless recognizes that it is a necessary condition for the maturation of the gonad of the female pigeon that it should see another member of its species, of either sex; so sufficient in itself is this condition that the desired effect may be obtained merely by placing the individual within reach of the field of reflection of a mirror. Similarly, in the case of the migratory locust, the transition within a generation from the solitary to the gregarious form can be obtained by the exposure of the individual, at a certain stage, to the exclusively visual action of a similar image, provided it is animated by movements of a style sufficiently close to that characteristic of the species. Such facts are inscribed in an order of homeomorphic identification which would itself fall within the larger question of the meaning of beauty as formative and erotogenic.

But facts of mimicry are no less instructive when conceived as cases of heteromorphic identification, inasmuch as they raise the problem of the significance of space for the living organism; psychological concepts hardly seem less appropriate for shedding light on these matters than ridiculous attempts to reduce them to the supposedly supreme law of adaptation. Let us only recall how Roger Caillois (who was then very young, and still fresh from his breach with the sociological school of his training) illuminated the subject by using the term *'legendary psychasthenia'* to classify morphological mimicry as an obsession with space in its derealizing effect.

We have ourselves shown in the social dialectic which structures human knowledge as paranoiac[4] why human knowledge has greater autonomy than animal knowledge in relation to the field of force of desire, but also why it is determined in the direction of that 'lack of

reality' which surrealist dissatisfaction denounces in it. These reflections lead us to recognize in the spatial ensnarement exhibited in the
mirror-phase, even before the social dialectic, the effect in man of an
organic insufficiency in his natural reality – in so far, that is, as we
attach any meaning to the word 'nature'.

We are therefore led to regard the function of the mirror-phase as a
particular case of the function of the *imago*, which is to establish a
relation of the organism to its reality – or, as they say, of the *Innenwelt* to
the *Umwelt*.

In man, however, this relation to nature is impaired by a kind of
dehiscence of the organism in the womb, a primordial Discord
betrayed by the signs of discomfort and motor inco-ordination of the
neonatal months. The objective notion of the anatomical incom-
pleteness of the pyramidal system and likewise the presence of certain
humoral residues of the maternal organism confirm the view we have
formulated as the fact of a real *specific prematurity of birth* in man.

Let us note, incidentally, that this is a fact fully recognized by
embryologists, by the term *foetalization*, which determines the prevalence of the so-called superior apparatus of the neurax, and especially
of the cortex, which psycho-surgical operations lead us to regard as the
intra-organic mirror.

This development is lived as a temporal dialectic which decisively
projects the formation of the individual into history; the *mirror-phase* is
a drama whose internal impulse rushes from insufficiency to anticipation and which manufactures for the subject, captive to the lure of
spatial identification, the succession of phantasies from a fragmented
body-image to a form of its totality which we shall call orthopaedic –
and to the assumption, finally, of the armour of an alienating identity,
which will stamp with the rigidity of its structure the whole of the
subject's mental development. Thus, to break out of the circle of the
Innenwelt into the *Umwelt* generates the endless quadrature of the
inventorying of the *ego*.

The Fragmented Body

This fragmented body, the term for which I have introduced into our
theoretical frame of reference, regularly manifests itself in dreams
when the movement of the analysis encounters a certain level of
aggressive disintegration in the individual. It then appears in the form
of disjointed limbs, or of those organs figured in exoscopy, growing
wings and taking up arms for intestinal persecutions – the very same
that the visionary Hieronymus Bosch has fixed, for all time, in

painting, as they climbed, in the fifteenth century, to the imaginary zenith of modern man, but this form is even tangibly revealed at the organic level, in the lines of 'fragilization' which define the anatomy of phantasy, as exhibited in the schizoid and spasmodic symptoms of hysteria.

Correlatively, the formation of the *I* is symbolized in dreams by a fortress, or a stadium – its inner arena and enclosure, surrounded by marshes and rubbish-tips, dividing it into two opposed fields of contest where the subject flounders in quest of the haughty and remote inner castle, which, in its shape (sometimes juxtaposed in the same scenario), symbolizes the *id* in startling fashion. Similarly, on the mental plane, we find realized the structures of fortified works, the metaphor of which arises spontaneously, and as if issuing from the symptoms themselves, to describe the mechanisms of obsessional neurosis – inversion, isolation, reduplication, cancellation and displacement.

But were we to build on this merely subjective data, and should this be detached from the experiential condition which would make us derive it from a language technique, our theoretical enterprise would remain exposed to the charge of projecting itself into the unthinkable of an absolute subject. That is why we have to find in the present hypothesis, grounded in a conjunction of objective data, the guiding grid for a *method of symbolic reduction*.

It establishes in the *defences of the ego* a genetic order, in accordance with the wish formulated by Miss Anna Freud, in the first part of her great work, and situates (as against a frequently expressed prejudice) hysterical repression and its returns at a more archaic stage than obsessional inversion and its isolating processes, and the latter in turn as preliminary to paranoiac alienation, which dates from the deflection of the mirror *I* into the social *I*.

This moment in which the mirror-phase comes to an end inaugurates, by the identification with the *imago* of the fellow and the drama of primordial jealousy (so well high-lighted by the school of Charlotte Bühler in the phenomenon of infantile *transitivism*), the dialectic which will henceforth link the *I* to socially elaborated situations.

It is this moment that decisively shakes the whole of human knowledge in the mediatization by the desire of the other, constitutes its objects in an abstract equivalence by virtue of the competition of the other, and makes the *I* into that system for which every instinctual thrust constitutes a danger, even though it should correspond to a natural maturation – the very normalization of this maturation being henceforth dependent, in man, on a cultural go-between, as exemplified, in the case of the sexual object, by the Oedipus complex.

In the light of this conception, the term primary narcissism, by which analytical doctrine denotes the libidinal investment characteristic of that moment, reveals in those who invented it the most profound awareness of semantic latencies. But it also illuminates the dynamic opposition of that libido to sexual libido, which they tried to define when they invoked destructive and, indeed, death instincts, in order to explain the evident connection between narcissistic libido and the alienating function of the *I*, the aggressiveness which it releases in any relation to the other, albeit that of the most Samaritan aid.

Existentialism

They were encountering that existential negativity whose reality is so warmly advocated by the contemporary philosophy of being and nothingness.

But unfortunately that philosophy grasps negativity only within the confines of a self-sufficiency of consciousness, which, as one of its premises, links to the constitutive mis-recognitions of the *ego*, the illusion of autonomy to which it entrusts itself. This flight of fancy, for all that it draws, to an unusual extent, on borrowings from psycho-analytic experience, culminates in the pretension to provide an existential psychoanalysis.

At the climax of the historical attempt of a society to refuse to recognize that it has any function other than the utilitarian one, and in the anguish of the individual confronting the concentrational form of the social bond which seems to arise to crown this attempt, existential-ism must be judged by the account it gives of the subjective dilemmas which it has indeed given rise to: the freedom which never claims more authenticity than when it is within the walls of a prison; the demand for commitment, expressing the impotence of a pure consciousness to master any situation; the voyeuristic-sadistic idealization of the sexual relationship; the personality which realizes itself only in suicide; the awareness of the other which can be satisfied only by Hegelian murder.

These propositions are denied by all our experience, inasmuch as it teaches us not to regard the *ego* as centred on the *perception-consciousness system*, or as organized by the 'reality principle' – a principle which is the expression of a scientistic prejudice most hostile to the dialectic of knowledge. Our experience shows that we should start instead from the *function of misrecognition* which characterizes the *ego* in all its structures, so markedly articulated by Miss Anna Freud. For, if the *Verneinung* represents the patent form of that function, its effects will, for the most part, remain latent, so long as they are not illuminated by a light reflected in the plane of fatality, where the *id* is revealed.

We can thus understand the inertia characteristic of the formations of the *I*, and find there the most extensive definition of neurosis – even as the ensnarement of the subject by the situation which gives us the most general formula for madness, not only the madness which lies behind the walls of asylums, but also the madness which deafens the world with its sound and fury.

The sufferings of neurosis and psychosis are for us the school of the passions of the soul, just as the scourge of the psychoanalytic scales, when we compute the tilt of their threat to entire communities, gives us the index of the deadening of the passions of the city.

At this junction of nature and culture which is so persistently scanned by modern anthropology, psychoanalysis alone recognizes this knot of imaginary servitude which love must always undo again, or sever.

For such a task we place no reliance on altruistic feeling, we who lay bare the aggressiveness that underlies the activity of the philanthropist, the idealist, the pedagogue, and even the reformer.

In the recourse of subject to subject which we preserve, psychoanalysis can accompany the patient to the ecstatic limit of the 'Thou art that', wherein is revealed to him the cipher of his mortal destiny, but it is not in our mere power as practitioners to bring him to that point where the real journey begins.

(1949 – *translated by Jean Roussel*)

Notes

1. *Translator's note*: 'I' is used here and throughout to translate Lacan's '*je*', in 'le *je*', 'la fonction du *je*', etc. '*Ego*' translates 'le *moi*' and is used in the normal sense of psychoanalytic literature. On '*je*', see Note 2 below.

2. Throughout this article we leave in its peculiarity the translation we have adopted for Freud's *Ideal-Ich* (i.e. '*je-idéal*'), without further comment, save that we have not maintained it since.

3. Cf. Claude Lévi-Strauss, *Structural Anthropology*, London 1968, Chapter X.

4. See Jacques Lacan, *Écrits*, Paris 1966, pp. 111, 180.

Ideology and Ideological State Apparatuses (Notes towards an Investigation)

Louis Althusser

On the Reproduction of the Conditions of Production[1]

As Marx said, every child knows that a social formation which did not reproduce the conditions of production at the same time as it produced would not last a year.[2] The ultimate condition of production is therefore the reproduction of the conditions of production. This may be 'simple' (reproducing exactly the previous conditions of production) or 'on an extended scale' (expanding them). Let us ignore this last distinction for the moment.

What, then, is *the reproduction of the conditions of production*?

Here we are entering a domain which is both very familiar (since *Capital* Volume Two) and uniquely ignored. The tenacious obviousness (ideological obviousness of an empiricist type) of the point of view of production alone or even of that of mere productive practice (itself abstract in relation to the process of production) are so integrated into our everyday 'consciousness' that it is extremely hard, not to say almost impossible, to raise oneself to the *point of view of reproduction*. Nevertheless, everything outside this point of view remains abstract (worse than one-sided: distorted) – even at the level of production, and, *a fortiori* at that of mere practice.

Let us try and examine the matter methodically.

To simplify my exposition, and assuming that every social formation arises from a dominant mode of production, I can say that the process of production sets to work the existing productive forces in and under definite relations of production.

It follows that, in order to exist, every social formation must reproduce the conditions of its production at the same time as it produces, and in order to be able to produce. It must therefore reproduce:

1. the productive forces;
2. the existing relations of production.

Reproduction of the Means of Production

Everyone (including the bourgeois economists whose work is national accounting, or the modern 'macro-economic' 'theoreticians') now recognizes, because Marx compellingly proved it in *Capital* Volume Two, that no production is possible which does not allow for the reproduction of the material conditions of production: the reproduction of the means of production.

The average economist, who is no different in this than the average capitalist, knows that each year it is essential to foresee what is needed to replace what has been used up or worn out in production: raw material, fixed installations (buildings), instruments of production (machines), etc. I say the average economist = the average capitalist, for they both express the point of view of the firm, regarding it as sufficient simply to give a commentary on the terms of the firm's financial accounting practice.

But thanks to the genius of Quesnay, who first posed this 'glaring' problem, and to the genius of Marx, who resolved it, we know that the reproduction of the material conditions of production cannot be thought at the level of the firm, because it does not exist at that level in its real conditions. What happens at the level of the firm is an effect, which only gives an idea of the necessity of reproduction, but absolutely fails to allow its conditions and mechanisms to be thought.

A moment's reflection is enough to be convinced of this: Mr X, a capitalist who produces woollen yarn in his spinning-mill, has to 'reproduce' his raw material, his machines, etc. But *he* does not produce them for his own production – other capitalists do: an Australian sheep-farmer, Mr Y, a heavy engineer producing machine-tools, Mr Z, etc., etc. And Mr Y and Mr Z, in order to produce those products which are the condition of the reproduction of Mr X's conditions of production, also have to reproduce the conditions of their own production, and so on to infinity – the whole in proportions such that, on the national and even the world market, the demand for means of production (for reproduction) can be satisfied by the supply.

In order to think this mechanism, which leads to a kind of 'endless chain', it is necessary to follow Marx's 'global' procedure, and to study in particular the relations of the circulation of capital between Department I (production of means of production) and Department II (production of means of consumption), and the realization of surplus-value, in *Capital*, Volumes Two and Three.

We shall not go into the analysis of this question. It is enough to have mentioned the existence of the necessity of the reproduction of the material conditions of production.

Reproduction of Labour-Power

However, the reader will not have failed to note one thing. We have discussed the reproduction of the means of production – but not the reproduction of the productive forces. We have therefore ignored the reproduction of what distinguishes the productive forces from the means of production, i.e. the reproduction of labour-power.

From the observation of what takes place in the firm, in particular from the examination of the financial accounting practice which predicts amortization and investment, we have been able to obtain an approximate idea of the existence of the material process of repro-duction, but we are now entering a domain in which the observation of what happens in the firm is, if not totally blind, at least almost entirely so, and for good reason: the reproduction of labour-power takes place essentially outside the firm.

How is the reproduction of labour-power ensured?

It is ensured by giving labour-power the material means with which to reproduce itself: by wages. Wages feature in the accounting of each enterprise, but as 'wage capital',[3] not at all as a condition of the material reproduction of labour-power.

However, that is in fact how it 'works', since wages represent only that part of the value produced by the expenditure of labour-power which is indispensable for its reproduction: sc. indispensable to the reconstitution of the labour-power of the wage-earner (the where-withal to pay for housing, food and clothing, in short, to enable the wage-earner to present himself again at the factory gate the next day – and every further day God grants him); and we should add: indispen-sable for raising and educating the children in whom the proletarian reproduces himself (in n models where n = 0, 1, 2, etc. . . .) as labour-power.

Remember that this quantity of value (wages) necessary for the reproduction of labour-power is determined not by the needs of a 'biological' Guaranteed Minimum Wage [*Salaire Minimum Interprofess-ionnel Garanti*] alone, but by the needs of a historical minimum (Marx noted that English workers need beer while French proletarians need wine) – i.e. a historically variable minimum.

I should also like to point out that this minimum is doubly historical in that it is defined not by the historical needs of the working class 'recognized' by the capitalist class, but by the historical needs imposed by the proletarian class struggle (a double class struggle: against the lengthening of the working day and against the reduction of wages).

However, it is not enough to ensure for labour-power the material conditions of its reproduction if it is to be reproduced as labour-power. I have said that the available labour-power must be 'competent', i.e. suitable to be set to work in the complex system of the process of production. The development of the productive forces and the type of unity historically constitutive of the productive forces at a given moment produce the result that the labour-power has to be (diversely) skilled and therefore reproduced as such. Diversely: according to the requirements of the socio-technical division of labour, its different 'jobs' and 'posts'.

How is the reproduction of the (diversified) skills of labour-power provided for in a capitalist regime? Here, unlike social formations characterized by slavery or serfdom, this reproduction of the skills of labour-power tends (this is a tendential law) decreasingly to be provided for 'on the spot' (apprenticeship within production itself), but is achieved more and more outside production: by the capitalist education system, and by other instances and institutions.

What do children learn at school? They go varying distances in their studies, but at any rate they learn to read, to write and to add – i.e. a number of techniques, and a number of other things as well, including elements (which may be rudimentary or, on the contrary, thorough-going) of 'scientific' or 'literary culture', which are directly useful in the different jobs in production (one instruction for manual workers, another for technicians, a third for engineers, a final one for higher management, etc.). Thus they learn 'know-how'.

But besides these techniques and knowledges, and in learning them, children at school also learn the 'rules' of good behaviour, i.e. the attitude that should be observed by every agent in the division of labour, according to the job he is 'destined' for: rules of morality, civic and professional conscience, which actually means rules of respect for the socio-technical division of labour and ultimately the rules of the order established by class domination. They also learn to 'speak proper French', to 'handle' the workers correctly, i.e. actually (for the future capitalists and their servants) to 'order them about' properly, i.e. (ideally) to 'speak to them' in the right way, etc.

To put this more scientifically, I shall say that the reproduction of labour-power requires not only a reproduction of its skills, but also, at the same time, a reproduction of its submission to the rules of the established order, i.e. a reproduction of submission to the ruling ideology for the workers, and a reproduction of the ability to manipulate the ruling ideology correctly for the agents of exploitation and repression, so that they, too, will provide for the domination of the ruling class 'in words'.

In other words, the school (but also other State institutions like the Church, or other apparatuses like the Army) teaches 'know-how', but in forms which ensure *subjection to the ruling ideology* or the mastery of its 'practice'. All the agents of production, exploitation and repression, not to speak of the 'professionals of ideology' (Marx), must in one way or another be 'steeped' in this ideology in order to perform their tasks 'conscientiously' – the tasks of the exploited (the proletarians), of the exploiters (the capitalists), of the exploiters' auxiliaries (the managers), or of the high priests of the ruling ideology (its 'functionaries'), etc.

The reproduction of labour-power thus reveals as its *sine qua non* not only the reproduction of its 'skills' but also the reproduction of its subjection to the ruling ideology or of the 'practice' of that ideology, with the proviso that it is not enough to say 'not only but also', for it is clear that *it is in the forms and under the forms of ideological subjection that provision is made for the reproduction of the skills of labour-power.*

But this is to recognize the effective presence of a new reality: *ideology.*

Here I shall make two comments.

The first is to round off my analysis of reproduction.

I have just given a rapid survey of the forms of the reproduction of the productive forces, i.e. of the means of production on the one hand, and of labour-power on the other.

But I have not yet approached the question of the *reproduction of the relations of production.* This is a *crucial question* for the Marxist theory of the mode of production. To let it pass would be a theoretical omission – worse, a serious political error.

I shall therefore discuss it. But in order to obtain the means to discuss it, I shall have to make another long detour.

The second comment is that in order to make this detour, I am obliged to re-raise my old question: what is a society?

Infrastructure and Superstructure

On a number of occasions[4] I have insisted on the revolutionary character of the Marxist conception of the 'social whole' in so far as it is distinct from the Hegelian 'totality'. I said (and this thesis only repeats famous propositions of historical materialism) that Marx conceived the structure of every society as constituted by 'levels' or 'instances' articulated by a specific determination: the *infrastructure*, or economic base (the 'unity' of the productive forces and the relations of production) and the *superstructure*, which itself contains two 'levels' or 'instances': the politico-legal (law and the State) and ideology (the different ideologies, religious, ethical, legal, political, etc.).

Besides its theoretico-didactic interest (it reveals the difference between Marx and Hegel), this representation has the following crucial theoretical advantage: it makes it possible to inscribe in the theoretical apparatus of its essential concepts what I have called their *respective indices of effectivity*. What does this mean?

It is easy to see that this representation of the structure of every society as an edifice containing a base (infrastructure) on which are erected the two 'floors' of the superstructure, is a metaphor, to be quite precise, a spatial metaphor: the metaphor of a topography [*topique*].[5] Like every metaphor, this metaphor suggests something, makes something visible. What? Precisely this: that the upper floors could not 'stay up' (in the air) alone, if they did not rest precisely on their base.

Thus the object of the metaphor of the edifice is to represent above all the 'determination in the last instance' by the economic base. The effect of this spatial metaphor is to endow the base with an index of effectivity known by the famous terms: the determination in the last instance of what happens in the upper 'floors' (of the superstructure) by what happens in the economic base.

Given this index of effectivity 'in the last instance', the 'floors' of the superstructure are clearly endowed with different indices of effectivity. What kind of indices?

It is possible to say that the floors of the superstructure are not determinant in the last instance, but that they are determined by the effectivity of the base; that if they are determinant in their own (as yet undefined) ways, this is true only in so far as they are determined by the base.

Their index of effectivity (or determination), as determined by the determination in the last instance of the base, is thought by the Marxist tradition in two ways: (1) there is a 'relative autonomy' of the superstructure with respect to the base; (2) there is a 'reciprocal action' of the superstructure on the base.

We can therefore say that the great theoretical advantage of the Marxist topography, i.e. of the spatial metaphor of the edifice (base and superstructure), is simultaneously that it reveals that questions of determination (or of index of effectivity) are crucial; that it reveals that it is the base which in the last instance determines the whole edifice; and that, as a consequence, it obliges us to pose the theoretical problem of the types of 'derivatory' effectivity peculiar to the superstructure, i.e. it obliges us to think what the Marxist tradition calls conjointly the relative autonomy of the superstructure and the reciprocal action of the superstructure on the base.

The greatest disadvantage of this representation of the structure of every society by the spatial metaphor of an edifice is obviously the fact that it is metaphorical: i.e. it remains *descriptive*.

It now seems to me that it is possible and desirable to represent things differently. NB: I do not mean by this that I want to reject the classical metaphor, for that metaphor itself requires that we go beyond it. And I am not going beyond it in order to reject it as outworn. I simply want to attempt to think what it gives us in the form of a description.

I believe that it is possible and necessary to think what characterizes the essential of the existence and nature of the superstructure *on the basis of reproduction*. Once one takes the point of view of reproduction, many of the questions whose existence was indicated by the spatial metaphor of the edifice, but to which it could not give a conceptual answer, are immediately illuminated.

My basic thesis is that it is not possible to pose these questions (and therefore to answer them) *except from the point of view of reproduction*.

I shall give a short analysis of Law, the State and Ideology *from this point of view*. And I shall reveal what happens both from the point of view of practice and production on the one hand, and from that of reproduction on the other.

The State

The Marxist tradition is strict, here: in the *Communist Manifesto* and the 'Eighteenth Brumaire' (and in all the later classical texts, above all in Marx's writings on the Paris Commune and Lenin's on *State and Revolution*), the State is explicitly conceived as a repressive apparatus. The State is a 'machine' of repression, which enables the ruling classes (in the nineteenth century the bourgeois class and the 'class' of big landowners) to ensure their domination over the working class, thus enabling the former to subject the latter to the process of surplus-value extortion (i.e. to capitalist exploitation).

The State is thus first of all what the Marxist classics have called *the State apparatus*. This term means: not only the specialized apparatus (in the narrow sense) whose existence and necessity I have recognized in relation to the requirements of legal practice, i.e. the police, the courts, the prisons; but also the army, which (the proletariat has paid for this experience with its blood) intervenes directly as a supplementary repressive force in the last instance, when the police and its specialized auxiliary corps are 'outrun by events'; and above this ensemble, the head of State, the government and the administration.

Presented in this form, the Marxist–Leninist 'theory' of the State has its finger on the essential point, and not for one moment can there be any question of rejecting the fact that this really is the essential point. The State apparatus, which defines the State as a force of repressive execution and intervention 'in the interests of the ruling classes' in the class struggle conducted by the bourgeoisie and its allies against the proletariat, is quite certainly the State, and quite certainly defines its basic 'function'.

From Descriptive Theory to Theory as such

Nevertheless, here too, as I pointed out with respect to the metaphor of the edifice (infrastructure and superstructure), this presentation of the nature of the State is still partly descriptive.

As I shall often have occasion to use this adjective (descriptive), a word of explanation is necessary in order to remove any ambiguity.

Whenever, in speaking of the metaphor of the edifice or of the Marxist 'theory' of the State, I have said that these are descriptive conceptions or representations of their objects, I had no ulterior critical motives. On the contrary, I have every grounds to think that great scientific discoveries cannot help but pass through the phase of what I shall call *descriptive 'theory'*. This is the first phase of every theory, at least in the domain which concerns us (that of the science of social formations). As such, one might – and in my opinion one must – envisage this phase as a transitional one, necessary to the development of the theory. That it is transitional is inscribed in my expression: 'descriptive theory', which reveals in its conjunction of terms the equivalent of a kind of 'contradiction'. In fact, the term theory 'clashes' to some extent with the adjective 'descriptive' which I have attached to it. This means quite precisely: (1) that the 'descriptive theory' really is, without a shadow of a doubt, the irreversible beginning of the theory; but (2) that the 'descriptive' form in which the theory is presented requires, precisely as an effect of this 'contradiction', a development of the theory which goes beyond the form of 'description'.

Let me make this idea clearer by returning to our present object: the State.

When I say that the Marxist 'theory' of the State available to us is still partly 'descriptive', that means first and foremost that this descriptive 'theory' is without the shadow of a doubt precisely the beginning of the Marxist theory of the State, and that this beginning gives us the essential point, i.e. the decisive principle of every later development of the theory.

Indeed, I shall call the descriptive theory of the State correct, since it is perfectly possible to make the vast majority of the facts in the domain with which it is concerned correspond to the definition it gives of its object. Thus, the definition of the State as a class State, existing in the repressive State apparatus, casts a brilliant light on all the facts observable in the various orders of repression whatever their domains: from the massacres of June 1848 and of the Paris Commune, of Bloody Sunday, May 1905 in Petrograd, of the Resistance, of Charonne, etc., to the mere (and relatively anodyne) interventions of a 'censorship' which has banned Diderot's *La Religieuse* or a play by Gatti on Franco; it casts light on all the direct or indirect forms of exploitation and extermination of the masses of the people (imperialist wars); it casts light on that subtle everyday domination beneath which can be glimpsed, in the forms of political democracy, for example, what Lenin, following Marx, called the dictatorship of the bourgeoisie.

And yet the descriptive theory of the State represents a phase in the constitution of the theory which itself demands the 'supersession' of this phase. For it is clear that if the definition in question really does give us the means to identify and recognize the facts of oppression by relating them to the State, conceived as the repressive State apparatus, this 'interrelationship' gives rise to a very special kind of obviousness, about which I shall have something to say in a moment: 'Yes, that's how it is, that's really true!' And the accumulation of facts within the definition of the State may multiply examples, but it does not really advance the definition of the State, i.e. the scientific theory of the State. Every descriptive theory thus runs the risk of 'blocking' the develop-ment of the theory, and yet that development is essential.

That is why I think that, in order to develop this descriptive theory into theory as such, i.e. in order to understand further the mechanisms of the State in its functioning, I think that it is indispensable to *add* something to the classical definition of the State as a State apparatus.

The Essentials of the Marxist Theory of the State

Let me first clarify one important point: the State (and its existence in its apparatus) has no meaning except as a function of *State power*. The whole of the political class struggle revolves around the State. By which I mean around the possession, i.e. the seizure and conservation of State power by a certain class or by an alliance between classes or class fractions. This first clarification obliges me to distinguish between State power (conservation of State power or seizure of State power), the objective of the political class struggle on the one hand, and the State apparatus on the other.

We know that the State apparatus may survive, as is proved by bourgeois 'revolutions' in nineteenth-century France (1830, 1848), by *coups d'état* (2 December, May 1958), by collapses of the State (the fall of the Empire in 1870, of the Third Republic in 1940), or by the political rise of the petty bourgeoisie (1890–95 in France), etc., without the State apparatus being affected or modified: it may survive political events which affect the possession of State power.

Even after a social revolution like that of 1917, a large part of the State apparatus survived after the seizure of State power by the alliance of the proletariat and the small peasantry: Lenin repeated the fact again and again.

It is possible to describe the distinction between State power and State apparatus as part of the 'Marxist theory' of the State, explicitly present since Marx's 'Eighteenth Brumaire' and *Class Struggles in France.*

To summarize the 'Marxist theory of the State' on this point, it can be said that the Marxist classics have always claimed that (1) the State is the repressive State apparatus, (2) State power and State apparatus must be distinguished, (3) the objective of the class struggle concerns State power, and in consequence the use of the State apparatus by the classes (or alliance of classes or of fractions of classes) holding State power as a function of their class objectives, and (4) the proletariat must seize State power in order to destroy the existing bourgeois State apparatus and, in a first phase, replace it with a quite different, proletarian, State apparatus, then in later phases set in motion a radical process, that of the destruction of the State (the end of State power, the end of every State apparatus).

In this perspective, therefore, what I would propose to add to the 'Marxist theory' of the State is already there in so many words. But it seems to me that even with this supplement, this theory is still in part descriptive, although it does now contain complex and differential elements whose functioning and action cannot be understood without recourse to further supplementary theoretical development.

The State Ideological Apparatuses

Thus, what has to be added to the 'Marxist theory' of the State is something else.

Here we must advance cautiously in a terrain which, in fact, the Marxist classics entered long before us, but without having systematized in theoretical form the decisive advances implied by their experiences and procedures. Their experiences and procedures were indeed restricted in the main to the terrain of political practice.

In fact, i.e. in their political practice, the Marxist classics treated the State as a more complex reality than the definition of it given in the 'Marxist theory of the State', even when it has been supplemented as I have just suggested. They recognized this complexity in their practice, but they did not express it in a corresponding theory.[6]

I should like to attempt a very schematic outline of this corresponding theory. To that end, I propose the following thesis.

In order to advance the theory of the State it is indispensable to take into account not only the distinction between *State power* and *State apparatus*, but also another reality which is clearly on the side of the (repressive) State apparatus, but must not be confused with it. I shall call this reality by its concept: the *ideological State apparatuses*.

What are the ideological State apparatuses (ISAs)?

They must not be confused with the (repressive) State apparatus. Remember that in Marxist theory, the State Apparatus (SA) contains: the Government, the Administration, the Army, the Police, the Courts, the Prisons, etc., which constitute what I shall in future call the Repressive State Apparatus. Repressive suggests that the State Apparatus in question 'functions by violence' – at least ultimately (since repression, e.g. administrative repression, may take non-physical forms).

I shall call Ideological State Apparatuses a certain number of realities which present themselves to the immediate observer in the form of distinct and specialized institutions. I propose an empirical list of these which will obviously have to be examined in detail, tested, corrected and reorganized. With all the reservations implied by this requirement, we can for the moment regard the following institutions as Ideological State Apparatuses (the order in which I have listed them has no particular significance):

- the religious ISA (the system of the different Churches);
- the educational ISA (the system of the different public and private 'Schools');
- the family ISA;[7]
- the legal ISA;[8]
- the political ISA (the political system, including the different Parties);
- the trade-union ISA;

- the communications ISA (press, radio and television, etc.);
- the cultural ISA (Literature, the Arts, sports, etc.).

I have said that the ISAs must not be confused with the (Repressive) State Apparatus. What constitutes the difference?

As a first moment, it is clear that while there is *one* (Repressive) State Apparatus, there is a *plurality* of Ideological State Apparatuses. Even presupposing that it exists, the unity that constitutes this plurality of ISAs as a body is not immediately visible.

As a second moment, it is clear that whereas the – unified – (Repressive) State Apparatus belongs entirely to the *public* domain, much the larger part of the Ideological State Apparatuses (in their apparent dispersion) are part, on the contrary, of the *private* domain. Churches, Parties, Trade Unions, families, some schools, most newspapers, cultural ventures, etc., etc., are private.

We can ignore the first observation for the moment. But someone is bound to question the second, asking me by what right I regard as Ideological *State* Apparatuses institutions which for the most part do not possess public status, but are quite simply *private* institutions. As a conscious Marxist, Gramsci already forestalled this objection in one sentence. The distinction between the public and the private is a distinction internal to bourgeois law, and valid in the (subordinate) domains in which bourgeois law exercises its 'authority'. The domain of the State escapes it because the latter is 'above the law': the State, which is the State *of* the ruling class, is neither public nor private; on the contrary, it is the precondition for any distinction between public and private. The same thing can be said from the starting point of our State Ideological Apparatuses. It is unimportant whether the institutions in which they are realized are 'public' or 'private'. What matters is how they function. Private institutions can perfectly well 'function' as Ideological State Apparatuses. A reasonably thorough analysis of any one of the ISAs proves it.

But now for what is essential. What distinguishes the ISAs from the (Repressive) State Apparatus is the following basic difference: the Repressive State Apparatus functions 'by violence', whereas the Ideological State Apparatuses *function 'by ideology'*.

I can clarify matters by correcting this distinction. I shall say rather that every State Apparatus, whether Repressive or Ideological, 'functions' both by violence and by ideology, but with one very important distinction which makes it imperative not to confuse the Ideological State Apparatuses with the (Repressive) State Apparatus.

This is the fact that the (Repressive) State Apparatus functions massively and predominantly *by repression* (including physical repression), while functioning secondarily by ideology. (There is no such thing as a purely repressive apparatus.) For example, the Army and the Police also function by ideology both to ensure their own cohesion and reproduction, and in the 'values' they propound externally.

In the same way, but inversely, it is essential to say that for their part the Ideological State Apparatuses function massively and predominantly *by ideology*, but they also function secondarily by repression, even if ultimately, but only ultimately, this is very attenuated and concealed, even symbolic. (There is no such thing as a purely ideological apparatus.) Thus Schools and Churches use suitable methods of punishment, expulsion, selection, etc., to 'discipline' not only their shepherds, but also their flocks. The same is true of the Family . . . . The same is true of the cultural IS Apparatus (censorship, among other things), etc.

Is it necessary to add that this determination of the double 'functioning' (predominantly, secondarily) by repression and by ideology, according to whether it is a matter of the (Repressive) State Apparatus or the Ideological State Apparatuses, makes it clear that very subtle explicit or tacit combinations may be woven from the interplay of the (Repressive) State Apparatus and the Ideological State Apparatuses? Everyday life provides us with innumerable examples of this, but they must be studied in detail if we are to go further than this mere observation.

Nevertheless, this remark leads us towards an understanding of what constitutes the unity of the apparently disparate body of the ISAs. If the ISAs 'function' massively and predominantly by ideology, what unifies their diversity is precisely this functioning, in so far as the ideology by which they function is always in fact unified, despite its diversity and its contradictions, *beneath the ruling ideology*, which is the ideology of 'the ruling class'. Given the fact that the 'ruling class' in principle holds State power (openly or more often by means of alliances between classes or class fractions), and therefore has at its disposal the (Repressive) State Apparatus, we can accept the fact that this same ruling class is active in the Ideological State Apparatuses in so far as it is ultimately the ruling ideology which is realized in the Ideological State Apparatuses, precisely in its contradictions. Of course, it is a quite different thing to act by laws and decrees in the (Repressive) State Apparatus and to 'act' through the intermediary of the ruling ideology in the Ideological State Apparatuses. We must go into the details of this difference – but it cannot mask the reality of a profound identity. To my knowledge, *no class can hold State power over a long period without at the same time exercising its hegemony over and in the State Ideological Apparatuses.* I need only one example and proof of this:

Lenin's anguished concern to revolutionize the educational Ideological State Apparatus (among others), simply to make it possible for the Soviet proletariat, who had seized State power, to secure the future of the dictatorship of the proletariat and the transition to socialism.[9]

This last comment puts us in a position to understand that the Ideological State Apparatuses may be not only the *stake*, but also the *site* of class struggle, and often of bitter forms of class struggle. The class (or class alliance) in power cannot lay down the law in the ISAs as easily as it can in the (Repressive) State Apparatus, not only because the former ruling classes are able to retain strong positions there for a long time, but also because the resistance of the exploited classes is able to find means and occasions to express itself there, either by the utilization of their contradictions, or by conquering combat positions in them in struggle.[10]

Let me run through my comments.

If the thesis I have proposed is well-founded, it leads me back to the classical Marxist theory of the State, while making it more precise in one point. I argue that it is necessary to distinguish between State power (and its possession by . . .) on the one hand, and the State Apparatus on the other. But I add that the State Apparatus contains two bodies: the body of institutions which represent the Repressive State Apparatus on the one hand, and the body of institutions which represent the body of Ideological State Apparatuses on the other.

But if this is the case, the following question is bound to be asked, even in the very summary state of my suggestions: what exactly is the extent of the role of the Ideological State Apparatuses? What is their importance based on? In other words: to what does the 'function' of these Ideological State Apparatuses, which do not function by repression but by ideology, correspond?

On the Reproduction of the Relations of Production

I can now answer the central question which I have left in suspense for many long pages: *how is the reproduction of the relations of production secured?*

In the topographical language (Infrastructure, Superstructure), I can say: for the most part,[11] it is secured by the legal-political and ideological superstructure.

But as I have argued that it is essential to go beyond this still descriptive language, I shall say: for the most part, it is secured by the exercise of State power in the State Apparatuses, on the one hand the

(Repressive) State Apparatus, on the other the Ideological State Apparatuses.

What I have just said must also be taken into account, and it can be assembled in the form of the following three features:

1. All the State Apparatuses function both by repression and by ideology, with the difference that the (Repressive) State Apparatus functions massively and predominantly by repression, whereas the Ideological State Apparatuses function massively and predominantly by ideology.

2. Whereas the (Repressive) State Apparatus constitutes an organized whole whose different parts are centralized beneath a commanding unity, that of the politics of class struggle applied by the political representatives of the ruling classes in possession of State power, the Ideological State Apparatuses are multiple, distinct, 'relatively autonomous' and capable of providing an objective field to contradictions which express, in forms which may be limited or extreme, the effects of the clashes between the capitalist class struggle and the proletarian class struggle, as well as their subordinate forms.

3. Whereas the unity of the (Repressive) State Apparatus is secured by its unified and centralized organization under the leadership of the representatives of the classes in power executing the politics of the class struggle of the classes in power, the unity of the different Ideological State Apparatuses is secured, usually in contradictory forms, by the ruling ideology, the ideology of the ruling class.

Taking these features into account, it is possible to represent the reproduction of the relations of production[12] in the following way, according to a kind of 'division of labour'.

The role of the Repressive State Apparatus, in so far as it is a repressive apparatus, consists essentially in securing by force (physical or otherwise) the political conditions of the reproduction of relations of production which are in the last resort *relations of exploitation*. Not only does the State apparatus contribute generously to its own reproduction (the capitalist State contains political dynasties, military dynasties, etc.), but also, and above all, the State apparatus secures by repression (from the most brutal physical force, via mere administrative commands and interdictions, to open and tacit censorship) the political conditions for the action of the Ideological State Apparatuses.

In fact, it is the latter which largely secure the reproduction specifically of the relations of production, behind a 'shield' provided by the Repressive State Apparatus. It is here that the role of the ruling ideology is heavily concentrated, the ideology of the ruling class, which holds State power. It is the intermediation of the ruling ideology that ensures a (sometimes teeth-gritting) 'harmony' between the Repressive State Apparatus and the Ideological State Apparatuses, and between the different State Ideological Apparatuses.

We are thus led to envisage the following hypothesis, as a function precisely of the diversity of ideological State Apparatuses in their single, because shared, role of the reproduction of the relations of production.

Indeed, we have listed a relatively large number of Ideological State Apparatuses in contemporary capitalist social formations: the educational apparatus, the religious apparatus, the family apparatus, the political apparatus, the trade-union apparatus, the communications apparatus, the 'cultural' apparatus, etc.

But in the social formations of that mode of production characterized by 'serfdom' (usually called the feudal mode of production), we observe that although there is a single Repressive State Apparatus which, since the earliest known Ancient States, let alone the Absolute Monarchies, has been formally very similar to the one we know today, the number of Ideological State Apparatuses is smaller and their individual types are different. For example, we observe that during the Middle Ages, the Church (the religious Ideological State Apparatus) accumulated a number of functions which have today devolved on to several distinct Ideological State Apparatuses, new ones in relation to the past I am invoking, in particular educational and cultural functions. Alongside the Church there was the family Ideological State Apparatus, which played a considerable part, incommensurable with its role in capitalist social formations. Despite appearances, the Church and the Family were not the only Ideological State Apparatuses. There was also a political Ideological State Apparatus (the Estates General, the *Parlement*, the different political factions and Leagues, the ancestors or the modern political parties, and the whole political system of the free Communes and then of the *Villes*). There was also a powerful 'proto-trade-union' Ideological State Apparatus, if I may venture such an anachronistic term (the powerful merchants' and bankers' guilds and the journeymen's associations, etc.). Publishing and Communications, even, saw an indisputable development, as did the theatre; initially both were integral parts of the Church, then they became more and more independent of it.

In the pre-capitalist historical period which I have examined extremely broadly, it is absolutely clear that *there was one dominant Ideological State Apparatus, the Church*, which concentrated within it not only religious functions, but also educational ones, and a large proportion of the functions of communications and 'culture'. It is no accident that all ideological struggle, from the sixteenth to the eighteenth century, starting with the first shocks of the Reformation, was *concentrated* in an anti-clerical and anti-religious struggle; rather, this is a function precisely of the dominant position of the religious Ideological State Apparatus.

The foremost objective and achievement of the French Revolution was not just to transfer State power from the feudal aristocracy to the merchant-capitalist bourgeoisie, to break part of the former Repressive State Apparatus and replace it with a new one (e.g. the national popular Army) – but also to attack the number-one Ideological State Apparatus: the Church. Hence the civil constitution of the clergy, the confiscation of ecclesiastical wealth, and the creation of new Ideological State Apparatuses to replace the religious Ideological State Apparatus in its dominant role.

Naturally, these things did not happen automatically: witness the Concordat, the Restoration and the long class struggle between the landed aristocracy and the industrial bourgeoisie throughout the nineteenth century for the establishment of bourgeois hegemony over the functions formerly fulfilled by the Church: above all by the Schools. It can be said that the bourgeoisie relied on the new political, parliamentary-democratic, Ideological State Apparatus, installed in the earliest years of the Revolution, then restored after long and violent struggles, for a few months in 1848 and for decades after the fall of the Second Empire, in order to conduct its struggle against the Church and wrest its ideological functions away from it – in other words, to ensure not only its own political hegemony, but also the ideological hegemony indispensable to the reproduction of capitalist relations of production.

That is why I believe that I am justified in advancing the following Thesis, however precarious it is. I believe that the Ideological State Apparatus which has been installed in the *dominant* position in mature capitalist social formations, as a result of a violent political and ideological class struggle against the old dominant Ideological State Apparatus, is the *educational ideological apparatus*.

This thesis may seem paradoxical, given that for everyone, i.e. in the ideological representation that the bourgeoisie has tried to give itself and the classes it exploits, it really seems that the dominant Ideological State Apparatus in capitalist social formations is not the Schools, but the political Ideological State Apparatus, i.e. the regime of parliamentary democracy combining universal suffrage and party struggle.

However, history, even recent history, shows that the bourgeoisie has been and still is able to accommodate itself to political Ideological State Apparatuses other than parliamentary democracy: the First and

Second Empires, Constitutional Monarchy (Louis XVIII and Charles X), Parliamentary Monarchy (Louis-Philippe), Presidential Democracy (de Gaulle), to mention only France. In England this is even clearer. The Revolution was particularly 'successful' there from the bourgeois point of view, since unlike France, where the bourgeoisie, partly because of the stupidity of the petty aristocracy, had to agree to being carried to power by peasant and plebeian '*journées révolutionnaires*', something for which it had to pay a high price, the English bourgeoisie was able to 'compromise' with the aristocracy and 'share' State power and the use of the State apparatus with it for a long time (peace among all men of goodwill in the ruling classes!). In Germany it is even more striking, since it was behind a political Ideological State Apparatus in which the imperial Junkers (epitomized by Bismarck), their army and their police, provided it with a shield and leading personnel, that the imperialist bourgeoisie made its shattering entry into history, before 'traversing' the Weimar Republic and entrusting itself to Nazism.

Hence I believe I have good reasons for thinking that behind the scenes of its political Ideological State Apparatus, which occupies the front of the stage, what the bourgeoisie has installed as its number-one, i.e. as its dominant Ideological State Apparatus, is the educational apparatus, which has in fact replaced in its functions the previously dominant Ideological State Apparatus, the Church. One might even add: the School–Family couple has replaced the Church–Family couple.

Why is the educational apparatus in fact the dominant Ideological State Apparatus in capitalist social formations, and how does it function?

For the moment it must suffice to say:

1. All Ideological State Apparatuses, whatever they are, contribute to the same result: the reproduction of the relations of production, i.e. of capitalist relations of exploitation.

2. Each of them contributes towards this single result in the way proper to it. The political apparatus by subjecting individuals to the political State ideology, the 'indirect' (parliamentary) or 'direct' (plebiscitary or Fascist) 'democratic' ideology. The communications apparatus by cramming every 'citizen' with daily doses of nationalism, chauvinism, liberalism, moralism, etc., by means of the press, the radio and television. The same goes for the cultural apparatus (the role of sport in chauvinism is of the first importance), etc. The religious apparatus by recalling in sermons and the other great ceremonies of Birth, Marriage and Death, that man is only ashes, unless

he loves his neighbour to the extent of turning the other cheek to whoever strikes first. The family apparatus . . . but there is no need to go on.

3. This concert is dominated by a single score, occasionally disturbed by contradictions (those of the remnants of former ruling classes, those of the proletarians and their organizations): the score of the Ideology of the current ruling class which integrates into its music the great themes of the Humanism of the Great Forefathers, who produced the Greek Miracle even before Christianity, and afterwards the Glory of Rome, the Eternal City, and the themes of Interest, particular and general, etc., nationalism, moralism and economism.

4. Nevertheless, in this concert, one Ideological State Apparatus certainly has the dominant role, although hardly anyone lends an ear to its music: it is so silent! This is the School.

It takes children from every class at infant-school age, and then for years, the years in which the child is most 'vulnerable', squeezed between the family State apparatus and the educational State apparatus, it drums into them, whether it uses new or old methods, a certain amount of 'know-how' wrapped in the ruling ideology (French, arithmetic, natural history, the sciences, literature) or simply the ruling ideology in its pure state (ethics, civic instruction, philosophy). Somewhere around the age of sixteen, a huge mass of children are ejected 'into production': these are the workers or small peasants. Another portion of scholastically adapted youth carries on: and, for better or worse, it goes somewhat further, until it falls by the wayside and fills the posts of small and middle technicians, white-collar workers, small and middle executives, petty bourgeois of all kinds. A last portion reaches the summit, either to fall into intellectual semi-employment, or to provide, as well as the 'intellectuals of the collective labourer', the agents of exploitation (capitalists, managers), the agents of repression (soldiers, policemen, politicians, administrators, etc.) and the professional ideologists (priests of all sorts, most of whom are convinced 'laymen').

Each mass ejected *en route* is practically provided with the ideology which suits the role it has to fulfil in class society: the role of the exploited (with a 'highly developed', 'professional', 'ethical', 'civic', 'national' and apolitical consciousness); the role of the agent of exploitation (ability to give the workers orders and speak to them: 'human relations'), of the agent of repression (ability to give orders and enforce obedience 'without discussion', or ability to manipulate the demagogy of a political leader's rhetoric), or of the professional ideologist (ability to treat consciousnesses with the respect, i.e. with the contempt, blackmail and demagogy they deserve, adapted to the accents of Morality, of Virtue, or 'Transcendence', of the Nation, of France's World Role, etc.).

Of course, many of these contrasting Virtues (modesty, resignation, submissiveness on the one hand; cynicism, contempt, arrogance, confidence, self-importance, even smooth talk and cunning on the other) are also taught in the Family, in the Church, in the Army, in Good Books, in films and even in the football stadium. But no other Ideological State Apparatus has the obligatory (and not least, free) audience of the totality of the children in the capitalist social formation, eight hours a day for five or six days out of seven.

But it is by an apprenticeship in a variety of know-how wrapped up in the massive inculcation of the ideology of the ruling class that the *relations of production* in a capitalist social formation, i.e. the relations of exploited to exploiters and exploiters to exploited, are largely repro-duced. The mechanisms which produce this vital result for the capitalist regime are naturally covered up and concealed by a univer-sally reigning ideology of the School, universally reigning because it is one of the essential forms of the ruling bourgeois ideology: an ideology which represents the School as a neutral environment purged of ideology (because it is . . . lay), where teachers respectful of the 'conscience' and 'freedom' of the children who are entrusted to them (in complete confidence) by their 'parents' (who are free, too, i.e. the owners of their children) open up for them the path to the freedom, morality and responsibility of adults by their own example, by knowledge, literature and their 'liberating' virtues.

I ask the pardon of those teachers who, in dreadful conditions, attempt to turn the few weapons they can find in the history and learning they 'teach' against the ideology, the system and the practices in which they are trapped. They are a kind of hero. But they are rare, and how many (the majority) do not even begin to suspect the 'work' the system (which is bigger than they are and crushes them) forces them to do, or worse, put all their heart and ingenuity into performing it with the most advanced awareness (the famous new methods!). So little do they suspect it that their own devotion contributes to the maintenance and nourishment of this ideological representation of the School, which makes the School today as 'natural', indispensable-useful and even beneficial for our contemporaries as the Church was 'natural', indispensable and generous for our ancestors a few centuries ago.

In fact, the Church has been replaced today *in its role as the dominant Ideological State Apparatus* by the School. It is coupled with the Family just as the Church was once coupled with the Family. We can now claim that the unprecedentedly deep crisis which is now shaking the education system of so many States across the globe, often in conjunction with a crisis (already proclaimed in the *Communist Manifesto*) shaking the family system, takes on a political meaning, given that the School (and the School–Family couple) constitutes the dominant Ideological State Apparatus, the Apparatus playing a determinant part in the reproduction of the relations of production of a mode of production threatened in its existence by the world class struggle.

On Ideology

When I put forward the concept of an Ideological State Apparatus, when I said that the ISAs 'function by ideology', I invoked a reality which needs a little discussion: ideology.

It is well known that the expression 'ideology' was invented by Cabanis, Destutt de Tracy and their friends, who assigned to it as an object the (genetic) theory of ideas. When Marx took up the term fifty years later, he gave it a quite different meaning, even in his Early Works. Here, ideology is the system of the ideas and representations which dominate the mind of a man or a social group. The ideologico-political struggle conducted by Marx as early as his articles in the *Rheinische Zeitung* inevitably and quickly brought him face to face with this reality, and forced him to take his earliest intuitions further.

However, here we come upon a rather astonishing paradox. Everything seems to lead Marx to formulate a theory of ideology. In fact, *The German Ideology* does offer us, after the *1844 Manuscripts*, an explicit theory of ideology, but . . . it is not Marxist (we shall see why in a moment). As for *Capital*, although it does contain many hints towards a theory of ideologies (most visibly, the ideology of the vulgar economists), it does not contain that theory itself, which depends for the most part on a theory of ideology in general.

I should like to venture a first and very schematic outline of such a theory. The theses I am about to put forward are certainly not off the cuff, but they cannot be sustained and tested, i.e. confirmed or rejected, except by much thorough study and analysis.

Ideology has no History

One word first of all to expound the reason in principle which seems to me to found, or at least to justify, the project of a theory of ideology *in general*, and not a theory of particular ideolog*ies*, which, whatever their form (religious, ethical, legal, political), always express *class positions*.

It is quite obvious that it is necessary to proceed towards a theory of ideolog*ies* in the two respects I have just suggested. It will then be clear that a theory of ideolog*ies* depends in the last resort on the history of social formations, and thus of the modes of production combined in social formations, and of the class struggles which develop in them. In this sense it is clear that there can be no question of a theory of ideolog*ies in general*, since ideolog*ies* (defined in the double respect suggested above: regional and class) have a history, whose determination in the last instance is clearly situated outside ideologies alone, although it involves them.

On the contrary, if I am able to put forward the project of a theory of ideology *in general*, and if this theory really is one of the elements on which theories of ideolog*ies* depend, that entails an apparently paradoxical proposition which I shall express in the following terms: *ideology has no history.*

As we know, this formulation appears in so many words in a passage from *The German Ideology*. Marx utters it with respect to metaphysics, which, he says, has no more history than ethics (meaning also the other forms of ideology).

In *The German Ideology*, this formulation appears in a plainly positivist context. Ideology is conceived as a pure illusion, a pure dream, i.e. as nothingness. All its reality is external to it. Ideology is thus thought as an imaginary construction whose status is exactly like the theoretical status of the dream among writers before Freud. For these writers, the dream was the purely imaginary, i.e. null, result of 'day's residues', presented in an arbitrary arrangement and order, sometimes even 'inverted' – in other words, in 'disorder'. For them, the dream was the imaginary, it was empty, null and arbitrarily 'stuck together' [*bricolé*], once the eyes had closed, from the residues of the only full and positive reality, the reality of the day. This is exactly the status of philosophy and ideology (since in this book philosophy is ideology *par excellence*) in *The German Ideology*.

Ideology, then, is for Marx an imaginary assemblage [*bricolage*], a pure dream, empty and vain, constituted by the 'day's residues' from the only full and positive reality, that of the concrete history of concrete material individuals materially producing their existence. It is on this basis that ideology has no history in *The German Ideology*, since its history is outside it, where the only existing history is, the history of concrete individuals, etc. In *The German Ideology*, the thesis that ideology has no history is therefore a purely negative thesis, since it means both:

1. ideology is nothing in so far as it is a pure dream (manufactured by who knows what power: if not by the alienation of the division of labour, but that, too, is a *negative* determination);

2. ideology has no history, which emphatically does not mean that there is no history in it (on the contrary, for it is merely the pale, empty and inverted reflection of real history) but that it has no history *of its own*.

Now, while the thesis I wish to defend formally speaking adopts the terms of *The German Ideology* ('ideology has no history'), it is radically different from the positivist and historicist thesis of *The German Ideology*.

For on the one hand, I think it is possible to hold that ideolog*ies have a history of their own* (although it is determined in the last instance by the class struggle); and on the other, I think it is possible to hold that ideology *in general has no history* – not in a negative sense (its history is external to it), but in an absolutely positive sense.

This sense is a positive one if it is true that the peculiarity of ideology is that it is endowed with a structure and a functioning such as to make it a non-historical reality, i.e. an *omni-historical* reality, in the sense in which that structure and functioning are immutable, present in the same form throughout what we can call history, in the sense in which the *Communist Manifesto* defines history as the history of class struggles, i.e. the history of class societies.

To give a theoretical reference point here, I might say that – to return to our example of the dream, in its Freudian conception this time – our proposition *ideology has no history* can and must (and in a way which has absolutely nothing arbitrary about it, but, quite the reverse, is theoretically necessary, for there is an organic link between the two propositions) be related directly to Freud's proposition that the *unconscious is eternal*, i.e. that it has no history.

If eternal means, not transcendent to all (temporal) history, but omnipresent, transhistorical and therefore immutable in form throughout the extent of history, I shall adopt Freud's expression word for word, and write: *ideology is eternal*, exactly like the unconscious. And I add that I find this comparison theoretically justified by the fact that the eternity of the unconscious is not unrelated to the eternity of ideology in general.

That is why I believe I am justified, hypothetically at least, in proposing a theory of ideology *in general*, in the sense that Freud presented a theory of the unconscious *in general*.

To simplify the phrase, it is convenient, taking into account what has been said about ideologies, to use the plain term ideology to designate ideology in general, which I have just said has no history, or – what comes to the same thing – is eternal, i.e. omnipresent in its immutable form throughout history (= the history of social formations containing social classes). For the moment I shall restrict myself to 'class societies' and their history).

Ideology is a 'Representation' of the Imaginary Relationship of Individuals to their Real Conditions of Existence

In order to approach my central thesis on the structure and functioning of ideology, I shall first present two theses, one negative, the other positive. The first concerns the object which is 'represented' in the imaginary form of ideology; the second concerns the materiality of ideology.

THESIS I: Ideology represents the imaginary relationship of individuals to their real conditions of existence.

We commonly call religious ideology, ethical ideology, legal ideology, political ideology, etc., so many 'world outlooks'. Of course, assuming that we do not live one of these ideologies as the truth (e.g. 'believe' in God, Duty, Justice, etc. . . .), we admit that the ideology we are discussing from a critical point of view, examining it as the ethnologist examines the myths of a 'primitive society', that these 'world outlooks' are largely imaginary, i.e. do not 'correspond to reality'.

However, while admitting that they do not correspond to reality, i.e. that they constitute an illusion, we admit that they do make allusion to reality, and that they need only be 'interpreted' to discover the reality of the world behind their imaginary representation of that world (ideology = *illusion/allusion*).

There are different types of interpretation, the most famous of which are the *mechanistic* type, current in the eighteenth century (God is the imaginary representation of the real King), and the *'hermeneutic'* interpretation, inaugurated by the earliest Church Fathers, and revived by Feuerbach and the theologico-philosophical school which descends from him, e.g. the theologian Barth (to Feuerbach, for example, God is the essence of real Man). The essential point is that on condition that we interpret the imaginary transposition (and inversion) of ideology, we arrive at the conclusion that in ideology 'men represent their real conditions of existence to themselves in an imaginary form'.

Unfortunately, this interpretation leaves one small problem unsettled: why do men 'need' this imaginary transposition of their real conditions of existence in order to 'represent to themselves' their real conditions of existence?

The first answer (that of the eighteenth century) proposes a simple solution: Priests or Despots are responsible. They 'forged' the Beautiful Lies so that, in the belief that they were obeying God, men would in fact obey the Priests and Despots, who are usually in alliance in their imposture, the Priests acting in the interests of the Despots or vice versa, according to the political positions of the 'theoreticians' concerned. There is therefore a cause for the imaginary transposition of the real conditions of existence: that cause is the existence of a small number of cynical men who base their domination and exploitation of the 'people' on a falsified representation of the world which they have imagined in order to enslave other minds by dominating their imaginations.

The second answer (that of Feuerbach, taken over word for word by Marx in his Early Works) is more 'profound', i.e. just as false. It, too, seeks and finds a cause for the imaginary transposition and distortion of men's real conditions of existence, in short, for the alienation in the imaginary of the representation of men's conditions of existence. This cause is no longer Priests or Despots, nor their active imagination and the passive imagination of their victims. This cause is the material alienation which reigns in the conditions of existence of men themselves. This is how, in *The Jewish Question* and elsewhere, Marx defends the Feuerbachian idea that men make themselves an alienated (= imaginary) representation of their conditions of existence because these conditions of existence are themselves alienating (in the *1844 Manuscripts*: because these conditions are dominated by the essence of alienated society – '*alienated labour*').

All these interpretations thus take literally the thesis which they presuppose, and on which they depend, i.e. that what is reflected in the imaginary representation of the world found in an ideology is the conditions of existence of men, i.e. their real world.

Now I can return to a thesis which I have already advanced: it is not their real conditions of existence, their real world, that 'men' 'represent to themselves' in ideology, but above all it is their relation to those conditions of existence which is represented to them there. It is this relation which is at the centre of every ideological, i.e. imaginary, representation of the real world. It is this relation that contains the 'cause' which has to explain the imaginary distortion of the ideological representation of the real world. Or rather, to leave aside the language of causality, it is necessary to advance the thesis that it is the *imaginary nature of this relation* which underlies all the imaginary distortion that we can observe (if we do not live in its truth) in all ideology.

To speak in a Marxist language: if it is true that the representation of the real conditions of existence of the individuals occupying the posts of agents of production, exploitation, repression, ideologization and scientific practice does in the last analysis arise from the relations of production, and from relations deriving from the relations of production, we can say the following: all ideology represents in its necessarily imaginary distortion not the existing relations of production (and the other relations that derive from them), but above all the (imaginary) relationship of individuals to the relations of production and the relations that derive from them. What is represented in ideology is therefore not the system of the real relations which govern the existence of individuals, but the imaginary relation of those individuals to the real relations in which they live.

If this is the case, the question of the 'cause' of the imaginary distortion of the real relations in ideology disappears and must be replaced by a different question: why is the representation given to individuals of their (individual) relation to the social relations which govern their conditions of existence and their collective and individual life necessarily an imaginary relation? And what is the nature of this imaginariness? Posed in this way, the question explodes the solution by a 'clique',[13] by a group of individuals (Priests or Despots) who are the authors of the great ideological mystification, just as it explodes the solution by the alienated character of the real world. We shall see why later in my exposition. For the moment I shall go no further.

THESIS II: Ideology has a material existence.

I have already touched on this thesis by saying that the 'ideas' or 'representations', etc., which seem to make up ideology do not have an ideal [*idéale* or *idéelle*] or spiritual existence, but a material existence. I even suggested that the ideal [*idéale* or *idéelle*] and spiritual existence of 'ideas' arises exclusively in an ideology of the 'idea' and of ideology, and let me add, in an ideology of what seems to have 'founded' this conception since the emergence of the sciences, i.e. what the practitioners of the sciences represent to themselves in their spontaneous ideology as 'ideas', true or false. Of course, presented in affirmative form, this thesis is unproven. I simply ask that the reader be favourably disposed towards it, say, in the name of materialism. A long series of arguments would be necessary to prove it.

This hypothetical thesis of the not spiritual but material existence of 'ideas' or other 'representations' is indeed necessary if we are to advance in our analysis of the nature of ideology. Or rather, it is merely useful to us in order the better to reveal what every at all serious analysis of any ideology will immediately and empirically show to every observer, however critical.

While discussing the Ideological State Apparatuses and their practices, I said that each of them was the realization of an ideology (the unity of these different regional ideologies – religious, ethical, legal, political, aesthetic, etc. – being assured by their subjection to the ruling ideology). I now return to this thesis: an ideology always exists in an apparatus, and its practice, or practices. This existence is material.

Of course, the material existence of the ideology in an apparatus and its practices does not have the same modality as the material existence of a paving stone or a rifle. But, at the risk of being taken for a Neo-Aristotelian (NB: Marx had a very high regard for Aristotle), I shall say that 'matter is discussed in many senses', or rather that it exists in different modalities, all rooted in the last instance in 'physical' matter.

Having said this, let me move straight on and see what happens to the 'individuals' who live in ideology, i.e. in a determinate (religious, ethical, etc.) representation of the world whose imaginary distortion depends on their imaginary relation to their conditions of existence; in other words, in the last instance, to the relations of production and to class relations (ideology = an imaginary relation to real relations). I shall say that this imaginary relation is itself endowed with a material existence.

Now I observe the following.

An individual believes in God, or Duty, or Justice, etc. This belief derives (for everyone, i.e. for all those who live in an ideological representation of ideology, which reduces ideology to ideas endowed by definition with a spiritual existence) from the ideas of the individual concerned, i.e. from him as a subject with a consciousness which contains the ideas of his belief. In this way, i.e. by means of the absolutely ideological 'conceptual' device [dispositif] thus set up (a subject endowed with a consciousness in which he freely forms or freely recognizes ideas in which he believes), the (material) attitude of the subject concerned naturally follows.

The individual in question behaves in such and such a way, adopts such and such a practical attitude, and, what is more, participates in certain regular practices which are those of the ideological apparatus on which 'depend' the ideas which he has in all consciousness freely chosen as a subject. If he believes in God, he goes to church to attend Mass, kneels, prays, confesses, does penance (once it was material in the ordinary sense of the term) and naturally repents, and so on. If he believes in Duty, he will have the corresponding attitudes, inscribed in ritual practices 'according to the correct principles'. If he believes in Justice, he will submit unconditionally to the rules of the Law, and may even protest when they are violated, sign petitions, take part in a demonstration, etc.

Throughout this schema we observe that the ideological represen-tation of ideology is itself forced to recognize that every 'subject' endowed with a 'consciousness', and believing in the 'ideas' that his 'consciousness' inspires in him and freely accepts, must '*act* according to his ideas', must therefore inscribe his own ideas as a free subject in the actions of his material practice. If he does not do so, 'that is wicked'.

Indeed, if he does not do what he ought to do as a function of what he believes, it is because he does something else, which, still as a function of the same idealist scheme, implies that he has other ideas in his head as well as those he proclaims, and that he acts according to these other ideas, as a man who is 'inconsistent' ('no one is willingly evil') or cynical, or perverse.

In every case, the ideology of ideology thus recognizes, despite its imaginary distortion, that the 'ideas' of a human subject exist in his actions, or ought to exist in his actions, and if that is not the case, it lends him other ideas corresponding to the actions (however perverse) that he does perform. This ideology talks of actions: I shall talk of actions inserted into *practices*. *And* I shall point out that these practices are governed by the *rituals* in which these practices are inscribed, within the *material existence of an ideological apparatus*, be it only a small part of that apparatus: a small Mass in a small church, a funeral, a minor match at a sports club, a school day, a political party meeting, etc.

Besides, we are indebted to Pascal's defensive 'dialectic' for the wonderful formula which will enable us to invert the order of the notional schema of ideology. Pascal says, more or less: 'Kneel down, move your lips in prayer, and you will believe.' He thus scandalously inverts the order of things, bringing, like Christ, not peace but strife, and in addition something hardly Christian (for woe to him who brings scandal into the world!) – scandal itself. A fortunate scandal which makes him stick with Jansenist defiance to a language that directly names the reality.

I will be allowed to leave Pascal to the arguments of his ideological struggle with the religious Ideological State Apparatus of his day. And I shall be expected to use a more directly Marxist vocabulary, if that is possible, for we are advancing in still poorly explored domains.

I shall therefore say that, where only a single subject (such and such an individual) is concerned, the existence of the ideas of his belief is material in that *his ideas are his material actions inserted into material practices governed by material rituals which are themselves defined by the material ideological apparatus from which derive the ideas of that subject.* Naturally, the four inscriptions of the adjective 'material' in my proposition must be affected by different modalities: the materialities of a displacement for going to Mass, of kneeling down, of the gesture of the sign of the cross, or of the *mea culpa*, of a sentence, of a prayer, of an act of contrition, of a penitence, of a gaze, of a handshake, of an external verbal discourse or an 'internal' verbal discourse (consciousness), are not one and the same materiality. I shall leave on one side the problem of a theory of the differences between the modalities of materiality.

It remains that in this inverted presentation of things, we are not dealing with an 'inversion' at all, since it is clear that certain notions have purely and simply disappeared from our presentation, whereas others on the contrary survive, and new terms appear.

Disappeared: the term *ideas*.

Survive: the terms *subject, consciousness, belief, actions*.

Appear: the terms *practices, rituals, ideological apparatus*.

It is therefore not an inversion or overturning (except in the sense in which one might say a government or a glass is overturned), but a reshuffle (of a non-ministerial type), a rather strange reshuffle, since we obtain the following result.

Ideas have disappeared as such (in so far as they are endowed with an ideal or spiritual existence), to the precise extent that it has emerged that their existence is inscribed in the actions of practices governed by rituals defined in the last instance by an ideological apparatus. It therefore appears that the subject acts in so far as he is acted by the following system (set out in the order of its real determination): ideology existing in a material ideological apparatus, prescribing material practices governed by a material ritual, which practices exist in the material actions of a subject acting in all consciousness according to his belief.

But this very presentation reveals that we have retained the following notions: subject, consciousness, belief, actions. From this series I shall immediately extract the decisive central term on which everything else depends: the notion of the *subject*.

And I shall immediately set down two conjoint theses:

1. there is no practice except by and in an ideology;
2. there is no ideology except by the subject and for subjects.

I can now come to my central thesis.

Ideology Interpellates Individuals as Subjects

This thesis is simply a matter of making my last proposition explicit: there is no ideology except by the subject and for subjects. Meaning: there is no ideology except for concrete subjects, and this destination for ideology is made possible only by the subject; meaning: *by the category of the subject* and its functioning.

By this I mean that, even if it appears under this name (the subject) only with the rise of bourgeois ideology, above all with the rise of legal ideology,[14] the category of the subject (which may function under other names: e.g. as the soul in Plato, as God, etc.) is the constitutive category of all ideology, whatever its determination (regional or class) and whatever its historical date – since ideology has no history.

I say: the category of the subject is constitutive of all ideology, but at the same time and immediately I add that *the category of the subject is constitutive of all ideology only in so far as all ideology has the function (which defines it) of 'constituting' concrete individuals as subjects*. In the interaction of this double constitution exists the functioning of all ideology, ideology being nothing but its functioning in the material forms of existence of that functioning.

In order to grasp what follows, it is essential to realize that both he who is writing these lines and the reader who reads them are themselves subjects, and therefore ideological subjects (a tautological proposition), i.e. that the author and the reader of these lines both live 'spontaneously' or 'naturally' in ideology in the sense in which I have said that 'man is an ideological animal by nature'.

That the author, in so far as he writes the lines of a discourse which claims to be scientific, is completely absent as a 'subject' from 'his' scientific discourse (for all scientific discourse is by definition a subjectless discourse, there is no 'Subject of science' except in an ideology of science) is a different question which I shall leave on one side for the moment.

As St Paul admirably put it, it is in the 'Logos', meaning in ideology, that we 'live, move and have our being'. It follows that, for you and for me, the category of the subject is a primary 'obviousness' (obviousnesses are always primary): it is clear that you and I are subjects (free, ethical, etc. . . . .). Like all obviousnesses, including those that make a word 'name a thing' or 'have a meaning' (therefore including the obviousness of the 'transparency' of language), the 'obviousness' that you and I are subjects – and that that does not cause any problems – is an ideological effect, the elementary ideological effect.[15] It is indeed a peculiarity of ideology that it imposes (without appearing to do so, since these are 'obviousnesses') obviousnesses as obviousnesses, which we cannot *fail to recognize* and before which we have the inevitable and natural reaction of crying out (aloud or in the 'still, small voice of conscience'): 'That's obvious! That's right! That's true!'

At work in this reaction is the ideological *recognition* function which is one of the two functions of ideology as such (its inverse being the function of *misrecognition – méconnaissance*).

To take a highly 'concrete' example: we all have friends who, when they knock on our door and we ask, through the door, the question 'Who's there?', answer (since 'it's obvious') 'It's me'. And we recognize that 'it is him', or 'her'. We open the door, and 'it's true, it really was she who was there'. To take another example: when we recognize somebody of our (previous) acquaintance [(re)-connaissance] in the street, we show him that we have recognized him (and have recognized that he has recognized us) by saying to him 'Hello, my friend', and shaking his hand (a material ritual practice of ideological recognition in everyday life – in France, at least; elsewhere, there are other rituals).

In this preliminary remark and these concrete illustrations, I wish only to point out that you and I are *always-already* subjects, and as such constantly practise the rituals of ideological recognition, which guarantee for us that we are indeed concrete, individual, distinguishable and (naturally) irreplaceable subjects. The writing I am currently executing and the reading you are currently[16] performing are also in this respect rituals of ideological recognition, including the 'obviousness' with which the 'truth' or 'error' of my reflections may impose itself on you.

But to recognize that we are subjects and that we function in the practical rituals of the most elementary everyday life (the handshake, the fact of calling you by your name, the fact of knowing, even if I do not know what it is, that you 'have' a name of your own, which means that you are recognized as a unique subject, etc.) – this recognition gives us only the 'consciousness' of our incessant (eternal) practice of ideological recognition – its consciousness, i.e. its *recognition* – but in no sense does it give us the (scientific) *knowledge* of the mechanism of this recognition. Now it is this knowledge that we have to reach, if you will, while speaking in ideology, and from within ideology we have to outline a discourse which tries to break with ideology, in order to dare to be the beginning of a scientific (i.e. subjectless) discourse on ideology.

Thus in order to represent why the category of the 'subject' is constitutive of ideology, which exists only by constituting concrete subjects as subjects, I shall employ a special mode of exposition: 'concrete' enough to be recognized, but abstract enough to be thinkable and thought, giving rise to a knowledge.

As a first formulation I shall say: *all ideology hails or interpellates concrete individuals as concrete subjects*, by the functioning of the category of the subject.

This is a proposition which entails that we distinguish for the moment between concrete individuals on the one hand and concrete subjects on the other, although at this level concrete subjects exist only in so far as they are supported by a concrete individual.

I shall then suggest that ideology 'acts' or 'functions' in such a way that it 'recruits' subjects among the individuals (it recruits them all), or 'transforms' the individuals into subjects (it transforms them all) by that very precise operation which I have called *interpellation* or hailing, and which can be imagined along the lines of the most commonplace everyday police (or other) hailing: 'Hey, you there!'[17]

Assuming that the theoretical scene I have imagined takes place in the street, the hailed individual will turn round. By this mere one-hundred-and-eighty-degree physical conversion, he becomes a *subject*. Why? Because he has recognized that the hail was 'really' addressed to him, and that 'it was *really him* who was hailed' (and not someone else). Experience shows that the practical telecommunication of hailings is such that they hardly ever miss their man: verbal call or whistle, the one hailed always recognizes that it is really him who is being hailed. And yet it is a strange phenomenon, and one which cannot be explained solely by 'guilt feelings', despite the large numbers who 'have something on their consciences'.

Naturally for the convenience and clarity of my little theoretical theatre I have had to present things in the form of a sequence, with a before and an after, and thus in the form of a temporal succession. There are individuals walking along. Somewhere (usually behind them) the hail rings out: 'Hey, you there!' One individual (nine times out of ten it is the right one) turns round, believing/suspecting/knowing that it is for him, i.e. recognizing that 'it really is he' who is meant by the hailing. But in reality these things happen without any succession. The existence of ideology and the hailing or interpellation of individuals as subjects are one and the same thing.

I might add: what thus seems to take place outside ideology (to be precise, in the street), in reality takes place in ideology. What really takes place in ideology seems therefore to take place outside it. That is why those who are in ideology believe themselves by definition outside ideology: one of the effects of ideology is the practical *denegation* of the ideological character of ideology by ideology: ideology never says 'I am ideological'. It is necessary to be outside ideology, i.e. in scientific knowledge, to be able to say: I am in ideology (a quite exceptional case) or (the general case): I was in ideology. As is well known, the accusation of being in ideology applies only to others, never to oneself (unless one is really a Spinozist or a Marxist, which, in this matter, is to be exactly the same thing). Which amounts to saying that ideology *has no outside* (for itself), but at the same time *that it is nothing but outside* (for science and reality).

Spinoza explained this completely two centuries before Marx, who practised it but without explaining it in detail. But let us leave this point, although it is heavy with consequences, consequences which are not just theoretical, but also directly political, since, for example, the whole theory of criticism and self-criticism, the golden rule of the Marxist–Leninist practice of the class struggle, depends on it.

Thus ideology hails or interpellates individuals as subjects. As ideology is eternal, I must now suppress the temporal form in which I have presented the functioning of ideology, and say: ideology has always-already interpellated individuals as subjects, which amounts to making it clear that individuals are always-already interpellated by ideology as subjects, which necessarily leads us to one last proposition: *individuals are always-already subjects*. Hence individuals are 'abstract' with respect to the subjects which they always-already are. This proposition might seem paradoxical.

That an individual is always-already a subject, even before he is born, is nevertheless the plain reality, accessible to everyone and not a paradox at all. Freud shows that individuals are always 'abstract' with respect to the subjects they always-already are, simply by noting the ideological ritual that surrounds the expectation of a 'birth', that 'happy event'. Everyone knows how much and in what way an unborn child is expected. Which amounts to saying, very prosaically, if we agree to drop the 'sentiments', i.e. the forms of family ideology (paternal/maternal/conjugal/fraternal) in which the unborn child is expected: it is certain in advance that it will bear its Father's Name, and will therefore have an identity and be irreplaceable. Before its birth, the child is therefore always-already a subject, appointed as a subject in and by the specific familial ideological configuration in which it is 'expected' once it has been conceived. I hardly need add that this familial ideological configuration is, in its uniqueness, highly struc-tured, and that it is in this implacable and more or less 'pathological' (presupposing that any meaning can be assigned to that term) structure that the former subject-to-be will have to 'find' 'its' place, i.e. 'become' the sexual subject (boy or girl) which it already is in advance. It is clear that this ideological constraint and pre-appointment, and all the rituals of rearing and then education in the family, have some relationship with what Freud studied in the forms of the pre-genital and genital 'stages' of sexuality, i.e. in the 'grip' of what Freud registered by its effects as being the unconscious. But let us leave this point, too, on one side.

Let me go one step further. What I shall now turn my attention to is the way the 'actors' in this *mise en scène* of interpellation, and their respective roles, are reflected in the very structure of all ideology.

An Example: The Christian Religious Ideology

As the formal structure of all ideology is always the same, I shall restrict my analysis to a single example, one accessible to everyone, that of religious ideology, with the proviso that the same demonstration can be produced for ethical, legal, political, aesthetic ideology, etc.

Let us therefore consider the Christian religious ideology. I shall use a rhetorical figure and 'make it speak', i.e. collect into a fictional discourse what it 'says' not only in its two Testaments, its Theologians, Sermons, but also in its practices, its rituals, its ceremonies and its sacraments. The Christian religious ideology says something like this:

It says: I address myself to you, a human individual called Peter (every individual is called by his name, in the passive sense, it is never he who provides his own name), in order to tell you that God exists and that you are answerable to him. It adds: God addresses himself to you through my voice (Scripture having collected the Word of God, Tradition having transmitted it, Papal Infallibility fixing it for ever on 'nice' points). It says: this is who you are: you are Peter! This is your origin, you were created by God for all eternity, although you were born in the 1920th year of Our Lord! This is your place in the world! This is what you must do! By these means, if you observe the 'law of love' you will be saved, you, Peter, and will become part of the Glorious Body of Christ! Etc. . . . .

Now this is quite a familiar and banal discourse, but at the same time quite a surprising one.

Surprising because if we consider that religious ideology is indeed addressed to individuals,[18] in order to 'transform them into subjects', by interpellating the individual, Peter, in order to make him a subject, free to obey or disobey the appeal, i.e. God's commandments; if it calls these individuals by their names, thus recognizing that they are always-already interpellated as subjects with a personal identity (to the extent that Pascal's Christ says: 'It is for you that I have shed this drop of my blood!'); if it interpellates them in such a way that the subject responds: '*Yes, it really is me!*' if it obtains from them the *recognition* that they really do occupy the place it designates for them as theirs in the world, a fixed residence: 'It really is me, I am here, a worker, a boss or a soldier!' in this vale of tears; if it obtains from them the recognition of a destination (eternal life or damnation) according to the respect or contempt they show to 'God's Commandments', Law become Love – if everything does happen in this way (in the practices of the well-known rituals of baptism, confirmation, communion, confession and extreme unction, etc. . . . .), we should note that all this 'procedure' to set up Christian religious subjects is dominated by a strange phenomenon: the fact that there can be such a multitude of possible religious subjects only on the absolute condition that there is a Unique, Absolute *Other Subject*, i.e. God.

It is convenient to designate this new and remarkable Subject by writing Subject with a capital S to distinguish it from ordinary subjects, with a small s.

It then emerges that the interpellation of individuals as subjects presupposes the 'existence' of a Unique and central Other Subject, in whose Name the religious ideology interpellates all individuals as subjects. All this is clearly[19] written in what is rightly called the Scriptures. 'And it came to pass at that time that God the Lord (Yahweh) spoke to Moses in the cloud. And the Lord cried to Moses, "Moses!" And Moses replied "It is (really) I! I am Moses thy servant, speak and I shall listen!" And the Lord spoke to Moses and said to him, "*I am that I am*".'

God thus defines himself as the Subject *par excellence*, he who is through himself and for himself ('I am that I am'), and he who interpellates his subject, the individual subjected to him by his very interpellation, i.e. the individual named Moses. And Moses, interpellated-called by his Name, having recognized that it 'really' was he who was called by God, recognizes that he is a subject, a subject *of* God, a subject subjected to God, *a subject through the Subject and subjected to the Subject*. The proof: he obeys him, and makes his people obey God's Commandments.

God is thus the Subject, and Moses and the innumerable subjects of God's people, the Subject's interlocutors-interpellates: his *mirrors*, his *reflections*. Were not men made *in the image* of God? As all theological reflection proves, whereas He 'could' perfectly well have done without men, God needs them, the Subject needs the subjects, just as men need God, the subjects need the Subject. Better: God needs men, the great Subject needs subjects, even in the terrible inversion of his image in them (when the subjects wallow in debauchery, i.e. sin).

Better: God duplicates himself and sends his Son to the Earth, as a mere subject 'forsaken' by him (the long complaint of the Garden of Olives which ends in the Crucifixion), subject by Subject, man but God, to do what prepares the way for the final Redemption, the Resurrection of Christ. God thus needs to 'make himself' a man, the Subject needs to become a subject, as if to show empirically, visibly to the eye, tangibly to the hands (see St Thomas) of the subjects, that, if they are subjects, subjected to the Subject, that is solely in order that finally, on Judgement Day, they will re-enter the Lord's Bosom, like Christ, i.e. re-enter the Subject.[20]

Let us decipher into theoretical language this wonderful necessity for the duplication of *the Subject into subjects* and of *the Subject itself into a subject-Subject*.

We observe that the structure of all ideology, interpellating individuals as subjects in the name of a Unique and Absolute Subject, is *speculary*, i.e. a mirror-structure, and *doubly* speculary: this mirror duplication is constitutive of ideology, and ensures its functioning. Which means that all ideology is *centred*, that the Absolute Subject occupies the unique place of the Centre, and interpellates around it the infinity of individuals into subjects in a double mirror-connection such that it *subjects* the subjects to the Subject, while giving them in the Subject in which each subject can contemplate its own image (present and future) the *guarantee* that this really concerns them and Him, and that since everything takes place in the Family (the Holy Family: the Family is in essence Holy), 'God will *recognize* his own in it', i.e. those who have recognized God, and have recognized themselves in Him, will be saved.

Let me summarize what we have discovered about ideology in general.

The duplicate mirror-structure of ideology ensures simultaneously:

1. the interpellation of 'individuals' as subjects;
2. their subjection to the Subject;
3. the mutual recognition of subjects and Subject, the subjects' recognition of each other, and finally the subject's recognition of himself;[21]
4. the absolute guarantee that everything really is so, and that on condition that the subjects recognize what they are and behave accordingly, everything will be all right: Amen – '*So be it*'.

Result: caught in this quadruple system of interpellation as subjects, of subjection to the Subject, of universal recognition and of absolute guarantee, the subjects 'work', they 'work by themselves' in the vast majority of cases, with the exception of the 'bad subjects' who on occasion provoke the intervention of one of the detachments of the (Repressive) State Apparatus. But the vast majority of (good) subjects work all right 'all by themselves', i.e. by ideology (whose concrete forms are realized in the Ideological State Apparatuses). They are inserted into practices governed by the rituals of the ISAs. They 'recognize' the existing state of affairs [*das Bestehende*], that 'it really is true that it is so and not otherwise', and that they must be obedient to God, to their conscience, to the priest, to de Gaulle, to the boss, to the engineer, that thou shalt 'love thy neighbour as thyself', etc. Their concrete, material behaviour is simply the inscription in life of the admirable words of the prayer: '*Amen – So be it*'.

Yes, the subjects 'work by themselves'. The whole mystery of this effect lies in the first two moments of the quadruple system I have just discussed, or, if you prefer, in the ambiguity of the term *subject*. In the ordinary use of the term, subject in fact means: (1) a free subjectivity, a centre of initiatives, author of and responsible for its actions; (2) a subjected being, who submits to a higher authority, and is therefore stripped of all freedom except that of freely accepting his submission. This last note gives us the meaning of this ambiguity, which is merely a reflection of the effect which produces it: the individual *is interpellated as a (free) subject in order that he shall submit freely to the commandments of the Subject, i.e. in order that he shall (freely) accept his subjection*, i.e. in order that he shall make the gestures and actions of his subjection 'all by himself'. *There are no subjects except by and for their subjection*. That is why they 'work all by themselves'.

'*So be it!* . . .' This phrase which registers the effect to be obtained proves that it is not 'naturally' so ('naturally': outside the prayer, i.e. outside the ideological intervention). This phrase proves that it *has* to be so if things are to be what they must be, and let us let the words slip: if the reproduction of the relations of production is to be assured, even in the processes of production and circulation, every day, in the 'consciousness', i.e. in the attitude of the individual-subjects occupying the posts which the socio-technical division of labour assigns to them in production, exploitation, repression, ideologization, scientific practice, etc. Indeed, what is really in question in this mechanism of the mirror-recognition of the Subject and of the individuals interpellated as subjects, and of the guarantee given by the Subject to the subjects if they freely accept their subjection to the Subject's 'commandments'? The reality in question in this mechanism, the reality which is necessarily *ignored* [*méconnue*] in the very forms of recognition (ideology = misrecognition/ignorance) is indeed, in the last resort, the reproduction of the relations of production and of the relations deriving from them.

January–April 1969

P.S. If these few schematic theses allow me to illuminate certain aspects of the functioning of the Superstructure and its mode of intervention in the Infrastructure, they are obviously *abstract* and necessarily leave several important problems unanswered, which should be mentioned:

1. The problem of the *total process* of the realization of the reproduction of the relations of production.

As an element of this process, the ISAs *contribute* to this reproduction. But the point of view of their contribution alone is still an abstract one.

It is only within the processes of production and circulation that this reproduction is *realized*. It is realized by the mechanisms of those processes, in which the training of the workers is 'completed', their posts are assigned them, etc. It is in the internal mechanisms of these processes that the effect of the different ideologies is felt (above all the effect of legal-ethical ideology).

But this point of view is still an abstract one. For in a class society the relations of production are relations of exploitation, and therefore relations between antagonistic classes. The reproduction of the re-lations of production, the ultimate aim of the ruling class, cannot therefore be a merely technical operation training and distributing individuals for the different posts in the 'technical division' of labour. In fact there is no 'technical division' of labour except in the ideology of the ruling class: every 'technical' division, every 'technical' organization of labour, is the form and mask of a *social* (= class) division and organization of labour. The reproduction of the relations of produc-tion can therefore only be a class undertaking. It is realized through a class struggle which counterposes the ruling class and the exploited class.

The *total process* of the realization of the reproduction of the relations of production is therefore still abstract, in so far as it has not adopted the point of view of this class struggle. To adopt the point of view of reproduction is therefore, in the last instance, to adopt the point of view of the class struggle.

2. The problem of the class nature of the ideolog*ies* existing in a social formation.

The 'mechanism' of ideology *in general* is one thing. We have seen that it can be reduced to a few principles expressed in a few words (as 'poor' as those which, according to Marx, define production *in general*, or in Freud, define *the* unconscious *in general*). If there is any truth in it, this mechanism must be *abstract* with respect to every real ideological formation.

I have suggested that the ideologies were *realized* in institutions, in their rituals and their practices, in the ISAs. We have seen that on this basis they contribute to that form of class struggle, vital for the ruling class, the reproduction of the relations of production. But the point of view itself, however real, is still an abstract one.

In fact, the State and its Apparatuses have meaning only from the point of view of the class struggle, as an apparatus of class struggle ensuring class oppression and guaranteeing the conditions of exploi-tation and its reproduction. But there is no class struggle without antagonistic classes. Whoever says class struggle of the ruling class says resistance, revolt and class struggle of the ruled class.

That is why the ISAs are not the realization of ideology *in general*, nor even the conflict-free realization of the ideology of the ruling class. The ideology of the ruling class does not become the ruling ideology by the grace of God, nor even by virtue of the seizure of State power alone. It is by the installation of the ISAs in which this ideology is realized and realizes itself that it becomes the ruling ideology. But this installation is not achieved all by itself; on the contrary, it is the stake in a very bitter and continuous class struggle: first against the former ruling classes and their positions in the old and new ISAs, then against the exploited class.

But this point of view of the class struggle in the ISAs is still an abstract one. In fact, the class struggle in the ISAs is indeed an aspect of the class struggle, sometimes an important and symptomatic one: e.g. the anti-religious struggle in the eighteenth century, or the 'crisis' of the educational ISA in every capitalist country today. But the class struggles in the ISAs is only one aspect of a class struggle which goes beyond the ISAs. The ideology that a class in power makes the ruling ideology in its ISAs is indeed 'realized' in those ISAs, but it goes beyond them, for it comes from elsewhere. Similarly, the ideology that a ruled class manages to defend in and against such ISAs goes beyond them, for it comes from elsewhere.

It is only from the point of view of the classes, i.e. of the class struggle, that it is possible to explain the ideolog*ies* existing in a social formation. Not only is it from this starting point that it is possible to explain the realization of the ruling ideology in the ISAs and of the forms of class struggle for which the ISAs are the seat and the stake. But it is also and above all from this starting point that it is possible to understand the provenance of the ideologies which are realized in the ISAs and confront one another there. For if it is true that the ISAs represent the *form* in which the ideology of the ruling class must *necessarily* be realized, and the form in which the ideology of the ruled class must *necessarily* be measured and confronted, ideologies are not 'born' in the ISAs but from the social classes at grips in the class struggle: from their conditions of existence, their practices, their experience of the struggle, etc.

April 1970

Notes

1. This text is made up of two extracts from an ongoing study. The subtitle 'Notes towards an Investigation' is the author's own. The ideas expounded should not be regarded as more than the introduction to a discussion.

2. Marx to Kugelmann, 11 July 1868, *Selected Correspondence*, Moscow 1955, p. 209.

3. Marx gave it its scientific concept: *variable capital*.

4. In *For Marx* (London 1969) and *Reading Capital* (London 1970).

5. *Topography* from the Greek *topos*: place. A topography represents in a definite space the respective *sites* occupied by several realities: thus the economic is *at the bottom* (the base), the superstructure *above it*.

6. To my knowledge, Gramsci is the only one who went any distance on the road I am taking. He had the 'remarkable' idea that the State could not be reduced to the (Repressive) State Apparatus, but included, as he put it, a certain number of institutions from '*civil society*': the Church, the Schools, the trade unions, etc. Unfortunately, Gramsci did not systematize his institutions, which remained in the state of acute but fragmentary notes (cf. Gramsci, *Selections from the Prison Notebooks*, International Publishers 1971, pp. 12, 259, 260–63; see also the letter to Tatiana Schucht, 7 September 1931, in *Gramsci's Prison Letters. Lettere del Carcere*, trans. Hamish Henderson, London 1988, pp. 159–62.

7. The family obviously has other 'functions' than that of an ISA. It intervenes in the reproduction of labour-power. In different modes of production it is the unit of production and/or the unit of consumption.

8. The 'Law' belongs both to the (Repressive) State Apparatus and to the system of the ISAs.

9. In a pathetic text written in 1937, Krupskaya relates the history of Lenin's desperate efforts and what she regards as his failure.

10. What I have said in these few brief words about the class struggle in the ISAs is obviously far from exhausting the question of the class struggle.

To approach this question, two principles must be borne in mind:

The first principle was formulated by Marx in the Preface to *A Contribution to the Critique of Political Economy*: 'In considering such transformations [a social revolution] a distinction should always be made between the material transformation of the economic conditions of production, which can be determined with the precision of natural science, and the legal, political, religious, aesthetic or philosophic – in short, ideological forms in which men become conscious of this conflict and fight it out.' The class struggle is thus expressed and exercised in ideological forms, thus also in the ideological forms of the ISAs. But the class struggle *extends far beyond* these forms, and it is because it extends beyond them that the struggle of the exploited classes may also be exercised in the forms of the ISAs, and thus turn the weapon of ideology against the classes in power.

This by virtue of the *second principle*: the class struggle extends beyond the ISAs because it is rooted elsewhere than in ideology, in the Infrastructure, in the relations of production, which are relations of exploitation and constitute the base for class relations.

11. For the most part. For the relations of production are first reproduced by the materiality of the processes of production and circulation. But it should not be forgotten that ideological relations are immediately present in these same processes.

12. *For that part* of reproduction to which the Repressive State Apparatus and the Ideological State Apparatus *contribute*.

13. I use this very modern term deliberately. For even in Communist circles, unfortunately, it is a commonplace to 'explain' some political deviation (left or right opportunism) by the action of a 'clique'.

14. Which borrowed the legal category of 'subject in law' to make an ideological notion: man is by nature a subject.

15. Linguists and those who appeal to linguistics for various purposes often run up against difficulties which arise because they ignore the action of the ideological effects in all discourses – including even scientific discourses.

16. NB: this double 'currently' is one more proof of the fact that ideology is 'eternal', since these two 'currentlys' are separated by an indefinite interval; I am writing these lines on 6 April 1969, you may read them at any subsequent time.

17. Hailing as an everyday practice subject to a precise ritual takes a quite 'special' form in the policeman's practice of 'hailing', which concerns the hailing of 'suspects'.

18. Although we know that the individual is always-already a subject, we go on using this term, convenient because of the contrasting effect it produces.

19. I am quoting in a combined way, not to the letter but 'in spirit and truth'.

20. The dogma of the Trinity is precisely the theory of the duplication of the Subject (the Father) into a subject (the Son) and of their mirror-connection (the Holy Spirit).

21. Hegel is (unknowingly) an admirable 'theoretician' of ideology in so far as he is a 'theoretician' of Universal Recognition who unfortunately ends up in the ideology of Absolute Knowledge. Feuerbach is an astonishing 'theoretician' of the mirror-connection, who unfortunately ends up in the ideology of the Human Essence. To find the material with which to construct a theory of the guarantee, we must turn to Spinoza.

The Mechanism of Ideological (Mis)recognition

Michel Pêcheux

On the Ideological Conditions of the Reproduction/ Transformation of the Relations of Production

I shall start by explicating the expression '*ideological conditions of the reproduction/transformation of the relations of production*'. This explication will be carried out within the limits of my objective, which is to lay the foundations of a materialist theory of discourse.

To avoid certain misunderstandings, however, I must also specify a number of points of more general import, concerning the theory of ideologies, the practice of the production of knowledges and political practice, without which everything that follows would be quite 'out of place'.

(a) If I stress '*ideological* conditions of the reproduction/ transformation of the relations of production', this is because the region of ideology is by no means the *sole element* in which the reproduction/transformation of the relations of production of a social formation takes place; that would be to ignore the economic determinations which condition that reproduction/transformation 'in the last instance', even within economic production itself, as Althusser recalls at the beginning of his article on the ideological state apparatuses.

(b) In writing 'reproduction/transformation', I mean to designate the nodally contradictory character of *any mode of production which is based on a division into classes, i.e. whose 'principle' is the class struggle*. This means, in particular, that I consider it mistaken to locate at different points on the one hand what contributes to the reproduction of the relations of production and on the other what contributes to their transformation: the class struggle traverses the mode of production as a whole, which, in the region of ideology, means that the class struggle 'passes through' what Althusser has called the ideological state apparatuses.

In adopting the term *ideological state apparatus*, I intend to underline certain aspects which I believe to be crucial (apart of course from the reminder that ideologies are not made up of 'ideas' but of practices):

1. Ideology does not reproduce itself in the general form of a *Zeitgeist* (i.e. the spirit of the age, the 'mentality' of an epoch, 'habits of thought', etc.) imposed in an even and homogeneous way on 'society' as a kind of space pre-existing class struggle: 'The ideological state apparatuses are not the realization of ideology *in general* . . .'

2. '. . . nor even the conflict-free realization of the ideology of the ruling class', which means that it is impossible to attribute *to each class its own ideology*, as if each existed 'before the class struggle' in its own camp, with its own conditions of existence and its specific institutions, such that the ideological class struggle would be the meeting point of two distinct and pre-existing worlds, each with its own practices and its 'world outlook', this encounter being followed by the victory of the 'stronger' class, which would then impose its ideology on the other. In the end this would only multiply the conception of Ideology as *Zeitgeist* by two.[1]

3. 'The ideology of the ruling class does not become the ruling ideology by the grace of God . . .', which means that the ideological state apparatuses are not the *expression* of the domination of the ruling ideology, i.e. the ideology of the ruling class (God knows how the ruling ideology would achieve its supremacy if that were so!), but are the *site* and the *means* of realization of that domination: '. . . it is by the installation of the ideological state apparatuses in which this ideology [the ideology of the ruling class] is realized and realizes itself, that it becomes the ruling ideology . . .'

4. But even so, the ideological state apparatuses are not pure instruments of the ruling class, ideological machines simply reproducing the existing relations of production: ' . . . this installation [of the ideological state apparatuses] is not achieved all by itself; on the contrary, it is the stake in a very bitter and continuous class struggle . . .'[2] which means that the ideological state apparatuses constitute simultaneously and contradictorily the site and the ideological conditions of the transformation of the relations of production (i.e. of revolution in the Marxist–Leninist sense). *Hence the expression 'reproduction/transformation'*.

I can now take one more step in the study of the ideological conditions of the reproduction/transformation of the relations of production, by stating that these contradictory conditions are constituted, at a given historical moment and for a given social formation, *by the complex set of ideological state apparatuses* contained in that social formation. I say *complex* set, i.e. a set with relations of contradiction-unevenness-subordination between its 'elements', and not a mere list of elements: indeed, it would be absurd to think that in a given conjuncture *all the ideological state apparatuses* contribute *equally* to the reproduction of the relations of production *and* to their transformation. In fact, their 'regional' properties – their 'obvious' specialization into religion, knowledge, politics, etc. – condition their relative importance (the unevenness of their relationships) inside the set of ideological state apparatuses, and that as a function of the state of the class struggle in the given social formation.

This explains why the ideological instance in its concrete materiality exists in the form of 'ideological formations' (referred to ideological state apparatuses) which both have a 'regional' character *and* involve class positions: the ideological 'objects' are always supplied together with 'the way to use them' – their 'meaning', i.e. their orientation, i.e. the class interests which they serve – which allows the commentary that practical ideologies are class practices (practices of class struggle) in Ideology. Which is to say that, in the ideological struggle (no less than in the other forms of class struggle) there are no 'class positions' which *exist abstractly* and *are then applied* to the different regional ideological 'objects' of concrete situations, in the School, the Family, etc. In fact, this is where the contradictory connection between the reproduction and the transformation of the relations of production is joined at the ideological level, in so far as it is not the regional ideological 'objects' taken one by one but the very division into regions (God, Ethics, Law, Justice, Family, Knowledge, etc.) and the relationships of *unevenness-subordination* between those regions that constitute what is at stake in the *ideological class struggle*.

The domination of the ruling ideology (the ideology of the ruling class), which is characterized, at the ideological level, by the fact that the reproduction of the relations of production 'wins out' over their transformation (obstructs it, slows it down or suppresses it in different cases) thus corresponds less to keeping each ideological 'region' considered by itself *the same* than to the reproduction of the relationships of unevenness-subordination between those regions (with their 'objects' and the practices in which they are inscribed):[3] this is what entitled Althusser to propose the apparently scandalous thesis that the set of ideological state apparatuses in a capitalist social formation includes also the *trade unions* and the *political parties* (without further specification; in fact all he meant to designate was the function *attributed* to political parties and trade unions within the complex of the ideological state apparatuses *under the domination of the ruling ideology (the ideology of the ruling class)*, i.e., the subordinate but unavoidable and so quite necessary function whereby the ruling class is assured of 'contact' and 'dialogue' with its class adversary, i.e. the proletariat and its allies, a function to which a proletarian organization cannot of course simply *conform*).

This example helps explain how the relationships of unevenness-subordination between different ideological state apparatuses (and the regions, objects and practices which correspond to them) constitute, as I have been saying, the stake in the ideological class struggle. The ideological aspect of the struggle for the transformation of the relations of production lies therefore, above all, in the struggle to impose, inside the complex of ideological state apparatuses, *new relationships of unevenness-subordination*[4] (this is what is expressed, for example, in the slogan 'Put politics in command!'), resulting in a transformation of the *set* of the 'complex of ideological state apparatuses' in its relationship with the state apparatus and a transformation of the state apparatus itself.[5]

To sum up: the material objectivity of the ideological instance is characterized by the structure of unevenness-subordination of the 'complex whole in dominance' of the ideological formations of a given social formation, a structure which is nothing but that of the reproduction/transformation contradiction constituting the ideological class struggle.

At the same time, where the form of this contradiction is concerned, it should be specified that, given what I have just said, it cannot be thought of as the opposition between two forces acting against one another *in a single space*. The form of the contradiction inherent to the ideological struggle between the two antagonistic classes is not *symmetrical* in the sense of each class trying to achieve to its own advantage *the same thing* as the other: if I insist on this point it is because many conceptions of the ideological struggle, as we have seen, take it as an *evident fact* before the struggle, as we have seen, take is an *evident fact* before the struggle that '*society*' exists (*with the 'State' over it*) *as a space, as the terrain of that struggle*. This is so because, as Étienne Balibar points out, the class relation is concealed in the operation of the state apparatus by the very mechanism that realizes it, such that society, the state and subjects in law (free and equal in principle in the capitalist mode of production) are produced-reproduced as 'naturally evident notions'. This flushes out a second error, the first one's twin, concerning the nature of this contradiction and opposing reproduction to transformation as *inertia* is opposed to *movement*: the idea that the reproduction of the relations of production needs no explanation because they 'go of their own accord' *so long as they are left alone*, the *flaws* and *failures* of the 'system' apart, is an eternalist and anti-dialectical illusion. In reality the reproduction, just as much as the transformation, of the relations of production is an *objective process* whose mystery must be penetrated, and not just a state of fact needing only to be observed.

I have already alluded several times to Althusser's central thesis: '*Ideology interpellates individuals as subjects*'. The time has come to examine how this thesis 'penetrates the mystery' in question, and, specifically, how the way it penetrates this mystery leads directly to the problematic of a materialist theory of discursive processes, articulated into the problematic of the ideological conditions of the reproduction/transformation of the relations of production.

But first a remark on terminology: in the development that has brought us to this point a certain number of terms have appeared such as ideological state apparatuses, ideological formation, dominant or ruling ideology, etc., but *neither the term 'ideology'* (except negatively in the sentence 'the ideological state apparatuses are not the realization of Ideology in general') *nor the term 'subject'* has appeared (and even less the term 'individual'). Why is it that as a result of the preceding development, and precisely *in order to be able to strengthen it in its conclusions*, I am obliged to change my terminology and introduce new words (Ideology in the singular, individual, subject, interpellate)? The answer lies in the following two intermediary propositions –

1. there is no practice except by and in *an* ideology;
2. there is no Ideology except by the subject and for subjects

– that Althusser states before presenting his 'central thesis': in transcribing these two intermediary propositions, I have emphasized the two ways the term 'ideology' is determined: in the first, the indefinite article suggests the differentiated multiplicity of the ideological instance in the form of a combination (complex whole in dominance) of elements each of which is *an ideological formation* (in the sense defined above); in short, *an ideology*. In the second proposition, the determination of the term 'Ideology' operates 'in general', as when one says 'there is no square root except of a positive number', implying that *every* square root is the square root of a positive number: in the same way, the signification of this second proposition, which in fact prefigures the 'central thesis',[6] is that 'the category of the subject . . . is the constitutive category of every ideology'. In other words, *the emergence of the term 'subject'* in the theoretical exposition (an emergence which, as we shall see, is characterized grammatically by the fact that the term is neither subject nor object but an attribute of the object) is strictly contemporaneous with *the use of the term 'Ideology' in the singular*, in the sense of 'every ideology'.

Naturally, this makes me distinguish carefully between *ideological formation, dominant ideology* and *Ideology*.

Ideology, Interpellation, 'Münchhausen Effect'

Ideology in general, which, as we have seen, is *not* realized in the ideological state apparatuses – so it cannot coincide with a historically concrete *ideological formation* – is also not the same thing as the *dominant ideology*, as the overall result, the historically concrete form resulting from the relationships of unevenness-contradiction-subordination characterizing in a historically given social formation the 'complex whole in dominance' of the ideological formations operating in it. In other words, whereas 'ideologies have a history of their own' because they have a concrete historical existence, 'Ideology in general has no history' in so far as it is 'endowed with a structure and an operation such as to make it a non-historical reality, i.e. an omni-historical reality, in the sense in which that structure and operation are immutable, present in the same form throughout what we can call history, in the sense in which the *Communist Manifesto* defines history as the history of class struggles, i.e. the history of class societies'.[7] The concept of *Ideology* in general thus appears very specifically as the way to designate, within Marxism–Leninism, the fact that the relations of production are relationships between 'men', *in the sense that they are not relationships between things, machines, non-human animals or angels; in this sense and in this sense only*: i.e. without introducing at the same time, and surreptitiously, a certain notion of 'man' as anti-nature, transcendence, subject of history, negation of the negation, etc. As is well known, this is the central point of the 'Reply to John Lewis'.[8]

Quite the contrary, the concept of *Ideology in general* makes it possible to think 'man' as an 'ideological animal', i.e. to think his specificity as *part of nature* in the Spinozist sense of the term: 'History is an immense *"natural-human"* system in movement, and the motor of history is class struggle'.[9] Hence history once again, *that is* the history of the class struggle, i.e. the reproduction/transformation of class relationships, with their corresponding infrastructural (economic) and superstructural (legal-political and ideological) characteristics: it is within this 'natural-human' process of history that 'Ideology is eternal' (omni-historical) – a statement which recalls Freud's expression 'the unconscious is eternal'; the reader will realize that these two categories do not meet here *by accident*. But he will also realize that on this question, and despite important recent studies, the *essential theoretical work* remains to be done, and I want above all else to avoid giving the impression, rather widespread today, that we already have the answers. In fact, slogans will not fill the yawning absence of a worked-out conceptual articulation between *ideology* and the *unconscious*: we are still at the stage of theoretical 'glimmers' in a prevailing obscurity, and in the present study I shall restrict myself to calling attention to certain connections whose importance may have been underestimated, without really claiming to pose the true question that governs the relationship between these two categories.[10] Let me simply point out that the common feature of the two structures called respectively *ideology* and the *unconscious* is the fact that they conceal their own existence within their operation by producing a web of *'subjective' evident truths*, 'subjective' here meaning not 'affecting the subject' but 'in which the subject is constituted':

> For you and for me, the category of the subject is a primary 'obviousness' (obviousnesses are always primary): it is clear that you and I are subjects (free, ethical, etc.)[11]

Now – and it is, I believe, at this precise point that the necessity for a materialist theory of discourse begins – the evidentness of the spontaneous existence of the subject (as origin or cause in itself) is immediately compared by Althusser with another evidentness, all-pervasive, as we have seen, in the idealist philosophy of language: the evidentness of meaning. Remember the terms of this comparison, which I evoked at the very beginning of this study:

> Like all obviousnesses, including *those that make a word 'name a thing'* or *'have a meaning'* (*therefore including the obviousness of the 'transparency' of language*), the obviousness that you and I are subjects – and that that does not cause any problems – is an ideological effect, the elementary ideological effect.[12]

It is I who have stressed this reference to the evidentness of *meaning* taken from a commentary on the evidentness of the *subject*, and I should add that in the text at this point there is a note which directly touches on the question I am examining here:

> Linguists and those who appeal to linguistics for various purposes often run up against difficulties which arise because they ignore the action of the ideological effects in all discourses – including even scientific discourses.[13]

All my work finds its definition here, in this linking of the question of
the *constitution of meaning* to that of the *constitution of the subject*, a linking
which is not marginal (for example the special case of the ideological
'rituals' of reading and writing), but located inside the 'central thesis'
itself, in the figure of *interpellation*.

I say in the *figure* of interpellation in order to designate the fact that,
as Althusser suggests, 'interpellation' is an 'illustration', an example
adapted to a particular mode of exposition, '"concrete" enough to be
recognized, but abstract enough to be thinkable and thought, giving
rise to a knowledge'.[14] This figure, associated both with religion and
with the police ('You, for whom I have shed this drop of my
blood'/'Hey, you there!'), has the advantage first of all that, through
this double meaning of the word 'interpellation', it makes palpable the
superstructural link – determined by the economic infrastructure –
between the *repressive* state apparatus (the legal-political apparatus
which assigns-verifies-checks 'identities') *and* the *ideological* state apparatuses, i.e. the link between the 'subject in law' (he who enters into
contractual relations with other subjects in law, his equals) *and* the
ideological subject (he who says of himself: 'It's me!'). It has the second
advantage that it presents this link in such a way that the theatre of
consciousness (I see, I think, I speak, I see you, I speak to you, etc.) is
observed from behind the scenes, from the place where one can grasp
the fact that the subject is spoken *of*, the subject is spoken *to*, before the
subject can say: 'I speak'.

The last, but not the least, advantage of this 'little theoretical theatre'
of interpellation, conceived as an illustrated critique of the theatre of
consciousness, is that it designates, by the discrepancy in the formulation 'individual'/'subject', the paradox by which *the subject is called into
existence*: indeed, the formulation carefully avoids presupposing the
existence of the subject on whom the operation of interpellation is
performed – it does not say: 'The subject is interpellated by Ideology.'

This cuts short any attempt simply to *invert* the metaphor linking the
subject with the various 'legal entities' [*personnes morales*] which might
seem at first sight to be subjects made up of a collectivity of subjects, and
of which one could say, inverting the relationship, that it is this
collectivity, as a pre-existing entity, that imposes its ideological stamp
on each subject in the form of a 'socialization' of the individual in 'social
relations' conceived of as intersubjective relations. In fact, what the
thesis 'Ideology interpellates individuals as subjects' designates is
indeed that 'non-subject' is interpellated-constituted as subject by
Ideology. Now, the paradox is precisely that interpellation has, as it
were, a *retroactive effect*, with the result that every individual is
'always-already a subject'.

The *evidentness of the subject* as unique, irreplaceable and identical with himself: the absurd and natural reply 'It's me!' to the question 'Who's there?'[15] echoes the remark; it is 'evident' that *I* am the only person who can say 'I' when speaking of myself; this evidentness conceals something, which escapes Russell and logical empiricism: the fact that the subject has always been 'an individual interpellated as a subject', which, to remain in the ambience of Althusser's example, might be illustrated by the absurd injunction children address to one another as a superb joke: 'Mister So-and-so, remind me of your name!', an injunction whose playful character masks its affinity with the police operation of assigning and checking *identities*. Because this is indeed what is involved: the 'evidentness' of identity conceals the fact that it is the result of an identification-interpellation of the subject, whose alien origin is nevertheless 'strangely familiar' to him.[16]

[. . .]

Now, taking into account what I have just set out, it is possible to regard *the effect of the preconstructed as the discursive modality of the discrepancy by which the individual is interpellated as subject . . . while still being 'always-already a subject'*, stressing that this discrepancy (*between* the familiar strangeness of this outside located before, elsewhere and independently, *and* the identifiable, responsible subject, answerable for his actions) operates 'by contradiction', whether the latter be suffered in complete ignorance by the subject or, on the contrary, he grasps it in the forefront of his mind, as 'wit': many jokes, turns of phrase, etc., are in fact governed by the contradiction inherent in this discrepancy; they constitute, as it were, the symptoms of it, and are sustained by the circle connecting the contradiction suffered (i.e. 'stupidity') with the contradiction grasped and displayed (i.e. 'irony'), as the reader can confirm using whatever example he finds especially 'eloquent'.[17]

The role of symptom I have discerned in the operation of a certain type of joke (in which what is ultimately involved is the *identity* of a subject, a thing or an event) with respect to the question of ideological interpellation-identification leads me to posit, in connection with this symptom, the existence of a *process of the signifier, in interpellation-identification*. Let me explain: it is not a matter here of evoking the 'role of language' in general or 'the power of words', leaving it uncertain whether what is invoked is the *sign, which designates something for someone*, as Lacan says, or the *signifier*, i.e. *what represents the subject for another signifier* (Lacan again). It is clear that, for my purposes, it is the second hypothesis which is correct, because it treats of *the subject as process (of representation) inside the non-subject constituted by the network of signifiers, in Lacan's sense: the subject is 'caught' in this network* – 'common nouns' and 'proper names', 'shifting' effects, syntactic constructions, etc. – *such that he results as 'cause of himself'*, in Spinoza's sense of the phrase. And it is precisely the existence of this contradiction (the production as a *result of a 'cause of itself'*, and its motor role for the process of the signifier in interpellation-identification, which justifies me in saying that it is indeed a matter of a *process*, in so far as the 'objects' which appear in it duplicate and divide to act on themselves as other than themselves.[18]

One of the consequences, I believe, of the necessary obliteration within the subject as 'cause of himself' of the fact that he is the result of a process, is a series of what one might call *metaphysical phantasies*, all of which touch on the question of causality: for example, the phantasy of the *two hands* each holding a pencil and *each drawing the other on the same sheet of paper*, and also that of the perpetual leap in which *one leaps up again with a great kick before having touched the ground*; one could extend the list at length. I shall leave it at that, with the proposal to call this phantasy effect – by which the individual is interpellated as subject – the 'Münchhausen effect', in memory of the immortal baron who *lifted himself into the air by pulling on his own hair*.

If it is true that ideology 'recruits' subjects from amongst individuals (in the way soldiers are recruited from amongst civilians) and that it recruits them *all*, we need to know how 'volunteers' are designated in this recruitment, i.e. in what concerns us, how all individuals *accept as evident* the meaning of what they hear and say, read and write (of what they *intend* to say and of what it is *intended* to be said to them) as 'speaking subjects': really to understand this is the only way to avoid repeating, in the form of a theoretical analysis, the 'Münchhausen effect', by positing the subject as the origin of the subject, i.e. in what concerns us, by positing the subject of discourse as the origin of the subject of discourse.

Notes

1. On this point, see the analysis of reformism in Althusser, 'Reply to John Lewis' (1972), in *Essays in Self Criticism*, trans. Grahame Lock, London 1976, pp. 49 ff.

2. Althusser, 'Ideology and Ideological State Apparatuses'; see this volume, Chapter 5, pp. 100–140.

3. 'The unity of the different Ideological State Apparatuses is secured, usually in contradictory forms, by the ruling ideology . . . of the ruling class'. Ibid., p. 114.

4. By a transformation of the subordinations in the class struggle: for example by a transformation of the relationship between the *school* and *politics*, which in the capitalist mode of production is a *relationship of disjunction* (denegation or simulation) based on the 'natural' place of the school between the family and economic production.

5. Étienne Balibar reminds us that it is a matter of replacing the bourgeois state apparatus *both* with another state apparatus *and* with *something other than* a state

apparatus. 'La Rectification du *Manifeste Communiste*' (1972), in *Cinq études du matérialisme historique*, Paris 1974, pp. 65–101.

6. 'This thesis [Ideology interpellates individuals as subjects] is simply a matter of making my last proposition explicit'. Althusser, 'Ideology', p. 128.

7. Ibid., p. 122.

8. In *Essays in Self Criticism*, pp. 49 ff.

9. Ibid., p. 51.

10. One of the merits of Elisabeth Roudinesco's work *Un Discours un réel. Théorie de l'inconscient et politique de la psychanalyse* (Tours 1973), is that she shows why the merits of the 'Freudo–Marxist' juxtaposition cannot be a solution.

It might be said that it is *this lack of a link between ideology and the unconscious* which today 'torments' psychoanalytic research, in diverse and often contradictory forms. There is no question of anticipating here what will result. Suffice it to say that the idealist reinscription of Lacan's work will have to be brought to book, and that this will above all be the business of those who are working today *inside* psychoanalysis.

11. Althusser, 'Ideology', p. 129.

12. Ibid.

13. Ibid., Note 15.

14. Ibid., p. 130.

15. This is Althusser's example. Ibid., p. 129.

16. Hence the well-known children's utterances of the type: 'I have three brothers, Paul, Michael and me'; or 'Daddy was born in Manchester, Mummy in Bristol and I in London: strange that the three of us should have met!'

17. Such examples might be multiplied indefinitely:

1. *on the family–school relationship*: the story of the lazy pupil who telephoned his headmaster to excuse himself from school, and when asked 'Who am I speaking to?' replied 'It's my father!';

2. *on ideological repetition*: 'There are no cannibals left in our area, we ate the last one last week';

3. *on the cultural apparatus and the cult of Great Men*: 'Shakespeare's works were not written by him but by an unknown contemporary of the same name';

4. *on metaphysics and the religious apparatus*: 'God is perfect in every way except one: he doesn't exist'; 'X didn't believe in ghosts, he wasn't even afraid of them', etc.

18. On this duplication and division in contradiction, and in the manner of a joke: 'What a shame they did not build the cities in the country – the air is so much cleaner there!'

7

Determinacy and Indeterminacy in the Theory of Ideology

Nicholas Abercrombie, Stephen Hill and Bryan S. Turner

The analysis of ideologies and forms of knowledge and belief is in a state of disorder. In contemporary Marxism, the autonomy and independent importance of ideology have been stressed at the expense of a discredited economic reductionism. In many ways this is a desirable development, although, as we have pointed out elsewhere,[1] it also carries with it some very misleading consequences. However, the critical problem that contemporary Marxist theories of ideology have to face is: how is one to reconcile materialism with the autonomy of ideology? This implies a second difficulty: namely, how is one to reconcile the notion of ideology as critique with a general theory of ideology? In terms of disciplinary definitions, there is a parallel question about the relationship of the Marxist theory of ideology to the sociology of knowledge which developed in opposition to classical Marxism.

The significance of these problems is nicely illustrated by Göran Therborn's *The Ideology of Power and the Power of Ideology*,[2] in which he attempts to clarify a variety of theoretical issues in contemporary Marxism and sociology. He conceives his project as taking 'Marx's insights as a point of departure for an attempt at a more systematic theory' (p. 41). Elsewhere he suggests that Marxism has a great deal to learn from the empirical findings of sociology, and in our view his own attempt to generate a new theory of ideology can also be seen as an attempt to synthesize a sociological perspective with Marxism. This is a most interesting project. Nevertheless, there is clearly a wide variety of possible destinations even if one takes Marx as one's point of departure, since one can as easily end outside the Marxist tradition as within it, nor need the terminus be a theory that is systematic or general.

Agents in Place

Therborn rejects the notion that ideology involves beliefs in people's heads, specifically beliefs that are false or mystified or misconstrued. He further denies that ideology is the opposite of science. Ideologies are defined as all social (in distinction to psychological) phenomena of a discursive (in distinction to non-discursive) nature. They include 'both everyday notions and "experience" and elaborate intellectual doctrines, both the "consciousness" of social actors and the institutionalized thought-systems and discourses of a given society' (p. 2). This is deliberately a broad definition, and one that in our view effectively reproduces the sociological notion of 'culture'. Following Althusser, Therborn suggests: 'The operation of ideology in human life basically involves the constitution and patterning of how human beings live their lives as conscious, reflecting initiators of acts in a structured, meaningful world. Ideology operates as discourse, addressing or, as Althusser puts it, interpellating human beings as subjects' (p. 15). This operation of ideology involves two processes: the constitution and subjection of human, conscious agents and their qualification to fulfil their positions in society. Therborn recognizes that an analysis of ideology in terms of inserting agents in their places is analogous to the traditional sociological analysis of social roles, but he maintains that traditional role analysis is too subjectivist. The main burden of ideology is to construct human subjectivity, so that 'to search for the structure of the ideological universe is to seek the dimensions of human subjectivity' (p. 17). These dimensions form 'a property space':

	Subjectivities of 'In-the-World'	Subjectivities of 'Being'
	Existential	Historical
Inclusive	1. Beliefs about meaning (e.g. life and death)	2. Beliefs about membership of historical social worlds (e.g. tribe, village, ethnicity, state, nation, church)
Positional	3. Beliefs about identity (e.g. individuality, sex, age)	4. Beliefs about 'social geography' (e.g. educational status, lineage, hierarchy, class)

Ideologies thus situate individuals in time and space by reference to personal, positional and social characteristics.

Therborn sees ideologies as being materially determined, and the definition of materialism is deliberately and unusually broad to encompass 'the structure of a given society and . . . its relationship to its natural environment and to other societies' (p. 43). Materialism, in the classical Marxist usage of the economic structure, is used to explain the determination of one specific ideological set which appears to comprise those class ideologies required for the subjection and qualification of economic agents, though Therborn's presentation is not clear on this point. He states explicitly, however: 'Any given combination of forces and relations of production of course requires a particular form of ideological subjection of the economic subjects . . .' (p. 47).

It is noteworthy that Therborn does not accept the contention, familiar from many classical Marxist accounts of ideology, that the principal function of ideology is to incorporate subordinates, to act as 'social cement'. He argues, by contrast, that subordinates will adhere to alter-ideologies which are oppositional, and he attempts to specify the conditions under which those alter-ideologies may arise. There are three possible explanations. The first and most general explanation, which Therborn emphasizes, is that, by its very nature, every positional ideology must generate an alter-ideology in the process of generating differences between self and other, us and them. These ideologies have thus 'an intrinsically dual character' (p. 27), and the implication is that any ideology of domination must generate resistance in the very act of setting up a Self/Other opposition. Such an argument links Therborn's position directly to that of current structural linguistics in that language subsists on the play of differences. A difficulty with the notion that the imposition of knowledge/ideology produces resistance is to show exactly how this comes about, and, more importantly, under what conditions resistance prevails – a difficulty manifest also in Foucault. Secondly, Therborn refers to the fact that class ideologies 'are inscribed in the relations of production' (p. 61). For example, feudalism involved a hierarchy of rights and obligations between peasant and landlord, and these were the foci of class struggle. Curtailment of peasant rights created alter-ideological conceptions of injustice that were the basis of peasant oppositions to the illegality of landlords' activities. In one place he also talks of 'the irreducibility of psychodynamic processes to complete social control', which creates 'a small margin of individual "misfits"' (p. 43). Thus it would seem that interpellation can never really be effective, as ideologies have an inherently dialectical character, while complex social processes mean that 'ideologies overlap, compete and clash, drown or reinforce each other' (p. vii). Indeed, ideologies actually operate 'in a state of disorder' (p. 77), so it is not surprising that ideological theory is itself disordered.

On the subject of class ideologies and alter-ideologies, which have mainly concerned Marxists and sociologists alike, Therborn has a number of comments. He suggests that class ideologies are typically core themes rather than elaborated forms of discourse; that they can only be derived theoretically, seemingly on the basis of the imputed functional requirements of a mode of production; that non-class ideologies are not reducible to class but are class patterned or overdetermined; and that class ideologies have to compete with and relate to non-class positional ideologies such as nationalism and religion. His brief analysis of nationalism and religion shows that the former is class patterned in different ways in different societies, while the latter seems scarcely patterned at all. The two-by-two matrix of the universe of ideological interpellations given above makes clear that class ideologies fall mainly into cell 4, with some dimensions in cell 2, and that they constitute a small part of the total population with which Therborn's theory is concerned.

Marxist Dilemmas

Contemporary Marxist theories of ideology are faced by a number of dilemmas, two of which are especially important. There is firstly the question of the autonomy of ideology. Almost all Marxist theorists have argued that ideology cannot be seen as determined by the economy but is, instead, relatively autonomous. This autonomy has three consequences. Firstly, ideology has its own laws of motion. In his earlier book, *Science, Class and Society*, Therborn quotes Engels: 'In a modern state, law must not only correspond to the general economic condition and be its expression, but must also be an internally coherent experience which does not, owing to inner contradictions, reduce itself to nought. In order to achieve this, the faithful reflection of economic conditions suffers increasingly.'[3] Secondly, ideology may be effective in giving a particular form to the economy. For example, one might argue that the prevalence of individualism in English culture from the seventeenth to the mid-nineteenth century may have given English capitalism its competitive form partly via the constitution of individuals as economic subjects. Thirdly, not all ideologies are reducible to class ideologies – a proposition that follows from the first two on a particular assumption of the relation between class and economy. This question of ideological autonomy constitutes a dilemma because, if too much autonomy is given, one loses the distinctiveness of Marxism's emphasis on the economy, while if ideology is seen as bound to the economy, all the familiar problems of economic reductionism arise.

The second dilemma facing contemporary Marxist theory of ideology is that of the falsity of ideology. If one holds a view of ideology-as-critique, then that appears to remove from analysis a whole range of ideologies that are not obviously false. If, on the other hand, the term ideology is seen as embracing all forms of knowledge, belief, or practice, then the critical edge of the concept is lost.

As we indicated earlier, Therborn holds that he is taking Marx's insights as a point of departure. He also suggests that the fact that 'the concrete forms of ideologies other than economic positional ones are not directly determined by the mode of production, indicates the limitations of historical materialism' (p. 48). Given this position, the problem is how Therborn resolves the dilemmas of Marxism. In the first place, his language has a distinctly Marxist ring to it. However, his conceptions of materialism are not necessarily Marxist. In his broad usage, which corresponds to the conventional sociology of knowledge, materialism amounts to little more than postulating a social explanation of ideology. In his narrower conception of economic materialism, he adopts a Marxist position. For Therborn, *class* ideologies appear to be determined by economic materialism, but the rest of the ideological universe rests on a material base that owes little to Marxism.

He also emphasizes the critical importance of class in the analysis of ideology. Although Therborn is at pains to show the significance of all kinds of ideology, including non-class elements such as those of gender, race or nation, class ideologies are not only fundamental, they are determining: ' . . . the structure of the ideological system, its class and non-class elements alike, is overdetermined by the constellation of class forces' (p. 39). For many critics, such an emphasis on class would be quite sufficient to place Therborn firmly in the Marxist camp (or *a* Marxist camp). That would, clearly, be quite wrong, for what is distinctive to Marxism is not the stress on class *per se*, but a *particular* theory of the generation, location and causal effects of classes.

A comparison with the work of Karl Mannheim is instructive here. Again many sociological commentators on Mannheim assume that he was a Marxist because of his belief that social class is the most significant social base of systems of belief. However, the whole point of Mannheim's work is that, for him, social classes are not constituted by their places in economic relations, but are instead essentially political entities, representing collectivities engaged in struggle. The explanation of these class struggles does not lie in the economy but in features of the human condition, particularly the apparently innate tendency to compete. We are not, of course, suggesting that Therborn adopts a Hegelian or essentialist position, which often seems to be implicit in Mannheim's work. None the less, the role of the economy in Therborn's theory of ideology could be rather clearer.

This lack of clarity does have some specific consequences. In the first place, it is not always clear why *particular* classes should have *particular* ideologies, although there is a sketch of the kinds of ideology that Therborn believes to be appropriate to specific classes (Chapter 3). Secondly, we are not told *why* the ideological system is 'over-determined by class forces' – an important point if one wishes to establish the primacy of class (although, it should be said, Therborn does suggest that he does not have the space to develop the point). Thirdly, the relationship between class and power is obscured. The title of Therborn's essay implies that power is his primary focus, and this attitude emerges at various points. For example, he starts by saying: 'The main concern of this essay is the operation of ideology in the organization, maintenance and transformation of power in society' (p. 1). That is by no means a peculiarly Marxist aim, and it is central, for example, to its main competitor, Weberian sociology. Power, class, and economy are analytically distinct and, as our analysis of Mannheim showed, one can have an interest in power, even in class power, without any commitment to a Marxist social theory. Marxists claim to be able to answer all three of these points by reference to an analysis of the economy.

Without a more detailed specification of the relationship between ideology and economy it is difficult to know how Therborn resolves the dilemmas. The tension here is further illustrated by a consideration of the second dilemma noted above, that of the definition of the concept of ideology itself:

> 'Ideology' will be used here in a very broad sense. It will not necessarily imply any particular content (falseness, miscognition, imaginary as opposed to real character), nor will it assume any necessary degree of elaboration and coherence. Rather it will refer to that aspect of the human condition under which human beings live their lives as conscious actors in a world that makes sense to them to varying degrees. Ideology is the medium through which this consciousness and meaningfulness operate. (p. 2)

Therborn clearly regards ideology as constituting human subjectivity, and he quite deliberately breaks with the conception of ideology as deficient: 'The broad definition of ideology adopted here departs from the usual Marxist one, by not restricting it to forms of illusion and miscognition' (p. 5). He is, of course, correct to identify ideology-as-critique as a central plank of Marxist theory. Indeed, unless it were the primacy of the economy, it would be difficult to imagine any other feature so characteristic of Marxist accounts of ideology. Marxists have often attacked the sociology of knowledge for adopting a conception of ideology as covering all kinds of knowledge, thus depriving the concept of what they see as its vital critical edge. To return to our original comparison, Lukács[4] felt that Mannheim's work obscured the crucial differences between true and false consciousness, while Adorno[5] suggested that Mannheim called everything into question but criticized nothing.

Constituting the (Human) Subject

We turn now to one of the central elements of Therborn's theory: the function of ideology. Therborn identifies four (and only four) dimensions of human subjectivity, and then argues that ideology's function is to construct those subjectivities: 'My thesis is that these four dimensions make up the fundamental forms of human subjectivity, and that the universe of ideologies is exhaustively structured by the four main types of interpellation that constitute these four forms of subjectivity' (p. 23). We see several difficulties arising out of Therborn's theoretical position. In the first place, he comes close to arguing that the forms of human subjectivity *determine* the forms of ideology, which would commit him to a problematic of the subject as the ground of all ideology. A second difficulty with this and other theories of interpellation is their assumption that the subject is an individual agent, the person, when on the contrary the constitution of 'persons' in late capitalism often requires the formation of collective agents such as business corporations, professional associations, trade unions and trade associations. It is perfectly possible to describe social epochs (classical Rome or late capitalism) in which legal, social or religious definitions of 'the person' do not coincide with effective economic agents. Therborn's argument may work for 'natural persons', but it needs to be shown how it applies in the case of 'juristic persons'. One can further ask whether the formation of corporate structures has to be by interpellation. In the third place, ideology does not invariably constitute persons; it can also de-constitute them. For example, the laws of *coverture* precluded women from personhood on entry into marriage. It is more pertinent to claim that ideologies function to differentiate persons from not-persons (for example, children, married women, slaves and aliens). These remarks raise the traditional philosophical problem of whether subjects require bodies and, indeed, what 'bodies' are. The variations on this union of subject/body are extensive. In medieval political thought, kings had two bodies reflecting their political and spiritual status. By contrast, corporations had legal personalities, but only fictive bodies, while slaves had bodies but not persons.

Leaving aside the question of how ideology constitutes collective agents, and adopting Therborn's frame of reference that the theory of ideology is concerned with the human subject, one may accept the logic of what he sets out to do in his classification of ideologies of the subject and still find the account somewhat incomplete and ambiguous. Because Therborn appears to take for granted the unity of body and subject, he does not consider, for example, how disease theories as medical ideologies fit into his model of interpellation. As Foucault has reminded us, medical classificatory schemas have enormous political significance. But are these addressed to diseases, bodies or persons? The debate about disease, illness behaviour and deviance comes eventually to the problem of the moral responsibility of the individual, and thus to the 'cause' and 'motives' of behaviour. However, it would be difficult to know where to locate, for example, the sociological notion of 'vocabularies of motive' within Therborn's categorization. Such vocabularies are not precisely elements of 'inclusive-existential ideologies', since they do not locate persons as members of the world; they simply specify what is to count as acceptable behaviour. This raises another issue concerning the classification of ideologies of the subject: there appears to be considerable and unclear overlap between boxes 1 and 4, and 2 and 3 in his table. It is not obvious, for example, why membership of a tribe (inclusive-historical) should be significantly different from membership of a system of tribes (positional-historical).

Therborn's approach to ideology represents a decisive move away from the problem of the falsity of ideological beliefs to the problem of possibility – what are the possibilities of subject construction? Therborn's work, like our *The Dominant Ideology Thesis*, is thus less concerned with questions of legitimation and incorporation and more concerned with the question of possibility. However, what he does not ask is: what are the variations in the effectivity of ideological systems, given differences in their apparatus, in establishing the possible? Such an omission is odd given the title of the work, and as a result it is never made explicit what the power of ideology actually is. What is clear is that, for Therborn, ideology is a very important social force. As he himself indicates, there is a definite Althusserian imprint here. Indeed, his conception could almost be described in Althusser's words: 'Human societies secrete ideology as the very element and atmosphere indispensable to their historical respiration and life',[6] and, more specifically, 'ideology (as a system of mass representations) is indispensable in any society if men are to be formed, transformed and equipped, to respond to the demands of their conditions of existence'.[7] Therborn's usage of interpellation is, however, a modification of Althusser's concept that comes closer to the traditional structural-functional sociological theory of roles than he admits. Again, Therborn discusses this parallel, but briefly and without much attention to more recent critical accounts of that theory from within sociology.

The general theory of ideology as interpellation, as constituting human subjectivity, therefore has echoes, not only of Althusser, but also of Parsons. It is also vulnerable to the criticism frequently made of both these authors: that their accounts manifest an *undesirable* functionalism. Parsons, in particular, adopts the strategy of identifying social needs and then explaining the existence of certain social practices by reference to the manner in which they serve those needs.

The same type of functionalist explanation is used to identify class ideologies, which, Therborn contends, have to be derived from a theoretical specification of the necessary requirements of a mode of production: 'it must be theoretically determined which ideologies are feudal, bourgeois, proletarian, petty-bourgeois or whatever; the question is not answerable by historical or sociological induction alone' (pp. 54–5). Such determination means finding the 'minimum subjection-qualification . . . necessary for a class of human beings to perform their economically defined roles' (p. 55). A major problem with Therborn's account of class ideologies is that he does not adequately explain *why* he chooses certain ideologies as functionally necessary, and his lists of ideological interpellations may not be theoretically or empirically well-grounded. For example, in specifying capitalist class ideologies, he asserts without explanation that bourgeois class ego-ideologies require 'individual achievement' (p. 57), a proposition that is contradicted in at least one advanced capitalist economy, Japan, where a corporate-collectivity orientation among capitalist managers is the typical bourgeois interpellation. Furthermore, Therborn's assertion that working-class ideology involves 'an orientation to work, to manual labour, including physical prowess, toughness, endurance and dexterity' (p. 59) is not appropriate to late capitalism, given changes in the occupational structure which have both created a sizeable non-manual proletariat and brought many women into waged economic roles.

The difficulties raised by this undesirable form of functionalist argument are, of course, similar to those presented by recent (and past) Marxist debates about the role of class struggle. The earlier Althusserian formulations emphasized the way in which the mode of production determined the form of social practices; the mode of production has requirements or conditions of existence which are provided by practices of various kinds. The difficulty with such arguments within Marxism, particularly acute given the centrality of the class struggle to Marxist theory, is that they leave no room for class struggles generated independently of the requirements of the mode of production.

Therborn does attempt to avoid some of the problems raised by his functionalist analysis by making the concept of ideology open-ended, by stressing the importance of ideological struggle and demonstrating the contradictions within ideological forms. He introduces an entirely welcome element of contingency into the debate which makes possible the analysis of ideology as a kind of functional circle in which subjects make ideology and ideology makes subjects. This contingency can be illustrated in a number of ways. For example, ideologies do not have uniform effects, operating in a single-minded fashion to create homogeneous subjectivities. At the level of the subject, who may be at the intersection of a number of conflicting ideologies, different subjectivities – for example, worker, husband or Protestant – may compete for dominance. Furthermore, contradictoriness may actually be inherent in the notion of ideology itself. Thus, for Therborn the creation of subjectivity actually involves two processes: of *subjecting* the subject to a particular definition of his role, and of *qualifying* him for his role. The reproduction of any social organization requires some basic correspondence between subjection and qualification. However, there is an inherent possibility of conflict between the two. For instance, 'new kinds of qualification may be required and provided, new skills that clash with the traditional forms of subjection' (p. 17).

Again, any smooth functioning of ideology may be interrupted by social struggles. In the case of subordinate classes, alter-ideologies provide the basis of ideological and, ultimately, class struggle. However, the difficulty with Therborn's account here is that he does not provide a convincing theoretical discussion of alter-ideologies. They are seen as logically an inevitable consequence of positional ideologies which produce differences, but there is no sociological account of how they are maintained and have effects in social struggles.

Further, Therborn quite rightly emphasizes the way in which ideologies are various and contradictory. It is not only the interpellated or interpellating subjects that have no fixed unity and consistency. Ideologies themselves are equally protean. For analytic purposes different ideologies may be identified according to their source, topic, content or interpellated subject. But as ongoing processes of interpellation, they have no natural boundaries, no natural criteria distinguishing one ideology from another or one element of an ideology from its totality. Particularly in today's open and complex societies different ideologies, however defined, 'not only coexist, compete and clash, but also overlap, affect and contaminate one another' (p. 79).

The Dilemmas of Indeterminacy

Contingency, of course, leads to an indeterminacy that makes it difficult to say much about ideological struggle that has *general* applicability. Despite Therborn's belief that there can be a general theory of ideology, he sensibly insists that ideologies, even within the capitalist mode, vary in their contents, and especially in their effects. For example, he notices that nationalism provides an interesting example of how a seemingly straightforward ideological discourse contains numerous contradictions. Therborn notes the historical association between bourgeois revolutions and nationalism 'which became linked to the bourgeois revolution by providing an ideology of struggle that counterposed to the dynastic and/or colonial power a state of legally free and equal citizens encompassing a certain territory' (p. 69). But bourgeois ideology is complex and inconsistent, because nationalism can be seen to be at odds with the internationalism ('cosmopolitanism') implied by bourgeois adherence to market rationality and competitive individualism (p. 69). Moreover, Therborn recognizes that nationalism, as one of the 'formulae of ruling-class legitimation' (p. 69), produces indeterminate outcomes, sometimes leading subordinate classes to rally to the 'national interest' and support of dominant interests, sometimes forming part of the '"national popular" tradition' of struggle (p. 70).

We endorse this argument and suggest, contrary to what a number of modern Marxists profess, that nationalism qualifies most uneasily as part of the dominant ideology of late capitalism, at least in Britain. Although capitalism developed within nation-states and still has an important national orientation, late capitalism also has a significant transnational character which means that the status of nationalism as a bourgeois ideology is ambiguous. Different economic interests within capitalism and their associated class fractions, national and international, have therefore created contradictory positions within the dominant ideology. In so far as nationalism has effects for subordinates, these are also contradictory. On the one hand, nationalism has often formed part of a popular counter-ideology. As Hobsbawm[8] has cogently reminded us, the combination of patriotism and working-class consciousness has been historically a powerful agency of radical social change, as it was in Britain in the aftermath of the Second World

War and earlier in the Chartist period. In recent years, nationalism has informed the political programme of the Left, notably in policies concerning the EEC and the reimposition of restrictions on the movement of capital abroad designed to protect popular interests against monopoly capital. On the other hand, we have to account for the apparently unifying effect of nationalism as a response to external threats, notably war. The 'Falklands Crisis' is obviously a case in point. However, while the Falklands issue did mobilize a wide cross-section of society behind conservative, jingoist symbols, patriotism is unlikely to change the underlying popular mood of 'hopelessness, apathy and defeatism'.[9] Such episodic socio-dramas may have little consequence for the formation of ideologies that have long-run effects. In addition to Hobsbawm's example of the historical affinity between working-class radicalism and patriotic nationalism in certain periods, we note that peripheral nationalism within peripheral regions – for example, Wales and Scotland – has divisive consequences for the nation-state and could not be regarded as a dominant ideology, certainly not a bourgeois one.

The point is that the fundamental ideological form of inclusive historical ideologies, even when specified more closely as nationalism, need have no explanatory power in predicting the outcome of ideological struggle. There is clearly something of a dilemma here between a general determinate analysis, which does not allow for the contingencies of ideology, and an indeterminate analysis which does not allow general claims. In our book we have tried to show the contingency of the relationship of ideology to capitalist economic activity.

Empirically it appears to be the case that a capitalist mode of production can coexist with a great variety of ideological superstructures. In religious ideologies, there is Catholicism in France, Catholicism and Protestantism in Holland, the 'civil religion' of America, and Islam in the Gulf States. In legal systems, there is the historical problem raised by Weber that 'judge-made law' in Britain and formal law in Germany were both compatible with capitalism. In politics, various political systems ranging from Fascism to liberal democracy appear to develop alongside capitalism. Social formations which share the same capitalist base thus display a variety of different ideological systems. From this perspective, while it may be possible to argue that ideology contributes under certain historical circumstances to the unity of classes or economic organization (such as family organization and Catholic teaching on sexuality in feudalism), it is difficult to draw any general conclusions from such particular observations. However, to conclude that, at the level of the social formation, ideology is always variable and contingent both in content and function may overstate the case.

One obvious objection is that there must be some limits to these variations, which are set by the basic requirements of the 'conditions of existence' of a mode of production. However, the ideological requirements of *capitalism* do appear to be unusual with respect to other modes. In *The Dominant Ideology Thesis*, we noted the paradox that in late capitalism the ideological apparatus is greatly extended, while the economic and political subordination of people makes ideological incorporation increasingly redundant. There are two reasons why we believe that ideological variation increases with the development of late capitalism: (1) 'dull compulsion' in everyday life is adequate for the subordination of the worker; and (2) there is no economic requirement for a dominant ideology. In short, capitalism can 'tolerate' contingency far better than any other mode of production.

Perhaps the mode of production ought to be regarded as establishing certain broad parameters which set the limits of ideological variation. In early capitalism, for example, the relations of production require certain legal supports in terms of private property and stability of economic contracts, but these may be guaranteed by a variety of legal systems. At the level of the social formation, ideology can be studied only, following Weber, in terms of certain historically specific, pre-existing ideologies which may or may not contribute to the growth of capitalist culture (the Protestant Ethic thesis). Ideology does not simply incorporate classes; it is, rather, a 'resource' of collective action. For example, as Marx noted,[10] the bourgeoisie, having mobilized individualism against feudalism, finds 'civil liberties' employed by oppositional groups against capitalist domination. Individualism can thus be regarded as a resource of political struggle. Furthermore, as we argued earlier, ideology, in the form of individualism, may be effective in actually forming the specific shape of capitalist society. It does not, however, *necessarily* have that function.

It follows from this discussion that Marxists should state the level of abstraction at which ideology is located. Ideology is not a necessary condition of existence of the economic base and, at the level of the social formation, class structure, political conflicts, ethnic composition, the nature of state development, etc., determine the variable role and content of ideology. There is no general theory which can specify the functions and content of ideology for different societies. The effectivity of an ideology is an issue entirely separate from the mere presence of an ideology. The effects of the apparatus of ideological transmission are variable (depending on the level of political education in the working class, the level of class organization, the presence of a tradition of working-class radicalism, etc.). In Marxism, the capacity of the ISAs and other socializing institutions to determine class consciousness, especially corporate consciousness, has been greatly exaggerated. It is not evident, in any case, that societies require the level of ideological support implied by Therborn. As Foucault argues, the individuation, construction and discipline of individuals can be secured by regulatory practices and institutions (panopticism) which do not require subjective consciousness on the part of individual persons.

The drift of our argument is that Therborn overstates the importance of ideology, an overstatement most prominent in his view of ideology constructing subjectivities. We would advocate a much more indeterminate approach: ideology has causally important effects only on some social phenomena at some times. For example, as we tried to show in *The Dominant Ideology Thesis*, ideology does not generally work to incorporate subordinate classes. Similarly, ideology may or may not have a role in the formation and maintenance of any economic practices. Or – to take a position advanced by Therborn – why should one assume that the role of ideology is to form subjectivities? Why, equally, should one not assume that subjectivities are only contingently formed by ideology and can, just as effectively, be created in other ways?

We believe that Therborn is not sufficiently indeterminate, and seems moreover to have allied very different Marxist and sociological forms of determinism. We do not, of course, wish to say that indeterminacy has no limits, a position of mindless empiricism, and in a review article of this length we cannot attempt to tackle the issue of what the limits are, although we have outlined a possible solution for Britain in *The Dominant Ideology Thesis*. Therborn has written an excellent essay which frees the study of ideology of many of its rigidities. However, in sum, we wish he would take space to say more on a number of issues, particularly on the relationship of the implicit functionalism of subjectivities to the contingent qualities of ideology, on the precise role of the economy, and on the mechanisms of the overdetermination of non-class ideologies by class.

Notes

1. Nicholas Abercrombie, Stephen Hill and Bryan S. Turner, *The Dominant Ideology Thesis*, London 1980.

2. Göran Therborn, *The Ideology of Power and the Power of Ideology*, London 1980. From this point onwards, page references to this book are given in the text.

3. Göran Therborn, *Science, Class and Society*, London 1976, p. 404.

4. Georg Lukács, *The Destruction of Reason*, London 1980.
5. Theodor W. Adorno, *Prisms*, London 1967.
6. Louis Althusser, *For Marx*, London 1969, p. 232.
7. Ibid., p. 235.
8. Eric Hobsbawm, 'Falklands Fallout', *Marxism Today*, January 1983.
9. Ibid., p. 19.
10. Karl Marx, 'The Eighteenth Brumaire of Louis Bonaparte', in *Surveys from Exile*, Harmondsworth 1974.

The New Questions of Subjectivity

Göran Therborn

The Dominant Ideology Thesis[1] by Nicholas Abercrombie, Stephen Hill and Bryan S. Turner is first of all the story of a hunting exploit. It relates how the authors hunt down and finally kill a beast called 'the dominant ideology thesis'. To save some space for due evaluation of this achievement, the beast will hereafter be shortened to DIT and its killers to AHT. Though told in the sometimes jarring tones of Sociologese, it is a fascinating story, which this reviewer read with considerable pleasure. Unfortunately it has become common for reviews to say far too much about the reviewer's pleasure or displeasure, or about his bright ideas in general, leaving the poor reader in the dark about the actual object which occasioned the review. Before embarking upon any further assessment, therefore, let us for a moment allow the authors to speak for themselves.

According to AHT: 'There exists a widespread agreement among Marxists, such as Habermas, Marcuse, Miliband and Poulantzas, that there is a powerful, effective, dominant ideology in contemporary capitalist societies and that this dominant ideology creates an acceptance of capitalism in the working class. It is with this dominant ideology thesis that our book is concerned' (p. 1). 'Ideology' AHT equate with 'beliefs' (p. 188), without any assumption of necessary falseness or misleading content. The authors' argumentation starts with two chapters surveying the theories they criticize and reject. The first focuses on three Marxist writers, Gramsci, Habermas and Althusser; the second on sociological 'theories of the common culture', particularly the work of Talcott Parsons and those influenced by him. AHT hold that there are 'considerable similarities' in the accounts of the social order given by the neo-Marxist DIT and the sociological common culture theory. It is argued that Parsons *et al.*, as well as

modern Marxists, tend to focus on the normative integration of societies, thereby departing from the emphasis on non-normative constraint central to classical social theory, in Durkheim and Weber as in
Marx himself.

Historical Arguments

The main part of the book then devotes one chapter each to medieval
feudalism, the early industrial capitalism of nineteenth-century
Britain, and the late capitalism of post-World War II Britain. Deploy-
ing a multitude of historiographic – and, in the third chapter, sociological – references, AHT affirm that DIT is an inaccurate theory. Thus,
under feudalism religion was not 'a dominant ideology which had the
consequence of successfully incorporating the peasantry' (p. 94);
rather, 'a dominant religious ideology among the landowning feudal
class had the consequence of helping the operation of the economic
conditions of feudalism' (p. 93), mainly through the contribution of
Catholic family morality to the regulation of inheritance in land. Early
British capitalism experienced the development of a new dominant
bourgeois ideology, provided by philosophic radicalism, which destroyed 'traditionalism' and its sanctioning of social and political authority by reference to natural law (p. 96). However, AHT emphasize as
their most important point that working-class culture and ideology
were all the time largely unpermeated by this dominant bourgeois
ideology. In feudalism and early capitalism there was a rather clearly
identifiable, though by no means completely unified, dominant ideology, which incorporated the *dominant* class, but the weakness of the
apparatus of ideological transmission left the subordinate classes
largely untouched by it. In late capitalism, however, a kind of inversion
has taken place. Transmission is more effective, but the 'limited ideological unity of previous periods has collapsed' (p. 156). State-
interventionist welfare capitalism, and the granting of trade-union and
individual employee rights by large corporations, indicate the internal
inconsistency of dominant bourgeois ideology and its limited sway
across the different fractions of the dominant class. AHT conclude that
'late capitalism operates largely without ideology' and, leaning upon
Max Weber's economic sociology and an expression of Marx, that 'the
coherence of capitalist societies is produced by the "dull compulsion of
economic relations"' (p. 165). 'Our position', they explain,

> is that the non-normative aspect of system integration provides a basis of a
> society's coherence, irrespective of whether or not there are common

values. Social integration and system integration can vary independently. Social classes do have different and conflicting ideologies but are, nevertheless, bound together by the network of objective social relations. (p. 168)

This is a very serious work on a very important topic: it makes a valuable contribution to our understanding of social order and social domination, two things which in human history have meant the same, alas. Since AHT have also been asked to review my own *The Ideology of Power and the Power of Ideology*, it may be of interest to note the areas of convergence with *The Dominant Ideology Thesis*. The two books appeared in the same year, partly addressing the same problems, but were written from very different intellectual, political and national backgrounds, with no apparent knowledge of each other. Both argue that existing order/domination is not maintained, to any significant extent, by a belief among the ruled in the rulers' right to rule. Both stress the crucial importance of non-normative constraint, the different relations of different classes to the same ideology, and the lack of coherence and consistency of most ideologies. It may also be the case that each of the two works would have benefited from knowledge and use of the other. Many of my propositions and conceptual distinctions could have been fruitfully concretized and corroborated by the empirical readings that AHT collect and introduce into their discussion. Their exposition could probably have been clarified and sharpened by parts of the analytical *instrumentarium* developed in my book. In spite of their partial confluence, however, *DIT* and *The Ideology of Power* . . . remain fundamentally different. In at least one sense they are even opposites. For while the latter is, above all, a constructive effort to develop new tools for grasping the complex relations of ideology and power, *DIT* is mainly a work of destruction. Not only is it about something which the authors are out to destroy. It ends with a call for *silence* about ideology: 'Since the real task is always to understand the economic and political forces which shape people's lives, too much has been said about ideology in recent decades' (p. 191). This sentence seems to imply two claims: that AHT have said virtually all there is to say about ideology, at least for the immediate future; and that, for all practical purposes, ideology has nothing to do with how economic and political forces shape people's lives. Let us test the weight of these claims.

If enough has been said about ideology with the publication of *DIT*, it must follow that enough has been said about DIT. That is what AHT were hunting throughout their book, and most readers will have noticed, even after a first reading, that their numerous shots scored several 'hits'. But what animal is it, whose hide the proud hunters have hung on the wall of the Sociology Staff Room? That is not very easy to say. DIT only got its name from its killers, just before the trigger was pulled.

A second, closer reading of *DIT* reveals a curious structure of the book. DIT is first defined by general reference to a number of Marxist theorists, then it is refuted by a series of arguments concerning what AHT hold to be false notions about the operation of ideology in feudal society and in early and late capitalism. This procedure assumes, with no systematic attempt at demonstration, that the criticized notions of feudal and capitalist ideology are those of the authors whose writings constitute the DIT. *DIT* contains a host of references, but the ones decisive for its authors' argument are conspicuously absent. A common and respectable procedure of scholarly debate is first to give a clear picture of what is to be scrutinized and criticized, and then to show the logical inconsistency of the object of analysis or to demonstrate its empirical inadequacy or falseness by bringing evidence to bear against it. For some reason, however, AHT have chosen a quite different path. The *criticandum*, DIT, is first defined in three different ways. Then the authors pool their knowledge to cast as much doubt as possible on one of the three objects of definition. The conclusion is that DIT is 'empirically false and theoretically unwarranted', presumably in all three meanings. To most people this will hardly be a convincing demonstration, however sympathetic they may feel towards much of the book's anti-idealist thrust. It remains to be seen whether AHT have arrived at a correct position, even though they have not succeeded in bringing their arguments together in a logically compelling way.

Three Definitions

The three definitions of 'the' DIT which AHT offer are the following. First, what we might call the 'identifiable DIT' is defined by reference to known authors 'such as Habermas, Marcuse, Miliband and Poulantzas' (p. 1), or 'Gramsci, Habermas and Althusser' (pp. 11 ff.). Secondly, we find something like a 'stress definition' of DIT: 'Our argument is that there has been an increased emphasis on the autonomy and causal efficacy of superstructural elements, and of ideology in particular, in modern Marxism. . . . This emphasis on ideology amounts to advocacy of what we have called the dominant ideology thesis' (p. 29). The third and final definition is of a 'constructed DIT', a product, most immediately, of AHT's talent for formulation:

The main elements of this thesis are as follows:
1. There is a dominant ideology . . .
2. Dominant classes 'benefit' from the effects of the dominant ideology . . .
3. The dominant ideology does incorporate the subordinate classes, making them politically quiescent . . .
4. The mechanisms by which ideology is transmitted have to be powerful enough to overcome the contradictions within the structure of capitalist society. (p. 29)

At least two minimal requirements must be satisfied if these definitions are to be used in conjunction with one another: it must be possible to locate, or at least to distil, the construct from the works making up the identifiable definition; and the 'modern Marxist' authors who lay such stress on ideology must be referring to the same thing that AHT understand by ideology. Otherwise, there would be no basis at all for the strange equation of 'emphasis on ideology' with 'advocacy of the dominant ideology thesis'. Crucial to the first requirement is the third of the elements given by AHT in their construct definition: the idea that 'the dominant ideology incorporates the subordinate classes'. All the others are irrelevant. AHT themselves hold elements (1) and (2), and element (4) is obviously not pertinent to their later discussion of medieval feudalism. AHT even give us a little help here in clarifying the meaning of the construct definition. They absolve Marx and Engels of the sin of DIT, in spite of ambiguous formulations in *The German Ideology*, because in the latter 'there was also an ideological conflict involved in the economic and political struggle. . . . We contend, therefore, that Marx and Engels did *not* adopt an incorporation theory' (p. 8). According to AHT's construct definition, then, those who hold a 'notion of class struggle at the ideological as well as the economic and political levels' (p. 8) should *not* be included among the proponents of DIT.

AHT never bother to argue that the notion of ideological class struggle has disappeared from the works of the DIT authors they mention. There is at least one good reason for their neglect, however, for a moment's reflection would reveal the sterility of any such attempt. To begin with Althusser, he took pains to emphasize his own view in the postscript to his essay on ideological state apparatuses:

Whoever says class struggle of the ruling class says resistance, revolt and class struggle of the ruled class. That is why the ISAs are not the realization of ideology in general, nor even the conflict-free realization of the ideology of the ruling class. . . . For if it is true that the ISAs represent the form in which the ideology of the ruling class must necessarily be realized, and the form in which the ideology of the ruled class must necessarily be measured and confronted, ideologies are 'born' not in the ISAs but from the social classes at grips in the class struggle: from their conditions of existence, their practices, their experience of the struggle, and so on.[2]

Ideology in Western Marxism

AHT indirectly admit that they had some difficulties in fitting Gramsci into their picture – difficulties avoided in other cases because of AHT's option to remain silent. On the one hand, we are told that Gramsci 'probably more than any other theorist [has] contributed to the contemporary dominant ideology thesis', with his 'conceptions of hegemony, and of ideology as cementing and unifying' (p. 14). On the other hand, a few lines later on the same page, we learn that 'Gramsci does not believe that the working class is completely subordinated *any more than Marx did*. He is no idealist. . . . Indeed, for Gramsci the economy is of prime importance.'[3] Some readers will, no doubt, wonder why Gramsci is included in the DIT company 'any more than Marx'. In fact, AHT proceed to give an answer. For Gramsci, 'despite the fact that there is a working-class consciousness at some level, its incorporation within a dominant ideology tends to produce "moral and political passivity"', which can be broken only 'as a result of struggle encouraged by a mass political party', the success of which 'depends partly on the party's intellectuals' (p. 15). Still, AHT would be unwise to make too much of any distinction between class and party or workers and intellectuals. In Gramsci's view, 'parties are only the nomenclature for classes', as the political organization of the latter: 'all members of a political party should be regarded as intellectuals', and between the 'spontaneous feeling' of the masses and the politically 'conscious leadership' there is but a '"quantitative" difference of degree, not one of quality'.[4] We shall consider presently whether Gramsci's view of the production of 'moral and political passivity' justifies AHT's assimilation of it to the 'empirically false and theoretically unwarranted' DIT. Let us just note that AHT do not take Marx to task for having said that 'the advance of capitalist production develops a working class which by education, tradition, habit, looks upon the conditions of that mode of production as self-evident laws of nature' (quoted on p. 166). If Marx escapes their indictment, there seems little reason to incorporate Gramsci into the construct definition of DIT.

It should be conceded that Habermas and Marcuse appear to qualify better for the ranks of the damned. But since that has more to do with their doubts about class struggle under contemporary capitalism than with any denial of *ideological* class struggle, it would seem preferable to consider them in relation to the stress definition of DIT. The case of Miliband is perhaps the simplest and most straightforward of all. If AHT had been less concerned with their image as *cavaliers seuls*, they could have enlisted Miliband in support of their more reasonable claims. Referring to *The German Ideology* and to 'the Gramscian concept of "hegemony"', or at least some interpretations of it, Miliband has written:

> What is involved is an overstatement of the ideological predominance of the 'ruling class' or of the effectiveness of that predominance. . . . It is at least as true now as it was when the words were written that 'the class which has the means of material production at its disposal has control at the same time over the means of mental production'. But it is only partially true . . . that 'thereby, generally speaking, the ideas of those who lack the means of mental production are subject to it'. The danger of this formulation, as of the notion of 'hegemony', is that it may lead to a quite inadequate account being taken of the many-sided and permanent challenge which is directed at the ideological predominance of the 'ruling class'. . . .[5]

Finally, Poulantzas. Again we can let the accused defend himself:

> To say that there is a working class in economic relations necessarily implies a specific place for this class in ideological and political relations, even if in certain countries and certain historical periods this class does not have its own 'class consciousness' or an autonomous political organization. This means that in such cases, even if it is heavily contaminated by bourgeois ideology, its economic existence is still expressed in certain specific material politico-ideological practices which burst through its bourgeois 'discourse'. . . . To understand this, of course, it is necessary to break with a whole conception of ideology as a 'system of ideas' or a coherent 'discourse', and to understand it as an ensemble of material practices. This gives the lie to all those ideologies arguing the 'integration' of the working class. . . .[6]

Construct and Reality

The first and the third of AHT's definitions do not fit together. With the possible exceptions of Habermas and Marcuse – both coming out of one particular tradition of Western Marxism – the identifiable or, so to speak, actually existing DITists cannot be covered by AHT's constructed DIT. This non-fit between the identifiable definition and the construct is also apparent in the fact that part of AHT's evidence against the latter is either fully compatible with, or a direct corroboration of, propositions advanced by identifiable DITists. A brief list of illustrations will suffice – indeed, it could not be made much longer, because AHT have hardly understood the purpose of Althusser *et al.*, and spend most of their time simply talking at a tangent. When Althusser wanted to argue that the Catholic Church was the central ISA in pre-capitalist Europe, he said: 'It is no accident that all ideological struggle, from the sixteenth to the eighteenth century . . . was *concentrated* in an anti-clerical and anti-religious struggle; rather, this is a function precisely of the dominant position of the religious ideological state apparatus.'[7] Poulantzas had earlier made a related point: 'The dominance of this [dominant] ideology is shown by the fact that the dominated classes live their conditions of political existence through the forms of dominant political discourse: this means that often they live even *their revolt* against the domination of the system within the frame of reference of the dominant legitimacy.'[8]

We cannot expect AHT to have looked for evidence for or against these notions. But in arguing against their own construct, they have come up with some rather telling illustrations of Althusser's and Poulantzas's arguments. Against the idea of Catholic incorporation of the peasantry, for example, they write:

> In the Black Mass in the region of Labor in 1609 the Catholic Mass was celebrated in reverse by a priest who had his face to the ground while elevating a black Host. In Catalan witchcraft in the same period, Latin prayers were recited backwards while in the Midi Feast of Fools, Mass-bouffe and Mass-farce turned the Church's sacred ritual into a public burlesque. In the absence of a real revolutionary strategy, the peasantry had to content itself with a purely farcical portrayal of the idea that 'the first shall be last'. (pp. 78–9)

When they come to mid-Victorian Britain, AHT invoke studies of the labour aristocracy to support their view that 'apparently bourgeois beliefs [of self-help, improvement, independence, respectability] had distinctive, corporate and class meanings for the proletariat' (p. 117).

In AHT's opinion, Althusser's essay 'Ideology and Ideological State Apparatuses' 'is moving to the conventional statement of the dominant ideology thesis. . . . This position is summarized well in Althusser's own words: "To my knowledge, no class can hold State power over a very long period without at the same time exercising its hegemony over and in the State Ideological Apparatuses"' (p. 24; emphasis omitted). AHT make no attempt to disprove Althusser's statement. But they do make various points which indirectly pertain to it. Their discussion of the supportive relationship between Church and feudal aristocracy is of the kind we might expect from an Althusserian perspective. Again, in their summary of Willis's *Learning to Labour* (p. 150) they refer to the

individualist, achievement-orientated, hierarchical and non-manual
values of the school – values which seem to involve 'bourgeois
hegemony' over and in the school system, the central ISA in Althusser's
view of mature capitalism. Of course, AHT introduce Willis in order to
show the school's failure to indoctrinate the adolescent working class.
But the evidence could equally be used, not to prove Althusser's
'conventional statement', but at least to make it rather plausible.
Suppose, for example, that the school had embodied the ideology of
this working-class youth: 'a refusal to submit to authority; the value of
solidaristic collectivism and the rejection of the various elements of the
individualist ethos; a glorification of manual labour; and an awareness
that labour has only a commodity status in the modern economy,
coupled with [rejection] of this fact'. Is it not rather plausible that
bourgeois state power would then have been in jeopardy?

A Question of Stress?

AHT's 'stress definition' of DIT – in which it is equated with emphasis
on ideology – is the loosest of the three but apparently the most
important to the authors. Whereas the identifiable definition identifies the target, and the construct provides an easy route of attack, as
well as a catchy title for the enterprise, the 'stress definition' commands and connects the other two across all logical hiatuses, supplying the energy and meaning for the whole polemic. It is precisely
with the 'stress definition', however, that the argument of *DIT* breaks
down. For AHT do not really seem to have appreciated that they have
a much more restricted definition of ideology than the people they
attack. Towards the end of the book AHT claim: 'In our argument we
have so far equated "ideology" with beliefs' (p. 188). That is not quite
true. In reality, they equate ideology with *normative* beliefs, without
making clear to themselves that there might be other beliefs – about
what exists and what does not, about who one is, about what is
possible and what is not, and so on. Quite correctly AHT assert that
'there is an important distinction between the acceptance of social
arrangements because they appear just, and acceptance simply because they are there, or because they appear as a coercive external
fact'. 'We do not understand this kind of pragmatic acceptance', they
continue, 'as entailing the possession of *any* set of beliefs, attitudes or
false consciousness. Instead pragmatic acceptance is the result of the
coercive quality of everyday life and of the routines that sustain it'
(p. 166; emphasis added).
    Now, AHT's conception of ideology is not shared by the theorists

mentioned in definition one as proponents of DIT. Marcuse, whose
One-Dimensional Man: The Ideology of Industrial Society would at first
glance seem the most qualified for inclusion under the construct
definition of DIT, did not at all adhere to the restrictive definition of
ideology. When he talked about how 'changes in the character of work
and the instruments of production change the attitude and the
consciousness of the labourer, which become manifest in the widely
discussed "social and cultural integration" of the labouring class', he was
referring to 'assimilation in needs and aspirations, in the standard of
living, in leisure activities, in politics'.[9] The point is not whether Marcuse
was right or wrong in his analysis of this process – AHT clearly think he
was wrong. The point is that he saw it as an outcome of what AHT call
'the massive and constraining quality of everyday life' (p. 166), of the
worker's being 'incorporated into the technological community of the
administered population', by means of 'an integration in the plant itself,
in the material process of production'.[10] AHT are closer to the mark in
their discussion of Habermas's concern with legitimation. To their
credit, however, they also register that Habermas's concept of
legitimation sometimes extends beyond beliefs of right and wrong. To
that extent, Habermas escapes the critical salvos directed at DIT (p. 16).

From another angle, Althusser's discussion of ideology was explicitly
concerned with, among other things, how we come 'to recognize that
we are subjects and that we function in the practical rituals of the most
elementary everyday life'.[11] As to Gramsci, the 'consent' he analysed in
relation to hegemony was neither an exclusively normative acceptance
in AHT's sense, nor simply an everyday routine. Rather, Gramsci held
that 'this consent is "historically" caused by the prestige (and consequent confidence) which the dominant group enjoys because of its
position and function in the world of production'.[12] While this
formulation may lend itself to different interpretations, Gramsci could
also be quite explicit about non-normative components of ideological
hegemony. In a reflection about the possibility of interpreting Italian
Fascism as a 'passive revolution', he wrote:

> The ideological hypothesis could be presented in the following terms: that
> there is a passive revolution involved in the fact that – through the legislative
> intervention of the State, and by means of the corporative organization –
> relatively far-reaching modifications are being introduced into the
> country's economic structure in order to accentuate the 'plan of production'
> element. . . . What is important from the political and the ideological point
> of view is that it is capable of creating – and indeed does create – a period of
> *expectation and hope*, especially in certain Italian social groups such as the
> great mass of urban and rural petty bourgeois. It thus reinforces the
> hegemonic system.[13]

Conceptions of Subjectivity

The Dominant Ideology Thesis should be read with a sense of humour. The vociferous and voracious animal, which Abercrombie, Hill and Turner claim to have hunted out of every lair from medieval France to contemporary Britain, is little more than a blown-up balloon, against which little more than a pin or a good pencil is required. (But it is a balloon which deserves to be punctured.) Beneath the extravagant claims, *DIT* contains some sound sociological sense. Its authors are quite correct in emphasizing the usually fractured and contradictory character of dominant ideologies and the resilient ideological autonomy of subordinate classes. They are right to underline the crucial function of 'non-normative aspects of system integration' – a stress already developed by David Lockwood a score or so years ago. Their book does, however, involve a celebration of obscurantism which, if it were to become influential, would have very serious implications. For in their declamatory references to 'the dull compulsion of economic relations' and their closing statement that 'too much has been said about ideology in recent decades', they are paying obscurantist homage to what might be called a 'black-box' conception of human subjectivity. Black-box theories do have certain legitimate functions in science: they are economic, and they make it possible to advance by circumventing terrains of ignorance that are difficult to penetrate. But to turn such a makeshift solution into a principle, some 115 years after it was first proposed, seems to merit the harsh designation of a celebration of obscurantism. What of the people who are 'dully compelled' to become and to remain wage-labourers, or salaried sociology lecturers? What do they know, what do they feel, what do they hope for, what do they fear, what do they consider 'fun', what do they think is possible or impossible? Or do they not have any beliefs at all? Abercrombie, Hill and Turner have a perfect right to regard such questions as boring or trivial. But social science and historiography would themselves become dull and boring if they restrained other people from trying to answer them.

AHT remain imprisoned in one of the traditional conceptions of ideology: that of normative beliefs of right and wrong. Modern analyses of ideology and discourse have to break out of – are breaking out of – that straitjacket. I might be allowed to refer to my own book as one little example. Instead of barricading itself against the notion of subjectivity, as AHT propose, historical materialism has to confront it and account for its vicissitudes. Unless we transcend what Marx and Weber knew about the 'dull compulsion' of the market, we cannot comprehend the new social movements (the student, the women's, the ecological and the peace movements), or the actually existing history and possible future of the labour movement.

Finally, dominant ideologies need to be rescued from their conversion into theses, whether by proponents or opponents. They should be developed as hypotheses of empirical research. As far as I can tell, AHT are quite right in rejecting the idea that all-pervasive normative doctrines govern the behaviour of members of developed societies. But, again, it would be obscurantist to refrain from looking into the dominant ideologies. Here a comparative approach seems to be the most fruitful. In complex societies, *what is* can be most easily discovered through comparison with what exists or has existed elsewhere. In my own research I have been looking at how political ideologies have changed in Swedish electoral campaigns from 1928 to 1982. In functioning democracies, what is said and what is not said, what is appealing and what is regarded as a campaign blunder, tap important aspects of ideological power relations in complex societies. Since they have a behavioural component, election campaigns also seem more reliable than international opinion polls. Another promising route – doubtless not the only one – is to look at the prevalence or absence and the historical trajectory of certain concepts or labels of identification. For instance, in Swedish parlance there has been no 'middle class' or 'middle estate' [*Mittelstand*] since about 1950: but there are 'bourgeois parties' and a 'workers' movement' (without a working class).

With all the respect due to *The Dominant Ideology Thesis* for its intelligence, erudition and sound scepticism of the past, my fundamental objection is that it is not silence which is now on the agenda, that serious analysis of ideology has to begin and is beginning. Let me end by expressing the hope that Abercrombie, Hill and Turner will bring their undeniable skills to bear on this task.

Notes

1. London 1980.
2. Louis Althusser, 'Ideology and Ideological State Apparatuses', this volume, Chapter 5.
3. Emphasis added.
4. Antonio Gramsci, *Selections from the Prison Notebooks*, London 1971, pp. 227, 16, 199.
5. Ralph Miliband, *Marxism and Politics*, Oxford 1977, p. 53.
6. Nicos Poulantzas, *Political Power and Social Classes*, London 1978, pp. 16–17.
7. Althusser, 'Ideology and Ideological State Apparatuses', p. 000.
8. Nicos Poulantzas, *Classes in Contemporary Capitalism*, London 1973, p. 223; original emphasis.
9. Herbert Marcuse, *One-Dimensional Man*, London 1968, p. 39.
10. Ibid., pp. 37, 39.
11. Althusser, 'Ideology and Ideological State Apparatuses, p. 130.
12. Gramsci, *Selections from the Prison Notebooks*, p. 12.
13. Ibid., p. 120; emphasis added.

Ideology and its Vicissitudes in Western Marxism

Terry Eagleton

From Lukács to Gramsci

To think of Marxism as the scientific analysis of social formations, and to think of it as ideas in active struggle, will tend to yield two quite different epistemologies. In the former case, consciousness is essentially contemplative, seeking to 'match' or 'correspond to' its object in the greater possible accuracy of cognition. In the latter case, consciousness is much more obviously *part* of social reality, a dynamic force in its potential transformation. And if this is so, then to a thinker like Georg Lukács it would not seem entirely appropriate to speak of whether such thought 'reflects' or 'fits' the history with which it is inseparably bound up.

If consciousness is grasped in this way as a transformative force at one with the reality it seeks to change, then there would seem to be no 'space' between it and that reality in which false consciousness might germinate. Ideas cannot be 'untrue' to their object if they are actually part of it. In the terms of the philosopher J. L. Austin, we can speak of a 'constative' utterance, one which aims to describe the world, as either true or false; but it would not make sense to speak of a 'performative' statement as either correctly or incorrectly 'reflecting' reality. I am not *describing* anything when I promise to take you to the theatre, or curse you for spilling ink on my shirt. If I ceremonially name a ship, or stand with you before a clergyman and say 'I do', these are material events in reality, acts as efficacious as ironing my socks, not 'pictures' of some state of affairs which could be said to be accurate or mistaken.

Does this mean, then, that the model of consciousness as *cognitive* (or miscognitive) should be ousted by an image of consciousness as *performative*? Not exactly: for it is clear that this opposition can be to

179

some degree deconstructed. There is no point in my promising to take you to the theatre if the theatre in question was closed down for gross obscenity last week and I am unaware of the fact. My act of cursing is empty if what I thought was an ink stain on my shirt is just part of the floral design. All 'performative' acts involve cognition of some kind, implicate some sense of how the world actually is; it is futile for a political group to hone its ideas in the struggle with some oppressive power if the power in question collapsed three years ago and they simply have not noticed.

In his great work *History and Class Consciousness* (1922), the Hungarian Marxist Georg Lukács takes full account of this point. 'It is true', Lukács writes there, 'that reality is the criterion for the correctness of thought. But reality is not, it becomes – and to become the participation of thought is needed.'[1] Thought, we might say, is at once cognitive and creative: in the act of understanding its real conditions, an oppressed group or class has begun in that very moment to fashion the forms of consciousness which will contribute to changing them. And this is why no simple 'reflection' model of consciousness will really do. 'Thought and existence', Lukács writes, 'are not identical in the sense that they "correspond" to each other, or "reflect" each other, that they "run parallel" to each other or "coincide" with each other (all expressions that conceal a rigid duality). Their identity is that they are aspects of one and the same real historical and dialectical process.'[2] The cognition of the revolutionary proletariat, for Lukács, is part of the situation it cognizes, and alters that situation at a stroke. If this logic is pressed to an extreme, then it would seem that we never simply know some 'thing', since our act of knowing is has already transformed it into something else. The model tacitly underlying this doctrine is that of *self*-knowledge; for to know myself is no longer to be the self that I was a moment before I knew it. It would seem, in any case, that this whole conception of consciousness as essentially active, practical and dynamic, which Lukács owes to the work of Hegel, will force us to revise any too simplistic notion of false consciousness as some lag, gap or disjunction between the way things are and the way we know them.

Lukács takes over from aspects of the Second International the positive, non-pejorative sense of the word ideology, writing unembarrassedly for Marxism as 'the ideological expression of the proletariat'; and this is at least one reason why the widespread view that ideology for him is synonymous with false consciousness is simply mistaken. But he retains at the same time the whole conceptual apparatus of Marx's critique of commodity fetishism, and thus keeps alive a more critical sense of the term. The 'other' or opposite of ideology in this negative sense, however, is no longer primarily

'Marxist science' but the concept of *totality*; and one of the functions of this concept in his work is to allow him to ditch the idea of some disinterested social science without thereby falling prey to historical relativism. All forms of class consciousness are ideological; but some, so to speak, are more ideological than others. What is specifically ideological about the bourgeoisie is its inability to grasp the structure of the social formation as a whole, on account of the dire effects of reification. Reification fragments and dislocates our social experience, so that under its influence we forget that society is a collective process and come to see it instead merely as this or that isolated object or institution. As Lukács's contemporary Karl Kosch argues, ideology is essentially a form of synecdoche, the figure of speech in which we take the part for the whole. What is peculiar to proletarian consciousness, in its fullest political development, is its capacity to 'totalize' the social order, for without such knowledge the working class will never be able to understand and transform its own conditions. A true recognition of its situation will be, inseparably, an insight into the social whole within which it is oppressively positioned; so that the moments in which the proletariat comes to self-consciousness, and knows the capitalist system for what it is, are in effect identical.

Science, truth or theory, in other words, are no longer to be strictly counterposed to ideology; on the contrary, they are just 'expressions' of a *particular* class ideology, the revolutionary world-view of the working class. Truth is just bourgeois society coming to consciousness of itself as a whole, and the 'place' where this momentous event occurs is in the self-awareness of the proletariat. Since the proletariat is the prototypical commodity, forced to sell its labour-power in order to survive, it can be seen as the 'essence' of a social order based on commodity fetishism; and the self-consciousness of the proletariat is therefore, as it were, the commodity form coming to an awareness of itself, and in that act transcending itself.

In coming to write *History and Class Consciousness*, Lukács found himself faced with a kind of Hobson's choice or impossible opposition. On the one hand, there was the positivist fantasy (inherited from the Second International) of a Marxist science which appeared to repress its own historical roots; on the other hand, there was the spectre of historical relativism. Either knowledge was sublimely external to the history it sought to know, or it was just a matter of this or that specific brand of historical consciousness, with no more firm grounding than that. Lukács's way of circumventing this dilemma is by introducing the category of *self-reflection*. There are certain forms of knowledge – notably, the *self*-knowledge of an exploited class – which, while thoroughly historical, are nevertheless able to lay bare the limits of other ideologies, and so to figure as an emancipatory force. Truth, in Lukács's 'historicist' perspective,[3] is always relative to a particular historical situation, never a metaphysical affair beyond history altogether; but the proletariat, uniquely, is so historically positioned as to be able in principle to unlock the secret of capitalism as a whole. There is thus no longer any need to remain trapped within the sterile antithesis of ideology as false or partial consciousness on the one hand, and science as some absolute, unhistorical mode of knowledge on the other. For not all class consciousness is false consciousness, and science is simply an expression or encodement of 'true' class consciousness.

Lukács's own way of phrasing this argument is unlikely to win much unqualified allegiance today. The proletariat, he claims, is a potentially 'universal' class, since it bears with it the potential emancipation of all humanity. Its consciousness is thus in principle universal; but a universal subjectivity is in effect identical with objectivity. So what the working class knows, from its own partial historical perspective, must be objectively true. One does not need to be persuaded by this rather grandly Hegelian language to rescue the important insight buried within it. Lukács sees, quite rightly, that the contrast between merely partial ideological standpoints on the one hand, and some dispassionate views of the social totality on the other, is radically misleading. For what this opposition fails to take into account is the situation of oppressed groups and classes, who need to get some view of the social system as a whole, and of their own place within it, simply to be able to realize their own partial, particular interests. If women are to emancipate themselves, they need to have an interest in understanding something of the general structures of patriarchy. Such understanding is by no means innocent or disinterested; on the contrary, it is in the service of pressing political interests. But without, as it were, passing over at some point from the particular to the general, those interests are likely to founder. A colonial people, simply to survive, may find itself 'forced' to inquire into the global structures of imperialism, as their imperialist rulers need not do. Those who today fashionably disown the need for a 'global' or 'total' perspective may be privileged enough to dispense with it. It is where such a totality bears urgently in on one's own immediate social conditions that the intersection between part and whole is most significantly established. Lukács's point is that certain groups and classes need to inscribe their own condition within a wider context if they are to change that condition; and in doing so they will find themselves challenging the consciousness of those who have an interest in blocking this emancipatory knowledge. It is in this sense that the bugbear of relativism is irrelevant: for to claim that all knowledge springs from a specific social standpoint is not to imply that any old social standpoint is as valuable for these purposes as any other. If what one is looking for is some understanding of the workings of imperialism as a whole, then one would be singularly ill-advised to consult the Governor General or the *Daily Telegraph*'s Africa correspondent, who will almost certainly deny its existence.

There is, however, a logical problem with Lukács's notion of some 'true' class consciousness. For if the working class is the potential bearer of such consciousness, from what viewpoint is *this* judgement made? It cannot be made from the viewpoint of the (ideal) proletariat itself, since this simply begs the question; but if only that viewpoint is true, then it cannot be made from some standpoint external to it either. As Bhikhu Parekh points out, to claim that only the proletarian perspective allows one to grasp the truth of society as a whole already assumes that one knows what that truth is.[4] It would seem that truth is either wholly internal to the consciousness of the working class, in which case it cannot be assessed *as* truth and the claim becomes simply dogmatic; or one is caught in the impossible paradox of judging the truth from outside the truth itself, in which case the claim that this form of consciousness is true simply undercuts itself.

If the proletariat, for Lukács, is in principle the bearer of a knowledge of the social whole, it figures as the direct antithesis of a bourgeois class sunk in the mire of immediacy, unable to totalize its own situation. It is a traditional Marxist case that what forestalls such knowledge in the case of the middle class is its atomized social and economic conditions: each individual capitalist pursues his own interest, with little or no sense of how all of these isolated interests combine into a total system. Lukács, however, places emphasis, rather, on the phenomenon of reification – a concept he derives from Marx's doctrine of commodity fetishism, but to which he lends a greatly extended meaning. Splicing together Marx's economic analysis and Max Weber's theory of rationalization, he argues in *History and Class Consciousness* that in capitalist society the commodity-form permeates every aspect of social life, taking the shape of a pervasive mechanization, quantification and dehumanization of human experience. The 'wholeness' of society is broken up into so many discrete, specialized, technical operations, each of which comes to assume a semi-autonomous life of its own and to dominate human existence as a quasi-natural force. Purely formal techniques of calculability suffuse every region of society, from factory work to political bureaucracy, journalism to the judiciary; and the natural sciences themselves are simply one more instance of reified thought. Overwhelmed by an opaque world of autonomous objects and institutions, the human subject is rapidly reduced to an inert, contemplative being, incapable of recognizing any longer in these petrified products its own creative practice. The moment of revolutionary recognition arrives when the working class acknowledges this alienated world as its own confiscated creation, reclaiming it through political praxis. In the terms of the Hegelian philosophy which underlies Lukács's thought, this would signal the reunification of subject and object, torn grievously asunder by the effects of reification. In knowing itself for what it is, the proletariat becomes both subject and object of history. Indeed, Lukács occasionally seems to imply that this act of self-consciousness is a revolutionary practice all in itself.

What Lukács has in effect done here is to replace Hegel's Absolute Idea – itself the identical subject–object of history – with the proletariat.[5] Or at least, to qualify the point, with the kind of politically desirable consciousness which the proletariat could in principle achieve – what he calls 'ascribed' or 'imputed' consciousness. And if Lukács is Hegelian enough in this, he is equally so in his trust that the truth lies in the whole. For the Hegel of *The Phenomenology of Spirit*, immediate experience is itself a kind of false or partial consciousness; it will yield up its truth only when it is dialectically mediated, when its latent manifold relations with the whole have been patiently uncovered. One might say, then, that on this view our routine consciousness is itself inherently 'ideological', simply by virtue of its partiality. It is not that the statements we make in this situation are necessarily false; it is rather that they are true only in some superficial, empirical way, for they are judgements about isolated objects which have not yet been incorporated into their full context. We can think back here to the assertion: 'Prince Charles is a thoughtful, conscientious fellow', which may be true enough as far as it goes, but which isolates the object known as Prince Charles from the whole context of the institution of royalty. For Hegel, it is only by the operations of dialectical reason that such static, discrete phenomena can be reconstituted as a dynamic, developing whole. And to this extent one might say that a certain kind of false consciousness is for Hegel our 'natural' condition, endemic to our immediate experience.

For Lukács, by contrast, such partial seeing springs from specific historical causes – the process of capitalist reification – but is to be overcome in much the same way, by the workings of a 'totalizing' or dialectical reason. Bourgeois science, logic and philosophy are his equivalent of Hegel's routine, unredeemed mode of knowledge, breaking down what is in fact a complex, evolving totality into artificially autonomous parts. Ideology for Lukács is thus not exactly a discourse untrue to the way things are, but one true to them only in a limited, superficial way, ignorant of their deeper tendencies and connections. And this is another sense in which, contrary to wide-spread opinion, ideology is not in his view false consciousness in the sense of simple error or illusion.

To seize history as totality is to grasp it in its dynamic, contradictory development, of which the potential realization of human powers is a vital part. To this extent, a particular kind of *cognition* – knowing the whole – is for both Hegel and Lukács a certain kind of moral and political *norm*. The dialectical method thus reunites not only subject and object, but also 'fact' and 'value', which bourgeois thought has ripped asunder. To understand the world in a particular way becomes inseparable from acting to promote the free, full unfolding of human creative powers. We are not left high and dry, as we are in positivist or empiricist thought, with a dispassionate, value-free knowledge on the one hand, and an arbitrary set of subjective values on the other. On the contrary, the act of knowledge is itself both 'fact' and 'value', an accurate cognition indispensable for political emancipation. As Leszek Kolakowski puts the point: 'In this particular case [i.e. that of emancipatory knowledge] the understanding and transformation of reality are not two separate processes, but one and the same phenomenon.'[6]

Lukács's writings on class consciousness rank among the richest, most original documents of twentieth-century Marxism. They are, nevertheless, subject to a number of damaging criticisms. It could be argued, for example, that his theory of ideology tends towards an unholy mixture of economism and idealism. Economism, because he uncritically adopts the later Marx's implication that the commodity-form is somehow the secret essence of all ideological consciousness in bourgeois society. Reification figures for Lukács not only as a central feature of the capitalist economy, but as 'the central structural problem of capitalist society in all aspects'.[7] A kind of essentialism of ideology is consequently at work here, homogenizing what are in fact very different discourses, structures and effects. At its worst, this model tends to reduce bourgeois society to a set of neatly layered 'expressions' of reification, each of its levels (economic, political, juridical, philosophical) obediently miming and reflecting the others. Moreover, as Theodor Adorno was later to suggest, this single-minded insistence upon reification as the clue to all crimes is itself overtly idealist: in Lukács's texts, it tends to displace such more fundamental concepts as economic exploitation. Much the same might be said of his use of the Hegelian category of totality, which sometimes pushes to one side an attention to modes of production, contradictions between the forces and relations of production, and the like. Is Marxism, like Matthew Arnold's ideal poetic vision, just a matter of seeing reality steadily and seeing it whole? To parody Lukács's case a little: is revolution simply a question of making *connections*? And is not the social totality, for Marxism if not for Hegel, 'skewed' and asymmetrical, twisted out of true by the preponderance within it of economic determinants? Properly cautious of 'vulgar' Marxist versions of 'base' and 'superstructure', Lukács wishes to displace attention from this brand of mechanistic determinism to the idea of the social whole; but this social whole then risks becoming a purely 'circular' one, in which each 'level' is granted equal effectivity with each of the others.

Commodity fetishism, for Lukács as much as for Marx, is an objective material structure of capitalism, not just a state of mind. But in *History and Class Consciousness* another, residually idealist model of ideology is also confusingly at work, which would seem to locate the 'essence' of bourgeois society in the collective subjectivity of the bourgeois class itself. 'For a class to be ripe for hegemony', Lukács writes, 'means that its interests and consciousness enable it to organise the whole of society in accordance with those interests.'[8] What is it, then, which provides the ideological linchpin of the bourgeois order? Is it the 'objective' system of commodity fetishism, which presumably imprints itself on all classes alike, or the 'subjective' strength of the dominant class's consciousness? Gareth Stedman Jones has argued that, as far as the latter view is concerned, it is as though ideology for Lukács takes grip through 'the saturation of the social totality by the ideological essence of a pure class subject'.[9] What this overlooks, as Stedman Jones goes on to point out, is that ideologies, far from being the 'subjective product of the "will to power" of different classes', are *'objective* systems determined by the *whole field* of social struggle between contending classes'. For Lukács, as for 'historicist' Marxism in general, it would sometimes appear as though each social class has its own peculiar, corporate 'world-view', one directly expressive of its material conditions of existence; and ideological dominance then consists in one of these world-views imposing its stamp on the social formation as a whole. It is not only that this version of ideological power is hard to square with the more structural and objective doctrine of commodity fetishism; it is also that it drastically simplifies the true unevenness and complexity of the ideological 'field'. For as Nicos Poulantzas has argued, ideology, like social class itself, is an inherently *relational* phenomenon; it expresses less the way a class lives its conditions of existence than the way it lives them *in relation to the lived experience of other classes.*[10] Just as there can be no bourgeois class without a proletariat, or vice versa, so the typical ideology of each of these classes is constituted to the root by the ideology of its antagonist. Ruling ideologies, as we have argued earlier, must engage effectively with the lived experience of subordinate classes; and the way in which those subaltern classes live their world will be typically shaped and influenced by the dominant ideologies. Historicist Marxism, in short, presumes too organic and internal a relation between a 'class subject' and its 'world-view'. There are social classes such as the petty bourgeoisie – 'contradiction incarnate', as Marx dubbed them – whose ideology is typically compounded of elements drawn from the classes both above and below them; and there are vital ideological themes such as nationalism which do not 'belong' to any particular social class but which, rather, provide a bone of contention between them.[11] Social classes do not manifest ideologies in the way that individuals display a particular style of walking: ideology is, rather, a complex, conflictive field of meaning, in which some themes will be closely tied to the experience of particular classes, while others will be more 'free-floating', tugged now this way and now that in the struggle between contending powers. Ideology is a realm of contestation and nego-tiation, in which there is a constant busy traffic: meanings and values are stolen, transformed, appropriated across the frontiers of different classes and groups, surrendered, repossessed, reinflected. A dominant class may 'live its experience' in part through the ideology of a previous dominant one: think of the aristocratic colouring of the English *haute bourgeoisie*. Or it may fashion its ideology partly in terms of the beliefs of a subordinated class – as in the case of Fascism, where a ruling sector of finance capitalism takes over for its own purposes the prejudices and anxieties of the lower middle class. There is no neat, one-to-one correspondence between classes and ideologies, as is evident in the case of revolutionary socialism. Any revolutionary ideology, to be politically effective, would have to be a good deal more than Lukács's 'pure' proletarian consciousness: unless it lent some provisional coherence to a rich array of oppositional forces, it would have scant chance of success.

The idea of social classes as 'subjects', central to Lukács's work, has also been contested. A class is not just some kind of collectivized individual, equipped with the sorts of attributes ascribed by humanist thought to the individual person: consciousness, unity, autonomy, self-determination, and so on. Classes are certainly for Marxism historical *agents*; but they are structural, material formations as well as 'intersubjective' entities, and the problem is how to think these two aspects of them together. We have seen already that ruling classes are generally complex, internally conflictive 'blocs', rather than homogen-ous bodies; and the same applies to their political antagonists. A 'class-ideology', then, is likely to display much the same kind of unevenness and contradictoriness.

The harshest criticism of Lukács's theory of ideology would be that, in a series of progressive conflations, he collapses Marxist theory into proletarian ideology; ideology into the expression of some 'pure' class subject; and this class subject to the essence of the social formation. But this case demands significant qualification. Lukács is not at all blind to the ways in which the consciousness of the working class is 'contaminated' by that of its rulers, and would seem to ascribe no organic 'world-view' to it in non-revolutionary conditions. Indeed, if the proletariat in its 'normal' state is little more than the commodity incarnate, it is hard to see how it can be a *subject* at all – and therefore hard to see how exactly it can make the transition to becoming a 'class for itself'. But this process of 'contamination' does not appear to work the other way round, in the sense that the *dominant* ideology seems in no way significantly shaped by a dialogue with its subordinates.

We have seen already that there are really two discrepant theories of ideology at work in *History and Class Consciousness* – the one deriving from commodity fetishism, the other from a historicist view of ideology as the world-view of a class subject. As far as the proletariat is concerned, these two conceptions would seem to correspond respectively to its 'normal' and revolutionary states of being. In non-revolutionary conditions, working-class consciousness is passively subject to the effects of reification; we are given no clue as to how this situation is actively *constituted* by proletarian ideology, or of how it interacts with less obediently submissive aspects of that experience. How does the worker constitute herself as a subject on the basis of her objectification? But when the class shifts – mysteriously – to becoming a revolutionary subject, a historicist problematic takes over, and what was true of their rulers – that they 'saturated' the whole social formation with their own ideological conceptions – can now become true of them too. What is said of these rulers, however, is inconsistent: for this *active* notion of ideology in their case is at odds with the view that they, too, are simply victims of the structure of commodity fetishism. How can the middle class govern by virtue of its unique, unified world-view when it is simply subjected, along with other classes, to the structure of reification? Is the dominant ideology a matter of the bourgeoisie, or of bourgeois society?

It can be claimed that *History and Class Consciousness* is marred by a typically idealist overestimation of 'consciousness' itself. 'Only the consciousness of the proletariat', Lukács writes, 'can point to the way that leads out of the impasse of capitalism';[12] and while this is orthodox enough in one sense, since an *unconscious* proletariat is hardly likely to do the trick, its emphasis is none the less revealing. For it is not in the first place the *consciousness* of the working class, actual or potential, which leads Marxism to select it as the prime agency of revolutionary change. If the working class figures as such an agent, it is for structural, material reasons – the fact that it is the only body so located within the productive process of capitalism, so trained and organized by that process and utterly indispensable to it, as to be capable of taking it over. In this sense it is capitalism, not Marxism, which 'selects' the instruments of revolutionary overthrow, patiently nurturing its own potential gravedigger. When Lukács observes that the strength of a social formation is always in the last resort a 'spiritual' one, or when he writes that 'the fate of the revolution . . . will depend on the ideological maturity of the proletariat, i.e. on its class consciousness',[13] he is arguably in danger of displacing these material issues into questions of pure consciousness – and a consciousness which, as Gareth Stedman Jones has pointed out, remains curiously disembodied and ethereal, a matter of 'ideas' rather than practices or institutions.

If Lukács is residually idealist in the high priority he assigns to consciousness, so is he also in his Romantic hostility to science, logic and technology.[14] Formal and analytic discourses are simply modes of bourgeois reification, just as all forms of mechanization and rationalization would seem inherently alienating. The progressive, emancipatory side of these processes in the history of capitalism is merely ignored, in an elegiac nostalgia typical of Romantic conservative thought. Lukács does not wish to deny that Marxism is a science; but this science is the 'ideological expression of the proletariat', not some set of timeless analytic propositions. This certainly offers a powerful challenge to the 'scientism' of the Second International – the belief that historical materialism is a purely objective knowledge of the immanent laws of historical development. But to react against such metaphysical fantasies by *reducing* Marxist theory to revolutionary ideology is hardly more adequate. Are the complex equations of *Capital* no more than a theoretical 'expression' of socialist consciousness? Is not that consciousness partly *constituted* by such theoretical labour? And if only proletarian self-consciousness will deliver us the truth, how do we come to accept this truth as true in the first place, if not by a certain theoretical understanding which must be relatively independent of it?

I have already argued that it is mistaken to see Lukács as equating ideology with false consciousness *tout court*. Working-class socialist ideology is not, of course, in his view false; and even bourgeois ideology is illusory only in a complex sense of the term. Indeed, we might claim that whereas for the early Marx and Engels, ideology is thought false to the true situation, for Lukács it is thought true to a false situation. Bourgeois ideas do indeed accurately mirror the state of things in bourgeois society; but it is this very state of affairs which is somehow twisted out of true. Such consciousness is faithful to the reified nature of the capitalist social order, and often enough makes true claims about this condition; it is 'false' in so far as it cannot penetrate this world of frozen appearances to lay bare the totality of tendencies and connections which underlies it. In the breathtaking central section of *History and Class Consciousness*, 'Reification and the Consciousness of the Proletariat', Lukács boldly rewrites the whole of post-Kantian philosophy as a secret history of the commodity-form, of the schism between empty subjects and petrified objects; and in this sense such thought is accurate to the dominant social categories of capitalist society, structured by them to its roots. Bourgeois ideology is false less because it distorts, inverts or denies the material world than because it is unable to press beyond certain limits structural to bourgeois society as such. As Lukács writes: 'Thus the barrier which converts the class consciousness of the bourgeoisie into "false" consciousness is objective; it is the class situation itself. It is the objective result of the economic set-up, and is neither arbitrary, subjective nor psychological.'[15] We have here, then, yet another definition of ideology, as 'structurally constrained thought', which runs back at least as far as Marx's 'The Eighteenth Brumaire of Louis Bonaparte'. In a discussion in that text of what makes certain French politicians representatives of the petty bourgeoisie, Marx comments that it is 'the fact that in their minds they do not get beyond the limits which the [petty bourgeoisie] does not get beyond in life'. False consciousness is thus a kind of thought which finds itself baffled and thwarted by certain barriers in society rather than in the mind; and only by transforming society itself could it therefore be dissolved.

One can put this point in another way. There are certain kinds of error which result simply from lapses of intelligence or information, and which can be resolved by a further refinement of thought. But when we keep running up against a limit to our conceptions which stubbornly refuses to give way, then this obstruction may be symptomatic of some 'limit' built into our social life. In this situation, no amount of intelligence or ingenuity, no mere 'evolution of ideas', will serve to get us further forward, for what is awry here is the whole cast and frame of our consciousness, conditioned as it is by certain material constraints. Our social practices pose the obstacle to the very ideas which seek to explain them; and if we want to advance those ideas, we will have to change our forms of life. It is precisely this which Marx argues of the bourgeois political economists, whose searching theoretical inquiries find themselves continually rebuffed by problems which mark the inscription on the interior of their discourse of the social conditions surrounding it.

It is thus that Lukács can write of bourgeois ideology as 'something which is *subjectively* justified in the social and historical situation, as something which can and should be understood, i.e. as "right". At the same time, *objectively*, it by-passes the essence of the evolution of society and fails to pinpoint and express it adequately.'[16] Ideology is now a long way from being some mere illusion; and the same is true if one reverses these terms 'objective' and 'subjective'. For one might equally claim, so Lukács remarks, that bourgeois ideology fails 'subjectively' to achieve its self-appointed goals (freedom, justice, and so on), but exactly in so failing helps to further certain objective aims of which it is ignorant. By which he means, presumably, helping to promote the historical conditions which will finally bring socialism to power. Such class consciousness involves an *un*consciousness of one's true social conditions, and is thus a kind of self-deception; but whereas Engels, as we have seen, tended to dismiss the conscious motivation involved here as sheer illusion, Lukács is prepared to accord it a certain limited truth. 'Despite all its objective falseness,' he writes, 'the self-deceiving "false" consciousness that we find in the bourgeoisie is at least in accord with its class situation.'[17] Bourgeois ideology may be false from the standpoint of some putative social totality, but this does not mean that it is false to the situation as it currently is.

This way of putting the point may perhaps help to make some sense of the otherwise puzzling notion of ideology as thought true to a false situation. For what seems spurious about this formulation is the very idea that a *situation* might be said to be false. Statements about deep-sea diving may be true or false, but not deep-sea diving itself. As a Marxist humanist, however, Lukács himself has a kind of answer to this problem. A 'false' situation for him is one in which the human 'essence' – the full potential of those powers which humanity has historically developed – is being unnecessarily blocked and estranged; and such judgements are thus always made from the standpoint of some possible and desirable future. A false situation can be identified only subjunctively or retrospectively, from the vantage point of what *might* be possible were these thwarting, alienating forces to be abolished. But this does not mean taking one's stand in the empty space of some speculative future, in the manner of 'bad' utopianism; for in Lukács's view, and indeed in the view of Marxism in general, the outline of that desirable future can already be detected in certain potentialities stirring within the present. The present is thus not identical with itself: there is that within it which points beyond it, as indeed the shape of every historical present is structured by its anticipation of a possible future.

If the critique of ideology sets out to examine the social foundations of thought, then it must logically be able to give some account of its own historical origins. What was the material history which gave rise to the notion of ideology itself? Can the study of ideology round upon its own conditions of possibility?

The concept of ideology, it can be argued, arose at the historical point where systems of ideas first became aware of their own partiality; and this came about when those ideas were forced to encounter alien or alternative forms of discourse. It was with the rise of bourgeois society, above all, that the scene was set for this occurrence. For it is characteristic of that society, as Marx noted, that everything about it, including its forms of consciousness, is in a state of ceaseless flux, in contrast to some more tradition-bound social order. Capitalism survives only by a restless development of the productive forces; and in this agitated social condition new ideas tumble upon one another's heels as dizzyingly as do fashions in commodities. The entrenched authority of any single world-view is accordingly undermined by the very nature of capitalism itself. Moreover, such a social order breeds plurality and fragmentation as surely as it generates social deprivation, transgressing time-hallowed boundaries between diverse forms of life and pitching them together in a *mêlée* of idioms, ethnic origins, lifestyles, national cultures. It is exactly this which the Soviet critic Mikhail Bakhtin means by 'polyphony'. Within this atomized space, marked by a proliferating division of intellectual labour, a variety of creeds, doctrines and modes of perception jostle for authority; and this thought should give pause to those postmodern theorists for whom difference, plurality and heterogeneity are unequivocally 'progressive'. Within this turmoil of competing creeds, any particular belief system will find itself wedged cheek by jowl with unwelcome competitors; and its own frontiers will thus be thrown into sharp relief. The stage is then set for the growth of philosophical scepticism and relativism – for the conviction that, within the unseemly hubbub of the intellectual marketplace, no single way of thinking can claim more validity than any other. If all thought is partial and partisan, then all thought is 'ideological'.

In a striking paradox, then, the very dynamism and mutability of the capitalist system threaten to cut the authoritative ground from under its own feet; and this is perhaps most obvious in the phenomenon of imperialism. Imperialism needs to assert the absolute truth of its own values at exactly the point where those values are confronting alien cultures; and this can prove a notably disorientating experience. It is hard to remain convinced that your own way of doing things is the only possible one when you are busy trying to subjugate another society which conducts its affairs in a radically different but apparently effective way. The fiction of Joseph Conrad turns on this disabling contradiction. In this as in other ways, then, the historical emergence of the concept of ideology testifies to a corrosive anxiety – to the embarrassed awareness that your own truths strike you as plausible only because of where you happen to be standing at the time.

The modern bourgeoisie is accordingly caught in something of a cleft stick. Unable to retreat to old-style metaphysical certainties, it is equally loath to embrace a full-blooded scepticism which would simply subvert the legitimacy of its power. One early-twentieth-century attempt to negotiate this dilemma is Karl Mannheim's *Ideology and Utopia* (1929), written under the influence of Lukács's historicism in the political tumult of the Weimar republic. Mannheim sees well enough that with the rise of middle-class society the old monological world-view of the traditional order has disappeared for ever. An authoritarian priestly and political caste, which once confidently monopolized knowledge, has now yielded ground to a 'free' intelligentsia, caught on the hop between conflicting theoretical perspectives. The aim of a 'sociology of knowledge' will thus be to spurn all transcendental truths and examine the social determinants of particular belief systems, while guarding at the same time against the disabling relativism which would level all these beliefs to one. The problem, as Mannheim is uneasily aware, is that any criticism of another's views as ideological is always susceptible to a swift *tu quoque*. In pulling the rug out from beneath one's intellectual antagonist, one is always in danger of pulling it out from beneath oneself.

Against such relativism, Mannheim speaks up for what he calls 'relationism', meaning the location of ideas within the social system which gives birth to them. Such an inquiry into the social basis of thought, he considers, need not run counter to the goal of objectivity; for though ideas are internally shaped by their social origins, their truth value is not reducible to them. The inevitable one-sidedness of any particular standpoint can be corrected by synthesizing it with its rivals, thus building up a provisional, dynamic totality of thought. At the same time, by a process of self-monitoring, we can come to appreciate the limits of our own perspective, and so attain a restricted sort of objectivity. Mannheim thus emerges as the Matthew Arnold of Weimar Germany, concerned to see life steadily and see it whole. Blinkered ideological viewpoints will be patiently subsumed into some greater totality by those dispassionate enough to do so – which is to say, by 'free' intellectuals with a remarkable resemblance to Karl Mannheim. The only problem with this approach is that it merely pushes the question of relativism back a stage; for we can always ask about the tendentious standpoint from which this synthesis is actually launched. Isn't the interest in totality just another interest?

Such a sociology of knowledge is for Mannheim a welcome alternative to the older style of ideology critique. Such critique, in his view, is essentially a matter of *unmasking* one's antagonist's notions, exposing them as lies, deceptions or illusions fuelled by conscious or unconscious social motivations. Ideology critique, in short, is here reduced to what Paul Ricoeur would call a 'hermeneutic of suspicion', and is plainly inadequate for the subtler, more ambitious task of eliciting the whole 'mental structure' which underlies a group's prejudices and beliefs. Ideology pertains only to specific deceptive assertions, whose roots, so Mannheim at one point argues, may be traced to the psychology of particular individuals. That this is something of a straw target of ideology is surely clear: Mannheim pays scant regard to such theories as the fetishism of commodities, where deception, far from springing from psychologistic sources, is seen as generated by an entire social structure.

The ideological function of the 'sociology of knowledge' is in fact to defuse the whole Marxist conception of ideology, replacing it with the less embattled, contentious conception of a 'world-view'. Mannheim, to be sure, does not believe that such world-views can ever be non-evaluatively analysed; but the drift of his work is to downplay concepts of mystification, rationalization and the power-function of ideas in the name of some synoptic survey of the evolution of forms of historical consciousness. In a sense, then, this post-Marxist approach to ideology returns to a *pre*-Marxist view of it, as simply 'socially determined thought'. And since this applies to any thought whatsoever, there is a danger of the concept of ideology cancelling all the way through.

In so far as Mannheim *does* retain the concept of ideology, he does so in a singularly unilluminating way. As a historicist, truth for Mannheim means ideas adequate to a particular stage of historical development; and ideology then signifies a body of beliefs incongruous with its epoch, out of sync with what the age demands. Conversely, 'Utopia' denotes ideas ahead of their time and so similarly discrepant with social reality, but capable none the less of shattering the structures of the present and transgressing its frontiers. Ideology, in short, is antiquated belief, a set of obsolescent myths, norms and ideals unhinged from the real; Utopia is premature and unreal, but should be reserved as a term for those conceptual prefigurations which really do succeed in realizing a new social order. Ideology emerges in this light as a kind of failed Utopia, unable to enter upon material existence; and this definition of it then simply throws us back to the patently insufficient early Marxian notion of ideology as ineffectual otherworldliness. Mannheim would appear to lack all sense of ideologies as forms of consciousness often all too well adapted to current social requirements, productively entwined with historical reality, able to organize practical social activity in highly effective ways. In his denigration of Utopia, which is similarly a 'distortion of reality', he is simply blinded to the ways in which what 'the age demands' may be precisely a thought which moves beyond it. 'Thought', he remarks, 'should contain neither less nor more than the reality in whose medium it operates'[18] – an identification of the concept with its object which Theodor Adorno, ironically enough, will denounce as the very essence of ideological thought.

In the end, Mannheim either stretches the term ideology beyond all serviceable use, equating it with the social determination of any belief whatsoever, or unduly narrows it to specific acts of deception. He fails to grasp that ideology cannot be synonymous with partial or perspectival thinking – for of what thinking is this not true? If the concept is not to be entirely vacuous it must have rather more specific connotations of power struggle and legitimation, structural dissemblance and mystification. What he does usefully suggest, however, is a third way between those who would hold that the truth or falsity of statements is sublimely untainted by their social genesis, and those who would abruptly reduce the former to the latter. For Michel Foucault, it would seem that the truth value of a proposition is entirely a matter of its social function, a reflex of the power interests it promotes. As the linguists might say, what is enunciated is wholly collapsible to the conditions of the enunciation; what matters is not so much what is said, but who says it to whom for what purposes. What this overlooks is that, while enunciations are certainly not independent of their social conditions, a statement such as 'Eskimos are, generally speaking, just as good as anyone else' is true no matter who says it for what end; and one of the important features of a claim such as 'Men are superior to women' is that, whatever power interests it may be promoting, it is also, as a matter of fact, false.

[. . .]

The key category in the writing of Lukács's Western Marxist colleague Antonio Gramsci is not ideology but *hegemony*; and it is worth pondering the distinction between these two terms. Gramsci normally uses the word hegemony to mean the ways in which a governing power wins consent to its rule from those it subjugates – though it is true that he occasionally uses the term to cover both consent and coercion together. There is thus an immediate difference from the concept of ideology, since it is clear that ideologies may be forcibly imposed. Think, for example, of the workings of racist ideology in South Africa. But hegemony is also a broader category than ideology: it *includes*

ideology, but is not reducible to it. A ruling group or class may secure
consent to its power by ideological means; but it may also do so, by, say,
altering the tax system in ways favourable to groups whose support it
needs, or creating a layer of relatively affluent, and thus somewhat
politically quiescent, workers. Or hegemony may take political rather
than economic forms: the parliamentary system in Western democracies is a crucial aspect of such power, since it fosters the illusion of
self-government on the part of the populace. What uniquely distinguishes the political form of such societies is that the people are
supposed to believe that they govern themselves, a belief which no slave
of antiquity or medieval serf was expected to entertain. Indeed, Perry
Anderson goes so far as to describe the parliamentary system as 'the
hub of the ideological apparatus of capitalism', to which such institutions as the media, churches and political parties play a critical but
complementary role. It is for this reason, as Anderson points out, that
Gramsci is mistaken when he locates hegemony in 'civil society' alone,
rather than in the state, for the political form of the capitalist state is
itself a vital organ of such power.[19]

    Another powerful source of political hegemony is the supposed
neutrality of the bourgeois state. This is not, in fact, simply an
ideological illusion. In capitalist society, political power is indeed
relatively autonomous of social and economic life, as opposed to the
political set-up in pre-capitalist formations. In feudal regimes, for
example, the nobility who economically exploit the peasantry also
exercise certain political, cultural and juridical functions in their lives,
so that the relation between economic and political power is here more
visible. Under capitalism, economic life is not subject to such continuous political supervision: as Marx comments, it is the 'dull compulsion
of the economic', the need simply to survive, which keeps men and
women at work, divorced from any framework of political obligations,
religious sanctions or customary responsibilities. It is as though in this
form of life the economy comes to operate 'all by itself', and the political
state can thus take something of a back seat, sustaining the general
structures within which this economic activity is conducted. This is the
real material basis of the belief that the bourgeois state is supremely
disinterested, holding the ring between contending social forces; and
in this sense, once again, hegemony is built into its very nature.

    Hegemony, then, is not just some successful kind of ideology, but
may be discriminated into its various ideological, cultural, political and
economic aspects. Ideology refers specifically to the way power
struggles are fought out at the level of signification; and though such
signification is involved in all hegemonic processes, it is not in all cases
the *dominant* level by which rule is sustained. Singing the National

Anthem comes as close to a 'purely' ideological activity as one could imagine; it would certainly seem to fulfil no other purpose, aside perhaps from annoying the neighbours. Religion, similarly, is probably the most purely ideological of the various institutions of civil society. But hegemony is also carried in cultural, political and economic forms – in non-discursive practices as well as in rhetorical utterances.

With certain notable inconsistencies, Gramsci associates hegemony with the arena of 'civil society', by which he means the whole range of institutions intermediate between state and economy. Privately owned television stations, the family, the Boy Scout movement, the Methodist Church, infant schools, the British Legion, the *Sun* newspaper: all of these would count as hegemonic apparatuses, which bind individuals to the ruling power by consent rather than by coercion. Coercion, by contrast, is reserved to the state, which has a monopoly on 'legitimate' violence. (We should note, however, that the coercive institutions of a society – armies, law courts and the rest – must themselves win a general consent from the people if they are to operate effectively, so that the opposition between coercion and consent can be to some extent deconstructed.) In modern capitalist regimes, civil society has come to assume a formidable power, in contrast to the days when the Bolsheviks, living in a society poor in such institutions, could seize the reins of government by a frontal attack on the state itself. The concept of hegemony thus belongs with the question: How is the working class to take power in a social formation where the dominant power is subtly, pervasively diffused throughout habitual daily practices, intimately interwoven with 'culture' itself, inscribed in the very texture of our experience from nursery school to funeral parlour? How do we combat a power which has become the 'common sense' of a whole social order, rather than one which is widely perceived as alien and oppressive?

[. . .]

If the concept of hegemony extends and enriches the notion of ideology, it also lends this otherwise somewhat abstract term a material body and political cutting edge. It is with Gramsci that the crucial transition is effected from ideology as 'systems of ideas' to ideology as lived, habitual social practice – which must then presumably encompass the unconscious, inarticulate dimensions of social experience as well as the workings of formal institutions. Louis Althusser, for whom ideology is largely unconscious and always institutional, will inherit both of these emphases; and hegemony as a 'lived' process of political domination comes close in some of its aspects to what Raymond Williams calls a 'structure of feeling'. In his own discussion of Gramsci, Williams acknowledges the *dynamic* character of hegemony, as against the potentially static connotations of 'ideology': hegemony is

never a once-and-for-all achievement, but 'has continually to be
renewed, recreated, defended, and modified'.[20] As a concept, then,
hegemony is inseparable from overtones of struggle, as ideology
perhaps is not. No single mode of hegemony, so Williams argues, can
exhaust the meanings and values of any society; and any governing
power is thus forced to engage with counter-hegemonic forces in ways
which prove partly constitutive of its own rule. Hegemony is thus an
inherently relational, as well as practical and dynamic, notion; and it
offers in this sense a signal advance on some of the more ossified,
scholastic definitions of ideology to be found in certain 'vulgar'
currents of Marxism.

Very roughly, then, we might define hegemony as a whole range of
practical strategies by which a dominant power elicits consent to its rule
from those its subjugates. To win hegemony, in Gramsci's view, is to
establish moral, political and intellectual leadership in social life by
diffusing one's own 'world-view' throughout the fabric of society as a
whole, thus equating one's own interests with the interests of society at
large. Such consensual rule is not, of course, peculiar to capitalism;
indeed one might claim that *any* form of political power, to be durable
and well-grounded, must evoke at least a degree of consent from its
underlings. But there are good reasons to believe that in capitalist
society in particular, the ratio between consent and coercion shifts
decisively towards the former. In such conditions, the power of the
state to discipline and punish – what Gramsci terms 'domination' –
remains firmly in place, and indeed in modern societies grows more
formidable as the various technologies of oppression begin to pro-
liferate. But the institutions of 'civil society' – schools, families,
churches, media and the rest – now play a more central role in the
processes of social control. The bourgeois state will resort to direct
violence if it is forced to it; but in doing so it risks suffering a drastic loss
of ideological credibility. It is preferable on the whole for power to
remain conveniently invisible, disseminated throughout the texture of
social life and thus 'naturalized' as custom, habit, spontaneous practice.
Once power nakedly reveals its hand, it can become an object of
political contestation.[21]

[. . .]

In his *Prison Notebooks*, Gramsci rejects out of hand any purely negative
use of the term ideology. This 'bad' sense of the term has become
widespread, he remarks, 'with the effect that the theoretical analysis of
the concept of ideology has been modified and denatured'.[22] Ideology
has been too often seen as pure appearance or mere obtuseness,
whereas a distinction must in fact be drawn between 'historically
organic' ideologies – meaning those necessary to a given social

structure – and ideology in the sense of the arbitrary speculations of individuals. This parallels to some extent the opposition we have observed elsewhere between 'ideology' and 'world-view', though we should note that for Marx himself the negative sense of ideology was by no means confined to arbitrary subjective speculation. Gramsci also dismisses any economistic reduction of ideology to the mere bad dream of the infrastructure: on the contrary, ideologies must be viewed as actively organizing forces which are psychologically 'valid', fashioning the terrain on which men and women act, struggle and acquire consciousness of their social positions. In any 'historical bloc', Gramsci comments, material forces are the 'content', and ideologies the 'form'.

[. . .]

For Gramsci, the consciousness of subordinated groups in society is typically fissured and uneven. Two conflicting conceptions of the world usually exist in such ideologies, the one drawn from the 'official' notions of the rulers, the other derived from an oppressed people's practical experience of social reality. Such conflicts might take the form of what we have seen earlier as a 'performative contradiction' between what a group or class says, and what it tacitly reveals in its behaviour. But this is not to be seen as mere self-deception: such an explanation, Gramsci thinks, might be adequate in the case of particular individuals, but not in the case of great masses of men and women. These contradictions in thought must have a historical base; and Gramsci locates this in the contrast between the emergent concept of the world which a class displays when it acts as an 'organic totality', and its submission in more 'normal' times to the ideas of those who govern it. One aim of revolutionary practice, then, must be to elaborate and make explicit the potentially creative principles implicit in the practical understanding of the oppressed – to raise these otherwise inchoate, ambiguous elements of its experience to the status of a coherent philosophy or 'world-view'.

[. . .]

To do this, however, means combating much that is negative in the empirical consciousness of the people, to which Gramsci gives the title of 'common sense'. Such common sense is a 'chaotic aggregate of disparate conceptions' – an ambiguous, contradictory zone of experience which is on the whole politically backward. How could we expect it to be otherwise, if a ruling bloc has had centuries in which to perfect its hegemony? In Gramsci's view there is a certain continuum between 'spontaneous' and 'scientific' consciousness, such that the difficulties of the latter should not be intimidatingly overestimated; but there is also a permanent war between revolutionary theory and the mythological or folkloric conceptions of the masses, and the latter is not to be patronizingly romanticized at the expense of the former. Certain 'folk' conceptions, Gramsci holds, do indeed spontaneously reflect important aspects of social life; 'popular consciousness' is not to be dismissed as purely negative, but its more progressive and more reactionary features must instead be carefully distinguished.[23] Popular morality, for example, is partly the fossilized residue of an earlier history, partly 'a range of often creative and progressive innovations . . . which go against, or merely differ from, the morality of the ruling strata of society'.[24] What is needed is not just some paternalist endorsement of existing popular consciousness, but the construction of 'a new common sense and with it a new culture and a new philosophy which will be rooted in the popular consciousness with the same solidity and imperative quality as traditional beliefs'.[25] The function of the organic intellectuals, in other words, is to forge the links between 'theory' and 'ideology', creating a two-way passage between political analysis and popular experience. And the term ideology here 'is used in its highest sense of a conception of the world that is implicitly manifest in art, in law, in economic activity and in all manifestations of individual and collective life.'[26] Such a 'world-view' cements together a social and political bloc, as a unifying, organizing, inspirational principal rather than a system of abstract ideas.

[. . .]

From Adorno to Bourdieu

We have seen how a theory of ideology can be generated from the commodity-form. But at the heart of Marx's economic analysis lies another category also of relevance to ideology, and this is the concept of exchange value. In the first volume of *Capital*, Marx explains how two commodities with quite different 'use values' can be equally exchanged, on the principle that both contain the same amount of abstract labour. If it takes the same quantity of labour-power to produce a Christmas pudding and a toy squirrel, then these products will have the same exchange value, which is to say that the same amount of money can buy them both. But the specific differences between these objects are thereby suppressed, as their use value becomes subordinate to their abstract equivalence.

If this principle reigns in the capitalist economy, it can also be observed at work in the higher reaches of the 'superstructure'. In the political arena of bourgeois society, all men and women are abstractly equal as voters and citizens; but this theoretical equivalence serves to mask their concrete inequalities within 'civil society'. Landlord and tenant, businessman and prostitute, may end up in adjacent polling booths. Much the same is true of the juridical institutions: all individuals are equal before the law, but this merely obscures the way in which the law itself is ultimately on the side of the propertied. Is there, then, some way of tracking this principle of false equivalence even further up the so-called superstructure, into the heady realms of ideology?

For the Frankfurt School Marxist Theodor Adorno, this mechanism of abstract exchange is the very secret of ideology itself. Commodity exchange effects an equation between things which are in fact incommensurable, and so, in Adorno's view, does ideological thought. Such thought is revolted by the sight of 'otherness', of that which threatens to escape its own closed system, and violently reduces it to its own image and likeness. 'If the lion had a consciousness,' Adorno writes in *Negative Dialectics*, 'his rage at the antelope he wants to eat would be ideology.' Indeed Fredric Jameson has suggested that the fundamental gesture of all ideology is exactly such a rigid binary opposition between the self or familiar, which is positively valorized, and the non-self or alien, which is thrust beyond the boundaries of intelligibility.[27] The ethical code of good versus evil, so Jameson considers, is then the most exemplary model of this principle. Ideology for Adorno is thus a form of 'identity-thinking' – a covertly paranoid style of rationality which inexorably transmutes the uniqueness and plurality of things into a mere simulacrum of itself, or expels them beyond its own borders in a panic-stricken act of exclusion.

On this account, the opposite of ideology would be not truth or theory, but difference or heterogeneity. And in this as in other ways, Adorno's thought strikingly prefigures that of the post-structuralists of our own day. In the face of this conceptual straitjacketing, he affirms the essential *non*-identity of thought and reality, the concept and its object. To suppose that the idea of freedom is identical with the poor travesty of it available in the capitalist marketplace is to fail to see that this object does not live up to its concept. Conversely, to imagine that the being of any object can be exhausted by the concept of it is to erase its unique materiality, since concepts are ineluctably general and objects stubbornly particular. Ideology *homogenizes* the world, spuriously equating distinct phenomena; and to undo it thus demands a 'negative dialectics', which strives, perhaps impossibly, to include within thought that which is heterogeneous to it. For Adorno, the highest paradigm of such negative reason is art, which speaks up for the differential and non-identical, promoting the claims of the sensuous particular against the tyranny of some seamless totality.[28]

Identity, then, is in Adorno's eyes the 'primal form' of all ideology. Our reified consciousness reflects a world of objects frozen in their

monotonously selfsame being, and in thus binding us to what *is*, to the
purely 'given', blinds us to the truth that 'what is, is more than it is'.[29] In
contrast with much post-structuralist thinking, however, Adorno
neither uncritically celebrates the notion of difference nor unequivocally denounces the principle of identity. For all its paranoid anxiety,
the identity principle carries with it a frail hope that one day true
reconciliation will come about; and a world of pure differences would
be indistinguishable from one of pure identities. The idea of Utopia
travels beyond both conceptions: it would be, instead, a 'togetherness
in diversity'.[30] The aim of socialism is to liberate the rich diversity of
sensuous use value from the metaphysical prison-house of exchange
value – to emancipate history from the specious equivalences imposed
upon it by ideology and commodity production. 'Reconciliation',
Adorno writes, 'would release the non-identical, would rid it of
coercion, including spiritualized coercion; it would open the road to
the multiplicity of different things and strip dialectics of its power over
them.[31]

How this is to come about, however, is not easy to see. For the critique
of capitalist society demands the use of analytic reason; and such
reason would seem for Adorno, at least in some of his moods,
intrinsically oppressive and reificatory. Indeed, logic itself, which Marx
once described as a 'currency of the mind', is a kind of generalized
barter or false equalization of concepts analogous to the exchanges of
the marketplace. A dominative rationality, then, can be unlocked only
with concepts already irredeemably contaminated by it; and this
proposition itself, since it obeys the rules of analytic reason, must
already be on the side of dominion. In *Dialectic of Enlightenment* (1947),
co-authored by Adorno and his colleague Max Horkheimer, reason
has become inherently violent and manipulative, riding roughshod
over the sensuous particularities of Nature and the body. Simply to
think is to be guiltily complicit with ideological domination; yet to
surrender instrumental thought altogether would be to lapse into
barbarous irrationalism.

The identity principle strives to suppress all contradiction, and for
Adorno this process has been brought to perfection in the reified,
bureaucratized, administered world of advanced capitalism. Much the
same bleak vision is projected by Adorno's Frankfurt School colleague
Herbert Marcuse, in his *One-Dimensional Man* (1964). Ideology, in
short, is a 'totalitarian' system which has managed and processed all
social conflict out of existence. It is not only that this thesis would come
as something of a surprise to those who actually run the Western
system; it is also that it parodies the whole notion of ideology itself. The
Frankfurt School of Marxism, several of whose members were

refugees from Nazism, simply projects the 'extreme' ideological universe of Fascism on to the quite different structures of liberal capitalist regimes. Does *all* ideology work by the identity principle, ruthlessly expunging whatever is heterogeneous to it? What, for example, of the ideology of liberal humanism, which, in however specious and restricted a fashion, is able to make room for variousness, plurality, cultural relativity, concrete particularity? Adorno and his fellow workers deliver us something of a straw target of ideology, in the manner of those post-structuralist theorists for whom all ideology without exception would appear to turn upon metaphysical absolutes and transcendental foundations. The real ideological conditions of Western capitalist societies are surely a good deal more mixed and self-contradictory, blending 'metaphysical' and pluralistic discourses in various measures. An opposition to monotonous self-identity ('It takes all kinds to make a world'); a suspicion of absolute truth claims ('Everyone's entitled to their point of view'); a rejection of reductive stereotypes ('I take people as I find them'); a celebration of difference ('It'd be a strange world if we all thought the same'): these are part of the stock in trade of popular Western wisdom, and nothing is to be politically gained by caricaturing one's antagonist. Simply to counterpose difference to identity, plurality to unity, the marginal to the central, is to lapse back into binary opposition, as the more subtle deconstructors are perfectly aware. It is pure formalism to imagine that otherness, heterogeneity and marginality are unqualified political benefits regardless of their concrete social content. Adorno, as we have seen, is not out simply to replace identity with difference; but his suggestive critique of the tyranny of equivalence leads him too often to 'demonize' modern capitalism as a seamless, pacified, self-regulating system. This, no doubt, is what the system would *like* to be told; but it would probably be greeted with a certain scepticism in the corridors of Whitehall and Wall Street.

The later Frankfurt School philosopher Jürgen Habermas follows Adorno in dismissing the concept of a Marxist science, and in refusing to assign any particular privilege to the consciousness of the revolutionary proletariat. But whereas Adorno is then left with little to pit against the system but art and negative dialectics, Habermas turns instead to the resources of communicative language. Ideology for him is a form of communication systematically distorted by power – a discourse which has become a medium of domination, and which serves to legitimate relations of organized force. For hermeneutical philosophers like Hans-Georg Gadamer, misunderstandings and lapses of

communication are textual blockages to be rectified by sensitive interpretation. Habermas, by contrast, draws attention to the possibility of
an entire discursive system which is somehow deformed. What warps
such discourse out of true is the impact upon it of extra-discursive
forces: ideology marks the point at which language is bent out of
communicative shape by the power interests which impinge upon it.
But this besieging of language by power is not just an external matter:
on the contrary, such dominion inscribes itself on the inside of our
speech, so that ideology becomes a set of effects internal to particular
discourses themselves.

If a communicative structure is *systematically* distorted, then it will
tend to present the appearance of normativity and justness. A distortion which is so pervasive tends to cancel all the way through and
disappear from sight – just as we would not describe as a deviation or
disability a condition in which everybody limped or dropped their
aitches all the time. A systematically deformed network of communication thus tends to conceal or eradicate the very norms by which it
might be judged to *be* deformed, and so becomes peculiarly invulner-
able to critique. In this situation, it becomes impossible to raise *within*
the network the question of its own workings or conditions of possibility, since it has, so to speak, confiscated these inquiries from the
outset. The system's historical conditions of possibility are redefined
by the system itself, thus evaporating into it. In the case of a 'successful' ideology, it is not as though one body of ideas is perceived to be
more powerful, legitimate or persuasive than another, but that the
very grounds for choosing rationally between them have been deftly
removed, so that it becomes impossible to think or desire outside the
terms of the system itself. Such an ideological formation curves back
upon itself like cosmic space, denying the possibility of any 'outside',
forestalling the generation of new desires as well as frustrating those
we already have. If a 'universe of discourse' is truly a *universe*, then
there is no standpoint beyond it where we might find a point of
leverage for critique. Or if other universes are acknowledged to exist,
then they are simply defined as incommensurable with one's own.

Habermas, to his credit, subscribes to no such fantastic dystopian
vision of an all-powerful, all-absorbent ideology. If ideology is language wrenched out of true, then we must presumably have some
idea of what an 'authentic' communicative act would like like. There
is, as we have noted, no appeal open for him to some scientific metalanguage which would adjudicate in this respect among competing
idioms; so he must seek instead to extract from our linguistic practices
the structure of some underlying 'communicative rationality' – some
'ideal speech situation' which glimmers faintly through our actual

debased discourses, and which may therefore furnish a norm or regulative model for the critical assessment of them.[32]

The ideal speech situation would be one entirely free of domination, in which all participants would have symmetrically equal chances to select and deploy speech acts. Persuasion would depend on the force of the better argument alone, not on rhetoric, authority, coercive sanctions, and so on. This model is no more than a heuristic device or necessary fiction, but it is in some sense implicit even so in our ordinary, unregenerate verbal dealings. All language, even of a dominative kind, is in Habermas's view inherently orientated to communication, and thus tacitly towards human consensus: even when I curse you I expect to be understood, otherwise why should I waste my breath? Our most despotic speech acts betray, despite themselves, the frail outlines of a communicative *rationality*: in making an utterance a speaker implicitly claims that what she says is intelligible, true, sincere and appropriate to the discursive situation. (Quite how this applies to such speech acts as jokes, poems and shouts of glee is not so apparent.) There is, in other words, a kind of 'deep' rationality built into the very structures of our language, regardless of what we actually say; and it is this which provides Habermas with the basis for a critique of our actual verbal practices. In a curious sense, the very *act* of enunciation can become a normative judgement on what is enunciated.

Habermas holds to a 'consensus' rather than 'correspondence' theory of truth, which is to say that he thinks truth less some adequation between mind and world than a question of the kind of assertion which everyone who could enter into unconstrained dialogue with the speaker would come to accept. But social and ideological domination currently prohibit such unconstrained communication; and until we can transform this situation (which for Habermas would mean fashioning a participatory socialist democracy), truth is bound to be, as it were, deferred. If we want to know the truth, we have to change our political form of life. Truth is thus deeply bound up with social justice: my truth claims refer themselves forward to some altered social condition where they might be 'redeemed'. It is thus that Habermas is able to observe that 'the truth of statements is linked in the last analysis to the intention of the good and the true life'.[33]

There is an important difference between this style of thought and that of the more senior members of the Frankfurt School. For them, as we have seen, society as it exists seems wholly reified and degraded, sinisterly successful in its capacity to 'administer' contradictions out of existence. This gloomy vision does not prevent them from discerning some ideal alternative to it, of the kind that Adorno discovers in modernist art; but it is an alternative with scant foundation in the given social order. It is less a dialectical function of that order than a 'solution' parachuted in from some ontological outer space. It thus figures as a form of 'bad' Utopianism, as opposed to that 'good' Utopianism which seeks somehow to anchor what is desirable in what is actual. A degraded present must be patiently scanned for those tendencies which are at once indissolubly bound up with it, yet which – interpreted in a certain way – may be seen to point beyond it. So it is that Marxism, for example, is not just some kind of wishful thinking, but an attempt to discover an alternative to capitalism latent in the very dynamic of that form of life. In order to resolve its structural contradictions, the capitalist order would *have* to transcend itself into socialism; it is not simply a matter of believing that it would be pleasant for it to do so. The idea of a communicative rationality is another way of securing an internal bond between present and future, and so, like Marxism itself, is a form of 'immanent' critique. Rather than passing judgement on the present from the Olympian height of some absolute truth, it installs itself *within* the present in order to decipher those fault lines where the ruling social logic presses up against its own structural limits, and so could potentially surpass itself. There is a clear parallel between such immanent critique and what is nowadays known as deconstruction, which seeks similarly to occupy a system from the inside in order to expose those points of impasse or indeterminacy where its governing conventions begin to unravel.

Habermas has often enough been accused of being a rationalist, and there is no doubt some justice in the charge. How far is it really possible, for example, to disentangle the 'force of the better argument' from the rhetorical devices by which it is conveyed, the subject positions at stake, the play of power and desire which will mould such utterances from within? But if a rationalist is one who opposes some sublimely disinterested truth to mere sectoral interests, then Habermas is certainly not of this company. On the contrary, truth and knowledge are for him 'interested' to their roots. We need types of instrumental knowledge because we need to control our environment in the interests of survival. Similarly, we need the sort of moral or political knowledge attainable in practical communication because without it there could be no collective social life at all. 'I believe that I can show', Habermas remarks, 'that a species that depends for its survival on the structures of linguistic communication and cooperative, purposive-rational action must *of necessity* rely on reason'.[34] Reasoning, in short, is in our interests, grounded in the kind of biological species we are. Otherwise why would we bother to find out anything at all? Such 'species-specific' interests move, naturally, at a highly abstract level, and will tell us little about whether we should vote Tory to keep the rates down. But as with communicative rationality, they can serve even so as a political norm; ideological interests which damage the structures of practical communication can be judged inimical to our interests as a whole. As Thomas McCarthy puts it, we have a practical interest in 'securing and expanding possibilities of mutual and self-understanding in the conduct of life',[35] so that a kind of politics is derivable from the sort of animals we are. Interests are *constitutive* of our knowledge, not just (as the Enlightenment believed) obstacles in its path. But this is not to deny that there are kinds of interest which threaten our fundamental requirements as a species, and these are what Habermas terms 'ideological'.

The opposite of ideology for Habermas is not exactly truth or knowledge, but that particular form of 'interested' rationality we call *emancipatory critique*. It is in our interests to rid ourselves of unnecessary constraints on our common dialogue, for unless we do, the kinds of truths we need to establish will be beyond our reach. An emancipatory critique is one which brings these institutional constraints to our awareness, and this can be achieved only by the practice of collective self-reflection. There are certain forms of knowledge that we need at all costs in order to be free; and an emancipatory critique such as Marxism or Freudianism is simply whatever form of knowledge this currently happens to be. In this kind of discourse, 'fact' (cognition) and 'value' (or interest) are not really separable: the patient in psychoanalysis, for example, has an interest in embarking on a process of self-reflection because without this style of cognition he will remain imprisoned in neurosis or psychosis. In a parallel way, an oppressed group or class, as we have seen in the thought of Lukács, has an interest in getting to understand its social situation, since without this self-knowledge it will remain a victim of it.

This analogy may be pursued a little further. Dominative social institutions are for Habermas somewhat akin to neurotic patterns of behaviour, since they rigidify human life into a compulsive set of norms and thus block the path to critical self-reflection. In both cases we become dependent on hypostasized powers, subject to constraints which are in fact cultural but which bear in upon us with all the inexorability of natural forces. The gratificatory instincts which such institutions thwart are then either driven underground, in the phenomenon Freud dubs 'repression', or sublimated into metaphysical world-views, ideal value systems of one kind or another, which help to console and compensate individuals for the real-life restrictions they must endure. These value systems thus serve to legitimate the social order, channelling potential dissidence into illusory forms; and this, in a nutshell, is the Freudian theory of ideology. Habermas, like Freud himself, is at pains to emphasize that these idealized world-views are not *just* illusions: however distortedly, they lend voice to genuine human desires, and thus conceal a Utopian core. What we can now only dream of might always be realized in some emancipated future, as technological development liberates individuals from the compulsion of labour.

Habermas regards psychoanalysis as a discourse which seeks to emancipate us from systematically distorted communication, and so as sharing common ground with the critique of ideology. Pathological be-haviour, in which our words belie our actions, is thus roughly equiv-alent to ideology's 'performative contradictions'. Just as the neurotic may vehemently deny a wish which nevertheless manifests itself in sym-bolic form on the body, so a ruling class may proclaim its belief in liberty while obstructing it in practice. To interpret these deformed discourses means not just translating them into other terms, but recon-structing their conditions of possibility and accounting for what Haber-mas calls 'the genetic conditions of the unmeaning'.[36] It is not enough, in other words, to unscramble a distorted text: we need, rather, to ex-plain the causes of the textual distortion itself. As Habermas puts the point, with unwonted pithiness: 'The mutilations [of the text] have meaning as such.'[37] It is not just a question of deciphering a language accidentally afflicted with slippages, ambiguities and non-meanings; it is, rather, a matter of explaining the forces at work of which these tex-tual obscurities are a necessary effect. 'The breaks in the text', Haber-mas writes, 'are places where an interpretation has forcibly prevailed that is ego-alien even though it is produced by the self. . . . The result is that the ego necessarily deceives itself about its identity in the symbolic structures that it consciously produces.'[38]

To analyse a form of systematically distorted communication, whether dream or ideology, is thus to reveal how its lacunae, repetitions, elisions and equivocations are themselves significant. As Marx puts the point in *Theories of Surplus Value*: 'Adam Smith's contradictions are of significance because they contain problems which it is true he does not resolve, but which he reveals by contradicting himself'.[39] If we can lay bare the social conditions which 'force' a particular discourse into certain deceptions and disguises, we can equally examine the repressed desires which introduce distortions into the behaviour of a neurotic patient, or into the text of a dream. Both psychoanalysis and 'ideology critique', in other words, focus upon the points where *meaning* and *force* intersect. In social life, a mere attention to meaning, as in hermeneutics, will fail to show up the concealed power interests by which these meanings are internally moulded. In psychical life, a mere concentration on what Freud calls the 'manifest content' of the dream will blind us to the 'dream-work' itself, where the forces of the unconscious are most stealthily operative. Both dream and ideology are in this sense 'doubled' texts, conjunctures of signs and power; so that to accept an ideology at face value would be like falling for what Freud terms 'secondary revision', the more or less coherent version of the dream text that the dreamer delivers when she wakes. In both cases, *what* is produced must be grasped in terms of its conditions of production; and to this extent Freud's own argument has much in common with *The German Ideology*. If dreams cloak unconscious motivations in symbolic guise, then so do ideological texts.

This suggests a further analogy between psychoanalysis and the study of ideology, which Habermas himself does not adequately explore. Freud describes the neurotic symptom as a 'compromise formation', since within its structure two antagonistic forces uneasily coexist. On the one hand there is the unconscious wish which seeks expression; on the other hand there is the censorious power of the ego, which strives to thrust this wish back into the unconscious. The neurotic symptom, like the dream text, thus reveals and conceals at once. But so also, one might claim, do dominant ideologies, which are not to be reduced to mere 'disguises'. The middle-class ideology of liberty and individual autonomy is no mere fiction: on the contrary, it signified in its time a real political victory over a brutally repressive feudalism. At the same time, however, it serves to mask the genuine oppressiveness of bourgeois society. The 'truth' of such ideology, as with the neurotic symptom, lies in neither the revelation nor the concealment alone, but in the contradictory unity they compose. It is not just a matter of stripping off some outer disguise to expose the truth, any more than an individual's self-deception is just a 'guise' he assumes. It is, rather, that what is revealed takes place in terms of what is concealed, and vice versa.

Marxists often speak of 'ideological contradictions', as well as of 'contradictions in reality' (though whether this latter way of talking makes much sense is a bone of contention amongst them). It might then be thought that ideological contradictions somehow 'reflect' or 'correspond to' contradictions in society itself. But the situation is in fact more complex than this suggests. Let us assume that there is a 'real' contradiction in capitalist society between bourgeois freedom and its oppressive effects. The ideological discourse of bourgeois liberty might also be said to be contradictory; but this is not exactly because it reproduces the 'real' contradiction in question. Rather, the ideology will tend to represent what is positive about such liberty, while masking, repressing or displacing its odious corollaries; and this masking or repressing work, as with the neurotic symptom, is likely to interfere from the inside with what gets genuinely articulated. One might claim, then, that the ambiguous, self-contradictory nature of the ideology springs precisely from its *not* authentically reproducing the real contradiction; indeed were it really to do so, we might hesitate about whether to term this discourse 'ideological' at all.

There is a final parallel between ideology and psychical disturbance which we may briefly examine. A neurotic pattern of behaviour, in Freud's view, is not simply *expressive* of some underlying problem, but is actually a way of trying to cope with it. It is thus that Freud can speak of neurosis as the confused glimmerings of a kind of solution to whatever is awry. Neurotic behaviour is a *strategy* for tackling, encompassing and 'resolving' genuine conflicts, even if it resolves them in an imaginary way. The behaviour is not just a passive reflex of this conflict, but an active, if mystified, form of engagement with it. Just the same can be said of ideologies, which are no mere inert by-products of social contradictions but resourceful strategies for containing, managing and imaginarily resolving them. Étienne Balibar and Pierre Macherey have argued that works of literature do not simply 'take' ideological contradictions, in the raw, as it were, and set about lending them some factitious symbolic resolution. If such resolutions are possible, it is because the contradictions in question have already been surreptitiously processed and transformed, so as to appear in the literary work *in the form of* their potential dissolution.[40] The point may be applied to ideological discourse as such, which *works* upon the conflicts it seeks to negotiate, 'softening', masking and displacing them as the dream-work modifies and transmutes the 'latent contents' of the dream itself. One might therefore attribute to the language of ideology something of the devices employed by the unconscious, in their respective labour upon their 'raw materials': condensation, displacement, elision, transfer of affect, considerations of symbolic representability, and so on. And the aim of this labour in both cases is to recast a problem in the form of its potential solution.

Any parallel between psychoanalysis and the critique of ideology must necessarily be imperfect. For one thing, Habermas himself tends in rationalist style to downplay the extent to which the psychoanalytic cure comes about less through self-reflection than through the drama of transference between patient and analyst. And it is not easy to think up an exact political analogy to this. For another thing, as Russell Keat has pointed out, the emancipation wrought by psychoanalysis is a matter of remembering or 'working through' repressed materials, whereas ideology is less a question of something we have *forgotten* than of something we never knew in the first place.[41] We may note finally that in Habermas's view the discourse of the neurotic is a kind of privatized symbolic idiom which has become split off from public communication, whereas the 'pathology' of ideological language belongs fully to the public domain. Ideology, as Freud might have said, is a kind of psychopathology of everyday life – a system of distortion so pervasive that it cancels all the way through and presents every appearance of normality.

Unlike Lukács, Theodor Adorno has little time for the notion of reified consciousness, which he suspects as residually idealist. Ideology, for him as for the later Marx, is not first of all a matter of consciousness, but of the material structures of commodity exchange. Habermas, too, regards a primary emphasis on consciousness as belonging to an outmoded 'philosophy of the subject', and turns instead to what he sees as the more fertile ground of social discourse.

    The French Marxist philosopher Louis Althusser is equally wary of the doctrine of reification, though for rather different reasons from Adorno's.[42] In Althusser's eyes, reification, like its companion category of alienation, presupposes some 'human essence' which then undergoes estrangement; and since Althusser is a rigorously 'anti-humanist' Marxist, renouncing all idea of an 'essential humanity', he can hardly found his theory of ideology upon such 'ideological' concepts. Neither, however, can he base it on the alternative notion of a 'world-view'; for if Althusser is anti-humanist he is equally anti-historicist, sceptical of the whole conception of a 'class subject' and firm in his belief that the science of historical materialism is quite independent of class consciousness. What he does, then, is to derive a theory of ideology, of impressive power and originality, from a combination of Lacanian psychoanalysis and the less obviously historicist features of Gramsci's work; and it is this theory that can be found in his celebrated essay 'Ideology and Ideological State Apparatuses', as well as in scattered fragments of his volume For Marx.[43]

    Althusser holds that all thought is conducted within the terms of an unconscious 'problematic' which silently underpins it. A problematic, rather like Michel Foucault's 'episteme', is a particular organization of categories which at any given historical moment constitutes the limits of what we are able to utter and conceive. A problematic is not in itself 'ideological': it includes, for example, the discourses of true science, which for Althusser is free of all ideological taint. But we can speak of the problematic of a specific ideology or set of ideologies; and to do so is to refer to an underlying structure of categories so organized as to exclude the possibility of certain conceptions. An ideological problematic turns around certain eloquent silences and elisions; and it is so constructed that the questions which are posable within it already presuppose certain kinds of answer. Its fundamental structure is thus closed, circular and self-confirming: wherever one moves within it, one will always be ultimately returned to what is securely known, of which what is unknown is merely an extension or a repetition. Ideologies can never be taken by surprise, since like a counsel leading a witness in a law court they signal what would count as an acceptable answer in the very form of their questions. A scientific problematic, by contrast, is characterized by its open-endedness: it can be 'revolutionized' as new scientific objects emerge and a new horizon of questions opens up. Science is an authentically exploratory pursuit, whereas ideologies give the appearance of moving forward while marching stubbornly on the spot.

   In a controversial move within Western Marxism,[44] Althusser insists on a rigorous distinction between 'science' (meaning, among other things, Marxist theory) and 'ideology'. The former is not just to be grasped in historicist style as the 'expression' of the latter; on the contrary, science or theory is a specific kind of labour with its own protocols and procedures, one demarcated from ideology by what Althusser calls an 'epistemological break'. Whereas historicist Marxism holds that theory is validated or invalidated by historical practice, Althusser holds that social theories, rather like mathematics, are verified by methods which are purely internal to them. Theoretical propositions are true or false regardless of who happens to hold them for what historical reasons, and regardless of the historical conditions which give birth to them.

[. . .]

There is a difference between holding that historical circumstances thoroughly condition our knowledge, and believing that the validity of our truth claims is simply *reducible* to our historical interests. The latter case is really that of Friedrich Nietzsche; and though Althusser's own case about knowledge and history is about as far from Nietzsche's as could be imagined, there is an ironic sense in which his major theses about ideology owe something to his influence. For Nietzsche, all human action is a kind of fiction: it presumes some coherent, autonomous human agent (which Nietzsche regards as an illusion); implies that the beliefs and assumptions by which we act are firmly grounded (which for Nietzsche is not the case); and assumes that the effects of our actions can be rationally calculated (in Nietzsche's eyes yet another sad delusion). Action for Nietzsche is an enormous, if necessary, oversimplification of the unfathomable complexity of the world, which thus cannot coexist with reflection. To act at all means to repress or suspend such reflectiveness, to suffer a certain self-induced amnesia or oblivion. The 'true' conditions of our existence, then, must necessarily be absent from consciousness at the moment of action. This absence is, so to speak, structural and determined, rather than a mere matter of oversight – rather as for Freud the concept of the unconscious means that the forces which determine our being cannot by definition figure within our consciousness. We become conscious agents only by virtue of a certain determinate lack, repression or omission, which no amount of critical self-reflection could repair. The paradox of the human animal is that it comes into being as a subject only on the basis of a shattering repression of the forces which went into its making.

The Althusserian antithesis of theory and ideology proceeds roughly along these lines. One might venture, in a first, crudely approximate formulation, that theory and practice are at odds for Nietzsche because he entertains an irrationalist suspicion of the former, whereas they are eternally discrepant for Althusser because he harbours a rationalist prejudice against the latter. All action for Althusser, including socialist insurrection, is carried on within the sphere of ideology; as we shall see in a moment, it is ideology alone which lends the human subject enough illusory, provisional coherence for it to become a practical social agent. From the bleak standpoint of theory, the subject has no such autonomy or consistency at all: it is merely the 'overdetermined' product of this or that social structure. But since we would be loath to get out of bed if this truth was held steadily in mind, it must disappear from our 'practical' consciousness. And it is in this sense that the subject, for Althusser as for Freud, is the product of a structure which must necessarily be repressed in the very moment of 'subjectivation'.

One can appreciate, then, why for Althusser theory and practice must always be somewhat at odds, in a way scandalous to the classical Marxism which insists on a dialectical relation between the two. But it is harder to see exactly what this discrepancy *means*. To claim that one cannot act and theorize simultaneously may be like saying that you cannot play the *Moonlight Sonata* and analyse its musical structure at one and the same time; or that you cannot be conscious of the grammatical rules governing your speech in the very heat of utterance. But this is hardly more significant than saying that you cannot chew a banana and play the bagpipes simultaneously; it has no *philosophical* import at all. It is certainly a far cry from maintaining, à la Nietzsche, that all action entails a necessary ignorance of its own enabling conditions. The trouble with *this* case, at least for a Marxist, is that it seems to rule out the possibility of theoretically informed practice, which Althusser, as an orthodox Leninist, would be hard put to it to abandon. To claim that your practice is theoretically informed is not, of course, the same as imagining that you could engage in intensive theoretical activity at the very moment you are closing the factory gates to lock out the police. What must happen, then, is that a theoretical understanding does indeed realize itself in practice, but only, as it were, through the 'relay' of ideology – of the 'lived fictions' of the actors concerned. And this will be a radically different form of understanding from that of the theorist in his study, involving as it does for Althusser an inescapable element of misrecognition.

What is misrecognized in ideology is not primarily the world, since ideology for Althusser is not a matter of knowing or failing to know reality at all. The misrecognition in question is essentially a *self*-misrecognition, which is an effect of the 'imaginary' dimension of human existence. 'Imaginary' here means not 'unreal' but 'pertaining to an image': the allusion is to Jacques Lacan's essay 'The Mirror-phase as Formative of the Function of the I', in which he argues that the small infant, confronted with its own image in a mirror, has a moment of jubilant misrecognition of its own actual, physically uncoordinated state, imagining its body to be more unified than it really is.[45] In this imaginary condition, no real distinction between subject and object has yet set in; the infant identifies with its own image, feeling itself at once within and in front of the mirror, so that subject and object glide ceaselessly in and out of each other in a sealed circuit. In the ideological sphere, similarly, the human subject transcends its true state of diffuseness or decentrement and finds a consolingly coherent image of itself reflected back in the 'mirror' of a dominant ideological discourse. Armed with this imaginary self, which for Lacan involves an 'alienation' of the subject, it is then able to act in socially appropriate ways.

Ideology can thus be summarized as 'a representation of the imaginary relationships of individuals to their real conditions of existence'. In ideology, Althusser writes, 'men do indeed express, not the relation between them and their conditions of existence, but *the way* they live the relation between them and their conditions of existence: this presupposes both a real relation and an '*imaginary*', '*lived*' relation. . . . In ideology, the real relation is inevitably invested in the imaginary relation.[46] Ideology exists only in and through the human subject; and to say that the subject inhabits the imaginary is to claim that it compulsively refers the world back to itself. Ideology is subject-centred or 'anthropomorphic': it causes us to view the world as somehow naturally orientated to ourselves, spontaneously 'given' to the subject; and the subject, conversely, feels itself a natural part of that reality, claimed and required by it. Through ideology, Althusser remarks, society 'interpellates' or 'hails' us, appears to single us out as uniquely valuable and address us by name. It fosters the illusion that it could not get on without us, as we can imagine the small infant believing that if *it* disappeared then the world would vanish along with it. In thus 'identifying' us, beckoning us personally from the ruck of individuals and turning its face benignly towards us, ideology brings us into being as individual subjects.

All of this, from the standpoint of a Marxist science, is in fact an illusion, since the dismal truth of the matter is that society has no need of me at all. It may need *someone* to fulfil my role within the process of production, but there is no reason why this particular person should be me. Theory is conscious of the secret that society has no 'centre' at all, being no more than an assemblage of 'structures' and 'regions'; and it is equally aware that the human subject is just as centreless, the mere 'bearer' of these various structures. But for purposive social life to get under way, these unpalatable truths must be masked in the register of the imaginary. The imaginary is thus in one sense clearly false: it veils from our eyes the way subjects and societies actually work. But it is not false in the sense of being mere arbitrary deception, since it is a wholly indispensable dimension of social existence, quite as essential as politics or economics. And it is also not false in so far as the *real* ways we live our relations to our social conditions are invested in it.

There are a number of logical problems connected with this theory. To begin with, how does the individual human being recognize and respond to the 'hailing' which makes it a subject if it is not a subject already? Are not response, recognition, understanding, subjective faculties, so that one would need to be a subject already in order to become one? To this extent, absurdly, the subject would have to pre-date its own existence. Conscious of this conundrum, Althusser argues that we are indeed 'always-already' subjects, even in the womb: our coming, so to speak, has always been prepared for. But if this is true then it is hard to know what to make of his insistence on the 'moment' of interpellation, unless this is simply a convenient fiction. And it seems odd to suggest that we are 'centred' subjects even as embryos. For another thing, the theory runs headlong into all the dilemmas of any notion of identity based upon self-reflection. How can the subject recognize its image in the mirror as itself, if it does not somehow recognize itself already? There is nothing obvious or natural about looking in a mirror and concluding that the image one sees is oneself. Would there not seem a need here for a third, higher subject, who could compare the real subject with its reflection and establish that the one was truly identical with the other? And how did this higher subject come to identify itself?

Althusser's theory of ideology involves at least two crucial misreadings of the psychoanalytic writings of Jacques Lacan – not surprisingly, given the sibylline obscurantism of the latter. To begin with, Althusser's imaginary subject really corresponds to the Lacanian *ego*, which for psychoanalytic theory is merely the tip of the iceberg of the self. It is the ego, for Lacan, which is constituted in the imaginary as a unified entity; the subject 'as a whole' is the split, lacking, desiring effect of the unconscious, which for Lacan belongs to the 'symbolic' as well as the imaginary order. The upshot of this misreading, then, is to render Althusser's subject a good deal more stable and coherent than Lacan's, since the buttoned-down ego is standing in here for the dishevelled unconscious. For Lacan, the imaginary dimension of our being is punctured and traversed by insatiable desire, which suggests a subject rather more volatile and turbulent than Althusser's serenely centred entities. The political implications of this misreading are clear: to expel desire from the subject is to mute its potentially rebellious clamour, ignoring the ways in which it may attain its allotted place in the social order only ambiguously and precariously. Althusser, in effect, has produced an ideology of the ego, rather than one of the human subject; and a certain political pessimism is endemic in this misrepresentation. Corresponding to this ideological misperception of his on the side of the 'little' or individual subject is a tendentious interpretation of the 'big' Subject, the governing ideological signifiers with which the individual identifies. In Althusser's reading, this Subject would seem more or less equivalent to the Freudian superego, the censorious power which keeps us obediently in our places; in Lacan's work, however, this role is played by the 'Other', which means something like the whole field of language and the unconscious. Since this, in Lacan's view, is a notoriously elusive, treacherous terrain in which nothing quite stays in place, the relations between it and the individual subject are a good deal more fraught and fragile than Althusser's model would imply.[47] Once again, the political implications of this misunderstanding are pessimistic: if the power which subjects us is singular and authoritarian, more like the Freudian superego than the shifting, self-divided Lacanian Other, the chances of opposing it effectively would seem remote.

If Althusser's subject were as split, desirous and unstable as Lacan's, then the process of interpellation might figure as a more chancy, contradictory affair than it actually does. 'Experience shows', Althusser writes with solemn banality, 'that the practical telecommunication of hailings is such that they hardly ever miss their man: verbal call or whistle, the one hailed always recognizes that it is really him who is being hailed.'[48] The fact that Louis Althusser's friends apparently never mistook his cheery shout of greeting in the street is offered here as irrefutable evidence that the business of ideological interpellation is invariably successful. But is it? What if we fail to recognize and respond to the call of the Subject? What if we return the reply: 'Sorry, you've got the wrong person'? That we have to be interpellated as *some* kind of subject is clear: the alternative, for Lacan, would be to fall outside the symbolic order altogether into psychosis. But there is no reason why we should always accept society's identification of us as this *particular* sort of subject. Althusser simply runs together the necessity of some 'general' identification with out submission to specific social roles. There are, after all, many different ways in which we can be 'hailed', and some cheery cries, whoops and whistles may strike us as more appealing than some others. Someone may be a mother, Methodist, house-worker and trade unionist all at the same time, and there is no reason to assume that these various forms of insertion into ideology will be mutually harmonious. Althusser's model is a good deal too monistic, passing over the discrepant, contradictory ways in which subjects may be ideologically accosted – partially, wholly, or hardly at all – by discourses which themselves form no obvious cohesive unity.

As Peter Dews has argued, the cry with which the Subject greets us must always be *interpreted*; and there is no guarantee that we will do this in the 'proper' fashion.[49] How can I know for sure what is being demanded of me, that it is *I* who am being hailed, whether the Subject has identified me aright? And since, for Lacan, I can never be fully present as a 'whole subject' in any of my responses, how can my accession to being interpellated be taken as 'authentic'? Moreover, if the response of the Other to me is bound up with my response to it, as Lacan would argue, then the situation becomes even more precarious. In seeking the recognition of the Other, I am led by this very desire to misrecognize it, grasping it in the imaginary mode; so the fact that there is desire at work here – a fact which Althusser overlooks – means that I can never quite grasp the Subject and its call as they really are, just as it can never quite know whether I have 'truly' responded to its invocation. In Lacan's own work, the Other just signifies this ultimately inscrutable nature of all individual subjects. No *particular* other can ever furnish me with the confirmation of my identity I seek, since my desire for such confirmation will always 'go beyond' this figure; and to write the other as Other is Lacan's way of signalling this truth.

The political bleakness of Althusser's theory is apparent in his very conception of how the subject emerges into being. The word 'subject' literally means 'that which lies beneath', in the sense of some ultimate foundation; and throughout the history of philosophy there have been a number of candidates for this function. It is only in the modern period that the individual subject becomes in this sense foundational. But it is possible by a play on words to make 'what lies beneath' mean 'what is kept down', and part of the Althusserian theory of ideology turns on this convenient verbal slide. To be 'subjectified' is to be 'subjected': we become 'free', 'autonomous' human subjects precisely by submitting ourselves obediently to the Subject, or Law. Once we have 'internalized' this Law, made it thoroughly our own, we begin to act it out spontaneously and unquestioningly. We come to work, as Althusser comments, 'all by ourselves', without need of constant coercive supervision; and it is this lamentable condition that we misrecognize as our freedom. In the words of the philosopher who stands behind all of Althusser's work – Baruch Spinoza – men and women 'fight for their slavery as if they were fighting for their liberation' (Preface to *Tractatus Theologico-Politicus*). The model behind this argument is the subjection of the Freudian ego to the superego, source of all conscience and authority. Freedom and autonomy, then, would seem to be sheer illusions: they signify simply that the Law is so deeply inscribed in us, so intimately at one with our desire, that we mistake it for our own free initiative. But this is only one side of the Freudian narrative. For Freud, the ego will rebel against its imperious master if his demands grow too insupportable; and the political equivalent of this moment would be insurrection or revolution. Freedom, in short, can transgress the very Law of which it is an effect; but Althusser maintains a symptomatic silence about this more hopeful corollary of his case. For him, as even more glaringly for Michel Foucault, subjectivity itself would seem just a form of self-incarceration; and the question of where political resistance springs from must thus remain obscure. It is this stoicism in the face of an apparently all-pervasive power or inescapable metaphysical closure which will flow into the current of post-structuralism.

[. . .]

Whatever its flaws and limits, Althusser's account of ideology represents one of the major breakthroughs in the subject in modern Marxist thought. Ideology is now not just a distortion or false reflection, a screen which intervenes between ourselves and reality or an automatic effect of commodity production. It is an indispensable medium for the production of human subjects. Among the various modes of production in any society, there is one whose task is the production of forms of subjectivity themselves; and this is quite as material and historically variable as the production of chocolate bars or automobiles. Ideology is not primarily a matter of 'ideas': it is a structure which imposes itself upon us without necessarily having to pass through consciousness at all. Viewed psychologically, it is less a system of articulated doctrines than a set of images, symbols and occasionally concepts which we 'live' at an unconscious level. Viewed sociologically, it consists in a range of material practices or rituals (voting, saluting, genuflecting, and so on) which are always embedded in material institutions. Althusser inherits this notion of ideology as habitual behaviour rather than conscious thought from Gramsci; but he presses the case to a quasi-behaviourist extreme in his claim that the subject's ideas '*are* his material actions inserted into material practices governed by material rituals which are themselves defined by the material ideological apparatus . . .'.[50] One does not abolish consciousness simply by a hypnotic repetition of the word 'material'. Indeed, in the wake of Althusser's work this term rapidly dwindled to the merest gesture, grossly inflated in meaning. If *everything* is 'material', even thought itself, then the word loses all discriminatory force. Althusser's insistence on the materiality of ideology – the fact that it is always a matter of concrete practices and institutions – is a valuable corrective to Georg Lukács's largely disembodied 'class consciousness'; but it also stems from a structuralist hostility to consciousness as such. It forgets that ideology is a matter of meaning, and that meaning is not material in the sense that bleeding or bellowing are. It is true that ideology is less a question of ideas than of feelings, images, gut reactions; but ideas often figure importantly within it, as is obvious enough in the 'theoretical ideologies' of Aquinas and Adam Smith.

 *If the term 'material' suffers undue inflation at Althusser's hands, so also does the concept of ideology itself. It becomes, in effect, identical with lived experience; but whether all lived experience can usefully be described as ideological is surely dubious. Expanded in this way, the concept threatens to lose all precise political reference. If loving God is ideological, then so, presumably, is loving Gorgonzola. One of Althusser's most controversial claims – that ideology is 'eternal', and will exist even in Communist society – then follows logically from this stretched sense of the word. For since there will be human subjects and lived experience under Communism, there is bound to be ideology as well. Ideology, Althusser declares, has no history – a formulation adapted from *The German Ideology*, but harnessed to quite different ends. Though its contents are, of course, historically variable, its structural mechanisms remain constant. In this sense, it is analogous to the Freudian unconscious: everyone dreams differently, but the operations of the 'dream-work' remain constant from one time or place to another. It is hard to see how we could ever know that ideology is unchanging in its basic devices; but one telling piece of evidence against this claim is the fact that Althusser offers as a *general* theory of ideology what is arguably specific to the bourgeois epoch. The idea that our freedom and autonomy lie in a submission to the Law has it sources in Enlightenment Europe. In what sense an Athenian slave regarded himself as free, autonomous and uniquely individuated is a question Althusser leaves unanswered. If ideological subjects work 'all by themselves', then some would seem to do so rather more than others.

Like the poor, then, ideology is always with us; indeed, the scandal of Althusser's thesis for orthodox Marxism is that it will actually outlast them. Ideology is a structure essential to the life of all historical societies, which 'secrete' it organically; and post-revolutionary societies would be no different in this respect. But there is a sliding in Althusser's thought here between three quite different views of why ideology is in business in the first place. The first of these, as we have seen, is essentially political: ideology exists to keep men and women in their appointed places in class society. So ideology in *this* sense would not linger on once classes had been abolished; but ideology in its more functionalist or sociological meaning clearly would. In a classless social order, ideology would carry on its task of adapting men and women to the exigencies of social life: it is 'indispensable in any society if men are to be formed, transformed and equipped to respond to the demands of their conditions of existence'.[51] Such a case, as we have seen, follows logically from this somewhat dubiously stretched sense of the term; but there is also another reason why ideology will persist in post-class society, which is not quite at one with this. Ideology will be necessary in such a future, as it is necessary now, because of the inevitable complexity and opaqueness of social processes. The hope that in Communism such processes might become transparent to human consciousness is denounced by Althusser as a humanist error. The workings of the social order as a whole can be known only to theory; as far as the practical lives of individuals go, ideology is needed to provide them with a kind of imaginary 'map' of the social totality, so that they can find their way around it. These individuals may also, of course, have access to a scientific knowledge of the social formation; but they cannot exercise this knowledge in the dust and heat of everyday life.

This case, we may note, introduces a hitherto unexamined element into the debate over ideology. Ideology, so the argument goes, springs from a situation in which social life has become too complex to be grasped as a whole by everyday consciousness. There is thus the need for an imaginary model of it, which will bear something of the oversimplifying relation to social reality that a map does to an actual terrain. It is a case which goes back at least as far as Hegel, for whom ancient Greece was a society immediately transparent as a whole to all its members. In the modern period, however, the division of labour, the fragmentation of social life and the proliferation of specialized discourses have expelled us from that happy garden, so that the concealed connections of society can be known only to the dialectical reason of the philosopher. Society, in the terminology of the eighteenth century, has become 'sublime': it is an object which cannot be *represented*. For the people as a whole to get their bearings within it, it is essential to construct a myth which will translate theoretical knowledge into more graphic, immediate terms. 'We must have a new mythology', Hegel writes,

> but this mythology must be in the service of Ideas; it must be a mythology of *Reason*. Until we express the Ideas aesthetically, that is, mythologically, they have no interest for *the people*; and conversely, until mythology is rational the philosopher must be ashamed of it. Thus in the end enlightened and unenlightened must clasp hands: mythology must become philosophical in order to make people rational, and philosophy must become mythological in order to make the philosophers sensible.[52]
>
> [. . .]

Hegel's myth, then, is Althusser's ideology, at least in one of its versions. Ideology adapts individuals to their social functions by providing them with an imaginary model of the whole, suitably schematized and fictionalized for their purposes. Since this model is symbolic and affective rather than austerely cognitive, it can furnish motivations for action as some mere theoretical comprehension might not. Communist men and women of the future will require such an enabling fiction just like anyone else; but meanwhile, in class society, it serves the additional function of helping to thwart true insight into the social system, thus reconciling individuals to their locations within it. The 'imaginary map' function of ideology, in other words, fulfils both a political and a sociological role in the present; once exploitation has been overcome, ideology will live on in its purely 'sociological' function, and mystification will yield to the *mythical*. Ideology will still be in a certain sense false; but its falsity will no longer be in the service of dominant interests.

I have suggested that ideology is not for Althusser a pejorative term; but this claim now requires some qualification. It would be more accurate to say that his texts are simply inconsistent on this score. There are times in his work when he speaks explicitly of ideology as false and illusory, *pace* those commentators who take him to have broken entirely with such epistemological notions.[53] The imaginary mappings of ideological fictions are false from the standpoint of theoretical knowledge, in the sense that they actually get society wrong. So it is not here simply a question of *self*-misrecognition, as we saw in the case of the imaginary subject. On the other hand, this falsity is absolutely indispensable and performs a vital social function. So although ideology is false, it is not *pejoratively* so. We need protest only when such falsehood is harnessed to the purpose of reproducing exploitative social relations. There need be no implication that in post-revolutionary society ordinary men and women will not be equipped with a theoretical understanding of the social totality; it is just that this understanding cannot be 'lived', so that ideology is essential here too. At other times, however, Althusser writes as though terms like 'true' and 'false' are quite inapplicable to ideology, since it is no kind of knowledge at all. Ideology implicates subjects; but for Althusser knowledge is a 'subjectless' process, so ideology must by definition be non-cognitive. It is a matter of experience rather than insight; and in Althusser's eyes it would be an empiricist error to believe that experience could ever give birth to knowledge. Ideology is a subject-centred view of reality; and as far as theory is concerned, the whole perspective of subjectivity is bound to get things wrong, viewing what is in truth a centreless world from some deceptively 'centred' standpoint. But though ideology is thus false when viewed from the external vantage point of theory, it is not false 'in itself' – for this subjective slant on the world is a matter of lived relations rather than controvertible propositions.

Another way of putting this point is to say that Althusser oscillates between a *rationalist* and a *positivist* view of ideology. For the rationalist mind, ideology signifies error, as opposed to the truth of science or reason; for the positivist, only certain sorts of statements (scientific, empirical) are verifiable, and others – moral prescriptions, for instance – are not even candidates for such truth/falsity judgements. Ideology is sometimes seen as wrong, and sometimes as not even propositional enough to be wrong. When Althusser relegates ideology to the false 'other' of true knowledge, he speaks like a rationalist; when he dismisses the idea that (say) moral utterances are in any sense cognitive, he writes like a positivist. A somewhat similar tension can be observed in the work of Emile Durkheim, for whose *The Rules of Sociological Method* ideology is simply an irrational obstruction to scientific knowledge, but whose *The Elementary Forms of Religious Life* views religion as an essential set of collective representations of social solidarity.

[. . .]

Althusser's thinking about ideology is on a fairly grand scale, revolving on such 'global' concepts as the Subject and ideological state apparatuses, whereas the French sociologist Pierre Bourdieu is more concerned to examine the mechanisms by which ideology takes hold in everyday life. To tackle this problem, Bourdieu develops in his *Outline of a Theory of Practice* (1977) the concept of *habitus*, by which he means the inculcation in men and women of a set of durable dispositions which generate particular practices. It is because individuals in society act in accordance with such internalized systems – what Bourdieu calls the 'cultural unconscious' – that we can explain how their actions can be objectively regulated and harmonized without being in any sense the result of conscious obedience to rules. Through these structured dispositions, human actions may be lent a unity and consistency without any reference to some conscious intention. In the very 'spontaneity' of our habitual behaviour, then, we reproduce certain deeply tacit norms and values; and habitus is thus the relay or transmission mechanism by which mental and social structures become incarnate in daily social activity. The habitus, rather like human language itself, is an open-ended system which enables individuals to cope with unforeseen, ever-changing situations; it is thus a 'strategy-generating principle' which permits ceaseless innovation, rather than a rigid blueprint.

The term ideology is not particularly central to Bourdieu's work; but if habitus is relevant to the concept, it is because it tends to induce in social agents such aspirations and actions as are compatible with the objective requirements of their social circumstances. At its strongest, it rules out all other modes of desiring and behaving as simply unthinkable. Habitus is thus 'history turned into nature', and for Bourdieu it is through this matching of the subjective and the objective, what we feel spontaneously disposed to do and what our social conditions demand of us, that power secures itself. A social order strives to naturalize its own arbitrariness through this dialectic of subjective aspirations and objective structures, defining each in terms of the other; so that the 'ideal' condition would be one in which the agents' consciousness would have the same limits as the objective system which gives rise to it. The recognition of legitimacy, Bourdieu states, 'is the misrecognition of arbitrariness'.

What Bourdieu calls *doxa* belongs to the king of stable, tradition-bound social order in which power is fully naturalized and unquestionable, so that no social arrangement different from the present could even be imagined. Here, as it were, subject and object merge indistinguishably into each other. What matters in such societies is what 'goes without saying', which is determined by tradition; and tradition is always 'silent', not least about itself as tradition. Any challenge to such doxa is then *heterodoxy*, against which the given order must assert its claims in a new *orthodoxy*. Such orthodoxy differs from doxa in that the guardians of tradition, of what goes without saying, are now compelled to speak in their own defence, and thus implicitly to present themselves as simply one possible position, among others.

Social life contains a number of different habitus, each system appropriate to what Bourdieu terms a 'field'. A field, he argues in *Questions de sociologie* (1980), is a competitive system of social relations which functions according to its own internal logic, composed of institutions or individuals who are competing for the same stake. What is generally at stake in such fields is the attainment of maximum dominance within them – a dominance which allows those who achieve it to confer legitimacy on other participants, or to withdraw it from them. To achieve such dominance involves amassing the maximum amount of the particular kind of 'symbolic capital' appropriate to the field; and for such power to become 'legitimate' it must cease to be recognized for what it is. A power which is tacitly rather than explicitly endorsed is one which has succeeded in legitimating itself.

Any such social field is necessarily structured by a set of unspoken rules for what can be validly uttered or perceived within it; and these rules thus operate as a mode of what Bourdieu terms 'symbolic violence'. Since symbolic violence is legitimate, it generally goes unrecognized *as* violence. It is, Bourdieu remarks in *Outline of a Theory of Practice*, 'the gentle, invisible form of violence, which is never recognised as such, and is not so much undergone as chosen, the violence of credit, confidence, obligation, personal loyalty, hospitality, gifts, gratitude, piety. . . .'[54] In the field of education, for example, symbolic violence operates not so much by the teacher speaking 'ideologically' to the students, but by the teacher being perceived as in possession of an amount of 'cultural capital' which the student needs to acquire. The educational system thus contributes to reproducing the dominant social order not so much by the viewpoints it fosters, but by this regulated distribution of cultural capital. As Bourdieu argues in *Distinction* (1979), a similar form of symbolic violence is at work in the whole field of culture, where those who lack the 'correct' taste are unobtrusively excluded, relegated to shame and silence. 'Symbolic violence' is thus Bourdieu's way of rethinking and elaborating the Gramscian concept of hegemony; and his work as a whole represents an original contribution to what one might call the 'microstructures' of ideology, complementing the more general notions of the Marxist tradition with empirically detailed accounts of ideology as 'everyday life'.

Notes

1. Georg Lukács, *History and Class Consciousness*, London 1971, p. 204.
2. Ibid., p. 204.
3. 'Historicism' in its Marxist sense is elegantly summarized by Perry Anderson as an

ideology in which 'society becomes a circular "expressive" totality, history a homo-geneous flow of linear time, philosophy a self-consciousness of the historical process, class struggle a combat of collective "subjects", capitalism a universe essentially defined by alienation, communism a state of true humanism beyond alienation' (*Considerations on Western Marxism*, London 1976, p. 70).

4. Bhikhu Parekh, *Marx's Theory of Ideology*, London 1982, pp. 171–2.

5. Like most analogies, this one limps: the Hegelian Idea is really its own creation, whereas the proletariat, far from being self-generating, is for Marxism an effect of the process of capital.

6. Leszek Kołakowski, *Main Currents of Marxism*, Oxford 1978, vol. 3, p. 270 (my parenthesis).

7. Lukács, *History and Class Consciousness*, p. 83. For useful discussions of Lukács's thought, see A. Arato and P. Breines, *The Young Lukács*, London 1979, ch. 8; and Michael Löwy, *Georg Lukács – From Romanticism to Bolshevism*, London 1979, part 4.

8. Lukács, *History and Class Consciousness*, p. 52.

9. Gareth Stedman Jones, 'The Marxism of the Early Lukács: An Evaluation', *New Left Review*, 70, November/December 1971.

10. Nicos Poulantzas, *Political Power and Social Classes*, London 1973, part 3, ch. 2. It should be pointed out that Lukács does in fact hold that there are heterogeneous 'levels' of ideology.

11. See Ernesto Laclau, *Politics and Ideology in Marxist Theory*, London 1977, ch. 3.

12. Lukács, *History and Class Consciousness*, p. 76.

13. Ibid., p. 70.

14. See Lucio Colletti, *Marxism and Hegel*, London 1973, ch. 10.

15. Lukács, *History and Class Consciousness*, p. 54.

16. Ibid., p. 50.

17. Ibid., p. 69.

18. Karl Mannheim, *Ideology and Utopia*, London 1954, p. 87. There are suggestive critiques of Mannheim in Jorge Larrain, *The Concept of Ideology*, London 1979; and in Nigel Abercrombie, *Class, Structure and Knowledge*, Oxford 1980. See also Bhikhu Parekh's essay in R. Benewick, ed., *Knowledge and Belief in Politics*, London 1973.

19. Perry Anderson, 'The Antinomies of Antonio Gramsci', *New Life Review*, 100, November 1976/January 1977.

20. Raymond Williams, *Marxism and Literature*, Oxford 1977, p. 112. For a historical study of political hegemony in eighteenth- and nineteenth-century England, see Francis Hearn, *Domination, Legitimation, and Resistance*, Westport, CT 1978.

21. See my *The Ideology of the Aesthetic*, Oxford 1990, chs 1 and 2.

22. Antonio Gramsci, *Selections from the Prison Notebooks*, ed. A. Hoare and G. Nowell-Smith, London 1971, p. 376.

23. See, on this topic, Alberto Maria Cirese, 'Gramsci's Observations on Folklore', in Anne Showstack Sassoon, ed., *Approaches to Gramsci*, London 1982.

24. Quoted in Cirese, 'Gramsci's Observations', p. 226.

25. Gramsci, *Prison Notebooks*, p. 424.

26. Ibid., p. 328.

27. See Fredric Jameson, *The Political Unconscious*, London 1981, pp. 114–15.

28. See Theodor W. Adorno, *Aesthetic Theory*, London 1984.

29. Theodor W. Adorno, *Negative Dialectics*, London 1973, p. 161.

30. Ibid., p. 150.

31. Ibid., p. 6.

32. See Jurgen Habermas, *The Theory of Communicative Action*, 2 vols, Boston, MA 1984.

33. Quoted by Thomas McCarthy, *The Critical Theory of Jürgen Habermas*, London 1978, p. 273.

34. Quoted in Peter Dews, ed., *Habermas: Autonomy and Solidarity*, London 1986, p. 51.

35. McCarthy, *The Critical Theory of Jürgen Habermas*, p. 56.

36. Quoted ibid., p. 201.

37. Jürgen Habermas, *Knowledge and Human Interests*, Cambridge 1987, p. 217. Habermas's account of Freud has been in my view justly criticized as excessively rationalistic.

38. Ibid., p. 227.

39. Karl Marx, *Theories of Surplus Value*, vol. 1, Moscow n.d., p. 147.

40. See Étienne Balibar and Pierre Macherey, 'On Literature as an Ideology Form', in Robert M. Young, ed., *Untying the Text*, London 1981.

41. Russell Keat, *The Politics of Social Theory*, Oxford 1981, p. 178.

42. For excellent accounts of Althusser's thought, see Alex Callinicos, *Althusser's Marxism*, London 1976; Ted Benton, *The Rise and Fall of Structural Marxism*, London 1984; and Gregory Elliott, *Althusser: The Detour of Theory*, London 1987.

43. See this volume, ch. 5.

44. For a coruscating account of Western Marxism, see Perry Anderson, *Considerations on Western Marxism*, London 1976.

45. Lacan's essay can be found in this volume, ch. 4; and in his *Écrits*, London 1977. See also Fredric Jameson, 'Imaginary and Symbolic in Lacan', *Yale French Studies*, 55/56, 1977.

46. Louis Althusser, *For Marx*, London 1969, pp. 233–4.

47. See Colin MacCabe, 'On Discourse', *Economy and Society*, 8, 3, August 1979.

48. Louis Althusser, *Lenin and Philosophy*, London 1971, p. 174.

49. Peter Dews, *Logics of Disintegration*, London 1987, pp. 78–9.

50. Althusser, *Lenin and Philosophy*, p. 169 (emphasis added).

51. Althusser, *For Marx*, p. 235.

52. Quoted by Jonathan Rée, *Philosophical Tales*, London 1958, p. 59.

53. See Althusser's unpublished essay of 1969, 'Théorie, Pratique Théorique et Formation Théorique, Idéologie et Lutte Idéologique', quoted by Elliott, *Althusser*, pp. 172–4.

54. Pierre Bourdieu, *Outline of a Theory of Practice*, Cambridge 1977, p. 192.

Feminism, Ideology, and Deconstruction: A Pragmatist View

Richard Rorty

Neither philosophy in general, nor deconstruction in particular, should be thought of as a pioneering, path-breaking, tool for feminist politics. Recent philosophy, including Derrida's, helps us see practices and ideas (including patriarchal practices and ideas) as neither natural nor inevitable – but that is all it does. When philosophy has finished showing that everything is a social construct, it does not help us decide which social constructs to retain and which to replace.

Most intellectuals would like to find ways of joining in the struggle of the weak against the strong. So they hope that their particular gifts and competences can be made relevant to that struggle. The term most frequently used in recent decades to formulate this hope is 'critique of ideology'. The idea is that philosophers, literary critics, lawyers, historians, and others who are good at making distinctions, redescribing, and recontextualizing can put these talents to use by 'exposing' or 'demystifying' present social practices.

But the most efficient way to expose or demystify an existing practice would seem to be by suggesting an alternative practice, rather than criticizing the current one. In politics, as in the Kuhnian model of theory-change in the sciences, anomalies within old paradigms can pile up indefinitely without providing much basis for criticism until a new option is offered. 'Immanent' criticism of the old paradigm is relatively ineffective. More specifically, the most effective way to criticize current descriptions of a given instance of the oppression of the weak as 'a necessary evil' (the political equivalent of 'a negligible anomaly') is to explain just why it is not in fact necessary, by explaining how a specific institutional change would eliminate it. That means sketching an alternative future and a scenario of political action that might take us from the present to the future.

Marx and Engels make this point in *The German Ideology* when they criticize Feuerbach for changing 'the word "communist", which in the real world means the follower of a definite revolutionary party, into a mere category'.[1] Their confidence that their criticisms of the German philosophical tradition substituted reality for illusion, science for fantasy, was greatly strengthened by the fact that they had a revolutionary party and a programme – a concrete proposal about how to provide empirical verification of their claim that certain contemporary evils (e.g. income differentials, unemployment) were unnecessary ones. The difference between their situation and ours is principally that no one now wants the revolution they had in mind; no longer does anyone want to nationalize the means of production or to abolish private property. So the contemporary Left lacks the sort of party and the sort of scenario that backed up Marx and Engel's claim that their thought was 'scientific' rather than 'Utopian' – the voice of reality rather than fantasy.[2]

The closest we leftist intellectuals in the rich democracies come nowadays to having such a party and a programme is the feminist movement. But on its political side feminism looks like a reformist rather than a revolutionary movement. For its political goals are fairly concrete and not difficult to envisage being achieved; these goals are argued for by appeals to widespread moral intuitions about fairness. So contemporary feminist politics is more analogous to eighteenth-century abolitionism than to nineteenth-century Communism. Whereas it was very difficult in the nineteenth century to envisage what things might be like without private ownership, it was relatively easy in the eighteenth and early nineteenth centuries to envisage a world without slaves and to see slavery as just a leftover of a barbarous age – morally repugnant to widely held intuitions. Analogously, it is relatively easy to envisage a world with equal pay for equal work, equally shared domestic responsibilities, as many women as men in positions of power, etc., and to see present inequities as repugnant to widely shared intuitions about what is right and just. Only in so far as feminism is more than a matter of specific reforms is it analogous to nineteenth-century Communism.

Feminists are in the following situation: like Marx and Engels, they suspect that piecemeal reforms will leave an underlying, and unnecessary, evil largely untouched. But unlike Marx and Engels, they cannot easily sketch a revolutionary political scenario or a post-revolutionary utopia. The result is a lot of talk about *philosophical* revolutions,

revolutions in *consciousness*; these revolutions, however, are not reflected at anything that Marx and Engels would recognize as 'the material level'. So it is easy to imagine Marx and Engels making the same kind of fun of a lot of contemporary feminist theory that they made of Hegel, Feuerbach, or Bauer. The feminist theorists, they might say, have made 'feminist' into 'a mere category'; nor can they hope to do more, as long as the term does not signify 'follower of a definite *revolutionary* party'.

These considerations lead one to ask whether feminists can keep the notion of 'critique of ideology' without invoking the distinction between 'matter' and 'consciousness' deployed in *The German Ideology*. There is a large and depressing literature about the equivocity of the term 'ideology', the latest example of which is the first chapter of Terry Eagleton's *Ideology*.[3] Eagleton rejects the frequent suggestion that the term has become more trouble than it is worth, and offers the following as a definition: 'ideas and beliefs which help to legitimate the interests of a ruling group or class specifically by distortion and dissimulation'. As an alternative he suggests 'false or deceptive beliefs' that arise 'not from the interests of a dominant class but from the material structure of society as a whole'.[4] The latter formulation incorporates the material/non-material contrast central to *The German Ideology*. But it is difficult for feminists to appropriate this contrast, which got whatever concrete relevance it had from the explication of 'material change' by reference to Marx's eschatological history of changes in the organization of mechanisms of production. That history is largely irrelevant to the oppression of women by men.[5]

If however, we drop the matter–consciousness distinction and fall back on the first of the two definitions of 'ideology' I quoted from Eagleton, we come into conflict with the philosophical views about truth, knowledge, and objectivity held by most of the contemporary feminist intellectuals who hope to put their gifts and competences to work criticizing masculinist ideology. For 'distortion' presupposes a medium of representation which, intruding between us and the object under investigation, produces an appearance that does not correspond to the reality of the object. This representationalism cannot be squared either with the pragmatist insistence that truth is not a matter of correspondence to the intrinsic nature of reality, or with the deconstructionist rejection of what Derrida calls 'the metaphysics of presence'.[6] Pragmatists and deconstructionists agree that everything is a social construct, and that there is no point in trying to distinguish between the 'natural' and the 'merely' cultural. They agree that the question is which social constructs to discard and which to keep, and that there is no point in appealing to 'the way things really are' in the course of struggles over who gets to construct what. Both philosophical schools can agree with Eagleton that 'if there are no values and beliefs not bound up with power, then the term ideology threatens to expand to the vanishing point'.[7] But, unlike Eagleton, both find this a reason to be dubious about the utility of the notion of 'ideology' (at least if it is supposed to mean more than 'a set of bad ideas').

The distinction that runs through *The German Ideology* between Marxist science and mere philosophical fantasy is an excellent example of a claim to have reached what Derrida calls 'a full presence which is beyond the reach of play'.[8] As a good Marxist, Eagleton has to echo the standard right-wing criticisms of Derrida when he says that 'the thesis that objects are entirely internal to the discourses which constitute them raises the thorny problem of how we could ever judge that a discourse had constructed its object validly' and goes on to ask 'if what validates my social interpretations are the political ends they serve, how am I to validate those ends?'[9] You cannot talk about 'distorted communication' or 'distorting ideas' without believing in objects external to discourses, and objects capable of being accurately or inaccurately, scientifically or merely fantastically, represented by those discourses.

Something, therefore, has to give. Feminist intellectuals who wish to criticize masculinist ideology, and to use deconstruction to do so, must (1) think of something new for 'ideology' to mean; or (2) disassociate deconstruction from anti-representationalism, from the denial that we can answer the question 'have I constructed the object *validly* (as opposed, for example, to usefully for feminist purposes)?'; or (3) say that the question of whether their criticisms of masculinist social practices are 'scientific' or 'philosophically well grounded', like the question of whether masculinism has 'distorted' things, is beside the point.

The best option is the last one. The first option is simply not worth the trouble, and I do not think that the second can be done at all. It seems to me unfortunate that some people identified with deconstruction have tried to reconstitute the Marxist matter–consciousness distinction – as when de Man said that 'it would be unfortunate to confuse the materiality of the signifier with the materiality of what it signifies', and went on to define 'ideology' as 'the confusion of linguistic with natural reality, of reference with phenomenalism'.[10] The way to rebut the accusation that literary theory, or deconstruction, is 'oblivious to social and historical reality' is to insist that 'constitution of objects by discourse' goes all the way down, and that 'respect for reality' (social and historical, astrophysical, or any other kind of reality) is just respect for past language, past ways of describing what is 'really' going on.[11] Sometimes such respect is a good thing, sometimes it is not. It depends on what you want.

Feminists want to change the social world, so they cannot have too much respect for past descriptions of social institutions. The most interesting question about the utility of deconstruction for feminism is whether, once Nietzsche, Dewey, Derrida, *et al.* have convinced us that there is nothing 'natural' or 'scientific' or 'objective' about any given masculinist practice or description, and that all objects (neutrinos, chairs, women, men, literary theory, feminism) are social constructs, there is any *further* assistance that deconstruction can offer in deciding which constructs to keep and which to replace, or in finding substitutes for the latter. I doubt that there is.

It is often said that deconstruction offers 'tools' which enable feminists to show, as Barbara Johnson puts it, that 'the differences between entities (prose and poetry, man and woman, literature and theory, guilt and innocence) are shown to be based on a repression of differences *within* entities, ways by which an entity differs from itself'.[12] The question of whether these differences were there (huddled together deep down within the entity, waiting to be brought to light by deconstructing excavators), or are there in the entity only after the feminist has finished reshaping the entity into a social construct nearer her heart's desire, seems to me of no interest whatever. Indeed, it seems to me an important part of the anti-metaphysical polemic common to post-Nietzcheans (pragmatists and deconstructionists alike) is to argue that this finding-vs-making distinction is of little interest. So I do not see that it is to any political purpose to say, as Johnson does, that '[d]ifference is a form of *work* to the extent that it *plays* beyond the control of any subject'.[13] It just doesn't matter whether God ordains, or 'the mass of productive forces' dialectically unfolds, or difference plays, beyond the control of any of us. All that matters is what we can do to persuade people to act differently than in the past. The question of what ultimately, deep down, determines whether they will or will not change their ways is the sort of metaphysical topic feminists can safely neglect.[14]

To sum up: anything that philosophy can do to free up our imagination a little is all to the political good, for the freer the imagination of the present, the likelier it is that future social practices will be different from past practices. Nietzsche's, Dewey's, Derrida's, and Davidson's treatments of objectivity, truth, and language have freed us up a bit, as did Marx's and Keynes's treatments of money and Christ's and Kierkegaard's treatments of love. But philosophy is not, as the Marxist tradition unfortunately taught us to believe, a source of tools for path-breaking political work. Nothing politically useful happens until people begin saying things never said before – thereby permitting us to visualize new practices, as opposed to analysing old ones. The moral of Kuhnian philosophy of science is important: there is no discipline called 'critique' that one can practise to get strikingly better politics, any more than there is something called 'scientific method' that one can apply in order to get strikingly better physics. Critique of ideology is, at best, mopping-up, rather than path-breaking. It is parasitic on prophecy rather than a substitute for it. It stands to the imaginative production of new descriptions of what has been going on (e.g. of what men have been doing to women) as Locke (who described himself as 'an under-labourer', clearing away the rubbish) stood to Boyle and Newton. The picture of philosophy as pioneer is part of a logocentric conception of intellectual work with which we fans of Derrida should have no truck.

One reason why many feminists resist this pragmatist view of the political utility of philosophy is that masculinism seems so thoroughly built into everything we do and say in contemporary society that it looks as if only some really *massive* intellectual change could budge it. So lots of feminists think that only by taking on some great big intellectual evil of the sort that philosophers specialize in spotting (something on the scale of logocentrism, or 'binarism', or 'technological thinking') – interpreting this evil as intrinsically masculinist and masculinism as standing or falling with it – can they achieve the radicality and scope their task seems to demand. Without such an alliance with a campaign against some large philosophical monster, the campaign against masculinism seems to them doomed to some form of complicity in present practices.[15]

This view seems to me to get the relative sizes all wrong. Masculinism is a much bigger and fiercer monster than any of the little, parochial monsters with which pragmatists and deconstructionists struggle. For masculinism is the defence of the people who have been on top since the beginning of history against attempts to topple them; that sort of monster is very adaptable, and I suspect that it can survive almost as well in an anti-logocentric as in a logocentric philosophical environment. It is true that, as Derrida has acutely noted, the logocentric tradition is bound up in subtle ways with the drive for purity – the drive to escape contamination by feminine messes – symbolized by what he calls 'the essential and essentially sublime figure of virile homosexuality'.[16] But that drive for purity and that 'sublime figure' are likely to survive in some still more highly sublimated form even if we philosophers somehow manage an overcoming (or even just a *Verwindung*) of metaphysics.

Pragmatism – considered as a set of philosophical views about truth, knowledge, objectivity, and language – is neutral between feminism and masculinism. So if one wants specifically feminist doctrines about these topics, pragmatism will not provide them. But feminists who (like MacKinnon) think of philosophy as something to be picked up and laid down as occasion demands, rather than as a powerful and indispensable ally, will find in pragmatism the same anti-logocentric doctrines they find in Nietzsche, Foucault and Derrida. The main advantage of the way pragmatists present these doctrines is that they make clear that they are not unlocking deep secrets, secrets that feminists must know in order to succeed. They admit that all they have to offer is occasional bits of *ad hoc* advice – advice about how to reply when masculinists attempt to make present practices seem inevitable. Neither pragmatists nor deconstructionists can do more for feminism than help rebut attempts to ground these practices on something deeper than a contingent historical fact – the fact that the people with the slightly larger muscles have been bullying the people with the slightly smaller muscles for a very long time.

Notes

1. Robert C. Tucker, ed., *The Marx–Engels Reader*, 2nd edn, New York 1978, p. 167.
2. For a good expression of this fantasy–reality contrast, see Engel's 'Socialism: Utopian and Scientific', in Tucker, *The Marx–Engels Reader*, pp. 693–4.
3. For a deflationary account of the Marxist use of 'ideology', see Daniel Bell, 'The Misreading of Ideology: The Social Determination of Ideas in Marx's Work', *Berkeley Journal of Sociology* 35, 1990, pp. 1–54. This article helps to make clear why Marx would have found the phrase 'Marxist ideology' objectionable, and how inseparable Marx's use of 'ideology' was from his characterization of his own thought as 'scientific'.
4. Terry Eagleton, *Ideology*, London 1991, p. 30. I cite the fifth and sixth of Eagleton's series of progressively fuller and sharper distinctions. For further discussion of this book, see Richard Rorty, 'We Anti-representationalists', *Radical Philosophy* 60, 1992, pp. 40–42.
5. As Catharine MacKinnon says, the history of the relations between men and women (unlike the history of sexuality – 'the history of what makes historians feel sexy') is flat: '[U]nderneath all of these hills and valleys, these ebbs and flows, there is this bedrock, this tide that has not changed much, namely male supremacy and the subordination of women' (MacKinnon, 'Does Sexuality Have a History?', *Michigan Quarterly Review* 30, 1991, p. 6). That subordination runs through the centuries like a monotone (and so usually inaudible) ground bass – the sound of men beating up on women. No dramatic orchestration seems possible.
6. I offer an account of pragmatism as anti-representationalism in a foreword to John Murphy, *Pragmatism: from Pierce to Davidson*, Boulder, CO 1990; and also in the introduction to Richard Rorty, *Objectivity, Relativism and Truth*, Cambridge 1992. For the parallels between Davidson's anti-representationalism and Derrida's anti-metaphysics, see Samuel Wheeler, 'Indeterminacy of French Interpretation: Derrida and Davidson', in Ernest Le Pore, ed., *Truth and Interpretation: Perspectives on the Philosophy of Donald Davidson*, Oxford 1986, pp. 477–94.
7. Eagleton, *Ideology* p. 7.
8. Jacques Derrida, *Writing and Difference*, Chicago 1978, p. 279.
9. Eagleton, *Ideology*, p. 205.
10. Paul de Man, *The Resistance to Theory*, Minneapolis, MN 1986, p. 11
11. Wallace Stevens said that the imagination is the mind pressing back against reality.

Derrida and Dewey both help us see that this amounts to pressing back against the imagination of the past.

12. Barbara Johnson, *The Critical Difference*, Baltimore, MD 1980, pp. x–xi. See the use of the passage from Johnson by Joan Scott in her 'Deconstructing Equality–vs.– Difference: Or, the Uses of Poststructuralist Theory for Feminism', in Marianne Hirsch and Evelyn Fox Keller, eds, *Conflicts in Feminism*, New York 1990, pp. 137–8.

13. Johnson, *The Critical Difference*, p. xi.

14. I develop this analogy between contemporary feminism and the New Science of the seventeenth century at somewhat greater length in 'Feminism and Pragmatism', *Michigan Quarterly Review* 30, 1991, pp. 231–58.

15. A good example of this charge of complicity is Drucilla Cornell's criticism of Catharine MacKinnon in *Beyond Accommodation: Ethical Feminism, Deconstruction and the Law*, New York 1991, ch. 3. Cornell thinks that although MacKinnon 'superficially rejects the dream of symmetry, which measures us against the male norm', she nevertheless 'cannot but fall into that very old dream given the limits of her own theoretical discourse, which necessarily repudiates the feminine as femininity because she can only 'see' from her own masculinist perspective' (p. 151). Cornell thinks that more philosophical reflection (of a specifically deconstructionist sort) than MacKinnon wishes to engage in will be needed to avoid complicity with masculinism. She also thinks that MacKinnon betrays feminism's distinctive ethical standpoint by reducing feminism to a power grab. My sympathies are with MacKinnon. I cannot see anything wrong with power grabs, and am less sanguine about the political utility of deconstructionist philosophy than is Cornell. (For more doubts about this utility, see Thomas McCarthy, 'The Politics of the Ineffable: Derrida's Deconstructionism', *The Philosophical Forum* 21, 1989, pp. 146–68. For MacKinnon's view that 'men are the way they are because they have the power' and that 'women who succeed to male forms of power will largely be that way too', see Catharine MacKinnon, *Feminism Unmodified*, Cambridge, MA 1987, p. 220.)

16. I agree with Cornell that one of Derrida's central contributions to feminism is that 'he explicitly argues that fundamental philosophical questions cannot be separated from the thinking of sexual difference' (*Beyond Accommodation*, p. 98). Indeed, I should go further and say that Derrida's most original and important contribution to philosophy is his weaving together of Freud and Heidegger, his association of 'ontological difference' with gender difference. This weaving together enables us to see for the first time the connection between the philosophers' quest for purity, the view that women are somehow impure, the subordination of women, and 'virile homosexuality' (the kind of male homosexuality that Eve Sedgwick calls 'homo-homosexuality', epitomized in Jean Genet's claim that 'the man who fucks another man is twice a man'). Compared to this insight (which is most convincingly put forward in Derrida's 'Geschlecht I'), the grab bag of easily reproduced gimmicks labelled 'deconstruction' seems to me relatively unimportant.

Ideology, Politics, Hegemony: From Gramsci to Laclau and Mouffe

Michèle Barrett

Gramsci is something of a paradox in radical political thought. On the one hand, his work is much admired as the most sympathetic treatment, within the classical Marxist tradition, of cultural and ideological politics. He has become the adopted theorist of, for example, the Eurocommunist strategy in Italy, Spain and other countries and, in Britain, the inspiration for many of those who wish to realign Labour politics in a new and realistic mode. His approach to ideology, his theory of hegemony, his account of the role of intellectuals, his insistence on the importance of tactics and persuasion and his detailed attention to questions of culture, and the politics of everyday culture, have all been taken up enthusiastically by a generation sick of the moralizing rules and precepts of both the Marxist–Leninist and Labourist lefts.

Yet, in theoretical terms, Gramsci's work has posed many unresolved questions in the area of a theory of ideology – partly because (like Marx, perhaps) his brilliant insights often stand alone or in some tension with each other. It is not clear, to take an example I shall discuss in more detail, exactly how his approach to ideology ties in with the now celebrated definition and use of the idea of hegemony. More generally, Gramsci's thought has taken on an iconic significance for the contemporary Left, both intellectual and cultural, but it is also Gramsci – at least the Gramsci read by Ernesto Laclau and Chantal Mouffe – who stands at the crucial breaking point of Marxism as a viable political theory. This latter argument, which hangs on the central status of the concept of class in Marxist theory and politics, will occupy much of this

chapter. As we shall see, a very important feature of that debate is the
question of whether particular ideologies necessarily pertain to different social classes, or whether this imputation of the 'class-belonging'
nature of political ideology is a mistake.

Gramsci, as is no doubt known to all readers, wrote most of what has
come down to us as the body of his writings in the extraordinarily
coercive circumstances of an Italian Fascist prison. The conditions
under which he wrote, including his progressively poor health,
obviously have a bearing on the nature of the texts we have, and a
further important consideration is the fact that his works incorporate
many strategies and detours related to the prison censor. These bald
facts explain, to some extent anyway, the relatively fragmentary and
'open' nature of these crucial writings.

If we look first at one passage from the *Prison Notebooks* where
Gramsci addresses directly the concept of ideology in the Marxist
tradition, we find the following points made. Gramsci refers to the
'negative value judgement' that has (erroneously) become attached to
the meaning of ideology in Marxist philosophy; here we should take
note of Jorge Larrain's point that, first and foremost, Gramsci must be
identified as taking a 'positive' rather than 'critical' stance on ideology.
Gramsci suggests – though not quite in these words – that the weak
understanding of ideology in Marxist thought can be blamed on those
who have seen ideology as merely determined by an economic base and
therefore '"pure" appearance, useless, rubbish etc.': in this regard he
lines himself up with Korsch's critique of 'vulgar-Marxism'. Gramsci
then stresses that 'historically organic ideologies' – those that are
'necessary' – have a psychological validity and they 'create the terrain
on which men move, acquire consciousness of their position, struggle
etc.': it is this attention to 'psychological validity' that has made Gramsci
in some senses unique in the Marxist tradition.

In the same brief, but highly condensed, set of theses Gramsci
suggests that 'organic' ideologies can be distinguished from the
polemics of individual ideologues, and he distinguishes between
ideology as the 'necessary superstructure of a particular structure' and
ideology in the sense of these 'arbitrary elucubrations' of individuals.
Gramsci refers to Marx's view that 'a popular conviction often has the
same energy as a material force', and concludes the passage with the
following formal statement:

> The analysis of these propositions tends, I think, to reinforce the conception
> of *historical bloc* in which precisely material forces are the content

and ideologies the form, though this distinction between form and content has purely didactic value, since the material forces would be inconceivable historically without form and the ideologies would be individual fancies without the material forces.[1]

A difficulty in considering these linked theses is that even such a short passage contains some complex, but distinct, shifts of position. The last sentence would be enough on its own to mark Gramsci out as a clear 'historicist', but this is tricky to assess when it falls at the end of a paragraph in which the now classically 'Gramscian' idea that ideology is a 'terrain of struggle' has been suggested – a view that sits rather ill with the historicist tendency to think in terms of 'expressive totalities'. Another problem is that frequently Gramsci is not explicit about whether something is or is not to be thought of as an 'organic ideology', hence his discussions of cultural and intellectual struggle are often somewhat ambiguous. (This is not a criticism, but it certainly has a bearing on the fact that Gramsci's work has become such a rich field for different interpretations.) These ambiguities surround even fairly basic questions. It is often assumed, for example, that Gramsci's general discussions of cultural and intellectual phenomena are couched under the rubric of ideology, but this is not exactly or necessarily the case. It is not clear whether Gramsci's illuminating classification of different levels of 'making sense of the world' – from philosophy to folklore – should be thought of as a treatment of ideology or not. Gramsci distinguishes, in another famous passage from the *Prison Notebooks*, between philosophy, religion, common sense and folklore as conceptions of the world with varying (decreasing) degrees of systematicity and coherence. Philosophy involves intellectual order, which religion and common sense do not, 'because they cannot be reduced to unity and coherence even within an individual consciousness, let alone collective consciousness'. Gramsci goes on to say that 'Every philosophical current leaves behind a sedimentation of "common sense": this is the document of its historical effectiveness. . . . "Common sense" is the folklore of philosophy, and is always half-way between folklore properly speaking and the philosophy, science and economics of the specialists. Common sense creates the folklore of the future.'[2]

Thus we have a hierarchy of forms, in which philosophies – systematic bodies of thought which can be espoused coherently – take their place above religion, which is subject to philosophical criticism. 'Common sense' will take many forms, but is a fragmented body of precepts; 'folklore' he describes as 'rigid' popular formulae. Gramsci points out that there may be considerable conflict between these levels, noting that there may be contradictions between the philosophy one

espouses at a systematic (rational) level and one's conduct as determined by 'common sense'. Hence we arrive at Gramsci's notion of
'contradictory consciousness' and of a distinction between intellectual
choice and 'real activity'.[3] Gramsci himself, as is now increasingly
appreciated in Britain from the new translations of his cultural
writings,[4] devoted considerable attention to popular culture and
ideology, ranging over topics as diverse as architecture, popular songs,
serial fiction, detective fiction, opera, journalism, and so on.

Yet it remains somewhat unclear how far Gramsci is thinking of
these various phenomena as ideology. Gramsci discusses these forms
under the heading of philosophy, but most people have tended to
assume that they are ideological forms. A rather impressionistic use of
the concept of ideology can occur with impunity in Gramsci's approach, largely because he has taken the explanatory weight from the
shoulders of ideology. This he can do as in turn he deploys another
concept to carry the theoretical burden that in other writers is taken by
the concept of ideology. Thus in order to see how Gramsci's treatment
of ideology meshes in with the tradition, we have to take it in
conjunction with its companion term – hegemony. Although the
Italian word *egemonia* was often seen as synonymous with Gramsci's
contribution, its roots, as Perry Anderson and others have emphasized,
lay in debates over the proletariat's need for 'hegemony' (persuasive
influence) over the peasantry in the pre-revolutionary period in
Russia.[5]

The concept of 'hegemony' is the organizing focus of Gramsci's
thought on politics and ideology, and his distinctive usage has
rendered it the hallmark of the Gramscian approach in general.
Hegemony is best understood as *the organization of consent* – the
processes through which subordinated forms of consciousness are
constructed without recourse to violence or coercion. The ruling bloc,
according to Gramsci, operates not only in the political sphere but
throughout the whole of society. Gramsci emphasized the 'lower' – less
systematic – levels of consciousness and apprehension of the world,
and in particular he was interested in the ways in which 'popular'
knowledge and culture developed in such a way as to secure the
participation of the masses in the project of the ruling bloc.

At this point it is worth remarking a significant difference of
interpretation about hegemony. It is not clear whether Gramsci uses
hegemony strictly to refer to the non-coercive (ideological?) aspects of
the organization of consent, or whether he uses it to explore the
relationship between coercive and non-coercive forms of securing
consent. Stuart Hall *et al.* suggest that Gramsci's fundamental question
– how can the state rule without coercion? – is one that causes him to

draw attention to non-coercive aspects of class rule. But, they argue, this is because of his underlying interest in the *relationship between* the state and 'civil society': it is not the product of a detached interest in the 'superstructures' or in 'culture' in the abstract.[6] Perry Anderson gives this question a somewhat different inflection; he notes that Gramsci's use of hegemony is inconsistent, since sometimes he uses it to mean consent rather than coercion; at other times it seems to mean a synthesis of the two. Anderson's explanation – based on his view that state power is the 'linchpin' of bourgeois hegemony – is to say that Gramsci 'slipped' towards focus on consent partly as a result of the difficulties of getting the coercion-related arguments past the prison censor.[7]

Leaving this on one side for a moment, we can say that Gramsci's emphasis was on hegemony in relation to a political and cultural strategy for socialism, and this was also where his greatest interest lay. His concepts of 'war of position' and 'war of manoeuvre' form the heart of a conceptualization of strategy that involves classes moving, on the analogy of trench warfare, to better vantage points and 'positions': hence the 'war of position' is the battle for winning political hegemony, the securing of consent, the struggle for the 'hearts and minds' of the people and not merely their transitory obedience or electoral support. 'War of manoeuvre', by contrast, comes at a later stage: it is the seizing of state power, but (in direct opposition to the Leninist tradition of political thought) cannot take place except in a situation where hegemony has already been secured.

This model of socialist strategy had built into it a theory of the political function of intellectuals. Gramsci did not see these as expressive of particular classes, or as locked into specific and socially defined roles; he saw intellectuals as important actors on the field where class conflict is 'played out' at the ideological level. In particular, he saw the hegemonic process – from the Left, that is – as one that would involve detaching 'traditional intellectuals from their base in the ruling bloc and developing what he called 'organic' intellectuals of the working class.

Gramsci's view of these processes is one that folds a theory of ideology, construed mainly as the varying forms of popular and systematic knowledge discussed earlier, into a more general political and cultural project that he theorizes in terms of the broader concept of hegemony. His interest in the relation between the state and civil society leads directly to his work on what has been called the socially 'cementing' functions of ideology and the ways in which consent is secured at a non-violent level.

[. . .]

Gramsci has come into his own as the exponent, *par excellence*, of a non-deterministic theory of ideology. Stuart Hall's article on 'base and superstructure' has, definitively, laid out the terms of the debate on determinism within the Marxist theory of ideology. Hall reads Gramsci as delivering a 'polemic against a reductionist account of the super-structure', and he argues that Gramsci has shown us how capitalism is not just a system of production, but a whole form of social life. The superstructures, in Hall's reading of Gramsci, are vital in that they draw culture and civil society into increasing conformity with the needs of capital. They *enlarge* capitalism's sway, creating new types of individual and civilization, working through the various institutions of civil society such as the family, law, education, cultural institutions, Church, and political parties. This is not a matter of economic interest alone, for Gramsci opposes economic reductionism and conceptualizes hegemony as political, cultural and social authority. Yet, concludes Stuart Hall, in Gramsci's view 'the superstructures *do* all this for capital'.[8]

There is, however, an issue that was never entirely articulated *within* the classical Marxist tradition but on which some aspects of Gramsci's ideas have recently been brought to bear with striking consequences: this is the question of whether or not ideologies should be described as 'class belonging'. As we shall see, the exploration of this issue has brought about a major challenge to Marxism, which Ernesto Laclau and Chantal Mouffe argue has now been superseded. It is an issue that was never raised within the Marxist tradition because it was taken for granted that whatever your theory of ideology it would be organized around social class as the essential and formative category of an analysis of capitalism. Hence it would not really matter if you saw ideologies as expressions of the consciousness of particular social classes (the most common, if 'historicist', variant of the positive approach), or if you saw ideology as mystification serving class interest. It would in either case, and with other definitions too, be axiomatic that in an analysis of capitalism the role and function of ideology was construed in terms of social class. It is precisely this that has now been problematized at a very fundamental level, with consequences that are of obvious interest to feminists and others who have been questioning the status of class analysis with reference to the competing theoretical and political claims that arise from other salient social divisions.

Class and Non-Class Political Ideologies

Let us begin by looking at the formulations of Ernesto Laclau's *Politics and Ideology in Marxist Theory* (1977), noting at the outset that the argument made in that book has proved far more acceptable to most Marxists than those of his later works, and particularly *Hegemony and Socialist Strategy* (1985), co-authored with Chantal Mouffe.[9] Laclau's earlier text was concerned with the problem of 'reductionism' in Marxist political theory, and in particular he was critical of those who had tended to see political ideology exclusively as, almost by definition, class ideology.

To 'reduce', philosophically speaking, is to explain a phenomenon that appears in term A by invoking (or reducing it to) something else – term B. Within Marxism, the problem of reductionism has been acute, for a classic explanatory strategy has been to say that a particular phenomenon (often an awkward one such as working-class conservatism, racism or homophobia) is *really* caused by, or functional to, the overriding dynamic of class and class conflict. Marxism has no monopoly on this style of thought: psychoanalysis, for example, has an even more pronounced tendency towards explanatory reductionism. But within Marxist theory the issue has in recent years been a much-debated one, particularly in response to the question of gender and race as competing explanatory factors in thinking about the generation of social inequality.[10] In any case, Laclau was interested in the ways in which Marxists had ignored aspects of political ideology that did not fit into an analysis in which political ideology was explained by, or reduced to, the effects of social class interests.

A key figure in this debate was Nicos Poulantzas, whose attempt to demarcate 'the specificity of the political' in Marxist theory met in general terms with Laclau's approbation. According to Laclau, however, the enormous contribution made by Poulantzas was vitiated by 'the general assumption that dominates his whole analysis: the reduction of every contradiction to a class contradiction, and the assignment of a class belonging to every ideological element'.[11] Laclau proposed a different, and entirely original, approach. He argued that Althusser's theory of the interpellation (hailing) process through which ideological subjects were constructed could be applied to the analysis of political ideology. This would enable us to see that non-class ideological elements operated, for example, in the integration of popular-democratic themes into Fascist ideological configurations and that these processes might, historically, be either independent of class or articulated with class but were in no circumstances *reducible* to class ideologies. He suggested that Fascist ideology could be understood, in particular historical instances which he described, as the articulation of 'popular-democratic' elements in political discourse rather than (as had been common in Marxist political analysis) the natural political discourse of extreme conservative groups. By 'popular-democratic'

Laclau means that the ideology addressed, and therefore constituted, its subjects as 'the people' rather than as 'the working class'. Laclau justifiably claimed that his rethinking of Fascism gave 'a perfect demonstration of the non-class character of popular interpellations'.[12]

Interestingly, then, Laclau was at pains in *Politics and Ideology in Marxist Theory* not to depart too radically from the received wisdom of Marxism. At one point he explicitly rehearses the doxa 'We do not intend to cast doubt on the priority of production relations in the ultimate determination of historical processes':[13] a formulation that he would now reject entirely. Even more interesting, perhaps, is the formulation he arrived at to express the relationship between the non-class ideological elements that he had so illuminatingly uncovered and the traditional ground of class struggle. In a passage that reveals the extent to which, in that period, he had not as yet emancipated himself from the logic of Marxism's theoretical closure, he veers himself towards a perverse form of reductionism:

> The popular-democratic interpellation not only has no precise class content, but is the domain of ideological class struggle par excellence. Every class struggles at the ideological level *simultaneously* as class and as the people, or rather, tries to give coherence to its ideological discourse by presenting its class objectives as the consummation of popular objectives.'[14]

This is interesting precisely because it takes away what, with the other hand, Laclau had just given us: instead of allowing us to savour the full independence of the non-class elements of political ideology that he so eloquently explained, we are enjoined here to restore 'class objectives' as the striven-for, if hidden, agenda of popular-democratic appearances. We shall return to these ambivalences in discussing Laclau's later work.

Meanwhile, it must be emphasized that Laclau's book – although highly contentious – had a terrific impact on work in the field of political ideology. Colin Mercer's study on Italian Fascism would be one example. Mercer discusses the fascinating material, brought to light by Maria Macciocchi among others, about Mussolini's operatic events where women swapped their gold wedding rings (in the interests of the production of armaments) for iron bands symbolizing their marriage to *Il Duce*. Mercer theorizes this and many other instances as a 'sexualization' of the social sphere and an 'aestheticiz- ation' of politics, seeing these as strategies that enabled popular- democratic discourses to circulate freely within Fascist political ideol- ogy. This he regards as a 'testament to Gramsci's assertion that in regimes of this nature, the terrains of the *people* and of *culture* are of key strategic importance and are foregrounded', and he concludes by quoting Gramsci's words that in these circumstances 'political questions are disguised as cultural ones'.[15]

Nothing could make more clear the thorny question that continues to dog the issue of political ideology and 'class belonging'. Mercer's quotation from Gramsci, the darling of the anti-reductionist school, reveals to us a Gramsci who certainly takes ideology, culture and populism seriously, but ultimately as a cover for 'political' (for which in practice read class) politics. Here lies the basis for much of the continuing disagreement over the interpretation of Gramsci.

Stuart Hall's work on 'Thatcherism' as a political ideology is perhaps one of the most well-known attempts to use Laclau's insights in the context of a Gramscian interpretation of contemporary British politics.[16] One of the most accessible routes into this style of thinking might be to consider the theme of patriotism – decisively 'captured' by Mrs Thatcher at the outbreak of the Falklands War as a Conservative party-political identification, which it had not previously been. The success of this has been striking, to the extent that the idea of a 'patriotic socialism' has become somewhat anomalous in Britain. We have for so long now heard the insistence on an identity between the government and the nation that, as Margaret Drabble recently remarked, we are actually surprised to encounter the old parliamentary expression 'Her Majesty's Loyal Opposition'.

Stuart Hall has analysed 'Thatcherism' as a political ideology which 'combines the resonant themes of organic Toryism – nation, family, duty, authority, standards, traditionalism – with the aggressive themes of a revived neo-liberalism – self-interest, competitive individualism, anti-statism.[17] In his successive writings in this area Hall has elaborated these arguments, originally developed in advance of the election of the Thatcher government and addressed, historically, to the consequences for the Left of the collapsing 'post-war consensus' of British politics. In the earlier statements of his analysis, Hall concentrated on explaining how Thatcherism was not to be seen as some error of judgement on the part of the masses, who had fallen for a political right wing that did not represent their true interests, but should be seen in terms of ideological developments that had spoken to real conditions, experiences and contradictions in the lives of the people and then recast them in new terms. The term 'authoritarian populism' was developed to try and explore these ideas.

Thatcherism was 'hegemonic' in its intention (if not successful as such) in that its project was to restructure the whole texture of social life, to alter the entire formation of subjectivity and political identity, rather than simply to push through some economic policies. In Gramscian mode Stuart Hall summarized this political intention:

'Thatcherite politics are 'hegemonic' in their conception and project: the
aim is to struggle on several fronts at once, not on the economic-corporate
one alone; and this is based on the knowledge that, in order really to
dominate and restructure a social formation, political, moral and intellectual leadership must be coupled to economic dominance. The Thatcherites
know they must 'win' in civil society as well as in the state.'[18]

Stuart Hall is noteworthy for having devoted considerable attention to
the inflection of Thatcherite themes, both 'organic Tory' and the
aggressive neo-liberal strands of the ideology, in political constructions
of gender, family and sexuality and with regard to racism and the
politics of ethnicity. So, if his analysis was frequently directed, as I
believe it was, to an audience of 'the Left' (particularly those who clung
to the hope that one morning they would wake up and find that it was
all a bad dream and the working class had come to its senses), it
nevertheless addressed 'the Left' as a group that is in significant ways
internally differentiated and divided by gender and race. That Stuart
Hall's interpretation of Thatcherism occasioned so much criticism
from the Left is, to my mind, symptomatic of the political weight
carried by the theory of ideology. Bob Jessop and others, in a lengthy
critical discussion of Hall's work, argued that one of his main errors was
'ideologism', or a tendency to neglect the 'structural underpinnings' of
Thatcherism in his concentration on ideological processes and his
analysis of patently ideological institutions such as the media.[19] This is
the classic charge of idealism and, as we shall see, it surfaces a great deal
in contemporary debates about ideology. Hall's reply – that he found it
'galling' to be accused of ideologism simply for tactically drawing
attention to important and specifically ideological aspects of Thatcherism – is an apt one.[20] For classical Marxists *any* serious consideration of
ideology is, in practice, nearly always too serious.

Post-Marxism

It might seem a long way from debates about whether or not all
elements of a political ideology should be designated as class-bound to
the position described by this subheading. Yet this is the end point of
Ernesto Laclau's trajectory (so far), and it marks the very interesting
point at which critical arguments made within Marxism have coincided
with some important 'post-structuralist' ideas in such a way as to
challenge the viability of Marxism as a systematic theory. It seems to me
that we can speak of a 'paradigm shift' here, however loosely such

expressions are often used, since the philosophical project of post-structuralist thought, whilst scarcely winning over all comers, brought about a rethinking of Marxist certainties that verges on a major transformation. 'Ideology' is a key element of this; indeed in my view it is a central focus of the debates, precisely because of the epistemological and political weight that theories of ideology have carried within Marxism.

In considering such a shift it is worth noting a prophetic point made by Laclau in his earlier book, where he suggests, following Althusser, that theoretical problems are never, strictly speaking 'solved': they are 'superseded'. This is because if they can be solved within the terms of the existing theory, they are not 'theoretical' problems as such but, rather, empirical or local difficulties of applying the theoretical framework in that particular case. By definition, says Laclau, if there is a genuine theoretical problem '(i.e. one involving an inconsistency in the logical structure of the theory)' then the only way forward is to accept that 'it cannot be resolved within the systems of postulates of the theory', which would mean that the theoretical system would then go into internal contradiction or conflict. From this, suggests Laclau, the 'only way forward is to deny the system of axioms on which the theory is based: that is, to move from one theoretical system to another'. And, as he correctly points out, the originating problem is 'dissolved' in the new system rather than 'solved' within the terms of the old.[21]

There is little point in reading Laclau and Mouffe's *Hegemony and Socialist Strategy* if you refuse to countenance the starting point that Marxism is one among several general theories that are not now viable: they state categorically in the introduction that 'Just as the era of normative epistemologies has come to an end, so too has the era of universal discourses.' The arguments that Laclau and Mouffe bring to bear on Marxism are central themes of post-structuralist thought, and they form part and parcel of that more general theoretical perspective. At times, their arguments are specifically indebted to those of Derrida (particularly), or Lacan. Laclau and Mouffe have themselves constructed, in the field of Marxism and political theory, theses that are complementary to, but distinct from, arguments that others have developed elsewhere – be this in literary criticism, psychoanalysis or economics, for example. It is important to note the depth of the theoretical critique of Marxism that Laclau and Mouffe are posing. They now believe that *theories such as* Marxism are not viable on general grounds, and it is inappropriate in my view for Marxists to respond to their arguments, as some have, with excoriation of them personally as lapsed, ex- or anti-Marxists.[22]

For Laclau and Mouffe, Marxism is founded on a political 'imaginary': it is a conception of socialism that rests on the assumption that the interests of social classes are pre-given, the axiom that the working class is both ontologically and politically privileged in its 'centrality', and the illusion that politics will become pointless after a revolution has founded a new, and homogeneous, social order. In one sentence describing this 'Jacobin imaginary' before its final stages of dissolution, Laclau and Mouffe condense some central themes of post-structuralist thought: 'Peopled with "universal" subjects and conceptually built around History in the singular, it has postulated "society" as an intelligible structure that could be intellectually mastered on the basis of certain class positions and reconstituted, as a rational, transparent order, through a founding act of a political character.'[23] It is worth noting here the allusions to post-structuralist critiques of 'foundationalism' in the epistemology of social and political theory, the critique of the (Cartesian) model of the unified subject, the critique of history as a monolithic and unilinear process, the glancing blow at phallocracy in the reference to mastery, and so on. It is also worth noting that 'the imaginary' (as opposed to the more everyday use of 'imaginary' as an adjective) is, of course, a Lacanian concept, and one that will trail particular resonances for some readers.[24]

Laclau and Mouffe insist that they are not obliterating Marxism without trace (an impossible project, of course, for good Derridians), but are in some senses working through it: they are post-*Marxist* as well as *post*-Marxist. This, as we shall see, has led to some critics of their book saying that Laclau and Mouffe are themselves not really free from the residues of totalizing and essentialist thought that they have acquired on their long tramp through Marxism. (One might ask: if you want to end up with a theory of the rainbow coalition, why pick Kautsky as the place to start?)

The substantive arguments of *Hegemony and Socialist Strategy* pivot on Laclau and Mouffe's reading of Gramsci, and here, as they say, 'everything depends on how ideology is conceived'.[25] Their account of Gramsci's theory of ideology and hegemony stresses – initially, anyway – his break with the critical conception of ideology, in favour of a positive (which they call 'material') perspective, and his rejection of the deterministic base/superstructure model of ideology. They insist, too, that for Gramsci 'the ideological elements articulated by a hegemonic class do not have a necessary class belonging'.[26]

Gramsci is a pivotal figure for Laclau and Mouffe because he represents the furthest point that can be reached within Marxism and the intrinsic limitations of the theoretical problematic. For even the 'articulatory' role of the working class is, in their reading of Gramsci, assigned to it on the basis of economic location, and thus has a necessary rather than their preferred contingent character. Gramsci's view is therefore, in the last analysis, as 'essentialist' one. It is essential with regard to the privileged position of the working class, and with regard to 'the last redoubt of essentialism: the economy'.

Their own conclusions, bracingly headed 'Facing the Consequences', are to deny that the economy is self-regulated and subject to endogenous laws, to deny that social agents are constituted, ultimately, in a class core, and to deny that class position is necessarily linked to 'interests'. The propositions of the new theory can be reduced to two, at its most simple. They are (1) a general philosophical position on 'the impossibility of society', explicated in the chapter entitled 'Beyond the Positivity of the Social'; and (2) a theorization of the issue of agency in radical democratic politics, in an epoch where class essentialism has given way to the pluralist demands of the 'new social movements' – feminism, anti-racism, lesbian and gay rights, ecology, peace, etc.

The Impossibility of Society

'The Impossibility of Society' is the title of an article published by Ernesto Laclau in 1983, prefiguring the more detailed argument on this theme to appear in *Hegemony and Socialist Strategy*.[27] Laclau and Mouffe are making a Derridean point here: not that there is no such 'thing' as society, but – as they put it, echoing Derrida's famous *Il n'y a* *pas de hors-texte* – '"Society" is not a valid object of discourse.'[28]

What do they mean by this? This is a decisive step in their argument, and it might be helpful to quote the passage at greater length, since it contains a number of key allusions and some characteristic 'moves'. They write: 'The incomplete character of every totality necessarily leads us to abandon, as a terrain of analysis, the premise of *"society"* as a sutured and self-defined totality. "Society" is not a valid object of discourse. There is no single underlying principle fixing – and hence constituting – the whole field of differences.'[29] The first and most obvious point to extract from this is the rejection of a model of society as a totality. Marxists have, it is true, differed as to how far they thought of societies as integrated totalities, but certainly they have tended to see them at least as bounded entities. In recent years, however, this notion of a social 'totality' has come under renewed scrutiny and reflection. In sociology, too, there has been a drift towards what we might call anti-totality models, with the rise of more micro-sociological and phenomenological approaches. Another aspect of this would be the reconsideration now under way of models of social entities that were, effectively, based on individual nation-states: as if 'the sociology of Britain' or 'of India' were a viable project in an increasingly global social environment. Anthony Giddens has provided incisive critiques of the naive assumptions underlying some conceptions of 'societies', and indeed, the slogan 'Think globally, act locally' has recently been held up to sociologists as a better model for the discipline than some of the previous ones.[30]

[. . .]

Laclau and Mouffe do not rest at a critique of the idea of social 'totality', but move into a more fundamental – philosophical rather than sociological – set of arguments about the 'impossibility' of society. Before going into these, it might be useful to summarize the schema of interlinked concepts that they propose for the analysis of social relations. They define four terms – *articulation, discourse, moment, element* – of which the second, 'discourse', has generated the most controversy. *Articulation* is defined as 'any practice establishing a relation among elements such that their identity is modified as a result of the articulatory practice'; *discourse* is 'the structured totality resulting from the articulatory practice'; *moments* are 'differential positions, in so far as they appear articulated within a discourse'; and an *element* is 'any difference that is not discursively articulated'.[31] The most important point to note about these definitions is that the very extended definition of 'discourse' by Laclau and Mouffe does not, as has been immediately concluded by several materialists, represent a vertiginous leap into idealism. The concept of discourse in their hands is a materialist one that enables them to rethink the analysis of social and historical phenomena in a different framework. Their concept of discourse has been developed in a mode of explicit criticism of the assumptions traditionally governing discussion of the 'material/ideal' split in Marxist theory, and thus cannot (or at least should not) be assimilated automatically to one position within a polarity that they have explicitly rejected. It has something in common with Foucault's use of 'discourse', but there are important differences too. As I shall clarify later, whatever the problems associated with their concept of discourse, Laclau and Mouffe, in their general epistemological orientation, do not occupy the 'idealist' and 'relativist' boxes into which their critics have tried to push them.

Departing, for the moment, from the contentious definition of 'discourse' in *Hegemony and Socialist Strategy*, I want to consider the related set of propositions put forward in the book as to the 'impossibility' of society and represented, in the passage under discussion, by the sentence 'There is no single underlying principle fixing – and hence constituting – the whole field of differences.' What does it mean for them to say that 'absolute fixity' of meaning (and absolute non-fixity) is not possible? A complication with their argument is that, as well as carrying its own considerable weight, it deploys concepts drawn from other theorists whose import to Laclau and Mouffe's argument will be differentially understood by readers. I propose to look at two key concepts of this type, as a way into Laclau and Mouffe's argument: *suture* and *difference*.

Suture is a term whose current theoretical use is drawn from Lacanian psychoanalysis and has been developed, as Laclau and Mouffe describe,[32] in semiotic film theory. Conventionally, in English, meaning 'stitch', the term suture is rendered by the *Oxford English Dictionary* as 'the joining of the lips of a wound', and this original surgical meaning is given a neat and modern gloss in Landry and Maclean's remark that 'a "suture" marks the absence of a former identity, as when cut flesh heals but leaves a scar marking difference'.[33] Laclau and Mouffe present us with a body politic whose skin is permanently split open, necessitating ceaseless duty in the emergency room for the surgeons of hegemony whose fate it is to try and close, temporarily and with difficulty, the gaps. (This patient never makes it to the recovery ward.) Their reference to Stephen Heath's account of suture stresses a 'double movement' – between on the one hand a Lacanian 'I' whose hallmark is division and lack, and on the other hand the simultaneous possibility of coherence or 'filling-in' of that lack. Their application of the concept of suture to the field of politics carries with it an idea that Derrida's work on deconstruction has made influential: the traces of the old cannot be destroyed but remain as sedimentary deposits – even, and indeed especially, where the new is trying hardest to exclude the old. (Deconstruction being the method of uncovering these buried traces.) Thus Laclau and Mouffe say: 'Hegemonic practices are suturing in so far as their field of operation is determined by the openness of the social, by the ultimately unfixed character of every signifier. This original lack is precisely what the hegemonic practices try to fill in.' They conclude that the closure implied in the idea of a totally sutured society is impossible.[34]

The 'ultimate fixity of meaning' is, explain Laclau and Mouffe, a proposition that has been challenged by a powerful strand of philosophical thought 'from Heidegger to Wittgenstein' and, most importantly perhaps for our purposes, by the post-structuralist philosopher Jacques Derrida. This is not the moment to attempt a summary of his views, but one might usefully refer here to Derrida's overarching insistence on meaning as positional rather than absolute. Derrida has elaborated a theory of language as the infinite 'play of signifiers', and of

linguistic meaning as constructed through relations of difference
within a chain.

Difference has come to stand, in a broad range of modern social
theory, as the exemplar of this approach to language and as the mark
of a rejection of absolute meaning or, as Laclau and Mouffe put it here,
of 'ultimate fixity' of meaning. At this point in their argument they
quote Derrida's generalization of the concept of discourse, in *Writing
and Difference*, as an approach that is 'coincident with that of our text'.
Derrida writes:

> This was the moment [he gives as temporal examples the works of
> Nietzsche, Freud and Heidegger] when language invaded the universal
> problematic, the moment when, in the absence of a centre or origin,
> everything became discourse – provided we can agree on this word – that is
> to say, a system in which the central signified, the original or transcendental
> signified, is never absolutely present outside a system of differences. The
> absence of the transcendental signified extends the domain and the play of
> signification infinitely.[35]

Hence, for Laclau and Mouffe, a discourse is 'constituted as an attempt
to dominate the field of discursivity, to arrest the flow of differences, to
construct a centre', and they describe the 'privileged discursive points
of this partial fixation' as *nodal points*, with reference to Lacan's *point de
capiton* (privileged signifiers that fix meaning in a chain).[36]

As far as the impossibility of society is concerned, we can see in
Laclau and Mouffe's perspective a very close and powerful fusing of
Lacan and Derrida. The images and metaphors cut across the divisions
of psychoanalytic, philosophical and political fields, and the guiding
principle is the analysis of a tension between the always-already
(indeed, essentially) split and decentred, be it the Lacanian psyche or
signification in Derrida, and the 'suturing' hegemonic project of
coherence. Thus Laclau and Mouffe conclude that 'If the social does
not manage to fix itself in the intelligible and instituted forms of a
society, the social only exists, however, as an effort to construct that
impossible object.'[37] 'Society' is the impossible object of the operations
of the social, just as, we might say, the 'Jacobin imaginary' figured as an
empty and illusory prospect for the operations of the political.

The Unsatisfactory Term 'New Social Movements'

If, in their constitution of 'society' as an impossibility, Laclau and
Mouffe draw on the ideas of other post-structuralist thinkers such as
Derrida and Lacan, it will be conceded even by their sternest critics that

in their analysis of the 'new social movements' they have delivered an original and highly influential development in political thought. An obvious explanation of the enormous current interest in their work is that it speaks to a problem – the weight to be attached to social class as opposed to other salient divisions such as gender, ethnicity or age, for example – that has exercised a major hold on both academic analyses and on practical political activity across the traditional Right/Left spectrum.

On the academic front, we have seen a variety of debates around this topic, largely (not surprisingly) in Marxisant treatments of sociology, politics and economics. Partly these debates concern the massive retheorization required to apply Marx's own concepts and descriptors to societies whose class structures and relationships have changed radically in the ensuing century – here one could point schematically to the debates around the work on class of Erik Olin Wright and Carchedi, around the questions that continue to arise from the writings of Poulantzas on politics and class and from the revolution in 'rethinking Marxism' spearheaded by the economists Steve Resnick and Rick Wolff, and indeed one could also mention the major developments known under the umbrella heading of 'rational choice theory' as it continues to sweep across the field of what we might still, rather loosely, call Marxism. In all of these debates, there has been a potential for engagement with the actualities of *non-class* divisions, but (to express the situation tactfully) this has remained in many instances a potential rather than a nettle to be grasped.

Partly, too, academic debates around class have taken place in a conscious dialogue with the work of feminists and the writings of those who have sought to rethink class in relation to the major concern of national identity and nationalist politics, as well as in relation to the issues of ethnicity and racism. It is perhaps worth stressing how rich and varied the challenge to 'class primacy' has become in social science: whole schools of thought now exist devoted to the ways in which housing, for example, or life-cycle effects, cut across cherished assumptions about the determining effects of social class. So it seems very clear that a radical new theorization of politics, in which the iconic factor of class is dramatically shifted from its privileged position, would be of great interest to many people. (Why Laclau and Mouffe's book has been taken up so extensively in literary critical theory is a more complex question, which I will not take up here.)

In terms of practical politics, there can be no doubt that *Hegemony and Socialist Strategy* addresses a problem of tremendous pertinence and significance. This is, perhaps, most obviously true of the belea-guered Left, which has had, in a variety of contexts, to rethink not only its images of class themselves but the role it should occupy in 'left' politics more generally, where it is in competition with the claims of environmentalism, gay rights, feminism, anti-racism, and so on. As we no doubt all know, dispute on this question has concerned the Left very deeply in recent years. The 'coalition politics' to emerge from some of these political interactions, of which perhaps the most notable example in recent years has been the Jesse Jackson campaign for the US presidency in 1988, are exactly what the book addresses at a theoretical level. Given, however, that it has been the Right and centre (certainly in Britain and the USA) that have articulated some of these new connections and meanings, we should not suppose at all that the phenomenon is restricted to the politics of the Left.

Laclau and Mouffe, presumably sensitive to the predicted charge that they are moving rightwards, suggest that their iconoclasm about social class paves the way for a new political radicalism:

> The rejection of privileged points of rupture and the confluence of struggles into a unified political space, and the acceptance, on the contrary, of the plurality and indeterminacy of the social, seem to us the two fundamental bases from which a new political imaginary can be constructed, radically libertarian and infinitely more ambitious in its objectives than the classic left.[38]

At the most elementary level the term 'new social movements' is unsatisfactory, to Laclau and Mouffe among others, in that it encodes its own historic marginality. These are, precisely, 'new' movements in that they are *not class* movements, and this reference back to class will remain there as long as we use that style of nomination. What is being referred to is the phenomenon, which Laclau and Mouffe try to locate historically in the web of post-1945 changes in labour process, state and cultural diffusion, of new antagonisms being articulated, in a novel way, in relation to increasingly numerous social relations. In practice, the term groups together struggles as diverse as 'urban, ecological, anti-authoritarian, anti-institutional, feminist, anti-racist, ethnic, regional or that of sexual minorities'.[39] Laclau and Mouffe see in these struggles the articulation of antagonisms in a wide range of sites beyond the traditional workplace in which class conflict has been situated by Marxism, and they point, for example, to consumption, services and habitat as terrains for these new conflicts.

As well as extending such antagonisms far beyond the limits conventionally operating in Marxist analyses, they suggest that the bureaucratization of postwar (Western, industrial capitalist) society has given rise to new forms of regulation of social relations. They thus recast the arguments of Foucault and Donzelot by seeing as 'consequences' of postwar bureaucratization the process of 'the imposition of multiple forms of vigilance and regulation in social relations which had previously been conceived as forming part of the private domain'.[40] Acknowledging the familiar political ambiguities surrounding political resistance in a 'welfare state' context, Laclau and Mouffe see, amongst the various factors in play in such struggles, a newly articulated broad sphere of social 'rights'. Categories such as 'justice' and 'equality' have been, in a sense, lifted from their liberal context and articulated within a democratic political discourse. Laclau and Mouffe conclude here that commodification and bureaucratization, and the reformulation of a liberal-democratic political ideology, form the context in which we should understand the expansion of social conflict and the constitution of new political subjects, which in turn they describe as 'a moment of deepening of the democratic revolution'.[41]

They add, however, that a third aspect of the new 'hegemonic formation of the post-war period' plays an important role: the expansion of mass communication and the retreat of traditional cultural identities. Laclau and Mouffe see, in the ambiguities of a cultural massification that interpellates subjects as theoretically equal consumers as well as providing some elements with subversive potential, a general homogenization of social life. They point, in a very interesting passage, to the fact that resistance to this has tended to take the form of a 'proliferation of particularisms' and the 'valorisation of "differences"', especially those geared to the creation of new cultural identities. In these demands for autonomy, so often slighted by the Left for their apparent individualism, Laclau and Mouffe see a reformulation of the demand for 'liberty' – one of the central themes of the democratic imaginary.[42]

In considering Laclau and Mouffe's argument in general, one might want to draw attention to a key emphasis on what they describe as 'the logic of equivalence'. This can be explained as follows: the French Revolution was an important moment in the development of a democratic imaginary in that it ushered out a hierarchical social order ('ruled by a theological-political logic in which the social order had its foundation in divine will') where political discourse could only be the repetition and reproduction of inequality. (A striking instance of this is the notorious English hymn verse 'The rich man in his castle, /The poor man at his gate, /God made them, high or lowly, /And ordered their estate.') Here let me quote a crucial sentence from Laclau and Mouffe: 'This break with the *ancien régime*, symbolised by the Declaration of the Rights of Man, would provide the discursive conditions which made it possible to propose the different forms of inequality as illegitimate and anti-natural, and thus make them equivalent as forms of oppression.'[43] Thus the 'logic of equivalence' is born: we have moved from a social order in which subjects are differentially, but fatefully, positioned, to a social order in which the democratic project can articulate itself in a political discourse which takes those differential positionings as an object of struggle. So the democratic revolution brings about a logic of equivalence, a logic of the comparison of subjects that are, essentially, construed as equals, through its new discourse of 'rights', 'liberty' and 'equality'.

There are ambiguities at the heart of Laclau and Mouffe's use of the idea of 'equivalence'. For one thing, it is not clear how the 'anti-natural' element of the democratic imaginary could ever operate without lapsing into the humanism and essentialism that they consistently deplore. Secondly, there is a more confusing ambiguity as to whether 'equivalence' is being construed as similar to 'equality', which is at times implied, or whether Laclau and Mouffe's logic of equivalence is more appropriately captured with reference to the chemical use of equivalence to denote the proportional weights of substances equal in their chemical value. This would emphasize a notion of equal value, but introducing the tension between equality and – precisely – *difference* is difficult to square with the 'one man one vote' [*sic*] logic of democratic equality.

There is, however, no ambiguity on one central point of the logic of equivalence, and this is the secondary place that class occupies with regard to the prior category of the democratic imaginary. Laclau and Mouffe write that socialist demands are not only 'a moment internal to the democratic revolution' but are 'only intelligible on the basis of the equivalential logic which the latter establishes'.[44] They write earlier of Marx that he had sought to rethink social division on a new principle – that of class – but that this was undermined from the start by 'a radical insufficiency, arising from the fact that class opposition is incapable of dividing the totality of the social body into two antagonistic camps', and they comment that Marx's sociological predictions (about capitalist society becoming increasingly polarized) were an effort to project a future simplification on a social world that in Marx's own time did not fit a crude class-reduced model.[45] Thus, in general, we have an account of Marxism's preoccupation with class as an articulation of political demands whose preconditions lay in the democratic revolution of the century before. Hence Laclau and Mouffe see no need for subsequent antagonisms, and the 'new' social movements articulating the demands of those oppressed by them, to cede place to class on the basis that social class is a founding principle. It is only, in their analysis, one of numerous contradictions that may by articulated within the parameters of democratic political discourse.

Post-Marxism, Discourse and Ideology

Several major considerations present themselves in thinking about the issues raised by *Hegemony and Socialist Strategy*. I have two reasons for taking its critique of Marxism very seriously, and both of them relate to longstanding difficulties with the arguments of Marxism: the first is the question of social class, in a political environment where it is increasingly obvious to everyone except the dogmatists of the far Right and far Left that social inequalities and political differences simply cannot plausibly be subsumed under or reduced to the question of class. Hence any attempt to advocate new ways of thinking about these different political struggles should be welcomed and considered.

Secondly, Laclau and Mouffe's argument addresses, although not in a predictable way (as I shall explain), the vexed question of how to theorize the concept of ideology. I say this is vexed, but its vexatiousness has a particular history and will be of more salience to some than to others. Within, roughly, 'socialist' versions of feminism there has been an attempt to use the concept of ideology to theorize the oppression of women in capitalist society, but this has remained problematic, since that theory is itself embedded in an analysis that not only argues/ assumes the primacy of class but also normally construes ideology in a determinist model such as the metaphor of 'base and superstructure'. The ensuing problem was raised by the arguments of an earlier book of mine in which, according to Johanna Brenner and Maria Ramas, 'ideology is Barrett's *deus ex machina*, her means of escape from the vexing dilemma of the Marxist-reductionist/dual systems idealist impasse of socialist-feminist thought'. What, they and other critics wanted to know, was the material basis – in a capitalist society – of this ideology that oppressed women?[46] Laclau and Mouffe, in rejecting the 'class-essentialist' logic of Marxism, in providing so many arguments against the automatic privileging of class in Marxist analysis, have, albeit very contentiously, struck at the heart of this problem.

In part this is a crisis of 'class politics' and, as Richard Wright has noted in a review of the divergent responses of Barry Hindess and Ellen Wood, it has produced polar reactions: a pragmatic approach to class that has been shorn of the theoretical pretension of the Marxist model, and a reaffirmation of classical class politics.[47] The reason the polarity has developed is because the position of arguing in detail for the complexities and specificities of gender in relation to class, against the ceaseless rehearsal of so-called received truths about class, is an unenviable one, and the 'centre' of the debate has, increasingly, been evacuated. It is not without interest that the theoretical models attempting to reconcile conflicts between the claims of class and

gender, as these emerge in social science anyway, have proved unequal
to the task of dealing with the 'newer' (to some) questions of ethnicity
and racism. As I have suggested elsewhere, it is as if existing theories of
social structure, already taxed by attempting to think about the
interrelations of class and gender, have been quite unable to integrate a
third axis of systematic inequality into their conceptual maps. And it is
easy to point, by contrast, to the veritable explosion of work that does
combine these three interests (the 'holy trinity' of class, race and
gender) in disciplines and genres where these structural/morphologi-
cal constraints do not hold back the exploration of new issues.[48]

It might be relevant to add, here, that the general orientation of
Laclau's earlier work rejecting the 'class-belonging' dimension of
political ideology has proved a useful framework for thinking about
political discourse in a nuanced manner. I have previously mentioned
the influence of that work on the exploration, by Colin Mercer and
Stuart Hall among others, of nationalism (the Gramscian 'national-
popular'), patriotism and Thatcherism, for example. The idea of
'political discourse', as a concept that can accommodate a variety of
groups, demands and interests as they are articulated, opens the way
for an analysis of gender that was by definition marginalized in the
'reflection of class' school of thought about political ideology. We have
certainly seen, drawing loosely on the ideas of 'early Laclau', several
analyses of contemporary political discourse as gendered: they consider the ways in which, for example, feminism and anti-feminism,
constructions of 'family' and sexuality, or articulations and denials of
women's reproductive rights, figure in the discourses.[49]

It remains to be seen, however, how far *Hegemony and Socialist Strategy*
really does carry through its iconoclastic project of the complete
dismantling of class privilege. To say this is not to make a cheap point of
the order of 'caught you using the word society' but to address a more
serious issue that surfaces in relation to the majority of post-structuralist
work. This is the intrusion, or return in disguise, of elements (often of
the kind that postmodernists refer to as 'metanarratives') which have
been explicitly rejected elsewhere in the texts in question.

As far as Laclau and Mouffe are concerned, we revert here to the
question of their post-Marxism. Let me take as an example the section
of their argument where they set out the hegemonic transformation of
the postwar social order, in which they locate the emergence of new
social antagonisms and their articulation in new social movements.[50]
Far from subscribing to a logic of 'contingency', the sequence of their
propositions, and the model of causality expounded in them, are
entirely characteristic of the traditional patterns of Marxist thought. If
we take the sequence of the argument first, it is astonishing that – in

their historical reconstruction of the new hegemonic social formation – they automatically move first to the 'economic point of view' which, drawing on the work of Michel Aglietta, they analyse in terms of that most orthodox of Marxist concepts, commodification. Then we have a brief registration of environmental and urban issues, though, interestingly, the argument here does not operate by means of any concept equivalent to commodification. Next (and by contrast we find the concept of bureaucratization mobilized) Laclau and Mouffe move, in fact, to the state, and then on to political articulation and the reformulation of liberal-democratic ideology. The classical Marxist mind-set – economy, then state, then ideology, then 'culture' – is then fully completed in the addition of the 'important aspect' of mass communication and its new cultural forms. So, whatever their theoretical protestations about the economy as 'the last redoubt of essentialism', it is undoubtedly true that in one of the rare places where a substantive social/historical account is offered in the book it exactly reproduces, in its own ordering, that economistic and determinist logic.

As does the content of the argument, too, at this point. The thesis about capitalist development in this period is concerned with the expansion of capitalist relations into previously non-capitalist areas, but it rests on an extraordinary construction of capitalism as being about 'commodification' but not necessarily about labour/capital contradictions. They write: 'Today it is not only as sellers of labour-power that the individual is subordinated to capital, but also through his or her incorporation into a multitude of other social relations: culture, free time, illness, education, sex and even death. There is practically no domain of individual or collective life which escapes capitalist relations.'[51] The entire discussion of this phenomenon is interesting in that it is uncritically couched within a Marxist reading of this historical process that has long been challenged – on the one hand by the Foucault/Donzelot position of the historical emergence of 'the social', and on the other by feminist insistence on the *non*-capitalist power relations at play in the world of the 'private domain'.[52] So, although Laclau and Mouffe gesture in the direction of feminism by noting the subordination of women in traditional community networks, they adopt a highly 'functionalist' and 'reductionist' and classically orthodox 'Marxist' formulation about the welfare state and the reproduction of labour-power, and one which has been explicitly criticized by feminists. And what is interesting about their constitution of 'capitalism' is that it remains an elemental and undefined agent in the argument – yet an agent whose existence they have, in general terms, challenged.

If all this is to say that Laclau and Mouffe are 'still too Marxist' – a position taken in Landry and Maclean's reading of the text[53] – it is a far cry from the usual tenor of responses to the book. Most of these have taken the form of polemical engagement with the apostasy, from a Marxist point of view, of Laclau and Mouffe's arguments. Ellen Wood, to take one of her criticisms at random, accuses them of 'not only a breathtaking misreading of Marx, but also a very substantial failure of reasoning'.[54] Many of these debates are concerned, which I am not, with a doxological restatement of the primacy of class to Marxist theory and practice, but some issues are worth recapitulating briefly. One of these is the question of materialism, and the issue of whether Laclau and Mouffe's rejection of the discursive/non-discursive distinction necessarily makes them 'idealist'. I have suggested earlier that it does not, and that their use of the category discourse is defensible in relation to what people like to call 'the real world': the elementary point to make is that discourse *is* 'real'. In their reply to a critique by Norman Geras, Laclau and Mouffe explain, with some examples, the sense in which they use the term 'discourse', which is defined in the book as the structured totality resulting from articulatory practice. First of all – but it is a source of some misunderstanding – they include within the category of discourse both linguistic and non-linguistic phenomena – discourse is not a text or speech or similar. The term is principally concerned with *meaning*, and they give the example (which Geras finds 'patronizing' but others have found useful) of football:

> If I kick a spherical object in the street or if I kick a ball in a football match, the *physical* fact is the same, but its *meaning* is different. The object is a football only to the extent that it establishes a system of relations with other objects, and these relations are not given by the mere referential materiality of the objects but are, rather, socially constructed.[55]

The example is helpful in that it answers those who think that their use of the term discourse is in some way a threat to ontological reality: they do not dispute referential materiality ('the discursive character of an object does not, by any means, imply putting its *existence* into question') but insist that the meaning of physical objects must be understood by apprehension of their place in a system (or discourse) of socially constructed rules. What applies to footballs, we could add, applies to tanks, police horses, jails, fighter bombers, and any other material appurtenances of the suppression of the working class. Laclau and Mouffe are not 'collapsing' or 'dissolving' everything into discourse: they are insisting that we cannot apprehend or think of the non-discursive other than in contextualizing discursive categories, be they scientific, political or whatever.

Related to this is the question of relativism. It is sometimes assumed that Laclau and Mouffe must be taking up a position of epistemological relativism, but nothing could be further from the case. As may readily be noted, although 'truth' is always theoretically contextual in their frame of reference, there is no shortage of truth claims in their own theoretical discourse. One interesting example here is to look at their treatment of the question of ideology, for so long a stumbling block in terms of the assignation of real interests, correct consciousness, and so on. Laclau and Mouffe's attachment to epistemological security is such that they even take on, within the terms of their own model, the old conundrum about whether people can be said to be 'oppressed' if they themselves do not think they are. This is the subject of a fascinating distinction that they draw between 'subordination' and 'oppression': the former simply marks a set of differential positions between social agents, whereas the latter requires a point *exterior* to the discourse from which – for 'oppression' to exist – the discourse of subordination can be interrupted. And just for those who still see relativism as indexically linked to privileging the discursive, let me quote their definition of 'relations of domination': 'those relations . . . which are considered as illegitimate from the perspective, or in the judgement, of a social agent external to them'.[56] Far from being 'relativist', these confident formulations, spoken naturally from the position of the judging external agent rather than that of the judges, err on the side of being hard to justify in epistemological terms.

So it is perhaps not surprising to find Laclau and Mouffe offering us a defence of the 'critical', 'epistemological' view of ideology, but of course a fundamentally reformulated one. There are points in the argument of *Hegemony and Socialist Strategy* where one can say that for Laclau and Mouffe something is 'essentially' of such and such a character, and this is an important recognition. A key point of interaction between epistemology and the general concerns I have indicated about ideology can be found in the conclusion of Laclau's article 'The Impossibility of Society'. Here Laclau clarifies the solid epistemological foundation of their 'anti-essentialism': 'We cannot do without the concept of misrecognition, precisely because the very assertion that the "identity and homogeneity of social agents is an illusion" cannot be formulated without introducing the category of misrecognition.' Hence Laclau concludes that both the category of ideology and that of misrecognition can be retained, but by inverting their traditional content: he suggests that 'the ideological would not consist of the misrecognition of a positive essence [an illusion as to real class interests, for example], but exactly the opposite: it would consist of the non-recognition of the precarious character of any positivity, of the impossibility of any ultimate suture.'[57] The substantive thesis put forward here – that ideology is a vain attempt to impose closure on a social world whose essential characteristic is the infinite play of differences and the impossibility of any ultimate fixing of meaning – is thus couched in a framework in which the traditional distinction within Marxism between knowledge and ideological 'misrecognition' is (paradoxically to some) retained.

In general, perhaps it would be a good thing for Marxists to look at the world, even if only for an experimental (but it would have to be open-minded) period, through the glasses of Laclau and Mouffe. It certainly is a different place, and despite all the refined and detailed arguments about their theses one is left with a sense that these people have woken up one morning and, simply, seen 'society' differently. This is a possible interpretation of Paul Hirst's differentiation between himself and Althusser: 'He conceives social relations . . . I, on the other hand, consider social relations . . . .' What makes the passage interesting is the assertion, cool and reflective with only a hint of the *ex cathedra*, of a simple difference of view. Much argued over in the past, but now a difference of vision rather than opinion.

Perhaps one could draw an analogy with the normal curve on which IQ testing rests. Leave aside for the moment the morass of detailed problems about whether IQ tests are culture-bound, or racist, and consider the more fundamental question of whether intelligence occurs through the population on the basis of a 'normal distribution' with regression to the mean. Strictly speaking, this cannot and could not be proved, but people continue to 'measure IQ' on a basis that makes sense only if this assumption is true. Some of Laclau and Mouffe's arguments can be responded to at the level of whether they are substantively accurate (if you like, the level of whether IQ testing is, within its own terms, objective), but some of their arguments are characteristically 'post-structuralist' in that they lift us out of the frame of reference in which we began (of denying, or querying, the proposition about the normal curve, and hence delegitimating the whole exercise). The most interesting example of this type of argument is the treatment, in *Hegemony and Socialist Strategy*, of the issue of 'positivity' and 'negativity' in a social context, and it is to here that I want to round off this discussion.

It is curiously disturbing to encounter the word 'positive' as a negative term, but this is indeed how it figures in Laclau and Mouffe's text. What does it mean to advocate a movement 'beyond the positivity of the social'? I have tried to explicate earlier what is meant by this in the context of the impossibility of 'society', and of the proposition that the social is always an attempt at suture rather than a complete closure. In more general terms, however, Laclau and Mouffe are in harmony with a strand of modern philosophy that might go under the headings of a celebration of negativity, a certain nihilism, a delight in destruction/deconstruction, an emphasis on meaninglessness. All these currents can be found, as is mentioned in the book, in modern European philosophy, from Sartre's existentialism to the more 'negative' side of the phenomenological tradition, in Heidegger, Nietzsche and parts of Wittgenstein. In this sense, contemporary post-structuralism has a long history in twentieth-century European philosophy, and this is the context in which we need to read Laclau and Mouffe. What is unique to them is the project of a rigorous re-engagement or rereading of the Marxist tradition of political thought through the lens of these ideas.

At the heart of their project is a recognition that Marxism delivers some elements of this 'negative' world-view, but is, in contrast, by and large what Timpanaro has called 'triumphalist' in its orientation. Marxism was born of a confident moment, indeed an imperialist one, and it speaks that 'Victorian' sense of conquest of the natural world in Marx's founding ideas about human nature and human labour.[58] As Laclau puts it: 'it would be absurd to deny that this dimension of mastery/ transparency/rationalism is present in Marxism'. Rather disarmingly, Laclau, in summarizing the 'negative' dimension of Marxism that he finds inspiring (negativity, struggle, antagonism, opacity, ideology, the gap between the real and the sensual), comments that for this reading to be possible, one has to ignore at least half of Marx's work.[59] It is for this reason that *Hegemony and Socialist Strategy* is '*post*- Marxist'. Laclau, in the slightly later article from which I am now quoting, sees the negative dimension as the founding one: 'it [the moment of negativity] shone for just a brief moment in theoretical discourse, only to dissolve an instant later into the full positivity which reabsorbed it – positivity of history and society as totalisations of their partial processes, the positivity of the subject – the social classes – as agents of history'.[60] Laclau's tone is elegiac here, and indeed he goes on to cite Stalin as the end point of the affirmation of positivity in Marxism.

There can be no doubt that the critique of 'positivity' and the critique of essentialist thought, which are applied by Laclau and Mouffe to Marxism, are aspects of a broader challenge to a wide variety of thought. The article to which I have just referred is, in fact, a consideration by Laclau of points of comparison between this 'reading' of Marxism (now 'post-Marxism') and psychoanalysis. Here, Laclau offers some links between the Laclau/Mouffe conception of hegemony (dislocation, the attempt at suture) and a Lacanian notion of 'lack', and

he recommends a possible confluence of post-Marxism and psychoanalysis 'around the logic of the signifier as a logic of unevenness and
dislocation'.[61] What Laclau does not mention at this point, however, is
that this reading of psychoanalysis requires us to ignore not just half
but almost all of 'psychoanalysis', and take up a strictly Lacanian
interpretation. For about 90 per cent of psychoanalysis is burdened
with a leaden weight of essentialism and it is, in fact, only the Lacanian
reworking of the theory that has stripped it of these positivities. Hence
it could be more appropriate to be discussing a confluence of
'post-psychoanalysis' with post-Marxism.

At this point we might turn to Charles Jencks's useful comment on
'the paradoxical dualism' that the hybrid term 'postmodernism' entails:
it is, he writes, at one and the same time the continuation of modernism
and its transcendence.[62] So it is with Laclau and Mouffe, whose work in
some respects remains locked inside a Marxist framework and in
others breaks out into an altogether different philosophical frame of
reference. And if you conclude that the 'axioms' of Marxism, particularly with regard to the relationships between class, ideology and
political discourse, are not self-evidently true in the contemporary
world, then their challenge to Marxism's class essentialism will represent a considerable cracking indeed, collapse – of the Marxist model.

Notes

1. Antonio Gramsci, *Selections from the Prison Notebooks*, eds, Quintin Hoare and
Geoffrey Nowell-Smith, London: Lawrence & Wishart 1976, pp. 376–7.
2. Ibid., pp. 325–6.
3. Ibid.
4. Antonio Gramsci, *Selections from Cultural Writings*, eds, David Forgacs and
Geoffrey Nowell-Smith, London: Lawrence & Wishart 1985.
5. Perry Anderson, 'The Antinomies of Antonio Gramsci', *New Left Review* 100,
1976–7.
6. Stuart Hall, Bob Lumley and Gregor McLennan, 'Politics and Ideology: Gramsci',
in Centre for Contemporary Cultural Studies, *On Ideology*, London: Hutchinson 1984;
originally pubd in *Working Papers in Cultural Studies* 10, 1977. I am indebted in this
account to the exposition of Gramsci in this admirably clear essay.
7. Anderson, 'Antinomies', p. 49.
8. Stuart Hall, 'Rethinking the "Base and Superstructure" Metaphor', in Jon
Bloomfield, ed., *Class, Hegemony and Party*, London: Lawrence & Wishart 1977, pp. 65–6.
9. Ernesto Laclau, *Politics and Ideology in Marxist Theory: Capitalism, Fascism, Populism*
London: New Left Books 1977; and *Hegemony and Socialist Strategy*, London: Verso 1985.
10. See the discussion of reductionism as a major problem in Marxist 'explanations' of
women's oppression in Michèle Barrett, *Women's Oppression Today: The Marxist/Feminist
Encounter*, 2nd edn with new Introduction, London: Verso 1988, pp. 23 ff. A more recent
trend is to clear away the entire problem of reductionism, by abandoning the focus on
pre-given interests characteristic of classical Marxism; see, for example, Barry Hindess,
'The Problem of Reductionism', in *Politics and Class Analysis*, Oxford: Basil Blackwell

1987; and Les Johnstone, 'Class and Political Ideology: A Non-reductionist Solution?', in *Marxism, Class Analysis and Socialist Pluralism*, London: Allen & Unwin 1986.

11. Laclau, *Politics and Ideology*, p. 113.

12. Ibid., p. 142.

13. Ibid., p. 135.

14. Ibid., pp. 108–9.

15. Colin Mercer, 'Fascist Ideology', in James Donald and Stuart Hall, eds, *Politics and Ideology*, Milton Keynes: Open Univeristy Press 1986, p. 237.

16. See Stuart Hall and Martin Jacques, eds, *The Politics of Thatcherism*, London: Lawrence & Wishart 1983; and especially Hall's 1979 essay 'The Great Moving Right Show'; Stuart Hall, *The Hard Road to Renewal*, London: Verso 1988.

17. Hall, 'Great Moving Right Show', p. 29.

18. Stuart Hall, 'Authoritarian Populism: A Reply', *New Left Review* 151, 1985, p. 119.

19. Bod Jessop *et al.*, 'Authoritarian Populism, Two Nations and Thatcherism', *New Left Review* 147, 1984.

20. Hall, 'Authoritarian Populism', p. 120.

21. Laclau, *Politics and Ideology*, pp. 60–61.

22. See, for example, Ellen Meiksins Wood, *The Retreat from Class: A New 'True' Socialism*, London: Verso 1986; Norman Geras, 'Post-Marxism?', *New Left Review* 163, 1987.

23. Laclau and Mouffe, *Hegemony and Socialist Strategy*, p. 2.

24. 'In the sense given to this term by Jacques Lacan (and generally used substantively): one of the three essential orders of the psycho-analytic field, namely the Real, the Symbolic and the Imaginary . . . .'. For further exposition of the concept, see J. Laplanche and J. -B. Pontalis, *The Language of Psycho-Analysis*, London: Hogarth Press 1973, p. 210.

25. Laclau and Mouffe, *Hegemony and Socialist Strategy*, p. 67.

26. Ibid.

27. Ernesto Laclau, 'The Impossibility of Society', *Canadian Journal of Political and Social Theory*, 7, 1 and 2, 1983.

28. Laclau and Mouffe, *Hegemony and Socialist Strategy*, p. 111; Jacques Derrida, *Of Grammatology*, trans. G. C. Spivak, Baltimore, MD: Johns Hopkins University Press 1974, p. 158.

29. Laclau and Mouffe, *Hegemony and Socialist Strategy*, p. 111.

30. John Urry, unpublished talk at the University of Surrey, 1990.

31. Laclau and Mouffe, *Hegemony and Socialist Strategy*, p. 105.

32. Ibid., p. 88, n. 1.

33. Donna Landry and Gerald Maclean, 'Reading Laclau and Mouffe' (forthcoming).

34. Laclau and Mouffe, *Hegemony and Socialist Strategy*, p. 88, n. 1.

35. Ibid., p. 112; Jacques Derrida, 'Structure, Sign and Play', in *Writing and Difference*, London: Routledge & Kegan Paul 1978, p. 280.

36. Laclau and Mouffe, *Hegemony and Socialist Strategy*, p. 112.

37. Ibid.

38. Ibid., p. 152.

39. Ibid., p. 159.

40. Ibid., p. 162; see also Jacques Donzelot, *The Policing of Families*, London: Hutchinson 1980.

41. Laclau and Mouffe, *Hegemony and Socialist Strategy*, p. 163.

42. Ibid., p. 164.

43. Ibid., p. 155.

44. Ibid., p. 156.

45. Ibid., p. 151.

46. Johanna Brenner and Maria Ramas, 'Rethinking Women's Oppression', *New Left Review* 144, 1984, pp. 68–9.

47. Richard Wright, review, *Rethinking Marxism* 1, 2, 1988, p. 170.

48. Barrett, *Women's Oppression Today*, p. x.

49. See Stuart Hall's work, especially *Politics of Thatcherism*; Gill Seidel, ed., *The Nature*

of the Right, Amsterdam: John Benjamins 1988; Ruth Levitas, ed., *The Ideology of the New Right*; and Michèle Jean *et al.*, 'Nationalism and Feminism in Quebéc, in R. Hamilton and M. Barrett, eds, *The Politics of Diversity*, London: Verso 1986.

50. Laclau and Mouffe, *Hegemony and Socialist Strategy*, pp. 160 ff.

51. Ibid., p. 161.

52. Donzelot, *Policing of Families*; Leonore Davidoff and Catherine Hall give a different account of the gendered character of the 'private sphere' in *Family Fortunes*, London: Hutchinson 1987.

53. Landry and Maclean, 'Reading Laclau and Mouffe'.

54. Wood, *Retreat from Class*, p. 59.

55. Ernesto Laclau and Chantal Mouffe, 'Post-Marxism without Apologies' (A Reply to Norman Geras), *New Left Review* 166, 1987, p. 82.

56. Laclau and Mouffe, *Hegemony and Socialist Strategy*, p. 154; see also Richard Rorty, *Consequences of Pragmatism*, Minneapolis: Minnesota University Press 1982, pp. 166–7.

57. Laclau, 'Impossibility of Society', p. 24.

58. See Sebastiano Timpanaro, *On Materialism*, London: Verso 1980.

59. Ernesto Laclau, 'Psychoanalysis and Marxism', in *The Trials of Psychoanalysis*, ed. Françoise Meltzer, Chicago University Press 1988, p. 143.

60. Ibid., p. 142.

61. Ibid., p. 144.

62. Charles Jencks, *What Is Post-modernism?* London: Academy Editions 1986, p. 7.

Doxa and Common Life: An Interview

Pierre Bourdieu and Terry Eagleton

Terry Eagleton Hello and welcome.* Pierre Bourdieu and I will discuss some of the themes in our new books – primarily his book, *Language and Symbolic Power*, but also my book, *Ideology*.[1] And then we will invite questions and comments.

I would like to welcome you, Pierre, on one of your too rare visits to this country. We are delighted to see you and to have these translated essays. One of the themes of your work is that language is as much – or is perhaps more – an instrument of power and of action than of communication. This is a theme that informs everything you write in this book and that leads you to be properly hostile, as I would see it, to any mere semiotics. You want to look instead at what you call at one point 'the social conditions of the production of utterances', and also, I suppose, at the conditions of the reception of utterances. In other words, you are arguing that what matters in talk, in discourse, is not some power inherent in language itself, but the kind of authority or legitimacy with which it is backed. And that leads you to mobilize concepts that, I think, many of us are very familiar with from your other work – such as 'symbolic power', 'symbolic violence', 'linguistic capital' and the rest. I would like to ask you whether I have got this right and to explain how these processes might relate to the concept of ideology – are they synonymous, or is ideology for you something quite different? The concept of ideology does sometimes crop up in your work, but it is not a central concern in this particular book.

* What follows is an edited transcript of a discussion – one in a series of 'Talking Ideas' – between Pierre Bourdieu and Terry Eagleton that took place at the Institute of Contemporary Arts, London, on 15 May 1991.

Pierre Bourdieu   Thank you for what you say about my book; in only
a few sentences you have summarized its main intention, so it is now
easier for me to answer the question. In fact, I tend to avoid the word
'ideology' because, as your own book shows, it has very often been
misused, or used in a very vague manner. It seems to convey a sort of
discredit. To describe a statement as ideological is very often an insult,
so that this ascription itself becomes an instrument of symbolic
domination. I have tried to substitute concepts like 'symbolic domination' or 'symbolic power' or 'symbolic violence' for the concept of
ideology in order to try to control some of the uses, or abuses, to which
it is subject. Through the concept of symbolic violence I try to make
visible an unperceived form of everyday violence. For example, here in
this auditorium now I feel very shy; I am anxious and have difficulty
formulating my thoughts. I am under a strong form of symbolic
violence which is related to the fact that the language is not mine and I
don't feel at ease in front of this audience. I think that the concept of
ideology could not convey that, or it would do so in a more general
manner. Sometimes we must refurbish concepts – first, to be more
precise, and second, to make them more alive. I am sure you agree that
the concept of ideology has been so used and abused that it does not
work any more. We no longer believe in it; and it is important, for
example in political uses, to have concepts that are efficient and
effective.

TE   This prompts me to explain why I still write about ideology, even
though I agree with what you say about the frequent vagueness of the
concept and that there are many different notions of ideology in
circulation. My book was partly an attempt to clarify the concept. I also
think there are reasons now why the concept of ideology seems to be
superfluous or redundant, and I try to look at these in my book too.
One is that the theory of ideology would seem to depend on a concept
of representation, and certain models of representation have been
called into question and thereby also, so it is thought, the notion of
ideology. Another reason – perhaps a more interesting one – is that it is
often felt now that in order to identify a form of thought as ideological
you would need to have some kind of access to absolute truth. If the
idea of absolute truth is called into question then the concept of
ideology would seem to fall to the ground with it.

There are two further reasons why it seems that ideology is no longer
a fashionable concept. One is what has been called 'enlightened false
consciousness', namely, that in a postmodern epoch the idea that we
simply labour under false consciousness is too simple – that people are
actually much more cynically or shrewdly aware of their values than

that would suggest. This again calls the concept of ideology into question. Finally, there is the argument that what keeps the system going is less rhetoric or discourse than, as it were, its own systemic logic: the idea that advanced capitalism works all by itself, that it doesn't any longer need to pass through consciousness to be validated, that it somehow secures its own reproduction. I actually am dubious about whether all of that is sufficient to ditch the concept of ideology. I accept there is a force in those various points, but I suppose one reason I want to retain the concept of ideology is that I do think there is something that corresponds to the notion of false consciousness, and I am interested in your own work in that respect. Can I put it this way: when you use concepts like doxa, spontaneous belief or opinion, then in a sense those are operating as notions of ideology for you, in that doxa would seem unquestionable and natural. On the other hand, does that allow you to talk about false consciousness in the sense of false notions or propositions that actually sustain unjust systems of power? Do you want to talk about false consciousness only in terms of naturalization or universalization, or would you want to talk in more epistemological terms about the relation of false or true ideas to social reality.

PB I agree with the first part of your reasoning – the doubts you expressed about the concept of ideology. I agree and can expand on your objections. In particular, I think that one of the main uses of the concept of ideology was to make a strong break between the scientist and others. For example, Althusser and those influenced by him made a very violent symbolic use of the concept. They used it as a sort of religious notion by which you must climb by degrees to the truth, never being sure to have achieved the true Marxist theory. The theorist was able to say 'You are an ideologist'. For example, Althusser would refer disparagingly to the '*so-called* social sciences'. It was a manner of making visible a sort of invisible separation between the true know-ledge – the possessor of science – and false consciousness. That, I think, is very aristocratic – indeed, one of the reasons why I don't like the word 'ideology' is because of the aristocratic thinking of Althusser.

So now to move on to more familiar ground: why do I think the notion of doxa is more useful? Many things that are called ideology in Marxist tradition in fact operate in a very obscure manner. For example, I could say that all the academic systems, all the educational systems, are a sort of ideological mechanism; they are a mechanism that produces an unequal distribution of personal capital, and they legitimate this production. Such mechanisms are unconscious. They are accepted and that is something very powerful, which is not grasped, in my view, in the traditional definition of ideology as representation, as false consciousness. I think that Marxism, in fact, remains a sort of Cartesian philosophy, in which you have a conscious agent who is the scholar, the learned person, and the others who don't have access to consciousness. We have spoken too much about consciousness, too much in terms of representation. The social world doesn't work in terms of consciousness; it works in terms of practices, mechanisms, and so forth. By using doxa we accept many things without knowing them, and that is what is called ideology. In my view we must work with a philosophy of change. We must move away from the Cartesian philosophy of the Marxist tradition towards a different philosophy in which agents are not aiming consciously towards things, or mistakenly guided by false representation. I think all that is wrong, and I don't believe in it.

TE   If I have understood you, the concept of doxa is what might be called a much more adequate theory of ideology. But I have two worries about that reformulation, which I would like to explain. One is that the concept of doxa stresses the naturalization of ideas. While this does allow you to look at unconscious mechanisms, isn't it too simple to claim that all symbolic violence or ideology is actually naturalized? That is, can't people be in some way more critical, even more sceptical, of those values and beliefs, and nevertheless continue to conform to them? Don't you rather overstress, in other words, the naturalizing function of ideology or doxa? And secondly, are you not in danger of accepting too quickly the idea that people do legitimate prevailing forms of power? There are presumably different kinds of legitimation, all the way from an absolute internalization of ruling ideas to a more pragmatic or sceptical acceptance. What room does your doctrine leave for that kind of dissent, criticism and opposition?

PB   That is a very good question. Even in the most economistic tradition that we know, namely Marxism, I think the capacity for resistance, as a capacity of consciousness, was overestimated. I fear that what I have to say is shocking for the self-confidence of intellectuals, especially for the more generous, left-wing intellectuals. I am seen as pessimistic, as discouraging the people, and so on. But I think it is better to know the truth; and the fact is that when we see with our own eyes people living in poor conditions – such as existed, when I was a young scholar, among the local proletariat, the workers in factories – it is clear that they are prepared to accept much more than we would have believed. That was a very strong experience for me: they put up with a great deal, and this is what I mean by doxa – that there are many things people accept without knowing. I will give you an example taken from our society. When you ask a sample of individuals what are the main factors of achievement at school, the further you go down the social scale the more they believe in natural talent or gifts – the more they believe that those who are successful are naturally endowed with intellectual capacities. And the more they accept their own exclusion, the more they believe they are stupid, the more they say, 'Yes, I was no good at English, I was no good at French, I was no good at mathematics.' Now that is a fact – in my view it is an appalling fact – one that intellectuals don't like to accept, but which they must accept. It doesn't mean that the dominated individuals tolerate everything; but they assent to much more than we believe and much more than they know. It is a formidable mechanism, like the imperial system – a wonderful instrument of ideology, much bigger and more powerful than television or propaganda. That is the main experience I want to convey. What you say about the capacity for dissent is very important; this indeed exists, but not where we look for it – it takes another form.

TE   Yes, you do talk about what you call 'heterodoxy', which is an oppositional kind of language. What Marxists call pessimism in your work, you yourself would see, presumably, as realism. One may agree with that, but on the other hand I know that you don't want to sound too much like Michel Foucault. You don't wish, by virtue of stressing that material realism, to move into a theory of power which you yourself have criticized, I think quite properly, as too abstract, too metaphysical, too all-pervasive; and you want to leave room for some kind of political opposition. My objection to the idea of doxa is that you seem to be saying that there is internalization of dominant and oppressive beliefs, but there is also, in a second movement, something that can be broken and thereby enable a heterodoxy to emerge. But isn't that too chronological? Maybe I'm caricaturing it, but is doxa not itself a more contradictory affair? That is, can people believe and not believe, or believe at different levels?

PB   No. That is related to the programme of the philosophy of man we have, of the philosophy of action, and so on. I would say that as long as you think in terms of consciousness, false consciousness, unconsciousness, and so on, you cannot grasp the main ideological effects, which most of the time are transmitted through the body. The main mechanism of domination operates through the unconscious manipulation of the body. For example, I have just written a paper about the processes of male domination in a so-called primitive society. They are the same as in our society, but a lot more visible. In the former case the dominated persons, the women, acquire domination through bodily education. I could go into detail – for instance, girls learn to walk in a determinate manner, they learn to move their feet in a particular way,

they learn to hide their breasts. When they learn to speak, they don't
say 'I know'; they say 'I don't know'. For example, if you ask a woman
for directions, she will say 'I don't know'. We have the equivalent
process, but it operates in a much more subtle manner – through
language, through the body, through attitudes towards things which
are below the level of consciousness. But this is not mechanistic; it does
not refer us to unconsciousness. As soon as we think in those terms, it
becomes clear that the work of emancipation is very difficult; it is a
question of mental gymnastics as much as consciousness-raising. And
as intellectuals we are not used to that. I call it a scholastic bias – a bias to
which we are all exposed: we think that the problems can be solved only
through consciousness. And that is where I differ from Foucault, and
would draw a contrast with his important concept of discipline.
Discipline, in French at least, points towards something external.
Discipline is enforced by a military strength; you must obey. In a sense
it is easy to revolt against discipline because you are conscious of it. In
fact, I think that in terms of symbolic domination, resistance is more
difficult, since it is something you absorb like air, something you don't
feel pressured by; it is everywhere and nowhere, and to escape from
that is very difficult. Workers are under this kind of invisible pressure,
and so they become much more adapted to their situation than we can
believe. To change this is very difficult, especially today. With the
mechanism of symbolic violence, domination tends to take the form of
a more effective, and in this sense more brutal, means of oppression.
Consider contemporary societies in which the violence has become
soft, invisible.

TE   I would suggest there is a kind of irony there, because on the one
hand you are reacting against what you see as an excessive emphasis on
consciousness. I think that is right, but some of the Marxist tradition
has registered that too. At the same time that you were developing
these theories, the Marxist tradition itself, in the work of Althusser,
whatever its limits, was trying to shift the concept of ideology on to a
much less conscious, and much more practical, institutional place,
which in a way comes closer perhaps to your own position.
   I would like to consider the point about political opposition or
pessimism from a different perspective, one that informs a vital area of
your work now. You talk very boldly and, I think, very imaginatively,
about linguistic markets and the price or the value of utterances – 'price
formation' – and you deliberately transpose a whole Marxist economic
language into the cultural or symbolic spheres; and you speak of the
field of struggle in which people try to amass an amount of *cultural
capital*, whether in education or the arts or whatever. I think this is very

illuminating, not least your stress that in looking at the phenomenon
of art, we can't go directly to the whole social field, but have to pass
through the particular artistic cultural field first. I think that is enor-
mously useful. However, couldn't it be argued that you come out with
a notion of the whole of human practice, action and language as a
war, in which players will try to increase their stakes, to invest more
effectively to the detriment of other players? That is a true description of many fields of our experience, but are there not other forms of
discourse, other forms of action, which you couldn't conceptualize so
easily in those agonistic terms?

PB You are yourself giving a good example of the fact that such
forms exist, through your sympathetic engagement with my ideas!
Anyway, that is an important question, and one that I ask myself; I
agree that it is a problem. I don't know why I tend to think in those
terms – I feel obliged to by reality. My sense is that the kind of exchange we are now engaged in is unusual. Where this happens, it is
the exception based on what Aristotle called φιλια ['philia'] – or
friendship, to use a more general expression. Φιλια is, according to
Aristotle, an economic exchange or symbolic exchange that you may
have within the family, among parents or with friends. I tend to think
that the structure of most of the fields, most of the social games, is
such that competition – a struggle for domination – is quasi-
inevitable. It is evident in the economic field; but even in the religious
field you will find the description is right. In most fields, we may observe what we characterize as competition for accumulation of different forms of capital (religious capital, economic capital, and so on),
and things being what they are, the undistorted communication referred to by Habermas is always an exception. We can achieve this undistorted communication only by a special effort when extraordinary
conditions are fulfilled.

I would just add a word on the analogy between linguistic exchange
and economic exchange, which you referred to just now. This analogy, in my view, is very fruitful in understanding many phenomena
that cannot be treated simply as communication, as language production. Some English philosophers, like Austin, made a point of this;
they saw the presence of very important things in language – like
giving orders, for example, or making announcements – which do not
conform to the communication model. Many things cannot be understood in terms of pure communication, and so by proposing my economic analogy I try only to generalize and to give to an insight of
analytical philosophy a sociological foundation which it lacks. I don't
criticize Austin; I say that he does not give a full account of the social

conditions of possibility of the process he describes. So, though I may
seem very far from this philosophy of language, I am in fact very close.

TE   Clearly, you are thinking sociologically as much as semiologically.
Running throughout the whole of your work is a sort of steady subtext
which is a deep preoccupation with the conditions of your own work
itself – or more generally, with the difficulty of a sociological discourse
that seeks, for whatever good, potentially emancipatory, reasons to
analyse the common life. That is, there is a very powerful commitment
in your work – not always explicit, but present as a kind of sensibility –
to what one might inadequately call 'the common life'. This is one of
many ways in which your work parallels that of Raymond Williams in
this country. But of course it is difficult for a sociologist involved in a
highly specialized discourse to take that common life as an object of
analysis or even of contemplation. You, like myself, don't come from
an intellectual background; and it seems to me that your work is very
interesting because it is marked by the tension between some sense of
common value that has nothing to do with intellect in the first place,
and the other dimension which is very much to analyse the academic
institution – the social condition of intellectuals and its implications. Do
you think this biographical circumstance helps to explain your
preoccupations?

PB   What you say is very sympathetic and generous. You have
expressed my personal feeling exactly. I try to put together the two
parts of my life, as many first-generation intellectuals do. Some use
different means – for instance, they find a solution in political action, in
some kind of social rationalization. My main problem is to try and
understand what happened to me. My trajectory may be described as
miraculous, I suppose – an ascension to a place where I don't belong.
And so to be able to live in a world that is not mine I must try to
understand both things: what it means to have an academic mind – how
such is created – and at the same time what was lost in acquiring it. For
that reason, even if my work – my full work – is a sort of autobiography,
it is a work for people who have the same sort of trajectory, and the
same need to understand.

TE   We have some time for questions or comments. Would anyone
like to take up any of the points raised in the discussion?

*It has been advanced as an argument against the concept of ideology that Marxism
credited people with too much ability to recognize the truth, and that those further
down the social scale are less likely to recognize it. Isn't it more the case that people
further down that scale don't have the economic power that would enable them to go to
discussion groups and escape from the narrow circle of their home life and recognize*

other possibilities? Do you think the part this has to play is more significant than intellectual capabilities – that people have the potential to recognize the wider truths, but their economic and family situations prevent them from reaching them?

TE   I argue in my book that the full business of internalizing, legitimating the authoritative power is itself a complex matter which requires capacity, intelligence. A degree of creativity is needed even to accept that one is being defined in a negative way, as low on the scale or as oppressed. And it is a paradox, I think, that the legitimation of a dominant power is never just a passive affair – a matter of taking it into yourself; so the capacities you are talking about must be there even for people to accept a dominant power, to define themselves in relation to it. I would have thought that much of Pierre Bourdieu's work is about the conditions in which people can or can't acquire capital.

PB   There is a sort of *de facto* division of labour of social production with respect to major varieties of experience. Very often the persons who are able to speak about the social world know nothing about the social world, and the people who do know about the social world are not able to speak about it. If so few true things are said about the social world, the reason lies in this division. For example, doxa implies a knowledge, a practical knowledge. Workers know a lot: more than any intellectual, more than any sociologist. But in a sense they don't know it, they lack the instrument to grasp it, to speak about it. And we have this mythology of the intellectual who is able to transform his doxic experiences, his mastery of the social world, to an explicit and nicely expressed presentation. That is a very difficult problem for social reasons. For example, if the intellectual tries to reproduce the experience of a worker, as in France after 1968, he encounters the experience of a worker who lacks the habits of an intellectual. Many of the things he is appalled at are in fact quite run-of-the-mill. He must be able to include in his vision a description of the worker's experience – the fact that it is an experience from *his* point of view. And that is very difficult. One of the reasons why intellectuals don't pay attention, in my view, is that they have very many interests related to cultural capital. I will give you an example: I was always shocked by what Marx said about Proudhon; he was very hard on him. Marx said: 'He is a stupid French petty-bourgeois'; that Proudhon only writes aesthetics from the point of view of the Greek aesthetes; that Proudhon was very naive. Marx, for his part, learnt Greek; when he was eighteen he was able to write in Greek. He condescended to Proudhon as a poorly educated petty-bourgeois, whereas Marx had had the classical education befitting the son of a high functionary of the Prussian monarchy. Such distinctions are very important. When you look for the crumbs of Marxism, they are there. They come from the arrogance of the intellectual with cultural capital. The behaviour and the many struggles of left-wing parties are related to that: intellectuals hate and despise the workers, or they admire them too much – which is a manner of despising them. It is very important to know all these things; and so, for that reason, the process of self-criticism, which one can practise by studying the intellectual, academic mind, is vital – it is, as it were, a necessary personal condition for any kind of communication on ideology.

Can I shift your attention to the arts for a moment. I am interested in the way the ideology of symbolic capital rests on arts and aesthetics, which you attack in both distinctions. At the end of your book you argue that people across the social scale subscribe to the universal classification system. They buy into Kantian aesthetics from the top to the bottom of the social range. What happens to the economy of symbolic goods when taking into account, say, Fredric Jameson's claim that there is a proliferation of new cultural codes? If it is true that there is a proliferation of new codes, how does it relate to your analysis of symbolic power?

PB   That is a difficult question. In my view, there are higher markets, places in which the dominant code remains absolutely efficient; and these places are where the main games are played – that is, the academic system (in France, the Grandes Écoles system, the places from which the executives are selected). Since I have worked on cultural themes, I will address these in my answer. We have a rehearsal of the old idea that mass culture, popular culture, and so on, is growing; that people are blind to that, that they are unconsciously attached to the difference of cultures. It is a form of dominant chic among intellectuals to say 'Look at these cartoons,' or some other cultural item, 'do they not display great cultural creativity?' Such a person is saying 'You don't see that, but I do, and I am the first to see it.' The perception may be valid; but there is an overestimation of the capacity of these new things to change the structure of the distribution of symbolic capital. To exaggerate the extent of change is, in a sense, a form of populism. You mystify people when you say 'Look, rap is great.' The question is: does this music really change the structure of the culture? I think it is fine to say that rap is great, and in a sense it is better than being ethnocentric and to suggest that such music has no value; but in fact it is a manner of being ethnocentric when you forget what remains the dominant form, and that you still can't realize symbolic profits from rap, in the main social games. I certainly think we must pay attention to these things, but there is a political and scientific danger in overestimating their cultural efficacy. Depending on the place in which I speak, I could be on one side or the other.

You say that symbolic violence is violence. What do you mean by that?

PB I believe that violence takes more sophisticated forms. One example is opinion polls – at least in France. (I was told that here it is different, but in France opinion polls are a more sophisticated form of grasping opinion than the simple contact between political men and their audience.) Opinion polls are an example of the kind of manipulation we have been discussing – a new form of symbolic violence for which nobody has full responsibility. I would need two hours to tell you how it works, since the manipulation is so complex. I think that no more than ten people understand what happens – not even the people who organize the polls. For example, the political men – those in government – don't know how the process operates, and it therefore governs them. It is a complex structure with a lot of different agents: journalists, opinion-poll makers, intellectuals who comment on polls, TV intellectuals (who are very important in terms of political effect), political men, and so on. All these persons are in a network of interconnections, and everyone mystifies the others and mystifies himself by mystifying the others. Nobody is conscious of the process, and it works in such a manner that no one could say that France is simply governed by opinion poll. To understand that, you need an instrument much more sophisticated than the methods traditionally used. I say that to all the union leaders. I tell them: you are late; we are three wars on, you are three class wars too late; you fight with instruments suited to the class struggle of the nineteenth century and you have in front of you forms of power that are very sophisticated.

I was very interested to hear the reference to the 'first-generation intellectual', and to the trajectory of such a person. For obvious reasons it is still a fairly rare breed; but since that breed is now itself at the age of breeding, what about the children of such people? Do they become second-generation intellectuals? Do they merge seamlessly into the middle classes or do they form some kind of subculture? I am asking this of both of you, partly because my own experience makes me despair of what seems to happen – the subsequent generation appears both to lose the strengths of the working-class tradition and somehow never completely goes into the middle-class tradition – and I would be interested in the comments of such first-generation intellectuals on this.

TE Well, my children wouldn't touch an intellectual with a barge-pole! I think they regard education as bourgeois ideology, which is very convenient for them! You are right. There is something in what you say about being neither one thing nor the other, but I don't see why that should necessarily be a source of despair. I think that could be an interesting position to be in, couldn't it? Such a generation, of course, are not working-class any more – just as their parents aren't any longer working-class – but they have also seen their parents in action and have a proper suspicion of intellectuals. In other words, they don't think that the answer is to be an intellectual.

I'd like to pick up on a point Pierre Bourdieu was making about the young intellectual talking about rap, and shifting the focus to culture. Don't you think that with your notion of 'habitus' you are in danger of obfuscating the basic economic determinants of people's possibility for emancipation – by talking about capital and culture and ideology, when, ultimately, if they haven't got the means to go and read a book then they don't get emancipated in that way? The other thing I would like to question is the notion of doxa. If people internalize their own domination, and in a sense it is subconscious and they are happy with it, then don't you run into trouble trying to justify the idea of emancipation?

PB   Are you saying that you suspect I have a sort of intellectual bias and that there is only one way to escape? Is that your impression?

You criticize the young intellectual for talking about rap as if this was a means of emancipation; but in your notion of 'habitus' you are incorporating culture as a determinant, and it could be that focusing on culture in that way shifts the emphasis from economic determinants that do still provide access to means for emancipation.

TE   I would like to formulate the point like this. Your concentration on culture is shifting the emphasis away from the economic determinants that prevent people from being emancipated. You are reacting to economism by lifting economic imagery into the cultural sphere rather than by registering the weight of the material and economic within culture.

PB   Maybe you are right. I tend to bend the stick too much, as Mao Tse-tung said, while trying to correct the previous bias. In this domain the dominant critical vision is in danger of economism. I tend to insist upon the other aspects, but maybe I am wrong. Even if in my head I have a better balance, I tend, in exposition of my ideas, to insist on the less probable, less visible, aspect – so you may be right.

TE   The second point is interesting – about people internalizing and so feeling happy with their oppression. Wouldn't one have to argue that they cannot be really happy if they are oppressed?

But if you are talking about the subconscious – if part of your subconscious habitus determines how you are – then it becomes very difficult to change it. Fair enough, you can't attribute happiness, but at the same time you can't attribute sadness; whereas Marxism and ideology would want to retain the notion of the actor fighting against something that seems wrong. With doxa you lose that; you don't begin to wonder what the point is – there is no drive to emancipation.

PB   I think this question of happiness is very important. The doxic attitude does not mean happiness; it means bodily submission, unconscious submission, which may indicate a lot of internalized tension, a lot of bodily suffering. I am currently conducting a survey in which I interview persons of indefinite social status – those who occupy places that are subject to powerful contradictions. And I try to be more Socratic than is usual when making positivistic surveys: I try to help them to express what they suffer. I have discovered a lot of suffering which had been hidden by this smooth working of habitus. It helps people to adjust, but it causes internalized contradictions. When this happens, some may, for instance, become drug addicts. I try to help the person who is suffering, to make their situation explicit in a sort of socioanalysis conducted in a friendly and supportive way. Often when I do that, the individuals experience a sort of intellectual pleasure; they say 'Yes, I understand what happens to me.' But at the same time it is very sad. I lack the positive confidence that psychoanalysts have; they expect consciousness to be a tale of sadness, and respond with sadness when the individual says 'Look what happened to me. Isn't it terrible?' To some extent social work is like that: when you do it, it punishes you. This is a situation that arises very often, and it does not contradict what I say about doxa. One may be very well adapted to this state of affairs, and the pain comes from the fact that one internalizes silent suffering, which may find bodily expression, in the form of self-hatred, self-punishment.

Note

1. Pierre Bourdieu, *Language and Symbolic Power*, Cambridge 1991; Terry Eagleton, *Ideology*, London 1991.

Postmodernism and the Market

Fredric Jameson

Linguistics has a useful scheme that is unfortunately lacking in ideological analysis: it can mark a given word as either 'word' or 'idea' by alternating slash marks or brackets. Thus the word *market*, with its various dialect pronunciations and its etymological origins in the Latin for trade and merchandise, is printed as /market/: on the other hand, the concept, as it has been theorized by philosophers and ideologues down through the ages, from Aristotle to Milton Friedman, would be printed ≪market≫. One thinks for a moment that this would solve so many of our problems in dealing with a subject of this kind, which is at one and the same time an ideology and a set of practical institutional problems, until one remembers the great flanking and pincer movements of the opening section of the *Grundrisse*, where Marx undoes the hopes and longings for simplification of the Proudhonists, who thought they would get rid of all the problems of money by abolishing money, without seeing that it is the very contradiction of the exchange system that is objectified and expressed in money proper and would continue to objectify and express itself in any of its simpler substitutes, like work-time coupons. These last, Marx observes dryly, would under ongoing capitalism simply turn back into money itself, and all the previous contradictions would return in force.

So also with the attempt to separate ideology and reality: the ideology of the market is unfortunately not some supplementary ideational or representational luxury or embellishment that can be removed from the economic problem and then sent over to some cultural or superstructural morgue, to be dissected by specialists over there. It is somehow generated by the thing itself, as its objectively necessary after-image: somehow both dimensions must be registered together, in their identity as well as in their difference. They are, to use

278

a contemporary but already outmoded language, semi-autonomous: which means, if it is to mean anything, that they are not really autonomous or independent from each other, but they are not really at one with each other, either. The Marxian concept of ideology was always meant to respect and to rehearse and flex the paradox of the mere semi-autonomy of the ideological concept, for example, the ideologies of the market, with respect to the thing itself – or in this case the problems of market and planning in late capitalism as well as in the socialist countries today. But the classical Marxian concept (including the very word *ideology*, itself something like the ideology of the thing, as opposed to its reality) often broke down in precisely this respect, becoming purely autonomous and then drifting off as sheer 'epiphenomenon' into the world of the superstructures, while reality remained below, the real-life responsibility of professional economists.

There are, of course, many professional models of ideology in Marx himself. The following one from the *Grundrisse* and turning on the delusions of the Proudhonists has been less often remarked and studied, but is very rich and suggestive indeed. Marx is here discussing a very central feature of our current topic, namely, the relationship of the ideas and values of freedom and equality to the exchange system: and he argues, just like Milton Friedman, that these concepts and values are real and objective, organically generated by the market system itself, and dialectically are indissolubly linked to it. He goes on to add – I was going to say now *unlike* Milton Friedman, but a pause for reflection allows me to remember that even these unpleasant consequences are also acknowledged, and sometimes even celebrated, by the neo-liberals – that in practice this freedom and equality turn out to be unfreedom and inequality. Meanwhile, however, it is a question of the attitude of the Proudhonists to this reversal, and of their miscomprehension of the ideological dimension of the exchange system and how that functions – both true and false, both objective and delusional, what we used to try to render with the Hegelian expression 'objective appearance':

> Exchange value, or, more precisely, the money system, is indeed the system of freedom and equality, and what disturbs [the Proudhonists] in the more recent development of the system are disturbances immanent to the system, i.e., the very realization of *equality* and *freedom*, which turn out to be inequality and unfreedom. It is an aspiration as pious as it is stupid to wish that exchange value would not develop into capital, or that labor which produces exchange value would not develop into wage labor. What distinguishes these gentlemen [in other words, the Proudhonists, or as we might say today, the social democrats] from the bourgeois apologists is, on the one hand, their awareness of the contradictions inherent in the system,

and, on the other, their utopianism, manifest in their failure to grasp the inevitable difference between the real and the ideal shape of bourgeois society, and the consequent desire to undertake the superfluous task of changing the ideal expression itself back into reality, whereas it is in fact merely the photographic image [*Lichtbild*] of this reality.[1]

So it is very much a cultural question (in the contemporary sense of the word), turning on the problem of representation itself: the Proud-honists are realists, we might say, of the correspondence model variety. They think (along with the Habermasians today, perhaps) that the revolutionary ideals of the bourgeois system – freedom and equality – are properties of real societies, and they note that, while still present in the Utopian ideal image or portrait of bourgeois market society, these same features are absent and woefully lacking when we turn to the reality which sat as the model for that ideal portrait. It will then be enough to change and improve the model and make freedom and equality finally appear, for real, in flesh and blood, in the market system.

But Marx is, so to speak, a modernist; and this particular theo-rization of ideology – drawing, only twenty years after the invention of photography, on very contemporary photographic figures (where previously Marx and Engels had favoured the pictorial tradition, with its various camera obscuras – suggests that the ideological dimension is intrinsically embedded within the reality, which secretes it as a necessary feature of its own structure. That dimension is thus profoundly imaginary in a real and positive sense; that is to say, it exists and is real in so far as it is an image, marked and destined to remain as such, its very unreality and unrealizability being what is real about it. I think of episodes in Sartre's plays which might serve as useful textbook allegories of this peculiar process: for example, the passionate desire of Electra to murder her mother, which, however, turns out not to have been intended for realization. Electra, after the fact, discovers that she did not really want her mother dead (≪dead≫, i.e. dead in reality); what she wanted was to go on longing in rage and resentment to have her /dead/. And so it is, as we shall see with those two rather contradictory features of the market system, freedom and equality: everybody wants to want them; but they cannot be realized. The only thing that can happen to them is for the system that generates them to disappear, thereby abolishing the 'ideals' along with the reality itself.

But to restore to 'ideology' this complex way of dealing with its roots in its own social reality would mean reinventing the dialectic, some-thing every generation fails in its own way to do. Ours has, indeed, not even tried; and the last attempt, the Althusserian moment, long since passed under the horizon along with the hurricanes of yesteryear. Meanwhile, I have the impression that only so-called discourse theory has tried to fill the void left when the concept of ideology was yanked along with the rest of classical Marxism into the abyss. One may readily endorse Stuart Hall's programme based, as I understand it, on the notion that the fundamental level on which political struggle is waged is that of the struggle over the legitimacy of concepts and ideologies: that political legitimation comes from that: and that, for example, Thatcherism and its cultural counterrrevolution were founded fully as much on the delegitimation of welfare-state or social-democratic (we used to call it liberal) ideology as on the inherent structural problems of the welfare state itself.

This allows me to express my thesis in its strongest form, which is that the rhetoric of the market has been a fundamental and central component of this ideological struggle, this struggle for the legitimation or delegitimation of left discourse. The surrender to the various forms of market ideology – on the *Left*, I mean, not to mention everybody else – has been imperceptible but alarmingly universal. Everyone is now willing to mumble, as though it were an inconsequential concession in passing to public opinion and current received wisdom (or shared communicational presuppositions), that no society can function efficiently without the market, and that planning is obviously impossible. This is the second shoe of the destiny of that older piece of discourse, 'nationalization', which it follows some twenty years later, just as, in general, full postmodernism (particularly in the political field) has turned out to be the sequel, continuation, and fulfilment of the old fifties 'end of ideology' episode. At any rate, we were then willing to murmur agreement to the increasingly widespread proposition that socialism had nothing to do with nationalization; the consequence is that today we find ourselves having to agree to the proposition that socialism really has nothing to do with socialism itself any longer. 'The market is in human nature' is the proposition that cannot be allowed to stand unchallenged; in my opinion, it is the most crucial terrain of ideological struggle in our time. If you let it pass because it seems an inconsequential admission or, worse yet, because you've really come to believe in it yourself, in your 'heart of hearts', then socialism and Marxism alike will have effectively become delegitimated, at least for a time. Sweezy reminds us that capitalism failed to catch on in a number of places before it finally arrived in England; and that if the actually existing socialisms go down the drain, there will be other, better, ones later on. I believe this also, but we don't have to make it a self-fulfilling prophecy. In the same spirit I want to add to the formulations and tactics of Stuart Hall's 'discourse analysis' the same kind of historical qualifier: the fundamental level on which political struggle is waged is that of the legitimacy of concepts like *planning* or *the market* – at least *right now* and in our current situation. At future times, politics will take more activist forms from that, just as it has done in the past.

It must finally be added, on this methodological point, that the conceptual framework of discourse analysis – although allowing us conveniently, in a postmodern age, to practise ideological analysis without calling it that – is no more satisfactory than the reveries of the Proudhonists: autonomizing the dimension of the /concept/ and calling it 'discourse' suggests that this dimension is potentially unrelated to reality and can be left to float off on its own, to found its own subdiscipline and develop its own specialists. I still prefer to call /market/ what it is, namely, an ideologeme, and to premise about it what one must premise about all ideologies: that, unfortunately, we have to talk about the realities fully as much as the concepts. Is market discourse merely a rhetoric? It is and isn't (to rehearse the great formal logic of the identity of identity and non-identity); and to get it right, you have to talk about real markets just as much as about metaphysics, psychology, advertising, culture, representations, and libidinal apparatuses.

But this means somehow skirting the vast continent of political philosophy as such, itself a kind of ideological 'market' in its own right, in which, as in some gigantic combinational system, all possible variants and combinations of political 'values', options and 'solutions' are available, on condition you think you are free to choose among them. In this great emporium, for example, we may combine the ratio of freedom to equality according to our individual temperament, as when state intervention is opposed because of its damage to this or that fantasy of individual or personal freedom: or equality is deplored because its values lead to demands for the correction of market mechanisms and the intervention of other kinds of 'values' and priorities. The theory of ideology excludes this optionality of political theories, not merely because 'values' as such have deeper class and unconscious sources than those of the conscious mind but also because theory is itself a kind of form determined by social content, and it reflects social reality in more complicated ways than a solution 'reflects' its problem. What can be observed at work here is the fundamental dialectical law of the determination of a form by its content – something not active in theories or disciplines in which there is no differentiation between a level of 'appearance' and a level of 'essence', and in which phenomena like ethics or sheer political *opinion* as such are modifiable by conscious decision or rational persuasion. Indeed, an extraordinary remark of Mallarmé – 'il n'existe d'ouvert à la recherche mentale que deux voies, en tout, où bifurque notre besoin, à savoir, l'esthétique d'une part et aussi l'économie politique'[2] – suggests that the deeper affinities between a Marxian conception of political economy in general and the realm of the aesthetic (as, for instance, in Adorno's or Benjamin's work) are to be located precisely here, in the perception shared by both disciplines of this immense dual movement of a plane of form and a plane of substance (to use an alternative language from the linguist Hjelmslev).

This would seem to confirm the traditional complaint about Marxism that it lacks any autonomous political reflection as such, something which, however, tends to strike one as a strength rather than a weakness. Marxism is indeed not a political philosophy of the *Weltan-schauung* variety, and in no way 'on all fours' with conservation, liberalism, radicalism, populism, or whatever. There is certainly a Marxist practice of politics, but political thinking in Marxism, when it is not practical in that way, has exclusively to do with the economic organization of society and how people co-operate to organize production. This means that 'socialism' is not exactly a political idea, or, if you like, that it presupposes the end of a certain political thinking. It also means that we do have our homologues among the bourgeois thinkers, but they are not the Fascists (who have very little in the way of thought in that sense, and have in any case become historically extinct) but, rather, the neo-liberals and the market people: for them also, political philosophy is worthless (at least once you get rid of the arguments of the Marxist, collectivist enemy), and 'politics' now means simply the care and feeding of the economic apparatus (in this case the market rather than the collectively owned and organized means of production). Indeed, I will argue the proposition that we have much in common with the neo-liberals, in fact virtually everything – save the essentials!

But the obvious must first be said, namely, that the slogan of the market not only covers a great variety of different referents or concerns but is also virtually always a misnomer. For one thing, no free market exists today in the realm of oligopolies and multinationals: indeed, Galbraith suggested long ago that oligopolies were our imperfect substitute for planning and planification of the socialist type.

Meanwhile, on its general use, market as a concept rarely has anything to do with choice or freedom, since those are all determined for us in advance, whether we are talking about new model cars, toys, or television programmes: we select among those, no doubt, but we can scarcely be said to have a say in actually choosing any of them. Thus the homology with freedom is at best a homology with parliamentary democracy of our representative type.

Then too, the market in the socialist countries would seem to have more to do with production than consumption, since it is above all a question of supplying spare parts, components, and raw materials to other production units that is foregrounded as the most urgent problem (and to which the Western-type market is then fantasized as a solution). But presumably the slogan of the market and all its accompanying rhetoric was devised to secure a decisive shift and displacement from the conceptuality of production to that of distribution and consumption: something it rarely seems in fact to do.

It also seems, incidentally, to screen out the rather crucial matter of property, with which conservatives have had notorious intellectual difficulty: here, the exclusion of 'the justification of original property titles'[3] will be viewed as a synchronic framing that excludes the dimension of history and systemic historical change.

Finally, it should be noted that in the view of many neo-liberals, not only do we not yet have a free market, but what we have in its place (and what is sometimes otherwise defended as a 'free market' against the Soviet Union)[4] – namely, a mutual compromise and buying off of pressure groups, special interests, and the like – is in itself, according to the New Right, a structure absolutely inimical to the real free market and its establishment. This kind of analysis (sometimes called public choice theory) is the right-wing equivalent of the left analysis of the media and consumerism (in other words, the obligatory theory of resistance, the account of what in the public area and the public sphere generally prevents people from adopting a better system and impedes their very understanding and reception of such a system).

The reasons for the success of market ideology can therefore not be sought in the market itself (even when you have sorted out exactly which of these many phenomena is being designated by the word). But it is best to begin with the strongest and most comprehensive metaphysical version, which associates the market with human nature. This view comes in many, often imperceptible, forms, but it has been conveniently formalized into a whole method by Gary Becker in his admirably totalizing approach: 'I am saying that the economic approach provides a valuable unified framework for understanding *all* human behavior.'[5] Thus, for example, marriage is susceptible to a kind of market analysis: 'My analysis implies that likes or unlikes mate when that maximizes total household commodity output over all marriages, regardless of whether the trait is financial (like wage rates and property income), or genetical (like height and intelligence), or psychological (like aggressiveness and passiveness).'[6] But here the clarifying footnote is crucial and marks a beginning towards grasping what is really at stake in Becker's interesting proposal: 'Let me emphasize again that commodity output is not the same as national product as usually measured, but includes children, companionship, health, and a variety of other commodities.' What immediately leaps to the eye, therefore, is the paradox – of the greatest symptomatic significance for the Marxian theoretical tourist – that this most scandalous of all market models is in reality a production model! In it consumption is explicitly described as the production of a commodity or a specific utility; in other words, a use value which can be anything from sexual gratification to a convenient place to take it out on your children if the outside world proves inclement. Here is Becker's core description:

> The household production function framework emphasizes the parallel services performed by firms and households as organizational units. Similar to the typical firm analyzed in standard production theory, the household invests in capital assets (savings), capital equipment (durable goods), and capital embodied in its 'labor force' (human capital of family members). As an organizational entity, the household, like the firm, engages in production using this labor and capital. Each is viewed as maximizing its objective function subject to resource and technological constraints. The production model not only emphasizes that the household is the appropriate basic unit of analysis in consumption theory, it also brings out the interdependence of several household decisions: decisions about family labor supply and time and goods expenditures in a single time-period analysis, and decisions about marriage, family size, labor force attachment, and expenditures on goods and human capital investments in a life cycle analysis.
>
> The recognition of the importance of time as a scarce resource in the household has played an integral role in the development of empirical applications of the household production function approach.[7]

I have to admit that I think one can accept this, and that it provides a perfectly realistic and sensible view not only of *this* human world but of *all* of them, going back to the earliest hominids. Let me underscore a few crucial features of the Becker model: the first is the stress on time itself as a resource (another fundamental essay is entitled 'A Theory of the Allocation of Time'). This is, of course, very much Marx's own view of temporality, as that supremely disengages itself from the *Grundrisse*, where finally all value is a matter of time. I also want to suggest the consistency and kinship between this peculiar proposal and much of contemporary theory or philosophy, which has involved a prodigious expansion in what we consider to be rational or meaningful behaviour. My sense is that, particularly after the diffusion of psychoanalysis but also with the gradual evaporation of 'otherness' on a shrinking globe

and in a media-suffused society, very little remains that can be
considered 'irrational' in the older sense of 'incomprehensible': the
vilest forms of human decision-making and behaviour – torture by
sadists and overt or covert foreign intervention by government leaders
– are now for all of us comprehensible (in terms of a Diltheyan
Verstehen, say), whatever we think of them. Whether such an enor-
mously expanded concept of Reason then has any further normative
value (as Habermas still thinks) in a situation in which its opposite, the
irrational, has shrunk to virtual non-existence, is another, and an
interesting, question. But Becker's calculations (and the word does not
at all in him imply *Homo economicus*, but rather very much unreflective,
everyday, 'preconscious' behaviour of all kinds) belong in that main-
stream; indeed, the system makes me think more than anything else of
Sartrean freedom in so far as it implies a responsibility for everything
we do – Sartrean choice (which, of course, in the same way takes place
on a non-self-conscious everyday behavioural level) means the individual or collective production at every moment of Becker's 'commodities'
(which need not be hedonistic in any narrow sense, altruism being, for
example, just such a commodity or pleasure). The representational
consequences of a view like this will now lead us belatedly to pronounce
the word postmodernism for the first time. Only Sartre's novels,
indeed (and they are samples; enormous, unfinished fragments), give
any sense of what a representation of life that interpreted and narrated
every human act and gesture, desire and decision, in terms of Becker's
maximization model would look like. Such representation would
reveal a world peculiarly without transcendence and without perspective (death is here, for example, just another matter of utility
maximization), and indeed without plot in any traditional sense, since
all choices would be equidistant and on the same level. The analogy
with Sartre, however, suggests that this kind of reading – which ought
to be very much a demystifying eyeball-to-eyeball encounter with daily
life, with no distance and no embellishments – might not be altogether
postmodern in the more fantastic senses of that aesthetic. Becker seems
to have missed the wilder forms of consumption available in the
postmodern, which is elsewhere capable of staging a virtual delirium of

the consumption of the very idea of consumption: in the postmodern,
indeed, it is the very idea of the market that is consumed with the most
prodigious gratification; as it were, a bonus or surplus of the
commodification process. Becker's sober calculations fall far short of
that, not necessarily because postmodernism is inconsistent or incompatible with political conservatism but, rather, primarily because his is
finally a production and not a consumption model at all, as has been
suggested above. Shades of the great introduction to the *Grundrisse*, in

which production turns into consumption and distribution and then ceaselessly returns to its basic productive form (in the enlarged systemic category of production Marx wishes to substitute for the thematic or analytic one)! Indeed, it seems possible to complain that the current celebrants of the market – the theoretical conservatives – fail to show much enjoyment or *jouissance* (as we will see below, their market mainly serves as a policeman meant to keep Stalin from the gates, where in addition one suspects that Stalin in turn is merely a code word for Roosevelt).

As description, then, Becker's model seems to me impeccable and very faithful indeed to the facts of life as we know it; when it becomes prescriptive, of course, we face the most insidious forms of reaction (my two favourite practical consequences are, first, that oppressed minorities only make it worse for themselves by fighting back; and, second, that 'household production', in his special sense [see above], is seriously lowered in productivity when the wife has a job). But it is easy to see how this should be so. The Becker model is postmodern in its structure as a transcoding; two separate explanatory systems are combined here by way of the assertion of a fundamental identity (about which it is always protested that it is *not metaphorical*, the surest sign of an intent to metaphorize): human behaviour (pre-eminently the family or the *oikos*), on the one hand, the firm or enterprise, on the other. Much force and clarity are then generated by the rewriting of phenomena like spare time and personality traits in terms of potential raw materials. It does not follow, however, that the figural bracket can then be removed, as a veil is triumphantly snatched from a statue, allowing one then to reason about domestic matters in terms of money or the economic as such. But that is very precisely how Becker goes about 'deducing' his practical-political conclusions. Here too, then, he falls short of absolute postmodernity, where the transcoding process has as a consequence the suspension of everything that used to be 'literal'. Becker wants to marshal the equipment of metaphor and figural identification, only to return in a final moment to the literal level (which has in the meantime, in late capitalism, evaporated out from under him).

Why do I find none of this particularly scandalous, and what could possibly be its 'proper use'? As with Sartre, in Becker choice takes place within an already pre-given environment, which Sartre theorizes as such (he calls it the 'situation') but which Becker neglects. In both we have a welcome reduction of the old-fashioned subject (or individual, or ego), who is now little more than a point of consciousness directed on to the stockpile of materials available in the outside world, and making decisions on that information which are 'rational' in the new enlarged

sense of what any other human being could understand (in Dilthey's
sense, or in Rousseau's, what every other human being could 'sympath-
ize' with). That means that we are freed from all kinds of more
properly 'irrational' myths about subjectivity and can turn our attention to that situation itself, that available inventory of resources, which
is the outside world itself and which must now indeed be called History.
The Sartrean concept of the situation is a new way of thinking history
as such: Becker avoids any comparable move, for good reasons. I have
implied that even under socialism (as in earlier modes of production)
people can very well be imagined operating under the Becker model.
What will be different is then the situation itself: the nature of the
'household', the stock of raw materials; indeed, the very form and
shape of the 'commodities' therein to be produced. Becker's market
thus by no means ends up as just another celebration of the market
system but, rather, as an involuntary redirection of our attention
towards history itself and the variety of alternative situations it offers.

We must suspect, therefore, that essentialist defences of the market
in reality involve other themes and issues altogether: the pleasures of
consumption are little more than the ideological fantasy consequences
available for ideological consumers who buy into the market theory, of
which they are not themselves a part. Indeed, one of the great crises in
the new conservative cultural revolution – and by the same token one
of its great internal contradictions – was displayed by these same
ideologues when some nervousness began to appear over the success
with which consumer America had overcome the Protestant ethic and
was able to throw its savings (and future income) to the winds in
exercising its new nature as the full-time professional shopper. But
obviously you can't have it both ways; there is no such thing as a
booming, functioning market whose customer personnel is staffed by
Calvinists and hard-working traditionalists knowing the value of the
dollar.

The passion for the market was indeed always political, as Albert O.
Hirschman's great book *The Passions and the Interests* taught us. The
market, finally, for 'market ideology', has less to do with consumption
than it has to do with government intervention, and indeed with the
evils of freedom and human nature itself. A representative description
of the famous market 'mechanism' is provided by Barry:

By a natural process Smith meant what would occur, or which pattern of
events would emerge, from individual interaction in the absence of some
specific human intervention, either of a political kind or from violence.
    The behaviour of a market is an obvious example of such natural
phenomena. The self-regulating properties of the market system are not

the product of a designing mind but are a spontaneous outcome of the price mechanism. Now from certain uniformities in human nature, including, of course, the natural desire to 'better ourselves,' it can be deduced what will happen when government disturbs this self-regulating process. Thus Smith shows how apprenticeship laws, restraints on international trade, the privileges of corporations, and so on, disrupt, but cannot entirely suppress, natural economic tendencies. The spontaneous order of the market is brought about by the *interdependency* of its constituent parts and any intervention with this order is simply self-defeating: 'No regulation of commerce can increase the quantity of industry in any part of society beyond what its capital can maintain. It can only divert a part of it into a direction which it otherwise would not have gone'. By the phrase 'natural liberty' Smith meant that system in which every man, provided that he does not violate the (negative) laws of justice, is left perfectly free to pursue his own interest in his own way and bring both his industry and capital into competition with those of any other man.[8]

The force, then, of the concept of the market lies in its 'totalizing' structure, as they say nowadays: that is, in its capacity to afford a model of a social totality. It offers another way of displacing the Marxian model: distinct from the now familiar Weberian and post-Weberian shift from economics to politics, from production to power and domination. But the displacement from production to circulation is no less a profound and ideological one, and it has the advantage of replacing the rather antediluvian fantasy representations that accompanied the 'domination' model from *1984* and *Oriental Despotism* all the way to Foucault – narratives rather comical for the new post-modern age – with representations of a wholly different order. (I will argue in a moment that these are not primarily consumptive ones, either.)

What we first need to grasp, however, are the conditions of possibility of this alternate concept of the social totality. Marx suggests (again, in the *Grundrisse*) that the circulation of market model will historically and epistemologically precede other forms of mapping and offer the first representation by which the social totality is grasped:

Circulation is the movement in which general alienation appears as general appropriation, and general appropriation as general alienation. Though the whole of this movement may well appear as a social process, and though the individual elements of this movement originate from the conscious will and particular purposes of individuals, nevertheless the totality of the process appears as an objective relationship arising spontaneously; a relationship which results from the interaction of conscious individuals, but which is neither part of their consciousness nor as a whole subsumed under them. Their collisions give rise to an *alien* social power standing above them.

Their own interaction (appears) as a process and force independent of them. Because circulation is a totality of the social process, it is also the first form in which not only the social relation appears as something independent of individuals as, say, in a coin or an exchange value, but the whole of the social movement itself.[9]

What is remarkable about the movement of these reflections is that they seem to identify two things which have most often been thought to be very different from each other as concepts: Hobbes's 'bellum omnium contra omnes' and Adam Smith's 'invisible hand' (here appearing disguised as Hegel's 'ruse of reason'). I would argue that Marx's concept of 'civil society' is something like what happens when these two concepts (like matter and anti-matter) are unexpectedly combined. Here, however, what is significant is that what Hobbes fears is somehow the same as what gives Smith confidence (the deeper nature of Hobbesian terror is in any case peculiarly illuminated by the complacency of Mr Milton Friedman's definition: 'A liberal is fundamentally fearful of concentrated power.'[10] The conception of some ferocious violence inherent in human nature and acted out in the English revolution, whence it is theorized ('fearfully') by Hobbes, is not modified and ameliorated by Hirschman's 'douceur du commerce':[11] it is rigorously identical (in Marx) with market competition as such. The difference is not political-ideological but historical: Hobbes needs state power to tame and control the violence of human nature and competition; in Adam Smith (and Hegel on some other metaphysical plane) the competitive system, the market, does the taming and controlling all by itself, no longer needing the absolute state. But what is clear throughout the conservative tradition is its motivation by fear and by anxieties in which civil war or urban crime are themselves mere figures for class struggle. The market is thus Leviathan in sheep's clothing: its function is not to encourage and perpetuate freedom (let alone freedom of a political variety) but, rather, to repress it; and about such visions, indeed, one may revive the slogans of the existential years – the fear of freedom, the flight from freedom. Market ideology assures us that human beings make a mess of it when they try to control their destinies ('socialism is impossible') and that we are fortunate in possessing an interpersonal mechanism – the market – which can substitute for human *hubris* and planning, and replace human decisions altogether. We only need to keep it clean and well oiled, and it now – like the monarch so many centuries ago – will see to us and keep us in line.

Why this consoling replacement for the divinity should be so universally attractive at the present time, however, is a different kind of historical question. The attribution of the new-found embrace of market freedom to the fear of Stalinism and Stalin is touching but just slightly misplaced in time, although certainly the current Gulag Industry has been a crucial component in the 'legitimation' of these ideological representations (along with the Holocaust Industry, whose peculiar relations to the rhetoric of the Gulag demand closer cultural and ideological study).

The most intelligent criticism ever offered me on a long analysis of the sixties I once published[12] I owe to Wlad Godzich, who expressed Socratic amazement at the absence, from my global model, of the Second World, and in particular the Soviet Union. Our experience of perestroika has revealed dimensions of Soviet history that powerfully reinforce Godzich's point and make my own lapse all the more deplorable; so I will here make amends by exaggerating in the other direction. My feeling has, in fact, come to be that the failure of the Khrushchev experiment was not disastrous merely for the Soviet Union, but somehow fundamentally crucial for the rest of global history, and not least the future of socialism itself. In the Soviet Union, indeed, we are given to understand that the Khruschev generation was the last to believe in the possibility of a renewal of Marxism, let alone socialism: or rather, the other way around: that it was their failure which now determines the utter indifference to Marxism and socialism of several generations of younger intellectuals. But I think this failure was also determinant of the most basic developments in other countries as well, and while one does not want the Russian comrades to bear all the responsibility for global history, there does seem to me to be some similarity between what the Soviet revolution meant for the rest of the world positively and the negative effects of this last, missed, opportunity to restore that revolution and to transform the Party in the process. Both the anarchism of the sixties in the West and the Cultural Revolution in China are to be attributed to that failure, whose prolongation, long after the end óf both, explains the universal triumph of what Sloterdijk calls 'cynical reason' in the omnipresent consumerism of the postmodern today. It is therefore no wonder that such profound disillusionment with political praxis should result in the popularity of the rhetoric of market abnegation and the surrender of human freedom to a now lavish invisible hand.

None of these things, however, which still involve thinking and reasoning, goes very far towards explaining the most astonishing feature of this discursive development; namely, how the dreariness of business and private property, the dustiness of entrepreneurship, and the well-nigh Dickensian flavour of title and appropriation, coupon-clipping, mergers, investment banking, and other such transactions (after the close of the heroic, or robber-baron, stage of business) should in our time have proved to be so sexy. In my opinion, the excitement of the once tiresome old fifties representation of the free market derives from its illicit metaphorical association with a very different kind of representation; namely, the media themselves in their largest contemporary and global sense (including an infrastructure of all the latest media gadgets and high technology). The operation is the postmodern one alluded to above, in which two systems of codes are identified in such a way as to allow the libidinal energies of the one to suffuse the other, without, however (as in older moments of our cultural and intellectual history), producing a synthesis, a new combination, a new combined language, or whatever.

Horkheimer and Adorno observed long ago, in the age of radio, the peculiarity of the structure of a commercial 'culture industry' in which the products were free.[13] The analogy between media and market is in fact cemented by this mechanism: it is not because the media are *like* a market that the two things are comparable; rather, it is because the 'market' is as *unlike* its 'concept' (or Platonic idea) as the media are unlike their own concept that the two things are comparable. The media offer free programmes in whose content and assortment the consumer has no choice whatsoever but whose selection is then rebaptized 'free choice'.

In the gradual disappearance of the physical marketplace, of course, and the tendential identification of the commodity with its image (or brand name or logo), another, more intimate, symbiosis between the market and the media is effectuated, in which boundaries are washed over (in ways profoundly characteristic of the postmodern) and an indifferentiation of levels gradually takes the place of an older separation between thing and concept (or indeed, economics and culture, base and superstructure). For one thing, the products sold on the market become the very content of the media image, so that, as it were, the same referent seems to maintain in both domains. This is very different from a more primitive situation in which to a series of informational signals (news reports, feuilletons, articles) a rider is appended touting an unrelated commercial product. Today the products are, as it were, diffused throughout the space and time of the entertainment (or even news) segments, as part of that content, so that in a few well-publicized cases (most notably the series *Dynasty*[14]) it is sometimes not clear when the narrative segment has ended and the commercial has begun (since the same actors appear in the commercial segment as well).

This interpenetration by way of the content is then augmented in a somewhat different way by the nature of the products themselves:

one's sense, particularly when dealing with foreigners who have been enflamed by American consumerism, is that the products form a kind of hierarchy whose climax lies very precisely in the technology of reproduction itself, which now, of course, fans out well beyond the classical television set and has come in general to epitomize the new informational or computer technology of the third stage of capitalism. We must therefore also posit another type of consumption: consumption of the very process of consumption itself, above and beyond its content and the immediate commercial products. It is necessary to speak of a kind of technological bonus of pleasure afforded by the new machinery and, as it were, symbolically re-enacted and ritually devoured at each session of official media consumption itself. It is indeed no accident that the conservative rhetoric that often used to accompany the market rhetoric in question here (but that in my opinion represented a somewhat different strategy of delegitimation) had to do with the end of social classes – a conclusion always demonstrated and 'proved' by the presence of TV in the workers' housing. Much of the euphoria of postmodernism derives from this celebration of the very process of high-tech informatization (the prevalence of current theories of communication, language, or signs being an ideological spinoff of this more general 'world-view'. This is, then, as Marx might have put it, a second moment in which (like 'capital in general' as opposed to the 'many capitals') the media 'in general' as a unified process are somehow foregrounded and experienced (as opposed to the content of individual media projections); and it would seem to be this 'totalization' that allows a bridge to be made to fantasy-images of 'the market in general' or 'the market as a unified process'.

The third feature of the complex set of analogies between media and market that underlies the force of the latter's current rhetoric may then be located in the form itself. This is the place at which we need to return to the theory of the image, recalling Guy Debord's remarkable theoretical derivation (the image as the final form of commodity reification).[15] At this point the process is reversed, and it is not the commercial products of the market which in advertising become images but, rather, the very entertainment and narrative processes of commercial television, which are, in their turn, reified and turned into so many commodities: from the serial narrative itself, with its well-nigh formulaic and rigid temporal segments and breaks, to what the camera shots do to space, story, characters, and fashion, and very much including a new process of the production of stars and celebrities that seems distinct from the older and more familiar historical experience of these matters and that now converges with the hitherto 'secular' phenomena of the former public sphere itself (real people and events in your nightly news broadcast, the transformation of names into something like news logos, etc.). Many analyses have shown how the news broadcasts are structured exactly like narrative serials; meanwhile, some of us in that other precinct of an official, or 'high', culture have tried to show the waning and obsolescence of categories like 'fiction' (in the sense of something opposed to either the 'literal' or the 'factual'). But here I think a profound modification of the public sphere needs to be theorized: the emergence of a new realm of image reality which is both fictional (narrative) and factual (even the characters in the serials are grasped as real 'named' stars with external histories to read about), and which now – like the former classical 'sphere of culture' – becomes semi-autonomous and floats above reality, with this fundamental historical difference that in the classical period reality persisted independently of that sentimental and romantic 'cultural sphere', whereas today it seems to have lost that separate mode of existence. Today, culture impacts back on reality in ways that make any independent and, as it were, non- or extracultural form of it problematical (in a kind of Heisenberg principle of mass culture which intervenes between your eye and the thing itself), so that finally the theorists unite their voices in the new doxa that the 'referent' no longer exists.

At any rate, in this third moment the contents of the media themselves have now become commodities, which are then flung out on some wider version of the market with which they become affiliated until the two things are indistinguishable. Here, then, the media, as which the market was itself fantasized, now return into the market and, by becoming a part of it, seal and certify the formerly metaphorical or analogical identification as a 'literal' reality.

What must finally be added to these abstract discussions of the market is a pragmatic qualifier, a secret functionality such as sometimes sheds a whole new light – striking at a lurid mid-level height – on the ostensible discourse itself. This is what Barry, at the conclusion of his useful book, blurts out in either desperation or exasperation; namely, that the philosophical test of the various neo-liberal theories can be applied only in a single fundamental situation, which we may call (not without irony) 'the transition from socialism to capitalism'.[16] Market theories, in other words, remain Utopian in so far as they are not applicable to this fundamental process of systemic 'deregulation'. Barry himself has already illustrated the significance of the judgement in an earlier chapter when, discussing the rational choice people, he points out that the ideal market situation is for them as Utopian and unrealizable under present-day conditions as, for the Left, socialist revolution or transformation in the advanced capitalist countries today. One wants to add that the referent here is twofold: not merely the processes in the various Eastern countries which have been understood as an attempt to re-establish the market in one way or another, but also those efforts in the West, particularly under Reagan and Thatcher, to do away with the 'regulations' of the welfare state and return to some purer form of market conditions. We need to take into account the possibility that both of these efforts may fail for structural reasons; but we also need to point out tirelessly the interesting development that the 'market' turns out finally to be as Utopian as socialism has recently been held to be. Under these circumstances, nothing is served by substituting one inert institutional structure (bureaucratic planning) for another inert institutional structure (namely, the market itself). What is wanted is a great collective project in which an active majority of the population participates, as something belonging to it and constructed by its own energies. The setting of social priorities – also known in the socialist literature as planning – would have to be a part of such a collective project. It should be clear, however, that virtually by definition the market cannot be a project at all.

Notes

1. Marx and Engels, *Collected Works*, vol. 28, New York 1987, p. 180.
2. 'Only two paths stand open to mental research: aesthetics, and also political economy.' Stéphane Mallarmé, 'Magie', in *Variations sur un sujet*, in *Oeuvres complètes*, Paris 1945, p. 399. The phrase, which I used as an epigraph to *Marxism and Form*, emerges from a complex mediation on poetry, politics, economics, and class written in 1895 at the very dawn of high modernism itself.
3. Norman P. Barry, *On Classical Liberalism and Libertarianism*, New York 1987, p. 13.
4. Ibid., p. 194.
5. Gary Becker, *An Economic Approach to Human Behavior*, Chicago 1976, p. 14.
6. Ibid., p. 217.
7. Ibid., p. 141.
8. Barry, *On Classical Liberalism*, p. 30.
9. Marx and Engels, *Collected Works*, vol. 28, pp. 131–2.
10. Milton Friedman, *Capitalism and Democracy*, Chicago 1962, p. 39.
11. See Albert O. Hirschman, *The Passions and the Interests*, Princeton, NJ 1977, part 1.
12. 'Periodizing the Sixties', in *The Ideologies of Theory*, Minneapolis, MN 1988, vol. 2, pp. 178–208.
13. T. W. Adorno and Max Horkheimer, *Dialectic of Enlightenment*, trans. John Cumming, New York 1972, pp. 161–7.
14. See Jane Feuer, 'Reading *Dynasty*: Television and Reception Theory', *South Atlantic Quarterly*, 88, 2, September 1989, pp. 443–60.
15. Guy Debord, *The Society of the Spectacle*, Detroit, MI 1977, ch. 1.
16. See Barry, *On Classical Liberalism*, pp. 193–6.

How Did Marx Invent the Symptom?

Slavoj Žižek

Marx, Freud: The Analysis of Form

According to Lacan, it was none other than Karl Marx who invented the notion of symptom. Is this Lacanian thesis just a sally of wit, a vague analogy, or does it possess a pertinent theoretical foundation? If Marx really articulated the notion of the symptom as it is also at work in the Freudian field, then we must ask ourselves the Kantian question concerning the epistemological 'conditions of possibility' of such an encounter: how was it possible for Marx, in his analysis of the world of commodities, to produce a notion which applies also to the analysis of dreams, hysterical phenomena, and so on?

The answer is that there is a fundamental homology between the interpretative procedure of Marx and Freud – more precisely, between their analysis of commodity and of dreams. In both cases the point is to avoid the properly fetishistic fascination of the 'content' supposedly hidden behind the form: the 'secret' to be unveiled through analysis is not the content hidden by the form (the form of commodities, the form of dreams) but, on the contrary, *the 'secret' of this form itself.* The theoretical intelligence of the form of dreams does not consist in penetrating from the manifest content to its 'hidden kernel', to the latent dream-thoughts; it consists in the answer to the question: why have the latent dream-thoughts assumed such a form, why were they transposed into the form of a dream? It is the same with commodities: the real problem is not to penetrate to the 'hidden kernel' of the commodity – the determination of its value by the quantity of the work consumed in its production – but to explain why work assumed the form of the value of a commodity, why it can affirm its social character only in the commodity-form of its product.

The notorious reproach of 'pansexualism' addressed at the Freudian interpretation of dreams is already a commonplace. Hans-Jürgen Eysenck, a severe critic of psychoanalysis, long ago observed a crucial paradox in the Freudian approach to dreams: according to Freud, the desire articulated in a dream is supposed to be – as a rule, at least – unconscious and at the same time of a sexual nature, which contradicts the majority of examples analysed by Freud himself, starting with the dream he chose as an introductory case to exemplify the logic of dreams, the famous dream of Irma's injection. The latent thought articulated in this dream is Freud's attempt to get rid of the responsibility for the failure of his treatment of Irma, a patient of his, by means of arguments of the type 'it was not my fault, it was caused by a series of circumstances . . .'; but this 'desire', the meaning of the dream, is obviously neither of a sexual nature (it rather concerns professional ethics) nor unconscious (the failure of Irma's treatment was troubling Freud day and night).[1]

This kind of reproach is based on a fundamental theoretical error: the identification of the unconscious desire at work in the dream with the 'latent thought' – that is, the signification of the dream. But as Freud continually emphasizes, *there is nothing 'unconscious' in the 'latent dream-thought'*: this thought is an entirely 'normal' thought which can be articulated in the syntax of everyday, common language; topologically, it belongs to the system of 'consciousness/preconsciousness'; the subject is usually aware of it, even excessively so; it harasses him all the time. . . . Under certain conditions this thought is pushed away, forced out of the consciousness, drawn into the unconscious – that is, submitted to the laws of the 'primary process', translated into the 'language of the unconscious'. The relationship between the 'latent thought' and what is called the 'manifest content' of a dream – the text of the dream, the dream in its literal phenomenality – is therefore that between some entirely 'normal', (pre)conscious thought and its translation into the 'rebus' of the dream. The essential constitution of dream is thus not its 'latent thought' but this work (the mechanisms of displacement and condensation, the figuration of the contents of words or syllables) which confers on it the form of a dream.

Herein, then, lies the basic misunderstanding: if we seek the 'secret of the dream' in the latent content hidden by the manifest text, we are doomed to disappointment: all we find is some entirely 'normal' – albeit usually unpleasant – thought, the nature of which is mostly non-sexual and definitely not 'unconscious'. This 'normal', conscious/preconscious thought is not drawn towards the unconscious, repressed simply because of its 'disagreeable' character for the conscious, but because it achieves a kind of 'short circuit' between it and another desire which is already repressed, located in the unconscious, *a desire which has nothing whatsoever to do with the 'latent dream-thought'*. 'A normal train of thought' – normal and therefore one which can be articulated in common, everyday language: that is, in the syntax of the 'secondary process' – 'is only submitted to the abnormal psychical treatment of the sort we have been describing' – to the dream-work, to the mechanisms of the 'primary process' – 'if an unconscious wish, derived from infancy and in a state of repression, has been transferred on to it'.[2]

It is this unconscious/sexual desire which cannot be reduced to a 'normal train of thought' because it is, from the very beginning, constitutively repressed (Freud's *Urverdrängung*) – because it has no 'original' in the 'normal' language of everyday communication, in the syntax of the conscious/preconscious; its only place is in the mechanisms of the 'primary process'. This is why we should not reduce the interpretation of dreams, or symptoms in general, to the retranslation of the 'latent dream-thought' into the 'normal', everyday common language of intersubjective communication (Habermas's formula). The structure is always triple; there are always *three* elements at work: the *manifest dream-text*, the *latent dream-content* or thought and the *unconscious desire* articulated in a dream. This desire attaches itself to the dream, it intercalates itself in the interspace between the latent thought and the manifest text; it is therefore not 'more concealed, deeper' in relation to the latent thought, it is decidedly more 'on the surface', consisting entirely of the signifier's mechanisms, of the treatment to which the latent thought is submitted. In other words, its only place is in the *form* of the 'dream': the real subject matter of the dream (the unconscious desire) articulates itself in the dream-work, in the elaboration of its 'latent content'.

As is often the case with Freud, what he formulates as an empirical observation (although of 'quite surprising frequency') announces a fundamental, universal principle: 'The form of a dream or the form in which it is dreamt is used with quite surprising frequency for representing its concealed subject matter'.[3] This, then, is the basic paradox of the dream: the unconscious desire, that which is supposedly its most hidden kernel, articulates itself precisely through the dissimulation work of the 'kernel' of a dream, its latent thought, through the work of disguising this content-kernel by means of its translation into the dream-rebus. Again, as characteristically, Freud gave this paradox its final formulation in a footnote added in a later edition:

> I used at one time to find it extraordinarily difficult to accustom readers to the distinction between the manifest content of dreams and the latent

dream-thoughts. Again and again arguments and objections would be brought up based upon some uninterpreted dream in the form in which it had been retained in the memory, and the need to interpret it would be ignored. But now the analysts at least have become reconciled to replacing the manifest dream by the meaning revealed by its interpretation, many of them have become guilty of falling into another confusion which they cling to with an equal obstinacy. They seek to find the essence of dreams in their latent content and in so doing they overlook the distinction between the latent dream-thoughts and the dream-work.

At bottom, dreams are nothing other than a particular form of thinking, made possible by the conditions of the state of sleep. It is the dream-work which creates that form, and it alone is the essence of dreaming – the explanation of its peculiar nature.[4]

Freud proceeds here in two stages:

• First, we must break the appearance according to which a dream is nothing but a simple and meaningless confusion, a disorder caused by physiological processes and as such having nothing whatsoever to do with signification. In other words, we must accomplish a crucial step towards a *hermeneutical* approach and conceive the dream as a meaningful phenomenon, as something transmitting a repressed message which has to be discovered by an interpretative procedure;

• Then we must get rid of the fascination in this kernel of signification, in the 'hidden meaning' of the dream – that is to say, in the content concealed behind the form of a dream – and centre our attention on this form itself, on the dream-work to which the 'latent dream-thoughts' were submitted.

The crucial thing to note here is that we find exactly the same articulation in two stages with Marx, in his analysis of the 'secret of the commodity-form':

• First, we must break the appearance according to which the value of a commodity depends on pure hazard – on an accidental interplay between supply and demand, for example. We must accomplish the crucial step of conceiving the hidden 'meaning' behind the commodity-form, the signification 'expressed' by this form; we must penetrate the 'secret' of the value of commodities:

The determination of the magnitude of value by labour-time is therefore a secret, hidden under the apparent fluctuations in the relative values of commodities. Its discovery, while removing all appearance of mere accidentality from the determination of the magnitude of the values of products, yet in no way alters the mode in which that determination takes place.[5]

• But as Marx points out, there is a certain 'yet': the unmasking of the secret *is not sufficient.* Classical bourgeois political economy has already discovered the 'secret' of the commodity-form; its limit is that it is not able to disengage itself from this fascination in the secret hidden behind the commodity-form – that its attention is captivated by labour as the true source of wealth. In other words, classical political economy is interested only in contents concealed behind the commodity-form, which is why it cannot explain the true secret, not the secret *behind* the form but *the secret of this form itself.* In spite of its quite correct explanation of the 'secret of the magnitude of value', the commodity remains for classical political economy a mysterious, enigmatic thing – it is the same as with the dream: even after we have explained its hidden meaning, its latent thought, the dream remains an enigmatic phenomenon; what is not yet explained is simply its form, the process by means of which the hidden meaning disguised itself in such a form.

We must, then, accomplish another crucial step and analyse the genesis of the commodity-form itself. It is not sufficient to reduce the form to the essence, to the hidden kernel; we must also examine the process – homologous to the 'dream-work' – by means of which the concealed content assumes such a form, because, as Marx points out: 'Whence, then, arises the enigmatical character of the product of labour, as soon as it assumes the form of commodities? Clearly from this form itself.'[6] It is this step towards the genesis of the form that classical political economy cannot accomplish, and this is its crucial weakness:

> Political economy has indeed analysed value and its magnitude, however incompletely, and has uncovered the content concealed within these forms. But it has never once asked the question why this content has assumed that particular form, that is to say, why labour is expressed in value, and why the measurement of labour by its duration is expressed in the magnitude of the value of the product.[7]

The Unconscious of the Commodity-form

Why did the Marxian analysis of the commodity-form – which, *prima facie*, concerns a purely economic question – exert such an influence in the general field of social sciences; why has it fascinated generations of philosophers, sociologists, art historians, and others? Because it offers a kind of matrix enabling us to generate all other forms of the 'fetishistic inversion': it is as if the dialectics of the commodity-form presents us with a pure – distilled, so to speak – version of a mechanism offering us a key to the theoretical understanding of phenomena which, at first sight, have nothing whatsoever to do with the field of political economy (law, religion, and so on). In the commodity-form there is definitely more at stake than the commodity-form itself, and it was precisely this 'more' which exerted such a fascinating power of attraction. The theoretician who has gone furthest in unfolding the universal reach of the commodity-form is indubitably Alfred Sohn-Rethel, one of the 'fellow-travellers' of the Frankfurt School. His fundamental thesis was that

> the formal analysis of the commodity holds the key not only to the critique of political economy, but also to the historical explanation of the abstract conceptual mode of thinking and of the division of intellectual and manual labour which came into existence with it.[8]

In other words, in the structure of the commodity-form it is possible to find the transcendental subject: the commodity-form articulates in advance the anatomy, the skeleton of the Kantian transcendental subject – that is, the network of transcendental categories which constitute the a priori frame of 'objective' scientific knowledge. Herein lies the paradox of the commodity-form: it – this inner-worldly, 'pathological' (in the Kantian meaning of the word) phenomenon – offers us a key to solving the fundamental question of the theory of knowledge: objective knowledge with universal validity – how is this possible?

After a series of detailed analyses, Sohn-Rethel came to the following conclusion: the apparatus of categories presupposed, implied by the scientific procedure (that, of course, of the Newtonian science of nature), the network of notions by means of which it seizes nature, is already present in the social effectivity, already at work in the act of commodity exchange. Before thought could arrive at pure *abstraction*, the abstraction was already at work in the social effectivity of the market. The exchange of commodities implies a double abstraction: the abstraction from the changeable character of the commodity during the act of exchange and the abstraction from the concrete, empirical, sensual, particular character of the commodity (in the act of exchange, the distinct, particular qualitative determination of a commodity is not taken into account; a commodity is reduced to an abstract entity which – irrespective of its particular nature, of its 'use value' – possesses 'the same value' as another commodity for which it is being exchanged).

Before thought could arrive at the idea of a purely *quantitative* determination, a *sine qua non* of the modern science of nature, pure quantity was already at work in money, that commodity which renders possible the commensurability of the value of all other commodities notwithstanding their particular qualitative determination. Before physics could articulate the notion of a purely abstract *movement* going on in a geometric space, independently of all qualitative determinations of the moving objects, the social act of exchange had already realized such a 'pure', abstract movement which leaves totally intact the concrete-sensual properties of the object caught in movement: the transference of property. And Sohn-Rethel demonstrated the same about the relationship of substance and its accidents, about the notion of causality operative in Newtonian science – in short, about the whole network of categories of pure reason.

In this way, the transcendental subject, the support of the net of a priori categories, is confronted with the disquieting fact that it depends, in its very formal genesis, on some inner-worldly, 'pathological' process – a scandal, a nonsensical impossibility from the transcendental point of view, in so far as the formal-transcendental a priori is by definition independent of all positive contents: a scandal corresponding perfectly to the 'scandalous' character of the Freudian unconscious, which is also unbearable from the transcendental-philosophical perspective. That is to say, if we look closely at the ontological status of what Sohn-Rethel calls the 'real abstraction' [*das reale Abstraktion*] (that is, the act of abstraction at work in the very *effective* process of the exchange of commodities), the homology between its status and that of the unconscious, this signifying chain which persists on 'another Scene', is striking: *the 'real abstraction' is the unconscious of the transcendental subject*, the support of objective-universal scientific knowledge.

On the one hand, the 'real abstraction' is of course not 'real' in the sense of the real, effective properties of commodities as material objects: the object-commodity does not contain 'value' in the same way as it possesses a set of particular properties determining its 'use value' (its form, colour, taste, and so on). As Sohn-Rethel pointed out, its nature is that of a *postulate* implied by the effective act of exchange – in other words, that of a certain 'as if' [*als ob*]: during the act of exchange, individuals proceed *as if* the commodity is not submitted to physical, material exchanges; *as if* it is excluded from the natural cycle of generation and corruption; although on the level of their 'consciousness' they 'know very well' that this is not the case.

The easiest way to detect the effectivity of this postulate is to think of the way we behave towards the materiality of money: we know very well that money, like all other material objects, suffers the effects of use, that its material body changes through time; but in the social *effectivity* of the market we none the less *treat* coins as if they consist 'of an immutable substance, a substance over which time has no power, and which stands in antithetic contrast to any matter found in nature'.[9] How tempting to recall here the formula of fetishistic disavowal: 'I know very well, but still . . .'. To the current exemplifications of this formula ('I know that Mother has not got a phallus, but still . . . [I believe she has got one]'; 'I know that Jews are people like us, but still . . . [there is something in them]') we must undoubtedly add also the variant of money: 'I know that money is a material object like others, but still . . . [it is as if it were made of a special substance over which time has no power]'.

Here we have touched a problem unsolved by Marx, that of the *material* character of money: not of the empirical, material stuff money is made of, but of the *sublime* material, of that other 'indestructible and immutable' body which persists beyond the corruption of the body physical – this other body of money is like the corpse of the Sadeian victim which endures all torments and survives with its beauty immaculate. This immaterial corporality of the 'body within the body' gives us a precise definition of the sublime object, and it is in this sense only that the psychoanalytic notion of money as a 'pre-phallic', 'anal' object is acceptable – provided that we do not forget how this postulated existence of the sublime body depends on the symbolic order: the indestructible 'body-within-the-body' exempted from the effects of wear and tear is always sustained by the guarantee of some symbolic authority:

> A coin has it stamped upon its body that it is to serve as a means of exchange and not as an object of use. Its weight and metallic purity are guaranteed by the issuing authority so that, if by the wear and tear of circulation it has lost in weight, full replacement is provided. Its physical matter has visibly become a mere carrier of its social function.[10]

If, then, the 'real abstraction' has nothing to do with the level of 'reality', of the effective properties, of an object, it would be wrong for that reason to conceive of it as a 'thought-abstraction', as a process taking place in the 'interior' of the thinking subject: in relation to this 'interior', the abstraction appertaining to the act of exchange is in an irreducible way external, decentred – or, to quote Sohn-Rethel's concise formulation: 'The exchange abstraction *is not* thought, but it has the *form* of thought'.

Here we have one of the possible definitions of the unconscious: *the form of thought whose ontological status is not that of thought*, that is to say, the form of thought external to the thought itself – in short, some Other Scene external to the thought whereby the form of the thought is already articulated in advance. The symbolic order is precisely such a formal order which supplements and/or disrupts the dual relationship of 'external' factual reality and 'internal' subjective experience; Sohn-Rethel is thus quite justified in his criticism of Althusser, who conceives abstraction as a process taking place entirely in the domain of knowledge, and for that reason refuses the category of 'real abstraction' as the expression of an 'epistemological confusion'. The 'real abstraction' is unthinkable in the frame of the fundamental Althusserian epistemological distinction between the 'real object' and the 'object of knowledge' in so far as it introduces a third element which subverts the very field of this distinction: the form of the thought previous and external to the thought – in short: the symbolic order.

We are now able to formulate precisely the 'scandalous' nature of Sohn-Rethel's undertaking for philosophical reflection: he has confronted the closed circle of philosophical reflection with an external place where its form is already 'staged'. Philosophical reflection is thus subjected to an uncanny experience similar to the one summarized by the old oriental formula 'thou art that': there, in the external effectivity of the exchange process, is your proper place; there is the theatre in which your truth was performed before you took cognizance of it. The confrontation with this place is unbearable because philosophy as such *is defined by* its blindness to this place: it cannot take it into consideration without dissolving itself, without losing its consistency.

This does not mean, on the other hand, that everyday 'practical' consciousness, as opposed to the philosophical-theoretical one – the consciousness of the individuals partaking in the act of exchange – is not also subjected to a complementary blindness. During the act of exchange, individuals proceed as 'practical solipsists', they misrecognize the socio-synthetic function of exchange: that is the level of the 'real abstraction' as the form of socialization of private production through the medium of the market: 'What the commodity owners do in an exchange relation is practical solipsism – irrespective of what they think and say about it.'[11] Such a misrecognition is the *sine qua non* of the effectuation of an act of exchange – if the participants were to take note of the dimension of 'real abstraction', the 'effective' act of exchange itself would no longer be possible.

> Thus, in speaking of the abstractness of exchange we must be careful not to apply the term to the consciousness of the exchange agents. They are supposed to be occupied with the use of the commodities they see, but occupied in their imagination only. It is the action of exchange, and the

action alone, that is abstract . . . the abstractness of that action cannot be noted when it happens because the consciousness of its agents is taken up with their business and with the empirical appearance of things which pertain to their use. One could say that the abstractness of their action is beyond realization by the actors because their very consciousness stands in the way. Were the abstractness to catch their minds their action would cease to be exchange and the abstraction would not arise.[12]

This misrecognition brings about the fissure of the consciousness into 'practical' and 'theoretical': the proprietor partaking in the act of exchange proceeds as a 'practical solipsist': he overlooks the universal, socio-synthetic dimension of his act, reducing it to a casual encounter of atomized individuals in the market. This 'repressed' *social* dimension of his act emerges thereupon in the form of its contrary – as universal Reason turned towards the observation of nature (the network of categories of 'pure reason' as the conceptual frame of natural sciences).

The crucial paradox of this relationship between the social effectivity of the commodity exchange and the 'consciousness' of it is that – to use again a concise formulation by Sohn-Rethel – 'this non-knowledge of the reality is part of its very essence': the social effectivity of the exchange process is a kind of reality which is possible only on condition that the individuals partaking in it are *not* aware of its proper logic; that is, a kind of reality *whose very ontological consistency implies a certain non-knowledge of its participants* – if we come to 'know too much', to pierce the true functioning of social reality, this reality would dissolve itself.

This is probably the fundamental dimension of 'ideology': ideology is not simply a 'false consciousness', an illusory representation of reality; it is, rather, this reality itself which is already to be conceived as 'ideological' – '*ideological*' is a social reality whose very existence implies the non-knowledge of its participants as to its essence – that is, the social effectivity, the very reproduction of which implies that the individuals 'do not know what they are doing'. '*Ideological*' is not the '*false consciousness*' of a (*social*) being but this being itself in so far as it is supported by '*false consciousness*'. Thus we have finally reached the dimension of the symptom, because one of its possible definitions would also be 'a formation whose very consistency implies a certain non-knowledge on the part of the subject': the subject can 'enjoy his symptom' only in so far as its logic escapes him – the measure of the success of its interpretation is precisely its dissolution.

The Social Symptom

How, then, can we define the Marxian symptom? Marx 'invented the symptom' (Lacan) by means of detecting a certain fissure, an asymmetry, a certain 'pathological' imbalance which belies the universalism of bourgeois 'rights and duties'. This imbalance, far from announcing the 'imperfect realization' of these universal principles – that is, an insufficiency to be abolished by further development – functions as their constitutive moment: the 'symptom' is, strictly speaking, a particular element which subverts its own universal foundation, a species subverting its own genus. In this sense, we can say that the elementary Marxian procedure of 'criticism of ideology' is already 'symptomatic': it consists in detecting a point of breakdown *heterogeneous* to a given ideological field and at the same time *necessary* for that field to achieve its closure, its accomplished form.

This procedure thus implies a certain logic of exception: every ideological Universal – for example, freedom, equality – is 'false' in so far as it necessarily includes a specific case which breaks its unity, lays open its falsity. Freedom, for example: a universal notion comprising a number of species (freedom of speech and press, freedom of consciousness, freedom of commerce, political freedom, and so on) but also, by means of a structural necessity, a specific freedom (that of the worker to sell freely his own labour on the market) which subverts this universal notion. That is to say, this freedom is the very opposite of effective freedom: by selling his labour 'freely', the worker *loses* his freedom – the real content of this free act of sale is the worker's enslavement to capital. The crucial point is, of course, that it is precisely this paradoxical freedom, the form of its opposite, which closes the circle of 'bourgeois freedoms'.

The same can also be shown for fair, equivalent exchange, this ideal of the market. When, in pre-capitalist society, the production of commodities has not yet attained universal character – that is, when it is still so-called 'natural production' which predominates – the proprietors of the means of production are still themselves producers (as a rule, at least): it is artisan production; the proprietors themselves work and sell their products on the market. At this stage of development there is no exploitation (in principle, at least – that is, if we do not consider the exploitation of apprentices, and so on); the exchange on the market is equivalent, every commodity is paid its full value. But as soon as production for the market prevails in the economic edifice of a given society, this *generalization* is necessarily accompanied by the appearance of a new, paradoxical type of commodity: the labour force, the workers who are not themselves proprietors of the means of production and who are consequently obliged to sell on the market their own labour instead of the products of their labour.

With this new commodity, the equivalent exchange becomes its own negation – the very form of exploitation, of appropriation of the surplus-value. The crucial point not to be missed here is that this negation is strictly *internal* to equivalent exchange, not its simple violation: the labour force is not 'exploited' in the sense that its full value is not remunerated; in principle, at least, the exchange between labour and capital is wholly equivalent and equitable. The catch is that the labour force is a peculiar commodity, the use of which – labour itself – produces a certain surplus-value, and it is this surplus over the value of the labour force itself which is appropriated by the capitalist.

We have here again a certain ideological Universal, that of equivalent and equitable exchange, and a particular paradoxical exchange – that of the labour force for its wages – which, precisely as an equivalent, functions as the very form of exploitation. The 'quantitative' development itself, the universalization of the production of commodities, brings about a new 'quality', the emergence of a new commodity representing the internal negation of the universal principle of equivalent exchange of commodities; in other words, *it brings about a symptom*. And in the Marxian perspective, *Utopian* socialism consists in the very belief that a society is possible in which the relations of exchange are universalized and production for the market predominates, but workers themselves none the less remain proprietors of their means of production and are therefore not exploited – in short, 'Utopian' conveys a belief in the possibility of *a universality without its symptom*, without the point of exception functioning as its internal negation.

This is also the logic of the Marxian critique of Hegel, of the Hegelian notion of society as a rational totality: as soon as we try to conceive the existing social order as a rational totality, we must include in it a paradoxical element which, without ceasing to be its internal constituent, functions as its symptom – subverts the very universal rational principle of this totality. For Marx, this 'irrational' element of the existing society was, of course, the proletariat, 'the unreason of reason itself' (Marx), the point at which the Reason embodied in the existing social order encounters its own unreason.

Commodity Fetishism

In his attribution of the discovery of symptom to Marx, Lacan is, however, more distinct: he locates this discovery in the way Marx conceived the *passage* from feudalism to capitalism: 'One has to look for the origins of the notion of symptom not in Hippocrates but in Marx, in the connection he was first to establish between capitalism and what? – the good old times, what we call the feudal times.'[13] To grasp the logic of this passage from feudalism to capitalism we have first to elucidate its theoretical background, the Marxian notion of commodity fetishism.

In a first approach, commodity fetishism is 'a definite social relation between men, that assumes, in their eyes, the fantastic form of a relation between things'.[14] The *value* of a certain commodity, which is effectively an insignia of a network of social relations between producers of diverse commodities, assumes the form of a quasi-'natural' property of another thing-commodity, money: we say that the value of a certain commodity is such-and-such amount of money. Consequently, the essential feature of commodity fetishism does not consist of the famous replacement of men with things ('a relation between men assumes the form of a relation between things'); rather, it consists of a certain misrecognition which concerns the relation between a structured network and one of its elements: what is really a structural effect, an effect of the network of relations between elements, appears as an immediate property of one of the elements, as if this property also belongs to it outside its relation with other elements.

Such a misrecognition can take place in a 'relation between things' as well as in a 'relation between men' – Marx states this explicitly apropos of the simple form of the value-expression. Commodity A can express its value only by referring itself to another commodity, B, which thus becomes its equivalent: in the value relationship, the natural form of commodity B (its use value, its positive, empirical properties) functions as a form of value of commodity A; in other words, the body of B becomes for A the mirror of its value. To these reflections, Marx added the following note:

> In a sort of way, it is with man as with commodities. Since he comes into the world neither with a looking-glass in his hand, nor as a Fichtian philosopher, to whom 'I am I' is sufficient, man first sees and recognizes himself in other men. Peter only establishes his own identity as a man by first comparing himself with Paul as being of like kind. And thereby Paul, just as he stands in his Pauline personality, becomes to Peter the type of the genus homo.[15]

This short note anticipates in a way the Lacanian theory of the mirror-phase: only by being reflected in another man – that is, in so far as this other man offers it an image of its unity – can the ego arrive at its self-identity; identity and alienation are thus strictly correlative. Marx pursues this homology: the other commodity (B) is an equivalent only in so far as A relates to it as to the form-of-appearance of its own value, only within this relationship. But the appearance – and herein lies the effect of inversion proper to fetishism – the appearance is exactly opposite: A seems to relate to B as if, for B, to be an equivalent of A would not be a 'reflexive determination' (Marx) of A – that is as if B would *already in itself* be the equivalent of A; the property of 'being-an-equivalent' appears to belong to it even outside its relation to A, on the same level as its other 'natural' effective properties constituting its use value. To these reflections, Marx again added a very interesting note:

> Such expressions of relations in general, called by Hegel reflex-categories, form a very curious class. For instance, one man is king only because other men stand in the relation of subjects to him. They, on the contrary, imagine that they are subjects because he is king.[16]

'Being-a-king' is an effect of the network of social relations between a 'king' and his 'subjects'; but – and here is the fetishistic misrecognition – to the participants of this social bond, the relationship appears necessarily in an inverse form: they think that they are subjects giving the king royal treatment because the king is already in himself, outside the relationship to his subjects, a king; as if the determination of 'being-a-king' were a 'natural' property of the person of a king. How can one not remind oneself here of the famous Lacanian affirmation that a madman who believes himself to be a king is no more mad than a king who believes himself to be a king – who, that is, identifies immediately with the mandate 'king'?

What we have here is thus a parallel between two modes of fetishism, and the crucial question concerns the exact relationship between these two levels. That is to say, this relationship is by no means a simple homology: we cannot say that in societies in which production for the market predominates – ultimately, that is, in capitalist societies – 'it is with man as with commodities'. Precisely the opposite is true: commodity fetishism occurs in capitalist societies, but in capitalism relations between men are definitely *not* 'fetishized'; what we have here are relations between 'free' people, each following his or her proper egoistic interest. The predominant and determining form of their interrelations is not domination and servitude but a contract between free people who are equal in the eyes of the law. Its model is the market exchange: here, two subjects meet, their relation is free of all the lumber of veneration of the Master, of the Master's patronage and care for his subjects; they meet as two persons whose activity is thoroughly determined by their egoistic interest; every one of them proceeds as a good utilitarian; the other person is for him wholly delivered of all mystical aura; all he sees in his partner is another subject who follows his interest and interests him only in so far as he possesses something – a commodity – that could satisfy some of his needs.

The two forms of fetishism are thus *incompatible*: in societies in which commodity fetishism reigns, the 'relations between men' are totally de-fetishized, while in societies in which there is fetishism in 'relations between men' – in pre-capitalist societies – commodity fetishism is not yet developed, because it is 'natural' production, not production for the market, which predominates. This fetishism in relations between men has to be called by its proper name: what we have here are, as Marx points out, 'relations of domination and servitude' – that is to say, precisely the relation of Lordship and Bondage in a Hegelian sense;[17] and it is as if the retreat of the Master in capitalism was only a *displacement*: as if the de-fetishization in the 'relations between men' was paid for by the emergence of fetishism in the 'relations between things' – by commodity fetishism. The place of fetishism has just shifted from intersubjective relations to relations 'between things': the crucial social relations, those of production, are no longer immediately transparent in the form of the interpersonal relations of domination and servitude (of the Lord and his serfs, and so on); they disguise themselves – to use Marx's accurate formula – 'under the shape of social relations between things, between the products of labour'.

This is why one has to look for the discovery of the symptom in the way Marx conceived the passage from feudalism to capitalism. With the establishment of bourgeois society, the relations of domination and servitude are *repressed*: formally, we are apparently concerned with free subjects whose interpersonal relations are discharged of all fetishism; the repressed truth – that of the persistence of domination and servitude – emerges in a symptom which subverts the ideological appearance of equality, freedom, and so on. This symptom, the point of emergence of the truth about social relations, is precisely the 'social relations between things'. 'Instead of appearing at all events as their own mutual relations, the social relations between individuals are disguised under the shape of social relations between things' – here we have a precise definition of the hysterical symptom, of the 'hysteria of conversion' proper to capitalism.

Totalitarian Laughter

Here Marx is more subversive than the majority of his contemporary critics who discard the dialectics of commodity fetishism as outdated:

this dialectics can still help us to grasp the phenomenon of so-called 'totalitarianism'. Let us take as our starting point Umberto Eco's *The Name of the Rose*, precisely because there is something wrong with this book. This criticism does not apply only to its ideology, which might be called – on the model of *spaghetti* Westerns – *spaghetti* structuralism: a kind of simplified, mass-culture version of structuralist and post-structuralist ideas (there is no final reality, we all live in a world of signs referring to other signs . . .). What should bother us about this book is its basic underlying thesis: the source of totalitarianism is a dogmatic attachment to the official word: the lack of laughter, of ironic detachment. An excessive commitment to Good may in itself become the greatest Evil: real Evil is any kind of fanatical dogmatism, especially that exerted in the name of the supreme Good.

[. . .]

First, this idea of an obsession with (a fanatical devotion to) Good turning into Evil masks the inverse experience, which is much more disquieting: how an obsessive, fanatical attachment to Evil may in itself acquire the status of an ethical position, of a position which is not guided by our egoistical interests. Consider only Mozart's Don Giovanni at the end of the opera, when he is confronted with the following choice: if he confesses his sins, he can still achieve salvation; if he persists, he will be damned for ever. From the viewpoint of the pleasure principle, the proper thing to do would be to renounce his past, but he does not, he persists in his Evil, although he knows that by persisting he will be damned for ever. Paradoxically, with his final choice of Evil, he acquires the status of an ethical hero – that is, of someone who is guided by fundamental principles 'beyond the pleasure principle' and not just by the search for pleasure or material gain.

What is really disturbing about *The Name of the Rose*, however, is the underlying belief in the liberating, anti-totalitarian force of laughter, of ironic distance. Our thesis here is almost the exact opposite of this underlying premiss of Eco's novel: in contemporary societies, democratic or totalitarian, that cynical distance, laughter, irony, are, so to speak, part of the game. The ruling ideology is not meant to be taken seriously or literally. Perhaps the greatest danger for totalitarianism is people who take its ideology literally – even in Eco's novel, poor old Jorge, the incarnation of dogmatic belief who does not laugh, is rather a tragic figure: outdated, a kind of living dead, a remnant of the past, certainly not a person representing the existing social and political powers.

What conclusion should we draw from this? Should we say that we live in a post-ideological society? Perhaps it would be better, first, to try to specify what we mean by ideology.

Cynicism as a Form of Ideology

The most elementary definition of ideology is probably the well-known phrase from Marx's *Capital*: '*Sie wissen das nicht, aber sie tun es*' – '*they do not know it, but they are doing it*'. The very concept of ideology implies a kind of basic, constitutive naivety: the misrecognition of its own presuppositions, of its own effective conditions, a distance, a divergence between so-called social reality and our distorted representation, our false consciousness of it. That is why such a 'naive consciousness' can be submitted to a critical-ideological procedure. The aim of this procedure is to lead the naive ideological consciousness to a point at which it can recognize its own effective conditions, the social reality that it is distorting, and through this very act dissolve itself. In the more sophisticated versions of the critics of ideology – that developed by the Frankfurt School, for example – it is not just a question of seeing things (that is, social reality) as they 'really are', of throwing away the distorting spectacles of ideology; the main point is to see how the reality itself cannot reproduce itself without this so-called ideological mystification. The mask is not simply hiding the real state of things; the ideological distortion is written into its very essence.

We find, then, the paradox of a being which can reproduce itself only in so far as it is misrecognized and overlooked: the moment we see it 'as it really is', this being dissolves itself into nothingness or, more precisely, it changes into another kind of reality. That is why we must avoid the simple metaphors of demasking, of throwing away the veils which are supposed to hide the naked reality.

[. . .]

But all this is already well known: it is the classic concept of ideology as 'false consciousness', misrecognition of the social reality which is part of this reality itself. Our question is: Does this concept of ideology as a naive consciousness still apply to today's world? Is it still operating today? In the *Critique of Cynical Reason*, a great bestseller in Germany,[18] Peter Sloterdijk puts forward the thesis that ideology's dominant mode of functioning is cynical, which renders impossible – or, more precisely, vain – the classic critical-ideological procedure. The cynical subject is quite aware of the distance between the ideological mask and the social reality, but he none the less still insists upon the mask. The formula, as proposed by Sloterdijk, would then be: 'they know very well what they are doing, but still, they are doing it'. Cynical reason is no longer naive, but is a paradox of an enlightened false consciousness: one knows the falsehood very well, one is well aware of a particular interest hidden behind an ideological universality, but still one does not renounce it.

We must distinguish this cynical position strictly from what Sloterdijk calls *kynicism*. Kynicism represents the popular, plebeian rejection
of the official culture by means of irony and sarcasm: the classical
kynical procedure is to confront the pathetic phrases of the ruling
official ideology – its solemn, grave tonality – with everyday banality
and to hold them up to ridicule, thus exposing behind the sublime
noblesse of the ideological phrases the egotistical interests, the violence,
the brutal claims to power. This procedure, then, is more pragmatic
than argumentative: it subverts the official proposition by confronting
it with the situation of its enunciation; it proceeds *ad hominem* (for
example, when a politician preaches the duty of patriotic sacrifice,
kynicism exposes the personal gain he is making from the sacrifice of
others).

Cynicism is the answer of the ruling culture to this kynical subver-
sion: it recognizes, it takes into account, the particular interest behind
the ideological universality, the distance between the ideological mask
and the reality, but it still finds reasons to retain the mask. This
cynicism is not a direct position of immorality, it is more like morality
itself put in the service of immorality – the model of cynical wisdom is to
conceive probity, integrity, as a supreme form of dishonesty, and
morals as a supreme form of profligacy, the truth as the most effective
form of a lie. This cynicism is therefore a kind of perverted 'negation of
the negation' of the official ideology: confronted with illegal enrichment, with robbery, the cynical reaction consists in saying that legal
enrichment is a lot more effective and, moreover, protected by the law.
As Bertolt Brecht puts it in his *Threepenny Opera*: 'what is the robbery of
a bank compared to the founding of a new bank?'

It is clear, therefore, that confronted with such cynical reason, the
traditional critique of ideology no longer works. We can no longer
subject the ideological text to 'symptomatic reading', confronting it
with its blank spots, with what it must repress to organize itself, to
preserve its consistency – cynical reason takes this distance into account
in advance. Is then the only issue left to us to affirm that, with the reign
of cynical reason, we find ourselves in the so-called post-ideological
world? Even Adorno came to this conclusion, starting from the premiss
that ideology is, strictly speaking, only a system which makes a claim to
the truth – that is, which is not simply a lie but a lie experienced as truth,
a lie which pretends to be taken seriously. Totalitarian ideology no
longer has this pretension. It is no longer meant, even by its authors, to
be taken seriously – its status is just that of a means of manipulation,
purely external and instrumental; its rule is secured not by its truth
value but by simple extra-ideological violence and promise of gain.

It is here, at this point, that the distinction between *symptom* and *fantasy* must be introduced in order to show how the idea that we live in a post-ideological society proceeds a little too quickly: cynical reason, with all its ironic detachment, leaves untouched the fundamental level of ideological fantasy, the level on which ideology structures the social reality itself.

Ideological Fantasy

If we want to grasp this dimension of fantasy, we must return to the Marxian formula 'they do not know it, but they are doing it', and pose ourselves a very simple question: Where is the place of ideological illusion, in the '*knowing*' or in the '*doing*' in the reality itself? At first sight, the answer seems obvious: ideological illusion lies in the 'knowing'. It is a matter of a discordance between what people are effectively doing and what they think they are doing – ideology consists in the very fact that the people 'do not know what they are really doing', that they have a false representation of the social reality to which they belong (the distortion produced, of course, by the same reality). Let us take again the classic Marxian example of so-called commodity fetishism: money is in reality just an embodiment, a condensation, a materialization of a network of social relations – the fact that it functions as a universal equivalent of all commodities is conditioned by its position in the texture of social relations. But to the individuals themselves, this function of money – to be the embodiment of wealth – appears as an immediate, natural property of a thing called 'money', as if money is already in itself, in its immediate material reality, the embodiment of wealth. Here, we have touched upon the classic Marxist motive of 'reification': behind the things, the relation between things, we must detect the social relations, the relations between human subjects.

But such a reading of the Marxian formula leaves out an illusion, an error, a distortion which is already at work in the social reality itself, at the level of what the individuals are *doing*, and not only what they *think* or *know* they are doing. When individuals use money, they know very well that there is nothing magical about it – that money, in its materiality, is simply an expression of social relations. The everyday spontaneous ideology reduces money to a simple sign giving the individual possessing it a right to a certain part of the social product. So, on an everyday level, the individuals know very well that there are relations between people behind the relations between things. The problem is that in their social activity itself, in what they are *doing*, they are *acting* as if money, in its material reality, is the immediate embodiment of wealth as such. They are fetishists in practice, not in theory. What they 'do not know', what they misrecognize, is the fact that in their social reality itself, in their social activity – in the act of commodity exchange – they are guided by the fetishistic illusion.

To make this clear, let us again take the classic Marxian motive of the speculative inversion of the relationship between the Universal and the Particular. The Universal is just a property of particular objects which really exist, but when we are victims of commodity fetishism it appears as if the concrete content of a commodity (its use value) is an expression of its abstract universality (its exchange value) – the abstract Universal, the Value, appears as a real Substance which successively incarnates itself in a series of concrete objects. That is the basic Marxian thesis: it is already the effective world of commodities which behaves like a Hegelian subject-substance, like a Universal going through a series of particular embodiments. Marx speaks about 'commodity metaphysics', about the 'religion of everyday life'. The roots of philosophical speculative idealism are in the social reality of the world of commodities; it is this world which behaves 'idealistically' – or, as Marx puts it in the first chapter of the first edition of *Capital*:

> This *inversion* through which what is sensible and concrete counts only as a phenomenal form of what is abstract and universal, contrary to the real state of things where the abstract and the universal count only as a property of the concrete – such an inversion is characteristic of the expression of value, and it is this inversion which, at the same time, makes the understanding of this expression so difficult. If I say: Roman law and German law are both laws, it is something which goes by itself. But if, on the contrary, I say: 'THE Law, this abstract thing, realizes itself in Roman law and in German law, i.e. in these concrete laws, the interconnection becomes mystical.[19]

The question to ask again is: Where is the illusion here? We must not forget that the bourgeois individual, in his everyday ideology, is definitely not a speculative Hegelian: he does not conceive the particular content as resulting from an autonomous movement of the universal Idea. He is, on the contrary, a good Anglo-Saxon nominalist, thinking that the Universal is a property of the Particular – that is, of really existing things. Value in itself does not exist, there are just individual things which, among other properties, have value. The problem is that in his practice, in his real activity, he acts as if the particular things (the commodities) were just so many embodiments of universal Value. To rephrase Marx: *He knows very well that Roman law and German law are just two kinds of law, but in his practice, he acts as if the Law itself, this abstract entity, realizes itself in Roman law and in German law.*

So now we have made a decisive step forward; we have established a new way to read the Marxian formula 'they do not know it, but they are doing it': the illusion is not on the side of knowledge, it is already on the side of reality itself, of what the people are doing. What they do not know is that their social reality itself, their activity, is guided by an illusion, by a fetishistic inversion. What they overlook, what they misrecognize, is not the reality but the illusion which is structuring their reality, their real social activity. They know very well how things really are, but still they are doing it as if they did not know. The illusion is therefore double: it consists in overlooking the illusion which is structuring our real, effective relationship to reality. And this over-looked, unconscious illusion is what may be called the *ideological fantasy*.

If our concept of ideology remains the classic one in which the illusion is located in knowledge, then today's society must appear post-ideological: the prevailing ideology is that of cynicism; people no longer believe in ideological truth; they do not take ideological propositions seriously. The fundamental level of ideology, however, is not of an illusion masking the real state of things but that of an (unconscious) fantasy structuring our social reality itself. And at this level, we are of course far from being post-ideological society. Cynical distance is just one way – one of many ways – to blind ourselves to the structuring power of ideological fantasy: even if we do not take things seriously, even if we keep an ironical distance, *we are still doing them.*

It is from this standpoint that we can account for the formula of cynical reason proposed by Sloterdijk: 'they know very well what they are doing, but still, they are doing it'. If the illusion were on the side of knowledge, then the cynical position would really be a post-ideological position, simply a position without illusions: 'they know what they are doing, and they are doing it'. But if the place of the illusion is in the reality of doing itself, then this formula can be read in quite another way: 'they know that, in their activity, they are following an illusion, but still, they are doing it'. For example, they know that their idea of Freedom is masking a particular form of exploitation, but they still continue to follow this idea of Freedom.

The Objectivity of Belief

From this standpoint, it would also be worth rereading the elementary Marxian formulation of so-called commodity fetishism: in a society in which the products of human labour acquire the form of commodities, the crucial relations between people take on the form of relations between things, between commodities – instead of immediate relations between people, we have social relations between things. In the 1960s and 1970s, this whole problem was discredited through Althusserian anti-humanism. The principal reproach of the Althusserians was that the Marxian theory of commodity fetishism is based on a naive, ideological, epistemologically unfounded opposition between persons (human subjects) and things. But a Lacanian reading can give this formulation a new, unexpected twist: the subversive power of Marx's approach lies precisely in the way he uses the opposition of persons and things.

[. . .]

The point of Marx's analysis is that things (*commodities*) *themselves believe in the place of subjects*: it is as if all their beliefs, superstitions and metaphysical mystifications, supposedly surmounted by the rational, utilitarian personality, are embodied in the 'social relations between things'. They no longer believe, *but the things themselves believe for them.*

This seems also to be a basic Lacanian proposition, contrary to the usual thesis that a belief is something interior and knowledge something exterior (in the sense that it can be verified through an external procedure). Rather, it is belief which is radically exterior, embodied in the practical, effective procedure of people. It is similar to Tibetan prayer wheels: you write a prayer on a piece of paper, put the rolled paper into a wheel, and turn it automatically, without thinking (or, if you want to proceed according to the Hegelian 'cunning of reason', you attach it to a windmill, so that it is moved around by the wind). In this way, the wheel itself is praying for me, instead of me – or, more precisely, I myself am praying through the medium of the wheel. The beauty of it all is that in my psychological interiority I can think about whatever I want, I can yield to the most dirty and obscene fantasies, and it does not matter because – to use a good old Stalinist expression – whatever I am thinking, *objectively* I am praying.

[. . .]

'Law is Law'

The lesson to be drawn from this concerning the social field is above all that belief, far from being an 'intimate', purely mental state, is always *materialized* in our effective social activity: belief supports the fantasy which regulates social reality. Let us take the case of Kafka: it is usually said that in the 'irrational' universe of his novels, Kafka has given an 'exaggerated', 'fantastic', 'subjectively distorted' expression to modern bureaucracy and the fate of the individual within it. In saying this we overlook the crucial fact that it is this very 'exaggeration' which articulates the fantasy regulating the libidinal functioning of the 'effective', 'real' bureaucracy itself.

The so-called 'Kafka's universe' is not a 'fantasy-image of social reality' but, on the contrary, the *mise en scène of the fantasy which is at work in the midst of social reality itself*: we all know very well that bureaucracy is not all-powerful, but our 'effective' conduct in the presence of bureaucratic machinery is already regulated by a belief in its almightiness. . . . In contrast to the usual 'criticism of ideology' trying to deduce the ideological form of a determinate society from the conjunction of its effective social relations, the analytical approach aims above all at the ideological fantasy efficient in social reality itself.

What we call 'social reality' is in the last resort an ethical construction; it is supported by a certain *as if* (we act *as if* we believe in the almightiness of bureaucracy, *as if* the President incarnates the Will of the People, *as if* the Party expresses the objective interest of the working class . . .). As soon as the belief (which, let us remind ourselves again, is definitely not to be conceived at a 'psychological' level: it is embodied, materialized, in the effective functioning of the social field) is lost, the very texture of the social field disintegrates. This was already articulated by Pascal, one of Althusser's principal points of reference in his attempt to develop the concept of 'Ideological State Apparatuses'. According to Pascal, the interiority of our reasoning is determined by the external, nonsensical 'machine' – automatism of the signifier, of the symbolic network in which the subjects are caught:

> For we must make no mistake about ourselves: we are as much automaton as mind. . . . Proofs only convince the mind; habit provides the strongest proofs and those that are most believed. It inclines the automaton, which leads the mind unconsciously along with it.[20]

Here Pascal produces the very Lacanian definition of the unconscious: 'the automaton (i.e. the dead, senseless letter), which leads the mind unconsciously [*sans le savoir*] with it'. It follows, from this constitutively senseless character of the Law, that we must obey it not because it is just, good or even beneficial, but simply *because it is the law* – this tautology articulates the vicious circle of its authority, the fact that the last foundation of the Law's authority lies in its process of enunciation:

> Custom is the whole of equity for the sole reason that it is accepted. That is the mystic basis of its authority. Anyone who tries to bring it back to its first principle destroys it.[21]

The only real obedience, then, is an 'external' one: obedience out of conviction is not real obedience because it is already 'mediated' through our subjectivity – that is, we are not really obeying the authority but simply following our judgement, which tells us that the authority deserves to be obeyed in so far as it is good, wise, beneficent. . . . Even more than for our relation to 'external' social authority, this inversion applies to our obedience to the internal authority of belief: it was Kierkegaard who wrote that to believe in Christ because we consider him wise and good is a dreadful blasphemy – it is, on the contrary, only the act of belief itself which can give us an insight into his goodness and wisdom. Certainly we must search for rational reasons which can substantiate our belief, our obedience to the religious command, but the crucial religious experience is that these reasons reveal themselves only to those who already believe – we find reasons attesting our belief because we already believe; we do not believe because we have found sufficient good reasons to believe.

'External' obedience to the Law is thus not submission to external pressure, to so-called non-ideological 'brute force', but obedience to the Command in so far as it is 'incomprehensible', not understood; in so far as it retains a 'traumatic', 'irrational' character: far from hiding its full authority, this traumatic, non-integrated character of the Law is *a positive condition of it*. This is the fundamental feature of the psychoanalytic concept of the *superego*: an injunction which is experienced as traumatic, 'senseless' – that is, which cannot be integrated into the symbolic universe of the subject. But for the Law to function 'normally', this traumatic fact that 'custom is the whole of equity for the sole reason that it is accepted' – the dependence of the Law on its process of enunciation or, to use a concept developed by Laclau and Mouffe, its radically *contingent* character – must be repressed into the unconscious, through the ideological, imaginary experience of the 'meaning' of the Law, of its foundation in Justice, Truth (or, in a more modern way, functionality):

> It would therefore be a good thing for us to obey laws and customs because they are laws. . . . But people are not amenable to this doctrine, and thus, believing that truth can be found and resides in laws and customs, they believe them and take their antiquity as a proof of their truth (and not just of their authority, without truth).[22]

It is highly significant that we find exactly the same formulation in Kafka's *Trial*, at the end of the conversation between K. and the priest:

> 'I do not agree with that point of view,' said K., shaking his head, 'for if one accepts it, one must accept as true everything the door-keeper says. But you yourself have sufficiently proved how impossible it is to do that.' 'No,' said the priest, 'it is not necessary to accept everything as true, one must

only accept it as necessary.' 'A melancholy conclusion,' said K. 'It turns lying into a universal principle.'[23]

What is 'repressed', then, is not some obscure origin of the Law but the very fact that the Law is not to be accepted as true, only as necessary – the fact that *its authority is without truth*. The necessary structural illusion which drives people to believe that truth can be found in laws describes precisely the mechanism of *transference*: transference is this supposition of a Truth, of a Meaning behind the stupid, traumatic, inconsistent fact of the Law. In other words, 'transference' names the vicious circle of belief: the reasons why we should believe are persuasive only to those who already believe. The crucial text of Pascal here is the famous fragment 233 on the necessity of the wager; the first, largest part of its demonstrates at length why it is rationally sensible to 'bet on God', but this argument is invalidated by the following remark of Pascal's imaginary partner in dialogue:

> ... my hands are tied and my lips are sealed; I am being forced to wager and I am not free; I am being held fast and I am so made that I cannot believe. What do you want me to do then? – 'That is true, but at least get it into your head that, if you are unable to believe, it is because of your passions, since reason impels you to believe and yet you cannot do so. Concentrate then not on convincing yourself by multiplying proofs of God's existence but by diminishing your passions. You want to find faith and you do not know the road. You want to be cured of unbelief and you ask for the remedy: learn from those who were once bound like you and who now wager all they have. These are people who know the road you wish to follow, who have been cured of the affliction of which you wish to be cured: follow the way by which they began. They behaved just as if they did believe, taking holy water, having masses said, and so on. That will make you believe quite naturally, and will make you more docile.
>
> 'Now what harm will come to you from choosing this course? You will be faithful, honest, humble, grateful, full of good works, a sincere, true friend. . . . It is true you will not enjoy noxious pleasures, glory and good living, but will you not have others?
>
> 'I tell you that you will gain even in this life, and that at every step you take along this road you will see that your gain is so certain and your risk so negligible that in the end you will realize that you have wagered on something certain and infinite for which you have paid nothing.'[24]

Pascal's final answer, then, is: leave rational argumentation and submit yourself simply to ideological ritual, stupefy yourself by repeating the meaningless gestures, act *as if* you already believe, and the belief will come by itself.

[. . .]

What distinguishes this Pascalian 'custom' from insipid behaviourist wisdom ('the content of your belief is conditioned by your factual behaviour') is the paradoxical status of a *belief before belief*: by following a custom, the subject believes without knowing it, so that the final conversion is merely a formal act by means of which we recognize what we have already believed. In other words, what the behaviourist reading of Pascalian 'custom' misses is the crucial fact that the external custom is always a material support for the subject's unconscious.

[. . .]

Kafka, Critic of Althusser

The externality of the symbolic machine ('automaton') is therefore not simply external: it is at the same time the place where the fate of our internal, most 'sincere' and 'intimate' beliefs is in advance staged and decided. When we subject ourselves to the machine of a religious ritual, we already believe without knowing it; our belief is already materialized in the external ritual; in other words, we already believe *unconsciously*, because it is from this external character of the symbolic machine that we can explain the status of the unconscious as radically external – that of a dead letter. Belief is an affair of obedience to the dead, uncomprehended letter. It is this short circuit between the intimate belief and the external 'machine' which is the most subversive kernel of Pascalian theology.

Of course, in his theory of Ideological State Apparatuses,[25] Althusser gave an elaborated, contemporary version of this Pascalian 'machine'; but the weak point of his theory is that he or his school never succeeded in thinking out the link between Ideological State Apparatuses and ideological interpellation: how does the Ideological State Apparatus (the Pascalian 'machine', the signifying automatism) 'internalize' itself: how does it produce the effect of ideological belief in a Cause and the interconnecting effect of subjectivation, of recognition of one's ideological position? The answer to this is, as we have seen, that this external 'machine' of State Apparatuses exercises its force only in so far as it is experienced, in the unconscious economy of the subject, as a traumatic, senseless injunction. Althusser speaks only of the process of ideological interpellation through which the symbolic machine of ideology is 'internalized' into the ideological experience of Meaning and Truth: but we can learn from Pascal that this 'internalization', by structural necessity, never fully succeeds, that there is always a residue, a leftover, a stain of traumatic irrationality and senselessness sticking to it, and that *this leftover, far from hindering the full submission of the subject to the ideological command, is the very condition of it*: it is precisely this non-integrated surplus of senseless traumatism which confers on the Law its unconditional authority: in other words, which – in so far as it escapes ideological sense – sustains what we might call the ideological *jouis-sense*, enjoyment-in-sense (enjoy-meant), proper to ideology.

And again, it was no accident that we mentioned the name of Kafka: concerning this ideological *jouis-sense* we can say that Kafka develops a kind of criticism of Althusser *avant la lettre*, in letting us see that which is constitutive of the gap between 'machine' and its 'internalization'. Is not Kafka's 'irrational' bureaucracy, this blind, gigantic, nonsensical apparatus, precisely the Ideological State Apparatus with which a subject is confronted *before* any identification, any recognition – any *subjectivation* – takes place? What, then, can we learn from Kafka?

In a first approach, the starting point in Kafka's novels is that of an interpellation: the Kafkaesque subject is interpellated by a mysterious bureaucratic entity (Law, Castle). But this interpellation has a somewhat strange look: it is, so to say, an *interpellation without identification/subjectivation*; it does not offer us a Cause with which to identify – the Kafkaesque subject is the subject desperately seeking a trait with which to identify, he does not understand the meaning of the call of the Other.

This is the dimension overlooked in the Althusserian account of interpellation: before being caught in the identification, in the symbolic recognition/misrecognition, the subject ($) is trapped by the Other through a paradoxical object-cause of desire in the midst of it (a), through this secret supposed to be hidden in the Other: $\$ \lozenge a$ – the Lacanian formula of fantasy. What does it mean, more precisely, to say that ideological fantasy structures reality itself? Let us explain by starting from the fundamental Lacanian thesis that in the opposition between dream and reality, fantasy is on the side of reality: it is, as Lacan once said, the support that gives consistency to what we call 'reality'.

In his Seminar on the *Four Fundamental Concepts of Psycho-Analysis*, Lacan develops this through an interpretation of the well-known dream about the 'burning child':

> A father had been watching beside his child's sick-bed for days and nights on end. After the child had died, he went into the next room to lie down, but left the door open so that he could see from his bedroom into the room in which his child's body was laid out, with tall candles standing round it. An old man had been engaged to keep watch over it, and sat beside the body murmuring prayers. After a few hours' sleep, the father had a dream that *his child was standing beside his bed, caught him by the arm and whispered to him reproachfully: 'Father, don't you see I'm burning?'* He woke up, noticed a bright glare of light from the next room, hurried into it and found the old watchman had dropped off to sleep and that the wrappings and one of the arms of his

beloved child's dead body had been burned by a lighted candle that had fallen on them.[26]

The usual interpretation of this dream is based on a thesis that one of the functions of the dream is to enable the dreamer to prolong his sleep. The sleeper is suddenly exposed to an exterior irritation, a stimulus coming from reality (the ringing of an alarm clock, knocking on the door or, in this case, the smell of smoke), and to prolong his sleep he quickly, on the spot, constructs a dream: a little scene, a small story, which includes this irritating element. However, the external irritation soon becomes too strong and the subject is awakened.

The Lacanian reading is directly opposed to this. The subject does not awake himself when the external irritation becomes too strong; the logic of his awakening is quite different. First he constructs a dream, a story which enables him to prolong his sleep, to avoid awakening into reality. But the thing that he encounters in the dream, the reality of his desire, the Lacanian Real – in our case, the reality of the child's reproach to his father, 'Can't you see that I am burning?', implying the father's fundamental guilt – is more terrifying than so-called external reality itself, and that is why he awakens: to escape the Real of his desire, which announces itself in the terrifying dream. He escapes into so-called reality to be able to continue to sleep, to maintain his blindness, to elude awakening into the Real of his desire. We can rephrase here the old 'hippie' motto of the 1960s: reality is for those who cannot support the dream. 'Reality' is a fantasy-construction which enables us to mask the Real of our desire.[27]

It is exactly the same with ideology. Ideology is not a dreamlike illusion that we build to escape insupportable reality; in its basic dimension it is a fantasy-construction which serves as a support for our 'reality' itself: an 'illusion' which structures our effective, real social relations and thereby masks some insupportable, real, impossible kernel (conceptualized by Ernesto Laclau and Chantal Mouffe as 'antagonism': a traumatic social division which cannot be symbolized). The function of ideology is not to offer us a point of escape from our reality but to offer us the social reality itself as an escape from some traumatic, real kernel. To explain this logic, let us refer again to the *Four Fundamental Concepts of Psycho-Analysis*.[28] Here Lacan mentions the well-known paradox of Zhuang Zi, who dreamt of being a butterfly, and after his awakening posed himself a question: How does he know that he is not *now* a butterfly dreaming of being Zhuang Zi? Lacan's commentary is that this question is justified, for two reasons.

First, it proves that Zhuang Zi was not a fool. The Lacanian definition of a fool is somebody who believes in his immediate identity with himself; somebody who is not capable of a dialectically mediated distance towards himself, like a king who thinks he is a king, who takes his being-a-king as his immediate property and not as a symbolic mandate imposed on him by a network of intersubjective relations of which he is a part (example of a king who was a fool thinking he was a king: Ludwig II of Bavaria, Wagner's patron).

However, this is not all; if it were, the subject could be reduced to a void, to an empty place in which his or her whole content is procured by others, by the symbolic network of intersubjective relations: I am 'in myself' a nothingness, the positive content of myself is what I am for others. In other words, if this were all, Lacan's last word would be a radical alienation of the subject. His content, 'what he is', would be determined by an exterior signifying network offering him the points of symbolic identification, conferring on him certain symbolic mandates. But Lacan's basic thesis, at least in his last works, is that there is a possibility for the subject to obtain some contents, some kind of positive consistency, also outside the big Other, the alienating symbolic network. This other possibility is that offered by fantasy: equating the subject to an object of fantasy. When he was thinking that he was a butterfly dreaming of being Zhuang Zi, Zhuang Zi was in a way correct. The butterfly was the object which constituted the frame, the backbone, of his fantasy-identity (the relationship *Zhuang Zi–butterfly* can be written $ \$ \Diamond a $). In the symbolic reality he was Zhuang Zi, but in the real of his desire he was a butterfly. Being a butterfly was the whole consistency of his positive being outside the symbolic network. Perhaps it is not quite by accident that we find a kind of echo of this in Terry Gilliam's film *Brazil*, which depicts, in a disgustingly funny way, a totalitarian society: the hero finds an ambiguous point of escape from everyday reality in his dream of being a man-butterfly.

At first sight, what we have here is a simple symmetrical inversion of the so-called normal, ordinary perspective. In our everyday understanding, Zhuang Zi is the 'real' person dreaming of being a butterfly, and here we have something which is 'really' a butterfly dreaming of being Zhuang Zi. But as Lacan points out, this symmetrical relationship is an illusion: when Zhuang Zi is awakened, he can think to himself that he is Zhuang Zi who dreamed of being a butterfly, but in his dream, when he is a butterfly, he cannot ask himself if when awoken, when he thought he was Zhuang Zi, he was not this butterfly that is now dreaming of being Zhuang Zi. The question, the dialectical split, is possible only when we are awake. In other words, the illusion cannot be symmetrical, it cannot run both ways, because if it did we would find ourselves in a nonsensical situation described by Alphonse Allais: Raoul and Marguerite, two lovers, arrange to meet at a masked ball;

there they skip into a hidden corner, embrace and fondle each other. Finally, they both put down their masks, and – surprise – Raoul finds that he is embracing the wrong woman, that she is not Marguerite, and Marguerite also finds that the other person is not Raoul but some unknown stranger. . . .

Fantasy as a Support of Reality

This problem must be approached from the Lacanian thesis that it is only in the dream that we come close to the real awakening – that is, to the Real of our desire. When Lacan says that the last support of what we call 'reality' is a fantasy, this is definitely not to be understood in the sense of 'life is just a dream', 'what we call reality is just an illusion', and so forth. We find such a theme in many science-fiction stories: reality as a generalized dream or illusion. The story is usually told from the perspective of a hero who gradually makes the horrifying discovery that all the people around him are not really human beings but some kind of automatons, robots, who only look and act like real human beings; the final point of these stories is of course the hero's discovery that he himself is also such an automaton and not a real human being. Such a generalized illusion is impossible: we find the same paradox in a well-known drawing by Escher of two hands drawing each other.

The Lacanian thesis is, on the contrary, that there is always a hard kernel, a leftover which persists and cannot be reduced to a universal play of illusory mirroring. The difference between Lacan and 'naive realism' is that for Lacan, *the only point at which we approach this hard kernel of the Real is indeed the dream*. When we awaken into reality after a dream, we usually say to ourselves 'it was just a dream', thereby blinding ourselves to the fact that in our everyday, wakening reality we are *nothing but a consciousness of this dream*. It was only in the dream that we approached the fantasy-framework which determines our activity, our mode of acting in reality itself.

It is the same with the ideological dream, with the determination of ideology as a dreamlike construction hindering us from seeing the real state of things, reality as such. In vain do we try to break out of the ideological dream by 'opening our eyes and trying to see reality as it is', by throwing away the ideological spectacles: as the subjects of such a post-ideological, objective, sober look, free of so-called ideological prejudices, as the subjects of a look which views the facts as they are, we remain throughout 'the consciousness of our ideological dream'. The only way to break the power of our ideological dream is to confront the Real of our desire which announces itself in this dream.

Let us examine anti-Semitism. It is not enough to say that we must liberate ourselves of so-called 'anti-Semitic prejudices' and learn to see Jews as they really are – in this way we will certainly remain victims of these so-called prejudices. We must confront ourselves with how the ideological figure of the 'Jew' is invested with our unconscious desire, with how we have constructed this figure to escape a certain deadlock of our desire.

Let us suppose, for example, that an objective look would confirm – why not? – that Jews really do financially exploit the rest of the population, that they do sometimes seduce our young daughters, that some of them do not wash regularly. Is it not clear that this has nothing to do with the real roots of our anti-Semitism? Here, we have only to remember the Lacanian proposition concerning the pathologically jealous husband: even if all the facts he quotes in support of his jealousy are true, even if his wife really is sleeping around with other men, this does not change one bit the fact that his jealousy is a pathological, paranoid construction.

Let us ask ourselves a simple question: In the Germany of the late 1930s, what would be the result of such a non-ideological, objective approach? Probably something like: 'The Nazis are condemning the Jews too hastily, without proper argument, so let us take a cool, sober look and see if they are really guilty or not; let us see if there is some truth in the accusations against them.' Is it really necessary to add that such an approach would merely confirm our so-called 'unconscious prejudices' with additional rationalizations? The proper answer to anti-Semitism is therefore not 'Jews are really not like that' but 'the anti-Semitic idea of Jew has nothing to do with Jews; the ideological figure of a Jew is a way to stitch up the inconsistency of our own ideological system'.

That is why we are also unable to shake so-called ideological prejudices by taking into account the pre-ideological level of everyday experience. The basis of this argument is that the ideological construction always finds its limits in the field of everyday experience – that it is unable to reduce, to contain, to absorb and annihilate this level. Let us again take a typical individual in Germany in the late 1930s. He is bombarded by anti-Semitic propaganda depicting a Jew as a monstrous incarnation of Evil, the great wire-puller, and so on. But when he returns home he encounters Mr Stern, his neighbour, a good man to chat with in the evenings, whose children play with his. Does not this everyday experience offer an irreducible resistance to the ideological construction?

The answer is, of course, no. If everyday experience offers such a resistance, then the anti-Semitic ideology has not yet really grasped us.

An ideology is really 'holding us' only when we do not feel any opposition between it and reality – that is, when the ideology succeeds in determining the mode of our everyday experience of reality itself. How then would our poor German, if he were a good anti-Semite, react to this gap between the ideological figure of the Jew (schemer, wire-puller, exploiting our brave men, and so on) and the common everyday experience of his good neighbour, Mr Stern? His answer would be to turn this gap, this discrepancy itself, into an argument for anti-Semitism: 'You see how dangerous they really are? It is difficult to recognize their real nature. They hide it behind the mask of everyday appearance – and it is exactly this hiding of one's real nature, this duplicity, that is a basic feature of the Jewish nature.' An ideology really succeeds when even the facts which at first sight contradict it start to function as arguments in its favour.

Surplus-value and Surplus-enjoyment

Herein lies the difference with Marxism: in the predominant Marxist perspective the ideological gaze is a *partial* gaze overlooking the *totality* of social relations, whereas in the Lacanian perspective ideology, rather, designates *totality set on effacing the traces of its own impossibility.* This difference corresponds to the one which distinguishes the Freudian from the Marxian notion of fetishism: in Marxism a fetish conceals the positive network of social relations, whereas in Freud a fetish conceals the lack ('castration') around which the symbolic network is articulated.

In so far as we conceive the Real as that which 'always returns to the same place', we can deduce another, no less crucial difference. From the Marxist point of view, the ideological procedure *par excellence* is that of *'false' eternalization and/or universalization*: a state which depends on a concrete historical conjunction appears as an eternal, universal feature of the human condition; the interest of a particular class disguises itself as universal human interest . . . and the aim of the 'criticism of ideology' is to denounce this false universality, to detect behind man in general the bourgeois individual; behind the universal rights of man the form which renders possible capitalist exploitation; behind the 'nuclear family' as a transhistorical constant the historically specified and limited form of kinship relations, and so on.

In the Lacanian perspective, we should change the terms and designate as the most 'cunning' ideological procedure the very opposite of eternalization: an *over-rapid historicization*. Let us take one of the commonplaces of the Marxist–feminist criticism of psychoanalysis, the idea that its insistence on the crucial role of the Oedipus complex and the nuclear-family triangle transforms a historically conditioned form of patriarchal family into a feature of the universal human condition: is not this effort to historicize the family triangle precisely an attempt to *elude* the 'hard kernel' which announces itself through the 'patriarchal family' – the Real of the Law, the rock of castration? In other words, if over-rapid universalization produces a quasi-universal Image whose function is to make us blind to its historical, socio-symbolic determination, over-rapid historicization makes us blind to the real kernel which returns as the same through diverse historicizations/symbolizations.

It is the same with a phenomenon that designates most accurately the 'perverse' obverse of twentieth-century civilization: concentration camps. All the different attempts to attach this phenomenon to a concrete image ('Holocaust', 'Gulag' . . .), to reduce it to a product of a concrete social order (Fascism, Stalinism . . .) – what are they if not so many attempts to elude the fact that we are dealing here with the 'real' of our civilization which returns as the same traumatic kernel in all social systems? (We should not forget that concentration camps were an invention of 'liberal' England, dating from the Boer War; that they were also used in the USA to isolate the Japanese population, and so on.)

Marxism, then, did not succeed in taking into account, coming to terms with, the surplus-object, the leftover of the Real eluding symbolization – a fact all the more surprising if we recall that Lacan modelled his notion of surplus-enjoyment on the Marxian notion of surplus-value. The proof that Marxian surplus-value announces effectively the logic of the Lacanian *objet petit a* as the embodiment of surplus-enjoyment is already provided by the decisive formula used by Marx, in the third volume of *Capital*, to designate the logical-historical limit of capitalism: 'the limit of capital is capital itself, i.e. the capitalist mode of production'.

This formula can be read in two ways. The first, usual historicist-evolutionist reading conceives it, in accordance with the unfortunate paradigm of the dialectics of productive forces and relations of production, as that of 'content' and 'form'. This paradigm follows roughly the metaphor of the serpent which, from time to time, sheds its skin, which has grown too tight: one posits as the last impetus of social development – as its (so to speak) 'natural', 'spontaneous' constant – the incessant growth of the productive forces (as a rule reduced to technical development); this 'spontaneous' growth is then followed, with a greater or lesser degree of delay, by the inert, dependent moment, the relationship of production. We have thus epochs in which the relation of production are in accordance with the productive forces, then those forces develop and outgrow their 'social clothes', the frame of relationships; this frame becomes an obstacle to their further development, until social revolution again co-ordinates forces and relations by replacing the old relations with new ones which correspond to the new state of forces.

If we conceive the formula of capital as its own limit from this point of view, it means simply that the capitalist relation of production which at first made possible the fast development of productive forces became at a certain point an obstacle to their further development: that these forces have outgrown their frame and demand a new form of social relations.

Marx himself is, of course, far from such a simplistic evolutionary idea. If we need convincing of this, we have only to look at the passages in *Capital* where he deals with the relation between formal and real subsumption of the process of production under Capital: the formal subsumption *precedes* the real one; that is, Capital first subsumes the process of production as it found it (artisans, and so on), and only subsequently does it change the productive forces step by step, shaping them in such a way as to create correspondence. Contrary to the above-mentioned simplistic idea, it is then the *form* of the relation of production which drives the development of productive forces – that is, of its 'content'.

All we have to do to render impossible the simplistic evolutionary reading of the formula 'the limit of capital itself' is to ask a very simple and obvious question: How do we define, exactly, the moment – albeit only an ideal one – at which the capitalist relation of production becomes an obstacle to the further development of the productive forces? Or the obverse of the same question: When can we speak of an accordance between productive forces and relation of production in the capitalist mode of production? Strict analysis leads to only one possible answer: *never*.

This is exactly how capitalism differs from other, previous modes of production: in the latter, we can speak of periods of 'accordance' when the process of social production and reproduction goes on as a quiet, circular movement, and of periods of convulsion when the contradiction between forces and relation aggravates itself; whereas in capitalism this contradiction, the discord forces/relation, *is contained in its very concept* (in the form of the contradiction between the social mode of production and the individual, private mode of appropriation). It is this internal contradiction which compels capitalism to permanent extended reproduction – to the incessant development of its own conditions of production, in contrast to previous modes of production where, at least in their 'normal' state, (re)production goes on as a circular movement.

If this is so, then the evolutionist reading of the formula of capital as its own limit is inadequate: the point is not that, at a certain moment of its development, the frame of the relation of production starts to constrict further development of the productive forces; the point is that *it is this very immanent limit, this 'internal contradiction', which drives capitalism into permanent development.* The 'normal' state of capitalism is the permanent revolutionizing of its own conditions of existence: from the very beginning capitalism 'putrifies', it is branded by a crippling contradiction, discord, by an immanent want of balance: this is exactly why it changes, develops incessantly – incessant development is the only way for it to resolve again and again, come to terms with, its own fundamental, constitutive imbalance, 'contradiction'. Far from constricting, its limit is thus the very impetus of its development. Herein lies the paradox proper to capitalism, its last resort: capitalism is capable of transforming its limit, its very impotence, in the source of its power – the more it 'putrefies', the more its immanent contradiction is aggravated, the more it must revolutionize itself to survive.

It is this paradox which defines surplus-enjoyment: it is not a surplus which simply attaches itself to some 'normal', fundamental enjoyment, because *enjoyment as such emerges only in this surplus,* because it is constitutively an 'excess'. If we subtract the surplus we lose enjoyment itself, just as capitalism, which can survive only by incessantly revolutionizing its own material conditions, ceases to exist if it 'stays the same', if it achieves an internal balance. This, then, is the homology between surplus-value – the 'cause' which sets in motion the capitalist process of production – and surplus-enjoyment, the object-cause of desire. Is not the paradoxical topology of the movement of capital, the fundamental blockage which resolves and reproduces itself through frenetic activity, *excessive* power as the very form of appearance of a fundamental *impotence* – this immediate passage, this coincidence of limit and excess, of lack and surplus – precisely that of Lacanian *objet petit a*, of the leftover which embodies the fundamental, constitutive lack?

All this, of course, Marx 'knows very well . . . and yet': and yet, in the crucial formulation in the Preface to the *Critique of Political Economy*, he proceeds *as if he does not know it,* by describing the very passage from capitalism to socialism in terms of the above-mentioned vulgar evolutionist dialectics of productive forces and the relation of production: when the forces surpass a certain degree, capitalist relation becomes an obstacle to their further development: this discord brings about the need for socialist revolution, the function of which is to co-ordinate again forces and relation: that is, to establish relations of production rendering possible the intensified development of the productive forces as the end-in-itself of the historical process.

How can we not detect in this formulation the fact that Marx failed to cope with the paradoxes of surplus-enjoyment? And the ironic vengeance of history for this failure is that today there exists a society which seems to correspond perfectly to this vulgar evolutionary dialectics of forces and relation: 'real socialism', a society which legitimizes itself by reference to Marx. Is it not already a commonplace to assert that 'real socialism' has rendered possible rapid industrialization, but that as soon as the productive forces have reached a certain level of development (usually designated by the vague term 'post-industrial society'), 'real socialist' social relationships began to constrict their further growth?

Notes

1. Hans-Jürgen Eysenck, *Sense and Nonsense in Psychology*, Harmondsworth 1966.
2. Sigmund Freud, *The Interpretation of Dreams*, Harmondsworth 1977, p. 757.
3. Ibid., p. 446.
4. Ibid., p. 650.
5. Karl Marx, *Capital*, vol. I, London 1974, p. 80.
6. Ibid., p. 76.
7. Alfred Sohn-Rethel, *Intellectual and Manual Labor*, London 1978, p. 31.
8. Ibid., p. 33.
9. Ibid., p. 59.
10. Ibid.
11. Ibid., p. 42.
12. Ibid., pp. 26–7.
13. Jacques Lacan, 'R.S.I.', *Ornicar?* 4, Paris 1975, p. 106.
14. Marx, *Capital*, p. 77.
15. Ibid., p. 59.
16. Ibid., p. 63.
17. G. W. F. Hegel, *Phenomenology of Spirit*, Oxford 1977.
18. Peter Sloterdijk, *Kritik der zynischen Vernunft*, Frankfurt 1983; translated as *Critique of Cynical Reason*, London 1988.
19. Marx, *Capital*, p. 132.
20. Blaise Pascal, *Pensées*, Harmondsworth 1966, p. 271.
21. Ibid., p. 46.
22. Ibid., p. 216.
23. Franz Kafka, *The Trial*, Harmondsworth 1985, p. 243.
24. Pascal, *Pensées*, pp. 152–3.
25. Louis Althusser, 'Ideology and Ideological State Apparatuses', see this volume, ch. 5.
26. Freud, *The Interpretation of Dreams*, p. 652.
27. Lacan, *The Four Fundamental Concepts of Psycho-Analysis*, Harmondsworth 1979, chs 5, 6.
28. Ibid., ch. 6.

List of Sources

Theodor W. Adorno, from the original manuscript of *Minima Moralia*, but omitted from the final publication. This translation first published in *New Left Review* 200, July/August 1993.

Peter Dews, *New Left Review* 157, May/June 1986.

Jacques Lacan, *New Left Review* 51, September/October 1968.

Louis Althusser, first published in *La Pensée*, 1970; this translation from *Essays on Ideology*, London: Verso 1984.

Michel Pêcheux, *Language, Semantics and Ideology*, London: Macmillan 1982.

Nicholas Abercrombie, Stephen Hill and Bryan S. Turner, *New Left Review* 142, November/December 1983.

Göran Therborn, *New Left Review* 143, January/February 1984.

Terry Eagleton, *Ideology*, London: Verso 1991, chapters 4 & 5.

Richard Rorty, *Hypatia*, 8, 2, Spring 1993.

Michèle Barrett, *The Politics of Truth: From Marx to Foucault*, Cambridge: Polity Press 1991, chapter 4.

Pierre Bourdieu and Terry Eagleton, Interview, *New Left Review* 191, January/February 1992.

Fredric Jameson, *Postmodernism or, the Cultural Logic of Late Capitalism*, London: Verso 1991, chapter 8.

Slavoj Žižek, *The Sublime Object of Ideology*, London: Verso 1989, chapter 1.

Index